Social Work Practice with Lesbian, Gay, Bisexual, and Transgender People

Second Edition

Social Work Practice with Lesbian, Gay, Bisexual, and Transgender People

Second Edition

Gerald P. Mallon, DSW
Editor

Routledge
Taylor & Francis Group

NEW YORK AND LONDON

First published 1998
by The Haworth Press, Inc.

This edition published 2008
by Routledge
270 Madison Ave, New York NY 10016

Simultaneously published in the UK
by Routledge
2 Park Square, Milton Park, Abingdon, Oxon, OX14 4RN

Routledge is an imprint of the Taylor & Francis Group, an informa business

Transferred to Digital Printing 2009

© 2008 Routledge

Cover design by Marylouise E. Doyle.

Library of Congress Cataloging in Publication Data
    Social work practice with lesbian, gay, bisexual, and transgender people / [edited by] Gerald P. Mallon.—2nd ed. p. cm.
    Rev. ed. of: Foundations of social work practice with lesbian and gay persons.
    Includes bibliographical references and index.
    ISBN: 978-0-7890-3357-4 (hard : alk. paper)
    ISBN: 978-0-7890-3358-1 (soft : alk. paper)
    1. Social work with gays—United States. 2. Gaymen—Services for—United States. 3. Lesbians—Services for—United States. 4. Bisexuals—Services for—United States. 5. Transgender people—Services for—United States. I. Mallon, Gerald P. II. Foundations of social work practice with lesbian and gay persons.
    HV1449.F68 2007
    362.8—dc22
                                2007034356

ISBN 10: 0-7890-3357-7 (hbk)
ISBN 10: 0-7890-3358-5 (pbk)

ISBN 13: 978-0-7890-3357-4 (hbk)
ISBN 13: 978-0-7890-3358-1 (pbk)

For Nancy Ramputi

Who was there for me on day one as a colleague when
I began my career, and has been there for me every day since
as my friend, reminding me always of why we wanted
to be social workers in the first place

CONTENTS

ABOUT THE EDITOR

Gerald P. Mallon, DSW, is Professor and Executive Director of the National Resource Center for Family-Centered Practice and Permanency Planning at the Hunter College School of Social Work in New York City. For more than thirty years, Dr. Mallon has been a child welfare practitioner, advocate, educator, and researcher. He is the author or editor of eighteen books and numerous peer-reviewed publications, most recently *Lesbian and Gay Foster and Adoptive Parents: Recruiting, Assessing, and Supporting an Untapped Resource for Children and Youth* and *Child Welfare for the Twenty-First Century.*

CONTRIBUTORS

George A. Appleby, DSW, is Professor of Social Work and Dean, School of Health and Human Services, at Southern Connecticut State University, New Haven, Connecticut. Dr. Appleby can be contacted via e-mail at serafingp@aol.com.

Laura C. Booker, LCSW, is a social worker in private practice. Ms. Booker can be contacted via e-mail at lcbooker@comcast.net.

Edgar Colon, DSW, is Professor of Social Work at Southern Connecticut State University, New Haven, Connecticut. Dr. Colon can be reached via e-mail at colone1@southernct.edu.

Carrie Davis, LCSW, is Director of Counseling and Social Services at the Lesbian, Gay, Bisexual, Transgender Community Services Center in New York City and an alumni of the Hunter College School of Social Work in New York City. Ms. Davis can be contacted via e-mail at carrie@gaycenter.org.

Sarah Jane Dodd, PhD, is Associate Professor, Hunter College School of Social Work in New York City. Dr. Dodd can be contacted via e-mail at sdodd@hunter.cuny.edu.

Nancy Feldman, PhD, is Assistant Professor, Hunter College School of Social Work in New York City. Dr. Feldman can be contacted via e-mail at nancy.feldman@hunter.cuny.edu.

Brian J. Flynn, MSW, LCSW, is Coordinator of Admissions and Service Learning, Department of Social Work, College of Community and Public Affairs, at the State University of New York, Binghamton, New York. Dr. Flynn can be contacted via e-mail at bjflynn@binghamton.edu.

Kathy T. Heffern, MSW, is a graduate from the Hunter College School of Social Work in New York City. Ms. Heffern can be reached via e-mail at kth210@nyu.edu.

Social Work Practice with LGBT People

Peg McCartt Hess, PhD, is Senior Consultant at the National Resource Center for Family-Centered Practice and Permanency Planning at the Hunter College School of Social Work in New York City. Dr. Hess can be contacted via e-mail at peghess@charternet.com.

L. Donald McVinney, LCSW, is Director of the Harm Reduction Program in New York City. Mr. McVinney can be contacted at mcvinney@harmreduction.org.

Eli C. Nealy, LCSW, is Associate Executive Director of the Lesbian, Gay, Bisexual, Transgender Community Services Center in New York City and a PhD candidate at the Hunter College School of Social Work in New York City. Mr. Nealy can be contacted via e-mail at enealy@gaycenter.org.

Roy L. Old Person Jr., MSW, is a National Institute of Mental Health Research Fellow and a Doctoral Student at the University of Washington School of Social Work, Seattle, Washington. Mr. Old Person can be contacted via e-mail at royo@u.washington.edu.

Mitchell Rosenwald, PhD, is Associate Professor of Social Work, Barry University School of Social Work, Miami Shores, Florida. Dr. Rosenwald can be contacted via e-mail at mrosenwa@mail.barry.edu.

Michael Shernoff, LCSW, is a private practitioner and Adjunct Professor at the Columbia University School of Social Work in New York City. Mr. Shernoff can be contacted via e-mail at mshernoff@aol.com.

Karina L. Walters, PhD, is the William B. and Ruth Gerberding Endowed Professor, University of Washington School of Social Work, Seattle, Washington. Dr. Walters can be contacted via e-mail at kw5@u.washington.edu.

Geordana Weber, MSW, is a graduate of the Hunter College School of Social Work in New York City. Ms. Weber can be reached via e-mail at geordala@yahoo.com.

Acknowledgments

Although the task of writing can be and often is a lonely endeavor, no one truly writes alone. One of the nicest things about completing a manuscript is having the opportunity to thank those who made the process more satisfying.

The idea for writing the original book, *Foundations of Social Work Practice with Lesbian and Gay Persons,* initially came from Ray Berger, who was one of the first social workers to write about social work practice with gay men and lesbians. His courage in writing about gay and lesbian persons, even though he was warned by friends and colleagues to "be careful," has allowed me and many other scholars to write books that speak to the needs of persons whose voices have been silenced by the majority.

A great deal has changed in the world since 1998 when this text was first published. Reissuing this text in its revised form as *Social Work Practice with Lesbian, Gay, Bisexual, and Transgender Persons* is important in that it expands the conversation to include two important population groups that were not discussed in the first text—bisexual and transgender persons. This new edition also includes new scholarship, new practices, and new research that has been published since 1998. In some cases, the chapters in this revised text are completely new, written by new authors and including new content; in other cases, the original chapters written in 1998 were expanded to include content on bisexual and transgender persons and to identify new research and new scholarship published in the professional literature and online since that first edition was published.

My immediate thanks in this newly revised edition are due to those scholars and practitioners who agreed to author or rework the chapters collected in this revised volume. One criterion for asking each of these professionals to participate in this project, both in the first edition and in this revised edition, was that they be trained social work practitioners and educators. In writing this text about social work practice with LGBT persons, it was important to me that all of the authors not only claim to have an understanding of a social work perspective, but that they actually practice from a social worker's perspective.

Social Work Practice with LGBT People

I would also like to acknowledge my colleagues and students at the Hunter College School of Social Work in New York City, several of whom are contributors to this volume, who have assisted me in completing this work by inviting me to a setting where the intellectual intensity, collegiality, and scholarly productivity are astounding. Our dean, Jacqueline Mondros, has been supportive of me as a faculty member and has been an inspiration to the entire school, and I am most appreciative of her support and guidance. I am proud to be a part of one of the finest schools of social work in the country—the Hunter College School of Social Work.

Above all, I treasure the loving encouragement of my partner, Mike Rendino, who has provided me with a nutritive environment that has been conducive to my own growth as a person, and to my writing. His patience when I took "just an hour" to clean up a reference list or hours to "fix" a chapter was commendable. The kind of writing that academics need to do requires that we spend many hours away from our families. All the time I was writing and editing, Mike was caring for our family: walking the dog, feeding the cats, cooking our meals, taking care of the kids, and much, much more. My thanks to Mike and to my family is, as always, inestimable.

Chapter 1

Knowledge for Practice with Lesbian, Gay, Bisexual, and Transgender (LGBT) People

Gerald P. Mallon

"You are the first gay person whom I have ever met that appears to be happy about who you are," said a graduate social work student to me over a decade ago. She meant it as a compliment, but it made me sad that she thought all gay people were unhappy. "How many gay people do you know?" I asked in response to her comment. "Oh, you're the first," she said. I felt even worse. Even though this student had been exposed to one openly gay man, who happened to be her research professor, I could not help but ask myself how well she was being prepared to practice with lesbians and gay men, not to mention bisexual or transgender persons, in her field placement and course work. The answer, I knew, was that she was not being prepared at all. She had no courses that expanded her knowledge about the needs of LGBT persons; she had few, if any, readings assigned that addressed this content; and apart from her one experience with her openly gay professor, she had no practice experiences in her professional training. It seemed woefully insufficient and somehow unethical to permit a student to graduate without any knowledge of the needs of this population. How were students, who would undoubtedly encounter LGBT persons in their professional lives, supposed to know how to practice with them? Unquestionably, there was a need to address these issues with graduate students preparing for practice in a diverse world. Apart from its significance as a practice dilemma, this experience also illustrates an important truth about LGBT persons in contemporary society: that most people have little or no accurate knowledge about the lives of this population. Fortunately, in the last ten years, there have been some changes in preparing MSW students for practice with LGBT populations.

AN ECOLOGICAL APPROACH

The person:environment* perspective (Germain, 1991), utilized throughout this text as a framework for practice, has been a central influence on the profession's theoretical base and has usefulness and relevance as an approach to social work practice with LGBT persons. Germain and Gitterman (1996) underscore the point that disempowerment, which threatens the health, social well-being, and life of those who are oppressed, imposes enormous adaptive tasks on LGBT persons. An understanding of the destructive relationships that exist between LGBT persons and a predominantly heterocentric environment is integral to the process of developing practice knowledge about working with LGBT persons as clients. The purpose of this chapter, therefore, is to define and describe the knowledge base of practice with LGBT persons and to review social work's response to the needs of this population.

What the social worker is supposed to do should dictate the boundaries of the profession's knowledge base, noted Meyer (1982). If social workers are supposed to be able to work with lesbians, gay men, bisexuals, and transgender persons, then a knowledge base for practice with them must be within those boundaries. An organized knowledge base is crucial to any profession. Anyone, notes Mattaini (1995, p. 6), "can act." The professional, however, is expected to act deliberately, taking the steps that are likely to be most helpful, least intrusive, and most consistent with the person's welfare. Making a conscious determination of these choices requires an extensive knowledge base.

SOURCES OF KNOWLEDGE

In his chapter focusing on the acquisition of knowledge for foundation practice, Mattaini (1995) identifies several key sources of knowledge that,

---

*The conventional use of "person:environment" in the social work field represents the connection between the individual and his or her environmental context. Carel Germain, a pillar of social work education, felt so strongly about the interconnectedness of these concepts that she conceptualized them as inseparable, using a colon rather than a hyphen. I have chosen to use her concept in this text.

in a modified version herein, provide a framework for this chapter's discussion on knowledge for practice with LGBT persons. Sources identified by Mattaini include

1. practice wisdom derived from narrative experiences of the profession and professional colleagues,
2. the personal experiences of the practitioner,
3. a knowledge of the professional literature,
4. a knowledge of history and current events,
5. research issues that inform practice (both qualitative and quantitative),
6. theoretical and conceptual analyses, and
7. information that is provided by the case itself.

All of these, understood within an ecological framework of person:environment, while being conscious of the reality of oppression in the lives of LGBT persons, are called upon to inform social work practice with LGBT persons, and each source contributes to the development of the knowledge base of practice with this population.

Practice wisdom can be viewed as that which is derived from the narrative experiences of the profession, gathered from both professional colleagues and from clients. Interest in narrative theory has grown in recent years, and the use of life stories in practice has in some organizations replaced elaborate, formalized intake histories. Life stories, which tend to be rich in detail, are usually obtained early in the work with a client, and can be a useful means toward not only gathering important data to enhance one's knowledge base, but also in establishing a rapport and a trusting relationship with a gay or lesbian client. As the client talks and the social worker listens empathically—that is, in the course of the telling and the listening—the story gains personal and cultural meanings. This process, particularly with LGBT persons who may have experienced oppression and marginalization, can be a healing process. It is, as Germain and Gitterman (1996, p. 145) put it, "our human way of finding meaning in life events, of explaining our life experience to ourselves and others, so that we can move on."

Over the years, several notable social work practitioners (English, 1996; Hartman, 1992; MacPike, 1989; Muzio, 1996; Shernoff, 1991, 1996; White & Epston, 1990) have provided excellent examples of the use of personal narrative as a means to enhance local knowledge that can guide practice. Markowitz's (1991a) beautifully written and touching story of a lesbian daughter and her father as they struggle to forge a new understanding of each other is one almost perfect example of the power that personal narrative has to inform practice.

In addition to listening to the life stories of clients and the practice experiences of practitioners, social workers practicing with LGBT persons can rely on rules that have been handed down by experienced practitioners. Heuristic practice, which can be described as principles to guide patterns of professional behavior and which has shaped and refined practice, may also serve as a model for other workers. The acquisition of group-specific language to guide practice, and a knowledge of the myths and stereotypes about LGBT persons, can be extremely useful forms of heuristic practice. A glossary of terms and several of the most common myths about lesbians, gay men, bisexuals, and transgender persons can be found in the appendix of this text. These fragments of practice wisdom can be valuable as a guide for practitioners interested in enhancing their practice knowledge base in working with LGBT persons.

PERSONAL EXPERIENCE

The personal experiences of practitioners is the second powerful force that guides knowledge development. Social workers are guided not only by their own personal experiences but also by a professional code of ethics (see Chapter 2). Most social workers base some of their knowledge about clients on integrated and synthesized events gathered from their own life experiences. Within the guidelines provided by the professions' code of ethics, basic interpersonal and problem-solving skills that social workers have developed throughout their lives are important means toward informing their practices.

It is a myth that most people do not know anyone who is gay, lesbian, bisexual, or transgender. Unquestionably, social workers who have a close friend or a family member who is openly gay, lesbian, bisexual, or transgender may have additional personal experiences that can assist them in guiding their practice with these populations. In addition, social workers who are themselves lesbian, gay, bisexual, or transgender will without doubt have greater insights into LGBT clients. However, being a gay man, a lesbian, a bisexual, or a transgender person alone does not provide a practitioner with a complete knowledge for practice with LGBT clients. Practitioners who are gay, lesbian, bisexual, or transgender may be at various stages of their own sexual or gender identity development, and their knowledge may be, at best, incomplete.

Issues of self-disclosure become significant when a social worker has had personal experiences or shares something in common with a client, in this case an LGBT identity. A gay, lesbian, bisexual, or transgender practitioner may find it helpful to disclose his or her orientation with a client who is struggling with whether to come out; but in some cases, the worker's disclosure could inhibit the client from sharing genuine feelings (Gartrell, 1994; Messinger, 2004). Although self-disclosure can be useful in many cases (Cain, 1996; Rochlin, 1985), and practitioners are using self-disclosure more than they did in the past, social workers need, at a minimum, close supervision and consultation to process these issues. Although personal experiences are key in knowledge development, social workers should always be in touch with their own feelings (Greene, 1994) and should remember that self-disclosure is intended to bring about the well-being of the client, not the practitioner.

HISTORY AND CURRENT EVENTS

As practice is embedded in the broader social context of life, a working knowledge of the social policies and shifting social forces is important for knowledge development and working with LGBT persons. The media is an important source of information, since historical events are most often documented in newspapers, televised news reports, and weekly and monthly magazines. Television talk shows and news journals are often less than objective and in many cases replete with inaccuracies; however, for many, these are the only sources of knowledge about LGBT persons and an important basis to work from, even in a professional context.

Media attention has thrust a variety of LGBT issues out of the closet and into the homes of millions of people. These issues are as varied as gay and lesbian marriage (Cooperman, 2004; Ziran, 1996); transgender experiences (Denizet-Lewis, 2002); bisexual teens (Morris, 2006); same-gender parental adoptions (Gay Adoption, 1993; Judge Lets, 1992); gay and lesbian partnership (Bennet, 1993; Schmalz, 1993c); benefits for same-sex partners; gay and lesbian parents (Goleman, 1992; Gross, 1991; Vaughan, 1996); the struggle for civil rights (Naegle, 1993; Schmalz, 1993b; The Future, 1990) or the restriction of gay rights (Gross, 1992; Johnson, 1993); the anatomical idiosyncrasies of brains in gay men (Angier, 1991a,b, 1992, 1993; Bailey & Pillard, 1991; Burr, 1993; Gelman, 1992; Henry, 1993; LeVay, 1991); the sense of smell in gay men (Slavic, Berglund, & Lindström, 2005); the collective power of lesbians (Salholz et al., 1993); gay and lesbian content in school curriculums (Levy, 1992; Teaching About, 1992); gays and the Boy

Scouts (Boy Scouts, 1992); the first gay comic book character (The Comics, 1992); the movement to end the ban on gays and lesbians in the military (Gay Sailor, 1993; Gordon, 1993; Manegold, 1993; Schmitt, 1993a,b,c; Schmalz, 1993a); and gay conservativism (Robinson, 2006). It seems that after years of being no more than a whisper, the issues of gays, lesbians, bisexuals, and transgender persons are now ostensibly being dealt with by the media in more open and visible ways.

The Internet has provided, more than any other avenue, very important sources of information about LGBT persons, and, at the same time, has permitted those persons at early stages of disclosure of an LGBT identity to explore their sexual and gender identity in a private and anonymous manner within the confines of their own homes. The information superhighway has grown exponentially for several years now (even since the first edition of this book), and the Internet may be, for many, the first place to begin a search about the plethora of issues pertaining to LGBT persons. Although there are also inaccuracies on the Internet, one huge benefit for those seeking access to knowledge about LGBT persons is that the Web has a reach that exceeds geography. Consequently, persons in remote rural areas potentially have equal access to information about and communication with LGBT persons around the world, whereas in the past such data were only to be found in urban areas. Granted, one must have access to a computer to make such connections, but libraries, schools, and Internet cafés in many communities can provide individuals with such access.

A review of appropriate Web sites about LGBT persons is beyond the scope of this publication, as there are literally tens of thousands, maybe more, that exist on the topic. The reader may find appropriate sites by using one of the numerous search engines (Yahoo, Webcrawler, Lycos, Excite, and others) and by keying code words and phrases such as gay, lesbian, bisexual, transgender, and sexual or gender orientation.

It is, however, a trinity of historical phenomenon—the groundbreaking work of the late Dr. Evelyn Hooker (1957, 1967), which presented the first rigorous scientific research to provide indisputable evidence that homosexuality is not a mental illness; the commencement of the Stonewall Rebellion of 1969 in New York City, generally regarded as the nativity of the gay and lesbian liberation movement; and the 1973 decision to eliminate homosexuality as a psychiatric disorder from the *Diagnostic and Statistical Manual of Mental Disorders,* Third Edition (DSM-III)—that were the major forces in conceptualizing Western society's views on gay and lesbian persons. In many significant ways, the advent of the AIDS pandemic has been another defining event for LGBT persons. Bisexual issues began to be discussed for the first time in social work literature with Fox's (1993) article;

transgender issues came into public consciousness for social work professionals with an early article by Wick (1978), but more fully in the 1990s (Mallon, 1999).

The history of social work with LGBT persons can best be described as an ambivalent relationship. Although the Delegate Assembly of the National Association of Social Workers (1994a,b) adopted a policy statement on gay issues in 1977, reaffirmed its commitment to this statement in 1993, and updated its code of ethics in 1994 and 1996 to emphasize its ban on discrimination based on sexual orientation, social work has generally lagged behind other helping professionals in putting resources behind its commitment. Transgender issues were first addressed by the National Association of Social Workers (NASW) in 1999.

Although the Council on Social Work Education (CSWE, 1992) revised its accreditation standards to require schools of social work to include foundation content related to LGBT service needs and practice in the core course curriculum (see Humphreys, 1983; Morrow & Messinger, 2006; Newman, 1989), a motion was put forward at the council's 1996 annual meeting to waive this requirement for "certain religiously affiliated organizations." Such moves signal reluctance on the part of the profession to allow gay and lesbian persons full and equal access to being included in the curriculum (see Parr & Jones's 1996 "Point/Counterpoint" journal article for a more complete discussion on this topic).

Despite inclusive policies and accreditation mandates that call for nondiscriminatory professional practice, an inherent difficulty in separating personal attitudes from professional prerogatives with respect to LGBT persons appears to have made service provision to this population a complex process. Gay, lesbian, bisexual, and transgender identity has historically been and continues to be a taboo subject for discussion even within most professional environments (Gochros, 1985, 1995; Mallon, 1998).

THE PROFESSIONAL LITERATURE

Although a plethora of professional literature has been published on and about LGBT persons in the *Journal of Homosexuality,* and more recently in the *Journal of Gay and Lesbian Social Services,* the mainstream social work publications have lagged behind those of several other helping professions, most notably psychology, in recognizing the legitimacy of homosexuality in the professional literature (see Van Voorhis & Wagner, 2001, 2002).

If one were to look exclusively within the social work professional literature to develop a knowledge base for practice, one would find a very circumscribed discussion of LGBT practice issues in the mainstream social work literature. The major social work journals have been slow to respond to and to publish articles that address the wide and diverse needs of LGBT persons. A review of the literature (Van Voorhis & Wagner, 2001) found seventy-seven articles that addressed gay and lesbian issues in four major social work journals—*Social Work, Social Service Review, Child Welfare,* and *Families in Society.* This was 3.92 percent of the 1,964 articles published during the decade of this study. Ninety percent of the articles on gay and lesbian identity were published in two journals: *Social Work* and *Families in Society.* An overwhelming majority of articles addressed HIV/AIDS. Less than 35 percent of the total number of articles addressed aspects of practice with lesbian and gay clients other than HIV/AIDS. Furthermore, more than half the articles that addressed HIV/AIDS were published in four special issues of *Social Work* and *Families in Society* that dealt either exclusively or primarily with HIV/AIDS. Unquestionably, there is a pressing need to provide information on and about LGBT persons.

Although a great deal of it is cited in this text, it is beyond the scope of this chapter to review the literature that delineates the knowledge requisite to achieve competent practice with LGBT persons. One only needs to scan the literature in Social Services Abstracts or other online tools to uncover an exponential body of literature on the topic.

RESEARCH

Groups of people who have been oppressed and discriminated against are vulnerable to stereotyping, perpetuation of myths about them, and other forms of negative misinformation. The bedrock of such misinformation is heterocentrism, racism, ethnocentrism, ageism, sexism, ableism, or all of these. Consequently, individuals who are members of oppressed groups may also believe or internalize these negative stereotypes about their group and thereby suffer what has been called a "dual oppression" (MacEachron, 1996, p. 20) from self and others. An important way to uncover stereotypic misinformation and oppressive myths is to provide evidence that validates the uniqueness of each individual. The amount of affirmative research, however, is not always congruent to the extent of societal oppression directed toward a group of people.

Meezan and Martin's (2003a) work provides an excellent overview of the current themes and brings together a highly qualified group of social work researchers to discuss research with LGBT populations. Meezan and Martin's (2003b) chapter on applying ethical standards to research and evaluation involving LGBT populations, and Wheeler's (2003) chapter on methodological issues in conducting community based health and social services re-search among black and African-American LGBT populations are par-ticularly noteworthy. Both quantitative and qualitative methods of research, or a blend of the two, are important means toward generating knowledge that has a scientific basis. Naturalistic inquiry, which is the rigorous obser-vation of phenomena that are important to social work practice, is particu-larly useful in cases where there has been limited conceptualization of an empirical nature. With its epistemological roots in anthropology, naturalis-tic research has increasingly been seen as an effective means of informing social work practice, particularly with LGBT persons.

Quantitative research has also found its place in allowing social workers to test sanctioned wisdom and to try new methods that may result in an im-proved outcome for clients (Elze, 2003). Group designs and single-system designs are probably the most common subtypes of experimental research (Elze, 2003). In the context of an emerging managed care environment, and as a means toward addressing issues of accountability, utilizing standardized outcome measures to test the veracity of clinical interventions with clients has increasingly become a significant aspect of practice (Bloom, Fischer, & Orme, 1995; Blythe, Tripodi, & Briar, 1994; Fischer & Corcoron, 1994; Hudson, 1985). Although only one standardized instrument could be found in the literature (Nurius & Hudson, 1988) to measure sexual orientation, there are two instruments (Hudson & Ricketts, 1980; Lumby, 1976) that were developed to measure homophobia.

In addition to monitoring practice effectiveness, quantitative methods have primarily been utilized by investigators who have sought to examine broad issues pertaining to the origin of sexual orientation (Acosta, 1975; Angier, 1991a,b, 1992, 1993; Bailey & Pillard, 1991; Baranaga, 1991; Barringer, 1993; Bell, Weinberg, & Hammersmith, 1981; Burr, 1993; Jay & Young, 1977; LeVay, 1991; Saghir, Robbins, & Walbian, 1973) and in the many attempts that have been made to quantify the population of gay men and lesbians (Janus & Janus, 1993; Kinsey, Pomeroy, & Martin, 1948; Kinsey, Pomeroy, Martin, & Gebhard, 1953; National Opinion Research Center, 1989-1992; Rogers, 1993).

In one edited text, Tully (1996) and colleagues (Jacobson, 1996; MacEachron, 1996; Woodman, Tully, & Barranti, 1996) focus on research issues with a lesbian population. Although the research that has focused on gay men has been slim in comparison with other groups, the research that has specifically focused on lesbians is even more sparse. Tully (1996) and colleagues have provided researchers and scholars with an intelligent and comprehensive overview of the research issues that affect lesbians. Their work can serve as a useful guide to those interested in examining research issues as a means toward developing practice knowledge about working with LGBT persons.

The research on bisexual women and men (Fox, 2004a) is in the nascent stages of research development. In his text, Fox (2004b) provides an excellent review of the social science literature on bisexuality. Israel and Mohr (2004) also provide a fine chapter on attitudes toward bisexual women and men, suggesting implications for future directions with this population.

The research on trans persons remains focused on medical issues pertaining to trans persons (see Bockting & Avery, 2005; Harry Benjamin International Gender Dysphoria Association, 2001; www.Translife.net/ tg101/research). Much of the social science literature focuses on interventions and rights issues. Lev's (2004) massive volume on the transgender experience provides a wide range of important information on practice with trans persons. Mallon's (1998) edited volume focused on issues pertaining to transgender youth. Israel and Tarver's (1997) work on transgender care provides readers with invaluable information about the experiences of persons living as trans. Langer and Martin's (2004) article, although humorously titled ("How Dresses Can Make You Mentally Ill"), seriously examines mental health issues for trans children. Similarly, Scholinski's book (1994) remains one of the best books written about the consequences of trying to live as others force you to live. Lesser's (1999) work addresses the issues of parenting a trans child from a parent's perspective. Currah, Juang, and Minter's (2006) text focuses exclusively on trans rights issues.

THEORETICAL AND CONCEPTUAL ANALYSES

Theories to guide practice or theoretical constructs that help one to better understand practice with a client system also offer explanations to guide practice. Understanding the process of LGBT identity formation will undoubtedly enable the practitioner to carry out informed and sensitive intervention with clients and families struggling with issues of sexual orientation. However, practitioners must also be aware of the fact that it is not possible for them to utilize traditional developmental models taught in most human behavior and social environment sequences (Blos, 1979; Erikson, 1950; Marcia, 1980; Newman & Newman, 1987), which posit concepts of sex-role identifications that are concerned only with heterosexual development and presume heterosexual identity as an eventual outcome.

Since the 1960s, identity movements of oppressed people (e.g., women, people-of-color communities, people with disabilities, LGBT persons) have challenged both academia and the society as a whole by exposing the extent to which they have been neglected by prevailing theoretical models (Domenici & Lesser, 1995). By exposing the biases behind paradigms that were previously considered objective, these voices have revealed the extent to which all epistemology is discourse specific (Domenici & Lesser, 1995). Dominant groups have constructed narratives of oppressed people that strengthened their own needs, values, interests, and self-esteem. Utilizing traditional approaches, which view homosexuality from a developmentally pejorative perspective, does not assist or prepare the practitioner to work competently with LGBT persons.

Berger (1977, 1982, 1983, 1990, 1996), who has written broadly about social work practice with gay and lesbian persons, offered two models for working with persons who identify as gay or lesbian: an advocate model (1977) and a definitional model (1983). Falco (1991), Garnets, Hancock, Cochran, Goodchikls, and Peplau (1991), and Morin (1991) have also presented affirmative models of therapy with lesbians and gay men. Viewing gay and lesbian identity through a lens of biculturality, Lukes and Lands (1990) proposed a model of practice that linked cultural issues with issues of one's identity. Slater's (1995) work also provided an affirming framework for working with lesbian clients within the context of a family life cycle. Fox's work (2004a, 2005) has been instrumental in developing models for practitioners to understand bisexual identity development; Lev's (2004) text reviews developmental issues that will be very helpful to social work practitioners seeking to understand the trans experience of development. Davis's chapter in this text also provides a clear overview of practice issues for trans persons.

Unlike their counterparts in the heterosexual majority, LGBT persons experience a social condition that is attributable to their LGBT gender/sexual orientation oppression. Oppression, notes Pharr (1988), cannot be viewed in isolation because its various dimensions—sexism, racism, homophobia, classism, anti-Semitism, and ableism—are interconnected by a common origin—economic power and control. Backed by institutional power, economic power, and both institutional and individual violence, this trinity of elements acts as the "standard of rightness and often righteousness wherein all others are judged in relation to it" (p. 24). There are many ways that norms are enforced both by individuals and institutions. One way to view persons who fall outside the "norm" is to label such individuals as "the other." It is easy to discriminate against—view as deviant, marginal, or inferior—such groups that are not part of the mainstream. Those who are classified as such become part of an invisible minority, a group whose achievements are kept hidden from and unknown to those in the dominant culture. Stereotyping, blaming the victim, and distortion of reality can even lead these persons to feeling as though they deserve the oppression that they experience. This process is called internalized homophobia. Other elements of oppression include isolation, passing as heterosexual, self-hatred, underachievement or overachievement, substance abuse, problems with relationships, and a variety of other mental health matters (Peterson, 1996).

Violence, as suggested by several researchers (Gustavsson & MacEachron, 1998; Hanson, 1996; Herek, 1990; Hunter, 1990; Pharr, 1988), is also seen as a theoretical construct in the lives of LGBT persons. The threat of violence toward LGBT persons who step out of line is made all the more powerful by the fact that they do not have to do anything to receive the violence. It is their lives alone that precipitate such action. Therefore, LGBT persons always have a sense of safety that is fragile and tenuous, and they may never feel completely secure. Social workers who are unfamiliar with gay and lesbian persons may view such conditions as a pathology in need of treatment, but for the gay or lesbian person such insecurity is an adaptive strategy for living within in a hostile environment (Germain & Gitterman, 1996).

SELF-AWARENESS

Many students entering the world of social work think that they are open-minded, and while many may have a genuine desire to help others, some have not delved inside of themselves to assess the roles that power, privilege, and influence have played in their own lives.

As social work is a values-based profession (McGowan, 1995), we are ethically obligated to address these issues and to work toward increasing the levels of competence and awareness within both students entering the profession and colleagues who continue to make contributions. Although the professional literature has begun to address these areas, as professionals we also must focus on the issue of self-awareness.

The consequence of not considering theoretical analyses and concepts that are heterocentric is that many heterosexual social workers believe that avoiding society's fear and loathing of LGBT persons is all that they need to do to work effectively with gay men and lesbian clients. While most social workers have "politically correct" ideas about LGBT persons, many professionals have not always had the opportunity to deal with the deeper prejudices and heterosexual privileges that they, themselves, possess. Since most professionals continue to have an inadequate knowledge base about the real lives of LGBT persons, this causes them to be in many cases more homo/bi/transignorant than homo/bi/transphobic.

Many LGBT persons believe that heterosexually oriented social workers still harbor the heterocentric assumption that it is less than normal or less preferable to be gay or lesbian. Some social workers, particularly those from a more "psychoanalytically oriented perspective, believe that somewhere in the LGBT person's system you can find the roots or the cause of homosexuality and that it secretly has something to do with family dysfunction" (Markowitz, 1991b, p. 28). These are complex issues that need to be addressed within the overall context of diversity and yet at the same time from a specific LGBT perspective. Moral, religious, and cultural biases still run deep in many students preparing for practice and in professionals who currently practice. Although there are no simple solutions to helping individuals overcome their biases, beginning an honest dialogue and providing students with accurate and appropriate information about LGBT persons is an important place to start. Newman, Dannenfelser, and Benishek (2002) and Cluse-Tolar, Lambert, Ventura, and Pasupuleti (2004) look at assessing social work and counseling students' acceptance of lesbians and gay men. Herek (2002) also addresses heterosexual attitudes toward gay men and lesbians. There is, as yet, no comparable work for assessing student's attitudes toward bisexual or trans persons.

KNOWLEDGE DERIVED FROM THE INDIVIDUAL CASE

Information provided by the case itself is the final means toward the generation of knowledge about LGBT persons that will be discussed in this chapter. The clients within the individual, couple, family, community, or organizational system, and the environmental context within which they live, provide a great deal of information which is specific to the case and which can guide practice. Listening to what clients say and observing what they do, from initial engagement through assessment, intervention, and termination, can provide crucial information.

Eda Goldstein (1995), in her chapter on ego-oriented intervention with diverse and oppressed populations, speaks to this type of knowledge. As she succinctly points out,

> [h]omosexuality is not a psychiatric illness nor does its presence in men and women mean that they are suffering from a psychological maladjustment or some type of personality pathology. (p. 249)

Although some LGBT persons present concerns that relate specifically to issues of gender or sexual orientation, many of which will be discussed in Shernoff's, Dodd and Booker's, Davis's, and Weber and Heffern's chapters in this collection, these individuals "usually seek help for a range of issues that have little to do with their sexual orientation per se or are related to it in an indirect way" (Goldstein, 1995, p. 249). Like their heterosexual counterparts, LGBT persons seek help from social work practitioners to deal with a wide array of problems in living (Alexander, 1998).

A critical aspect of intervening with a client who identifies as gay, lesbian, bisexual, or transgender is for practitioners to have a firm understanding of the client's identity formation, or what is more commonly known as the coming-out process (Cass, 1979, 1983/1984, 1984; Coleman, 1981, 1987; DeMonteflores & Schultz, 1978; Troiden, 1979, 1988, 1989). Although the adolescent and young adult (Elze, 2002; Mallon, 1999) periods of development are extremely important for LGBT identity development, the coming-out process can occur at any point in the life course (Johnson & Jenkins, 2004), particularly for women (Anderson & Holliday, 2004; Cass, 1996; Falco, 1991; Gramick, 1984; Ponse, 1980; Sophie, 1985-1986; Swann & Anastas, 2003), and may extend over many years. The coming-out experiences for bisexual persons and trans persons, while similar in many ways to gay and lesbian persons, are also qualitatively different experiences (see Lev, 2004; Fox, 2005).

The practitioner who is sensitive and affirming in his or her work with LGBT persons needs to have a complete understanding of the psychological, behavioral, affectional, attitudinal, and internal sense of "goodness of fit" as the features of each of the stages of coming out, and should direct interventions accordingly. A lack of familiarity with this process will cause the practitioner to misinterpret the client's reactions and to miss opportunities to assist the client in moving forward in the process of being comfortable with his or her own identity.

Practitioners need to be aware that certain conditions may be intensified, if not caused, by oppression and stigmatization that LGBT persons may have been exposed to in their development, and which they may continue to experience as adults. For example, although the coming-out process has been conceptualized as a positive developmental step toward healthfulness, the societal or familial response to an individual's disclosure may be less than constructive. On the other hand, the psychological consequences of hiding or passing (Berger, 1990; Cain, 1991a,b) are great and often contribute to conflict experienced on individual, interpersonal, and group levels.

Social work practitioners need to be sensitive to the particular needs and concerns of LGBT persons and must also appreciate that the client's membership in a stigmatized and oppressed group (Goffman, 1963) has shaped his or her identity and may play a role in the presenting problem the client may or may not bring to the initial session. Whether or not the presenting problem is related to the client's sexual orientation, the practitioner who intervenes with the client must be well acquainted with the issues and features of LGBT life, develop an expertise in working with the population, and acquire a knowledge of the community resources that exist to help this client. It is also important to recognize that there is as much diversity in the LGBT community as in all other communities, and therefore, there is no one type of gay, lesbian, bisexual, or transgender individual.

Although Western society has taken some positive steps in altering negative attitudes toward LGBT persons, practitioners, in working with individuals, must be aware of the presence of internalized homophobia (Malyon, 1982; Martin, 1982), or transphobia (Currah et al., 2006; Lev, 2004), or biphobia (Ochs, 1996; Page, 2004; Rust, 1996) to keep from reinforcing it through their own biases and stereotypes. Isolation is another problem that frequently arises as a result of the stigma associated with an LGBT identity. Practitioners need to be knowledgeable about resources that exist in the community and, if necessary, to support the client by going with him or her to visit these resources. The development of social support networks through involvement in such programs can be an important task for the client and practitioner to work on together.

Despite the mitigating effects of oppression, stigma, and discrimination, LGBT persons are a resilient and resourceful group of people who possess many strengths (Berger, 1990; Mallon, 1998). Utilizing a strengths perspective in practice (Cowger, 1994; DeJong & Miller, 1995) is also an important strategy in not only gaining knowledge about clients, but also as a step toward affirming and acknowledging the dignity and worth of individuals.

Subsequent chapters in this book will focus on exploring social work practice with LGBT persons from the perspectives of several client systems: individuals, groups, couples, families, communities, and organizations.

CONCLUSION

Although the vast majority of LGBT persons are healthy, resilient, and hardy individuals who do not seek social work intervention, some LGBT persons have been or will be clients in the agencies where social workers practice. Training social workers in our Master of Science in Social Work (MSW) programs and in our agencies is not only a requirement of the

CSWE, which is affirmed by NASW, but is also an ethical responsibility of the profession. Cultivating a knowledge base of practice to prepare students and practitioners to work more competently and effectively with LGBT persons is an essential element of good practice and needs to be integrated into foundation level curriculum in meaningful and conscientious ways.

REFERENCES

Acosta, F. X. (1975). Etiology and treatment of homosexuality: A review. *Archives of Sexual Behavior, 4,* 9-29.

Alexander, C. J. (1998). Treatment planning for gay and lesbian clients. *Journal of Gay & Lesbian Social Services, 8*(4), 95-106.

Anderson, S. C., & Holliday, M. (2004). Normative passing in the lesbian community: An exploratory study. *Journal of Gay & Lesbian Social Services, 17*(3), 25-38.

Angier, N. (1991a, September 1). Zone of brain linked to men's sexual orientation. *The New York Times,* p. Al.

Angier, N. (1991b, September 7). The biology of what it means to be gay. *The New York Times,* p. Dl.

Angier, N. (1992, August 1). Researchers find a second anatomical idiosyncrasy in brains of homosexual men. *The New York Times,* p. Bl.

Angier, N. (1993, March 12). Study suggests genes sway lesbians' sexual orientation. *The New York Times,* p. A11.

Bailey, M., & Pillard, R. (1991, August 17). Are some people born gay? *The New York Times,* p. A33.

Baranaga, M. (1991, August 31). Is homosexuality biological? *Science, 252*(5023), 945-958.

Barringer, F. (1993, April 15). Sex survey of American men finds 1% are gay. *The New York Times,* p. A1.

Bell, A. P., Weinberg, M. S., & Hammersmith, S. K. (1981). *Sexual preference: Its development in men and women.* Bloomington, IN: University of Indiana Press.

Bennet, J. (1993, January 11). Registry for gay couples holds benefits and risks. *The New York Times,* p. B3.

Berger, R. M. (1977). An advocate model for intervention with homosexuals. *Social Work, 22*(4), 280-283.

Berger, R. M. (1982). The unseen minority: Older gays and lesbians. *Social Work, 27*(3), 236-242.

Berger, R. M. (1983). What is a homosexual? A definitional model. *Social Work, 28*(2), 132-135.

Berger, R. M. (1990). Passing: Impact on the quality of same-sex couple relationships. *Social Work, 35,* 328-332.

Berger, R. M. (1996). *Gay and gray* (2nd ed.). Boston: Alyson Publications.

Bloom, M., Fischer, J., & Orme, J. G. (1995). *Evaluating practice: Guidelines for the accountable professional* (2nd ed.). Needham Heights, MA: Allyn and Bacon.

Blos, P. (1979). *The adolescent passage: Development issues.* New York: International Universities Press.

Blythe, B., Tripodi, T., & Briar, S. (1994). *Direct practice research in human service agencies.* New York: Columbia University Press.

Bockting, W. O., & Avery, E. (Eds.) (2005). *Transgender health and HIV prevention.* Binghamton, NY: The Haworth Press.

Boy Scouts to allow homosexuals in the new program (1992, August 22). *The New York Times,* p. A15.

Burr, C. (1993, March). Homosexuality and biology. *The Atlantic Monthly, 271*(3), 47-65.

Cain, R. (1991a). Relational contexts and information management among gay men. *Families in Society, 72*(6), 344-352.

Cain, R. (1991b). Stigma management and gay identity development. *Social Work, 36*(1), 67-73.

Cain, R. (1996). Heterosexism and disclosure in the social work classroom. *Journal of Social Work Education, 32*(1), 65-76.

Cass, V. C. (1979). Homosexual identity formation: A theoretical model. *Journal of Homosexuality, 4,* 219-235.

Cass, V. C. (1983/1984). Homosexual identity: A concept in need of a definition. *Journal of Homosexuality, 9*(2/3), 105-126.

Cass, V. C. (1984). Homosexual identity formation: Testing a theoretical model. *Journal of Sex Research, 20,* 143-167.

Cass, V. C. (1996, July 16). Personal interview.

Cluse-Tolar, T., Lambert, E. G., Ventura, L. A., & Pasupuleti, S. (2004). The views of social work students toward gay and lesbian persons: Are they different from other undergraduate students? *Journal of Gay & Lesbian Social Services, 17*(3), 59-85.

Coleman, E. (1981). Developmental stages of the coming out process. *Journal of Homosexuality, 7*(2/3), 31-43.

Coleman, E. (1987). Assessment of sexual orientation. *Journal of Homosexuality, 13*(4), 9-23.

The comics break new ground again (1992, January 24). *The New York Times,* p. A33.

Cooperman, A. (2004, July 26). Gay marriage as "The New Abortion" debate becomes polarizing as both sides become better organized, spend millions. *The Washington Post,* p. A03.

Council on Social Work Education (1992). *Curriculum policy statement for master's degree programs in social work education.* Alexandria, VA: Council on Social Work Education.

Cowger, C. D. (1994). Assessing client strengths: Clinical assessment for client empowerment. *Social Work, 39*(3), 262-268.

Currah, P., Juang, R. M., & Minter, S. (2006). *Transgender rights.* Minneapolis, MN: University of Minnesota Press.

DeJong, P., & Miller, S. D. (1995). How to interview for client strength. *Social Work, 40*(6), 729-736.

DeMonteflores, C., & Schultz, S. J. (1978). Coming out: Similarities and differences for lesbians and gay men. *Journal of Social Issues, 34*(3), 59-72.

Denizet-Lewis, B. (2002, May 26). About a boy who isn't. *New York Times Magazine,* p. 30.

Domenici, T., & Lesser, R. C. (Eds.) (1995). *Disorienting sexuality: Psychoanalytic reappraisals of sexual identities.* New York: Routledge.

Elze, D. E. (2002). Risk factors for internalizing and externalizing problems among gay, lesbian, and bisexual adolescents. *Social Work Research, 26*(2), 89-101.

Elze, D. E. (2003). 8,000 miles and still counting . . . reaching gay, lesbian and bisexual adolescents for research. *Journal of Gay & Lesbian Social Services, 15*(1/2), 127-145.

English, M. (1996). Transgenerational homophobia in the family: A personal narrative. In J. Laird & R.-J. Green (Eds.), *Lesbians and gays in couples and families: A handbook for therapists* (pp. 15-27). San Francisco: Jossey-Bass Publishers.

Erikson, E. (1950). *Childhood and society.* New York: W.W. Norton and Co.

Falco, K. L. (1991). *Psychotherapy with lesbian clients.* New York: Brunner/Mazel.

Fischer, J., & Corcoron, K. (1994). *Measures for clinical practice: A sourcebook* (2nd ed., Vols. 1 & 2). New York: The Free Press.

Fox, R. (2004a). *Current research in bisexuality.* Binghamton, NY: The Haworth Press.

Fox, R. (2004b). Bisexuality: A reader's guide to the social science literature. In R. A. Fox (Ed.), *Current research in bisexuality* (pp. 161-256). Binghamton, NY: The Haworth Press.

The future of gay America (1990, March 12). *Newsweek,* pp. 20-27.

Garnets, L., Hancock, K. A., Cochran, S. D., Goodchikls, J., & Peplau, L. A. (1991). Issues in psychotherapy with lesbians and gay men: A survey of psychologists. *American Psychologist, 46,* 964-972.

Gartrell, N. K. (1994). Boundaries in lesbian therapist-client relationships. In B. Greene & G. M. Herek (Eds.), *Lesbian and gay psychology: Theory, research, and clinical applications* (pp. 98-117). Thousand Oaks, CA: Sage Publications.

Gay adoption cases go to appeals court (1993, April 18). *The New York Times,* p. A25.

Gay sailor tells of a "living hell" (1993, March 8). *The New York Times,* p. A15.

Gelman, D. (1992, February 24). Born or bred? *Newsweek,* pp. 46-53.

Germain, C. B. (1991). *Human behavior and the social environment.* New York: Columbia University Press.

Germain, C. B., & Gitterman, A. (1996). *The life model of social work practice* (2nd ed.). New York: Columbia University Press.

Gochros, H. (1995). Sex, AIDS, social work and me. *Reflections, 1*(2), 37-43.

Gochros, H. L. (1985). Teaching social workers to meet the needs of the homosexually oriented. In R. Schoenberg, R. Goldberg, & D. Shore (Eds.), *With compassion towards some: Homosexuality and social work in America* (pp. 137-156). Binghamton, NY: The Haworth Press.

Goffman, E. (1963). *Stigma: Notes of the management of a spoiled identity.* Englewood Cliffs, NJ: Prentice Hall.

Goldstein, E. (1995). *Ego psychology and social work practice* (2nd ed.). New York: The Free Press.

Goleman, D. (1992, December 2). Studies find no disadvantage in growing up in a gay home. *The New York Times,* p. C14.

Gordon, M. R. (1993, March 30). Senate hearings open on homosexuals in military. *The New York Times,* p. Al.

Gramick, J. (1983). Homophobia: A new challenge. *Social Work, 28*(2), 131-141.

Gramick, J.J. III. (1984). Developing a lesbian identity. In T. Darty & S. Potter (Eds.), *Women identified women* (pp. 31-44). Palo Alto, CA: Mayfield.

Greene, B. (1994). Lesbian and gay sexual orientations: Implications for clinical training, practice and research. In B. Greene & G. M. Herek (Eds.), *Lesbian and gay psychology: Theory, research, and clinical applications* (pp. 1-24). Thousand Oaks, CA: Sage Publications.

Gross, J. (1991, February 11). New challenges of youth: Growing up in a gay home. *The New York Times,* p. Al.

Gross, J. (1992, September 26). In reversal, California governor signs a bill extending gay rights. *The New York Times,* p. Al.

Gustavsson, N. S., & MacEachron, A. E. (1998). Violence and lesbian and gay youth. *Journal of Gay & Lesbian Social Services, 8*(3), 41-50.

Hanson, B. (1996). The violence we face as lesbians and gay men: The landscape both outside and inside our communities. In M. Shernoff (Ed.), *Human services for gay people: Clinical and community practice* (pp. 95-114). Binghamton, NY: The Haworth Press.

Harry Benjamin International Gender Dysphoria Association (2001). *The HBIGDA standards of care for gender identity disorders* (6th version). Minneapolis, MN: The Harry Benjamin International Gender Dysphoria Association. Accessed April 5, 2006, from www.hbigda.org.

Hartman, A. (1992). In search of subjugated knowledge. *Social Work, 37,* 483-484.

Henry, W. A. (1993, July 26). Born gay? *Newsweek,* pp. 36-39.

Herek, G. M. (1990). The context of anti-gay violence: Notes on cultural psychological heterosexism. *Journal of Interpersonal Violence, 5*(3), 316-333.

Herek, G. M. (2002). Heterosexuals' attitudes toward bisexual men and women in the United States. *Journal of Sex Research, 39*(4), 264-275.

Hooker, E. (1957). The adjustment of the male overt homosexual. *Journal of Protective Techniques, 21,* 18-31.

Hooker, E. (1967). The homosexual community. In J. Gagnon & W. Simon (Eds.), *Sexual deviance* (pp. 380-392). New York: Harper and Row.

Hudson, W. W. (1985). *The clinical assessment system* [computer program]. Tempe, AZ: University of Arizona School of Social Work.

Hudson, W. W., & Ricketts, W. A. (1980). A strategy for measurement of homophobia. *Journal of Homosexuality, 5,* 357-371.

Humphreys, G. E. (1983). Inclusion of content on homosexuality in the social work curriculum. *Journal of Social Work Education, 19*(1), 55-60.

Hunter, J. (1990). Violence against lesbian and gay male youths. *Journal of Interpersonal Violence, 5*(3), 295-300.

Israel, G., & Tarver, D. (1997). *Transgender care: Recommended guidelines, practical information, and personal accounts.* Philadelphia: Temple University Press.

Israel, T., & Mohr, J. J. (2004). Attitudes toward bisexual women and men: Current research, future directions. In R. A. Fox (Ed.), *Current research in bisexuality* (pp. 117-134). Binghamton, NY: The Haworth Press.

Jacobson, S. (1996). Methodological research issues in research on older lesbians. In C. Tully (Ed.), *Lesbian social services: Research issues* (pp. 43-56). Binghamton, NY: The Haworth Press.

Janus, S. S., & Janus, C. L. (1993). *The Janus report on sexual behavior.* New York: John Wiley & Sons.

Jay, K., & Young, A. (1977). *The gay report: Lesbians and gay men speak out about their sexual experiences and lifestyles.* New York: Summit.

Johnson, D. (1993, January 16). A ban on gay-rights laws is put on hold in Colorado. *The New York Times,* p. A16.

Johnston, L. B., & Jenkins, D. (2004). Coming out in mid-adulthood: Building a new identity. *Journal of Gay & Lesbian Social Services, 16*(2), 19-42.

Judge lets gay partner adopt child: Companion of mother becomes foster parent (1992, January 31). *The New York Times,* p. Bl.

Kinsey, A. C., Pomeroy, W. B., & Martin, C. E. (1948). *Sexual behavior in the human male.* Philadelphia: W. B. Saunders.

Kinsey, A. C., Pomeroy, W. B., Martin, C. E., & Geghard, P. H. (1953). *Sexual behavior in the human female.* Philadelphia: W.B. Saunders.

Langer, S. J., & Martin, J. I. (2004). How dresses can make you mentally ill: Examining gender identity disorder in children. *Child and Adolescent Social Work Journal, 21*(1), 5-23.

Lesser, J. G. (1999). When your son becomes your daughter: Counseling the mother of a transsexual. *Families in Society, 80*(2), 182-189.

Lev, A. I. (2004). *Transgender emergence: Therapeutic guidelines for working with gender-variant people and their families.* Binghamton, NY: The Haworth Press.

LeVay, S. (1991). A difference in hypothalamic structure between heterosexual and homosexual men. *Science, 253*(5023), 1034-1037.

Levy, E. F. (1992). Strengthening the coping resources of lesbian families. *Families in Society, 73*(1), 23-31.

Lloyd, G. A. (1992). Contextual and clinical issues in providing services to gay men. In H. Land (Ed.), *AIDS: A complete guide to psychosocial intervention* (pp. 91-105). Milwaukee, WI: Family Services of America.

Lukes, C. A., & Lands, H. (1990). Biculturality and homosexuality. *Social Work, 35*(2), 155-161.

Lumby, M. E. (1976). Homophobia: The quest for a valid scale. *The Journal of Homosexuality, 2*(1), 39-47.

MacEachron, A. E. (1996). Potential use of single-system design for evaluating affirmative psychotherapy with lesbian women and gay men. In C. Tully (Ed.), *Lesbian social services: Research issues* (pp. 19-28). Binghamton, NY: The Haworth Press.

MacPike, L. (Ed.) (1989). There's something I've been meaning to tell you. Tallahassee, FL: The Naiad Press.

Mallon, G. P. (1998). *We don't exactly get the welcome wagon: The experience of gay and lesbian adolescents in child welfare systems.* New York: Columbia University Press.

Mallon, G. P. (Ed.) (1999). *Social services for transgendered youth.* Binghamton, NY: The Haworth Press.

Malyon, A. K. (1982). Psychotherapeutic implications of internalized homophobia in gay men. *Journal of Homosexuality, 7*(2/3), 59-69.

Marcia, J. E. (1980). Identity in adolescence. In J. Adelson (Ed.), *Handbook of adolescent psychiatry* (pp. 159-187). New York: John Wiley & Sons.

Markowitz, L. (1991a). You can go home again. *The Family Therapy Networker, 2,* 55-60.

Markowitz, L. (1991b). Homosexuality: Are we still in the dark? *The Family Therapy Networker, 2,* 27-35.

Martin, A. D. (1982). Learning to hide: The socialization of the gay adolescent. In S. C. Feinstein, J. G. Looney, A. Schartzberg, & A. Sorosky (Eds.), *Adolescent psychiatry: Developmental and clinical studies* (Vol. 10, pp. 52-65). Chicago: University of Chicago Press.

Mattaini, M. (1995). Knowledge for practice. In C. Meyer & M. Mataini (Eds.), *Foundations of social work practice* (pp. 59-85). Washington, DC: National Association of Social Workers.

McGowan, B. (1995, October 16). Personal communication.

Meezan, W., & Martin, J. (Eds.) (2003a). *Research methods with gay, lesbian, bisexual, and transgender populations.* Binghamton, NY: The Haworth Press.

Meezan, W., & Martin, J. (2003b). Applying ethical standards to research and evaluation involving LGBT populations. In W. Meezan & J. Martin (Eds.), *Research methods with gay, lesbian, bisexual, and transgender populations* (pp. 161-202). Binghamton, NY: The Haworth Press.

Messinger, L. (2004). Out in the field: Gay and lesbian social work students' experiences in field placement. *Journal of Social Work Education, 40*(2), 187-205.

Meyer, C. (1982). Issues in clinical social work: In search of a consensus. In P. Carloff (Ed.), *Treatment formulations and clinical social work* (pp. 19-26). Silver Spring, MD: National Association of Social Workers.

Morin, S. F. (1991). Removing the stigma: Lesbian and gay affirmative counseling. *The Counseling Psychologist, 19,* 245-247.

Morris, A. (2006, February 6). The cuddle puddle of Stuyvesant High School. *New York Magazine,* pp. 214-231.

Morrow, D. F., & Messinger, L. (2006). *Sexual orientation and gender expression in social work practice: Working with gay, lesbian, bisexual, and transgender people.* New York: Columbia University Press.

Muzio, C. (1996). Lesbians choosing children: Creating families, creating narratives. In J. Laird & R.-J. Green (Eds.), *Lesbians and gays in couples and families: A handbook for therapists* (pp. 358-369). San Francisco: Jossey-Bass Publishers.

Naegle, W. (1993, May 8). Group rights advocates fan flames of bias. *The New York Times,* p. A19.

National Association of Social Workers (1994a). Lesbian and gay issues. In National Association of Social Workers (Eds.), *Social work speaks* (pp. 162-165). Washington, DC: NASW.

National Association of Social Workers (1994b). *NASW code of ethics.* Washington, DC: NASW.

National Opinion Research Center (1989-1992). *General social survey.* University of Chicago: National Opinion Research Center.

Newman, B. M., & Newman, P. R. (1987). *Development through life: A psychosocial approach* (4th ed.). Belmont, CA: Dorsey Press.

Newman, B. S. (1989). Including curriculum content on lesbian and gay issues. *Journal of Social Work Education, 25*(3), 202-211.

Newman, B. S., Dannenfelser, P. L., & Benishek, L. (2002). Assessing beginning social work and counseling student's acceptance of lesbians and gay men. *Journal of Social Work Education, 38*(2), 273-289.

Nurius, P., & Hudson, W. (1988). Sexual activity and preference: Six quantifiable dimensions. *The Journal of Sex Research, 24,* 30-46.

Ochs, R. (1996). Biphobia: It goes more than two ways. In B. A. Firestein (Ed.), *Bisexuality: The psychology and politics of an invisible minority* (pp. 217-239). Thousand Oaks, CA: Sage Publications.

Page, E. H. (2004). Mental health services experiences of bisexual women and men: An empirical study. *Journal of Bisexuality, 3*(3/4), pp. 138-160.

Parr, R. G., & Jones, L. E. (1996). Point/counterpoint: Should CSWE allow social work programs in religious institutions an exemption from the accreditation non-discrimination standard related to sexual orientation? *Journal of Social Work Education, 52*(3), 297-313.

Peterson, K. J. (Ed.) (1996). Health care for lesbians and gay men: Confronting homophobia and heterosexism. *Journal of Gay & Lesbian Social Services, 5*(1) 112-131.

Pharr, S. (1988). *Homophobia: A weapon of sexism.* Little Rock, AR: Chardon Press.

Ponse, B. (1980). Finding self in the lesbian community. In M. Kirkpatrick (Ed.), *Women's sexual development* (pp. 181-200). New York: Plenum.

Robinson, P. (2006). *Queer wars: The new gay right and its critics.* Chicago: University of Chicago Press.

Rochlin, M. (1985). Sexual orientation of the therapist and therapeutic effectiveness with gay clients. In J. C. Gonsiorek (Ed.), *A guide to psychotherapy with gay and lesbian clients* (pp. 21-30). Binghamton, NY: The Haworth Press.

Rogers, P. (1993, February 15). How many gays are there? *Newsweek,* p. 46.

Rust, P. C. (1996). Managing multiple identities: Diversity among bisexual women and men. In B. A. Firestein, (Ed.), *Bisexuality: The psychology and politics of an invisible minority* (pp. 53-83). Thousand Oaks, CA: Sage Publications.

Saghir, M. T., Robbins, E., & Walbian, B. (1973). *Male and female homosexuality: A comprehensive study.* Baltimore: Williams and Wilkins.

Salholz, E., Glick, D., Beachy, L., Monserrate, C., King, P., Gordon, J., et al. (1993, June 21). The power and the pride: Lesbians, coming out strong. *Newsweek,* pp. 54-60.

Schmalz, J. (1993a, February 4). From midshipman to gay advocate. *The New York Times,* p. Cl.

Schmalz, J. (1993b, March 7). For gay people, a time of triumph and fear. *The New York Times,* p. L37.

Schmalz, J. (1993c, May 7). In Hawaii, step toward legalized gay marriage. *The New York Times,* p. 14.

Schmitt, E. (1993a, January 13). Clinton aides study indirect end to military ban on homosexuals. *The New York Times,* p. A1.

Schmitt, E. (1993b, January 23). Joint chiefs fighting Clinton's plan to allow homosexuals in military. *The New York Times,* p. Al.

Schmitt, E. (1993c, May 13). Family is unified in gay-ban debate. *The New York Times,* p. Al.

Scholinski, D. (1997). *The last time I wore a dress.* New York: Riverhead Books.

Shernoff, M. (1991). Eight years of working with people with HIV: Impact upon a therapist. In C. Silverstein (Ed.), *Gays, lesbians, and their therapists* (pp. 227-239). New York: W.W. Norton and Co.

Shernoff, M. (1996). The last journey. *Family Therapy Networker, 3,* 35-41.

Slater, S. (1995). *The lesbian family life cycle.* New York: The Free Press.

Slavic, I., Berglund, H., & Lindström, P. (2005, May). Brain response to putative pheromones in homosexual men. *The Proceedings of the National Academy of Sciences, 102*(20), 7356-7361.

Sophie, J. (1985/1986). A critical examination of stage theories of lesbian identity development. *Journal of Homosexuality, 12*(3/4), 39-51.

Swann, S. K., & Anastas, J. W. (2003). Dimensions of lesbian identity during adolescence and young adulthood. *Journal of Gay & Lesbian Social Services, 15*(1/2), 109-126.

Teaching about gays and tolerance (1992, September 27). *The New York Times,* p. E16.

Tievsky, D. L. (1988). Homosexual clients and homophobic social workers. *Journal of Independent Social Work, 2*(3), 51-62.

Translife. www.translife.net/tg101/. Accessed July 12, 2007.

Troiden, R. R. (1979). Becoming homosexual: A model of gay identity acquisition. *Psychiatry, 42,* 362-373.

Troiden, R. R. (1988). *Lesbian and gay identity: A sociological analysis.* Dix Hills: General Hall, Inc.

Troiden, R. R. (1989). The formation of homosexual identities. In G. Herdt (Ed.), *Lesbian and gay youth* (pp. 43-74). Binghamton, NY: The Haworth Press.

Tully, C. (Ed.) (1996). *Lesbian social services: Research issues.* Binghamton, NY: The Haworth Press.

Van Voorhis R., & Wagner, M. (2001). Coverage of gay and lesbian subject matter in social work journals. *Journal of Social Work Education, 37*(1), 147-159.

Van Voorhis R., & Wagner, M. (2002). Among the missing: Content on lesbian and gay people in social work journals. *Social Work, 47*(4), 345-54.

Van Wormer, K., & Wells, J. (2000). *Social work with lesbians, gays, and bisexuals: A strengths perspective.* New York: Allyn & Bacon.

Vaughan, M. (1996, September 3). Dad's out and baby goes too. *The Glasgow Herald,* p. 11.

Wheeler, D. (2003). Methodological issues in conducting community based health and social services research among Black and African-American LGBT populations. In W. Meezan & J. Martin (Eds.), *Research methods with gay, lesbian, bisexual, and transgender populations* (pp. 181-202). Binghamton, NY: The Haworth Press.

White, M., & Epston, D. (1990). *Narrative means to therapeutic ends.* New York: W.W. Norton.

Woodman, N., Tully, C. T., & Barranti, C. C. (1996). Research in lesbian communities: Ethical dilemmas. In C. Tully (Ed.), *Lesbian social services: Research issues* (pp. 57-66). Binghamton, NY: The Haworth Press.

Zirin, J. D. (1996, September 3). Vows that could alter marriage. *The London Times,* p. 37.

Chapter 2

Values and Ethics in Social Work Practice with Lesbian, Gay, Bisexual, and Transgender People

Peg McCartt Hess
Nancy Feldman

The codified values and ethics of the profession reflect the heart and conscience of social work practice. In this chapter, we explore the profession's values and ethical principles as they relate to social work practice with lesbian and gay clients. In order to clearly focus our discussion on the *profession's* value and ethical commitments, this chapter is organized around six core values and related ethical principles as outlined in the current National Association of Social Workers (NASW) *Code of Ethics* (1996). Within each section, the discussion highlights ways in which social workers should incorporate the stated values and ethical principles in practice with lesbian, gay, bisexual, and transgender (LGBT) persons and some of the obstacles that they are likely face in doing so. The chapter concludes with the identification of several frameworks useful in resolving ethical dilemmas.

Several professional documents identify the profession's core values and the expression and application of those values in practice. These include specific standards related to nondiscrimination against, social and economic justice for, and preparation for competent professional practice with a range of populations, including LGBT persons. The NASW *Code of Ethics,* revised and adopted by the Delegate Assembly of August 1996, states that social workers should "obtain education about and seek to understand the nature of social diversity and oppression with respect to race, ethnicity, national origin, color, sex, sexual orientation, age, marital status, political belief, religion and mental or physical disability" (1.05(c)) and "act to prevent and eliminate domination, exploitation, and discrimination against any person, group, or class on the basis of . . . sexual orientation . . . or any other preference, personal characteristic, or status" (6.04(d)). The Council on Social Work Education (CSWE, 1992) *Curriculum Policy Statement,* revised and adopted by the CSWE Board in 1992, stated that in both baccalaureate and master's programs, "The curriculum must provide content about people of color, women, and gay and lesbian persons" (pp. 101, 140). The revised CSWE *Evaluative Standards,* adopted by the board in 1994, state, "The program must be conducted without discrimination on the basis of . . . sexual orientation" (CSWE, 1994, pp. 84, 122).

More recently, the NASW (2003) supports curriculum policies in schools of social work that eliminate discrimination against people of diverse gender and encourages the implementation of continuing education programs on practice and policy issues relevant to gender diversity. In addition, to foster public awareness, NASW supports collaboration with organizations and groups supportive of the transgender community to develop programs to increase public awareness of the mistreatment and discrimination experienced by transgender people and of the contributions they make to society. The NASW also urges development of programs that educate students, faculty, and staff about gender diversity and the needs of transgender children and youth within schools and other child and youth services agencies (accessed August 15, 2006, from http://www.socialworkers.org/resources/abstracts/abstracts/transgender.asp).

Thus, the profession's commitment to prepare practitioners who demonstrate respect for the inherent dignity and worth of all persons and actively pursue social justice and social change on behalf of vulnerable and oppressed individuals and groups explicitly includes persons of differing sexual orientations. The realization of this commitment in social work education and practice, however, continues to challenge the profession as it attempts to move beyond the dictates and constraints of our homophobic and heterocentric social culture. In the following sections, these values and the related ethical principles are applied to practice with lesbian and gay persons.

THE PROFESSION'S CORE VALUES AND ETHICAL PRINCIPLES: APPLICATION IN PRACTICE WITH LESBIAN AND GAY CLIENTS

Consistent with the profession's historic and contemporary commitment to serving populations that are vulnerable and oppressed, the preamble of the NASW *Code of Ethics* (1996, p. 22) states:

The primary mission of the social work profession is to enhance human well-being and help meet basic human needs of all people, with particular attention to the needs and empowerment of people who are vulnerable, oppressed, and living in poverty. An historic and defining feature of social work is the profession's focus on individual well-being in a social context and the well-being of society. Fundamental to social work is attention to the environmental forces that create, contribute to, and address problems in living.

The mission of the social work profession is rooted in a set of core values. These core values, embraced by social workers throughout the profession's history, are the foundation of social work's unique purpose and perspective:

- Service
- Social justice
- Dignity and worth of the person
- Importance of human relationships
- Integrity
- Competence

The constellation of these core values reflects what is unique to the social work profession. Core values, and the principles which flow from them, must be balanced within the context and complexity of the human experience.

VALUE: *Service*

Ethical Principle: *Social workers' primary goal is to help people in need and to address social problems.*

Simply stated, the core value of service and the related goal of helping are the sine qua non of the social work profession. This simplicity, however, can be misleading. The determinations concerning whom, how, where, and in what ways one serves, and what in fact is experienced by others as helpful, are often complex and challenging to make. As introduced in the first chapter in this volume and discussed throughout, a client's sexual orientation may or may not be known to the practitioner and, in some instances, may be a matter of confusion and/or shame to the client. Therefore, in order to serve and be helpful, social work practitioners must be able to connect with persons who are lesbian and gay. Establishing such connections requires agency and practitioner messages that convey authentic inclusivity, acceptance, and affirmation; recognition of the varying role of sexual orientation in an individual client's service needs and of the range of appropriate interventive options; and an understanding of the relationship between the experiences of individual lesbians and gay men and the homophobic heterocentric culture in which they live.

First, in aspiring to serve and help individual LGBT persons, their family members and friends, and the LGBT communities, social work practitioners, and agencies that employ them must critically examine the degree to which their services are truly accessible. Enacting the professional value of service requires an organizational and individual professional commitment to intentional inclusivity in the development of policies, programs, and practices that are "user friendly" to lesbian and gay clients and couples, families headed by gay and lesbian parents, and families with gay and lesbian family members. Agency brochures, forms, and other written materials should portray images of LGBT staff and clientele. Particular attention must be given to the use of nonheterocentric language in telephone and in-person transactions between staff and potential clients. For example, changing the question "Are you married?" to "Do you have a partner?" conveys openness and the capacity to help LGBT clients as individuals and as couples. In a discussion of the promotion of organizational environments that are "user friendly" to all family forms, Hess and Jackson (1995) state:

> [T]he questions that families are asked directly and on intake forms either encourage clients to acknowledge openly their families' unique membership and set of relationships, roles, and needs or convey the assumption that client families must be traditionally constituted. Questions should anticipate that children may be biological, step-, adopted, or foster children or members of the extended family (nieces or nephews) and that they may have one caregiver (a single mother or father, a grandmother, an aunt, or a godparent), two caregivers, (such as a mother and a father, a mother and a mother, a father and a father, a mother and an aunt, or a grandmother and a grandfather), or two or more parents in separate household who share joint custody. Social workers must be mindful that simple questions about family membership can be posed in ways that shame or alienate the client or encourage deception. (pp. 134-135)

Helping LGBT persons also requires skill in assessing with the client whether sexual or gender orientation is in the foreground or background of her or his concern and service need. An assumption that sexual or gender orientation would be in the foreground conveys the practitioner's misconception that being LGBT is a "problem." On the other hand, a practitioner's assumption that sexual or gender orientation would be irrelevant conveys a lack of understanding of the many ways in which the client's life experience is affected by the homophobic and trans- or biphobic reactions of family members, friends, employers, and her or his own internalized heterocentrism. The discussions throughout this volume provide ample illustration of these and of the range of interventive options that may prove helpful.

Serving persons who are lesbian, gay, bisexual, or transgender also requires that organizations and practitioners identify and address social problems that affect them individually and collectively. These include discrimination in employment, health and other benefits, educational settings, and family courts, as well as violence perpetrated against LGBT persons. Addressing such problems requires social workers to advocate with and on behalf of LGBT clients, be vigilant against institutional discrimination against LGBT clients, and be visible in joining with the LGBT communities to address community and social problems. The following vignette illustrates the relevance of these dimensions.

A young couple, Ray and Jolene, sought help from a family service agency. Initially they identified concerns with the behavior of their four-year-old daughter Roxanne, who was attending day care. Day care staff reported that she was hitting other children, was unable to relax during nap time, and had frequent temper tantrums. Ray and Jolene were concerned that the center might refuse continued service, affecting their ability to retain their employment. The social worker engaged with Jolene and Ray to assess Roxanne's behaviors, the tensions within the marital relationship, and both parents' satisfaction with their lives. Ray was struggling with a worsening depression that he attributed to a growing distance between himself and Jolene, a distance he could not explain. Several times Jolene mentioned being unable to be herself in the relationship and alluded to a secret that she could not share.

Through a skillful series of individual and joint discussions, the social worker was able to help Jolene acknowledge the reality of her lesbian sexual orientation and share this with Ray. With the secret out, the social worker, Jolene, and Ray began to identify and work together on the many decisions that each faced individually and as parents. In reflecting upon their initial call to this particular family service agency, Jolene noted having seen a brochure in Roxanne's pediatrician's office describing the agency's service, including a group on parenting issues for lesbian and gay parents. Once connected to the agency, Jolene had experienced the social worker as being open in her ongoing assessment of the range of possible sources of Jolene's expressed ability to "be herself" in her relationship with Ray.

VALUE: *Social Justice*

Ethical Principle: *Social workers challenge social injustice.*

Historically and currently, the social work profession is strongly identified with the value of social justice. Challenging injustice and pursuing social change are integral to each professional social worker's job description. As described in Chapter 1 and throughout this volume, homophobia, biphobia, transphobia, and heterocentrism are powerful and insidious forces that have resulted in discrimination and inequality for LGBT persons in many aspects of their lives.

Social workers have an ethical responsibility to be informed about the degree to which LGBT persons in their communities are ensured equality of opportunity and access to needed information, services, resources, and meaningful participation in decision making. Social workers must use their professional knowledge, skills, and influence to enhance equal opportunity and access. As asserted by Hartman, "On the national level, we must press NASW to more actively take on the issue of gay rights and to make the weight of our profession felt by those who would reverse the movement toward acceptance and equity for gay men and lesbians" (1993, p. 360). Ann Hartman and her partner, Joan Laird, expand on this theme further in their subsequent work (Hartman & Laird, 1998) that focuses on the moral and ethical issues in working with lesbians and gay persons.

Informing oneself about one's own organization's policies, programs, and practices is a responsible beginning point. What are LGBT clients' experiences in the school, community mental health clinic, family service agency, residential treatment facility, hospital, shelter, or other setting in which you are employed or are placed as a social work intern? In your community, what are the experiences of people who are LGBT when they seek to access health benefits for themselves and/or their families, run for president of the local high school student council or of the school's PTA, become licensed as a foster parent, volunteer as a Big Brother or a Big Sister, adopt a child, join a health club, attend parenting classes, or apply for a mortgage?

In practice with LGBT clients, it is important to recognize the close relationship between case and cause. Given the extent to which oppression is ever present in the lives of persons who are LGBT it is often essential to include advocacy as a service component. The following example illustrates this point.

A child care agency in a metropolitan community was concerned about the length of time spent by "hard to place" infants and young children in foster care and institutional settings. Identified as hard to place because of special medical, physical, and emotional needs, the children typically required extensive parental involvement in daily care and parental involvement with a range of professionals. In response to the agency's outreach to potential adoptive parents, a number of single gay men and lesbians and gay and lesbian couples applied. Some applicants were parents; others, in adopting a child, would become a parent for the first time.

Following extensive assessment of the applicant pool, the agency selected several persons who were gay and lesbian for preadoptive placement preparation and planning. Upon challenges from other applicants in the pool regarding their selection, the agency stated the position that it would not discriminate against applicants on the basis of sexual orientation. A number of individuals and groups subsequently approached agency administrators and staff, portraying the lesbian and gay applicants as wishing to "convert" children to their sexual orientation and accusing the agency of subjecting children to a "deviant" lifestyle.

Recognizing that both the well-being of the applicants and of the children were at stake, agency administrators, supervisors, and staff in the program engaged in both education and advocacy. For example, staff initiated meetings with members of the agency's board, social workers in key positions in the community, and other influential community professionals to provide information, respond to concerns, and secure support. Agency staff contacted several national organizations in order to identify educational materials and individuals available for consultation. The PBS documentary *We Are Family* (Sands, 1986), which depicts gay and lesbian parents and their biological, foster, and adoptive children, was provided to community agencies and professional groups. While recognizing some risk to community support of the agency, the staff concluded that the issue of social justice must be confronted. The program remained intact and efforts to prevent the placements of children with lesbian and gay parents were thwarted.

VALUE: *Dignity and Worth of the Person*

Ethical Principle: *Social workers respect the inherent dignity and worth of the person.*

Respect for the dignity and worth of all people is perhaps the most basic of social work values. However, its application in practice with lesbian and gay persons requires a profound commitment to self-determination and strong skills in facilitating the enhancement of self-esteem in others. As articulated in the NASW *Code of Ethics,* "Social workers respect and promote the right of clients to self-determination and assist clients in their efforts to identify and clarify their goals" (p. 12).

In promoting the self-determination of their LGBT clients, some social workers may confront a sense of dissonance as they weigh their professional knowledge, their personal beliefs, their feelings for their clients, and professional standards. Valuing the dignity and worth of each person is a matter of thinking, feeling, and acting. Although our respect for the inherent dignity and worth of persons who are LGBT is primarily demonstrated through our professional behaviors, our capacity to behave respectfully is inevitably shaped by our personal experiences and values, professional knowledge and training, openness to feedback from others, and personal and professional commitment to a disciplined use of self.

Internalized heterocentrism often undermines an LGBT client's own sense of value and self-worth. In some instances, a client's confusion about her or his sexual or gender orientation potentially undermines self-determination and clarity about life goals. In such instances, the practitioner's expression of respect for the client's struggle, potential, and worth must be unwavering. The following vignette demonstrates a social worker's skill in communicating his valuing of a young transgender client.

Joshua began meeting with a social worker in his high school at the age of fifteen. He was experiencing depression, insomnia, and difficulties in completing his schoolwork. After finding a popular trans magazine *Tapestry* on the kitchen table, Joshua's sister asked Joshua if it was his. In the course of their conversation, Joshua acknowledged his gender identity issues, telling her that he has always felt that he was born in the wrong body. His sister urged him to "talk with someone."

After several further conversations with his sister, Joshua "stopped by" to talk with the social worker who had presented in several of his health classes about different issues that teenagers confront, including suicidal thoughts and confusion about sexual and gender orientation. The social worker began meeting with Joshua and learned that Joshua had always felt like he was a girl, not a boy, or as he sometimes said, "like a girl-boy." The youngest in his family, Joshua said he often looked in the mirror and saw someone else reflected back at him. His father seemed particularly upset by Joshua's "gender-atypical behavior." Joshua described having kissed several girls and having felt nothing, but he was very attracted to some boys in his school. He told the social worker he believed initially he might be gay, but had discussed his feelings with no one.

After exploring how he felt on an Internet chat room with other young trans people, Joshua now identifies as transgender and has a female name that he prefers to use—Janice. Joshua asked the social worker to begin calling her by her girl name, Janice, and the social worker complied. Janice was deeply distressed about her belief that her father was disappointed in her. She was experiencing increased attraction to men and a recurring sense of panic in her isolation from family and friends. At the same time, Janice felt different from some of the gay boys she met at the school's support group. The social worker concluded that Janice was confused and sad about accepting herself as a trans person.

The social worker helped Janice initiate a discussion with her mother about her belief that she might be transgender. Though initially frightened by this disclosure, her mother was reassured that Joshua/Janice had confided in her. The social worker actively engaged in helping Janice assess and recognize her inherent worth and value, clarifying and then challenging the negative self-statements that characterized Janice's conversations with him. The social worker also facilitated Janice's participation in a group of trans youth in the community. Through an intricate process involving conversations with the social worker, her mother and sister, and other trans youth, Janice was able to begin to express hopefulness about her life and her worth. She began to construct a self-concept as a bright, talented, and sensitive young woman. As she became clearer about her gender orientation and her identity, she began to come out to her friends, and, with the support of her mother and her sister, to her father. Her relationships and academic work began to stabilize. She maintained her connection to the social worker as she began to explore the transition from high school and family to college.

VALUE: *Importance of Human Relationships*

Ethical Principle: *Social workers recognize the central importance of human relationships.*

Social workers understand that human development, change, and opportunity occur within the context of nurturing, accepting, and supportive relationships. Perhaps the greatest cost of homophobia, biphobia, and transphobia occurs in relationships. Therefore, a central focus of practice with persons who are lesbian, gay, bisexual, or transgender is on relationships—bringing honesty into relationships, reducing tensions in relationships, redefining or ending relationships, and developing new relationships.

In practicing with LGBT persons, it is important to recognize the vital importance of supportive social networks. Reflective of the social isolation faced by many LGBT persons, close interpersonal ties are often limited or constrained. As illustrated by the situations described previously, intimate relationships with parents, siblings, children, and friends may become compromised and incomplete. Many LGBT clients need assistance in healing current relationships and/or in developing new relationships in order to decrease their sense of isolation, achieve their goals, and enhance their well-being. The following vignette demonstrates the potency of group intervention in working with gay men who are HIV positive.

A community-based HIV/AIDS service organization recognized the social isolation experienced by many gay men newly diagnosed with HIV infection. Fearful of disclosure to families, co-workers, and sometimes even close friends, this population of clients grew increasingly fearful and depressed. In addition to case management, emergency financial aid, and buddy services, the agency initiated several support groups for recently diagnosed HIV-positive men. The purpose of the groups was defined as mutual aid. Group membership was voluntary and expected to change depending on members' needs. Meeting on a weekly basis, one of the groups consisted of approximately twenty-two members, including two HIV-negative partners.

A simple format was used in which each member briefly checked in and an agenda was developed from those items. Occasionally, lecturers were invited into the group and social events were scheduled. However, the simple process of sharing openly in a safe place where confidentiality was assured set in motion a powerful process of mutual support and caring. Members reported their struggles with health issues, unresponsive professional caregivers, struggles with families and partners, and fears about death. As a result, members achieved a level of intimacy with one another unlike that found in most areas of their lives. Many group members described the group as their substitute family. Over time, group members developed family-like practices such as having a Thanksgiving buffet on Thanksgiving eve and dinner together on Christmas Day. Many group members had been estranged from their immediate and extended families for long periods of time. Most members identified this estrangement as more related to being gay than to being HIV positive.

Group members often planned other social activities, including traveling to see the AIDS Quilt and developing several fund-raising events. As the group members developed friendships based on honest expressions of their identities, fears, and needs, members reported an increase in positive self-esteem and an overall sense of empowerment. As some group members became ill and subsequently died, they were supported through these experiences by other members of the group. Many reported that their capacity to confront illness, pain, and possible death was greatly enhanced by helping others and knowing that others were committed to helping them. Group members came to trust that they were not alone.

VALUE: *Integrity*

Ethical Principle: *Social workers behave in a trustworthy manner.*

The NASW *Code of Ethics* rightfully holds that social workers should aspire to be trustworthy in all professional activities. When working with LGBT persons, integrity is particularly crucial to effective practice. Given the extent to which matters of sexual or gender orientation have been cloaked in secrecy, it is often unrealistic to expect that openness and clarity will be present with our clients, our colleagues, or even within ourselves. The pervasive presence of heterocentrism in our society has tended to discourage these qualities. Consequently, in a purposeful way, professional social workers must engage in a process of self-examination and change that in turn will contribute to the creation of more trustworthy professional relationships with clients and trustworthy programs and organizations for gay and lesbian clients.

The ongoing process of developing self-awareness is central to integrity in practice with persons who are lesbian and gay. In spite of the general professional social work awareness that discrimination on the basis of gender or sexual orientation is unacceptable, basic attitudes about persons who are LGBT continue to be strongly influenced by heterocentrism. It is reasonable to expect that just as all persons reared in our culture have internalized some elements of racism, homophobia/biphobia/transphobia have been internalized as well. This is often as true for LGBT persons as for those who are heterosexual. Consequently, it is imperative that professional social workers challenge their own attitudes and beliefs about gender and sexual orientation through a process of systematic self-exploration. Social workers need to be comfortable with the feminine and masculine aspects of themselves, as well as the ambiguous aspects, and be capable of empathy with clients whose emotional lives and gender or sexual orientations are similar to or different from their own. For all social workers, it is important to explore one's own gender and sexual orientation fully in order not to displace upon clients issues that grow out of one's own concerns and life experiences. Whatever one's own gender or sexual orientation, it is important to be able to accept and tolerate the variety of choices that may be made by LGBT clients about self-disclosure to family, friends, co-workers, and others.

Issues of practitioner self-disclosure regarding gender and sexual orientation have both practice and ethical dimensions. For practitioners who are themselves lesbian, gay, bisexual, or transgender, practice with LGBT clients may present particular challenges as discussed in several of the chapters in this collection. In small communities particularly, the ethical directives concerning dual or multiple relationships with clients or former clients and concerning clients' rights to privacy require attention and care.

Respect for the confidential nature of practice with persons who identify as LGBT is essential to the definition of trustworthiness. While all clients are rightfully concerned about privacy and confidentiality, clients who are LGBT are likely to be acutely sensitive to the nature of information shared among agency co-workers and maintained in agency records and practitioners' personal notes. Davidson and Davidson (1996) thoughtfully describe the vulnerability of clients in a "culture of information processing" (p. 215). Confidential information regarding clients' gender or sexual orientation must be carefully protected. Social workers should question under what circumstances information concerning the gender or sexual orientation of clients should be recorded and maintained as a part of agency records, particularly when information is to be passed on to managed care companies. Inadvertently "outing" a client or client's family member is tantamount to betrayal and an egregious breach of professional ethics.

VALUE: *Competence*

Ethical Principle: *Social workers practice within their areas of competence and develop and enhance their professional expertise.*

It is the expectation of the NASW that professionals should limit their practice to those areas in which they have established a necessary degree of competence. However, such a principle should not provide an easy rationale for refusing to work with lesbians and gay men. Rather, we agree with the standard established by the CSWE in 1992 that preparation for social work practice fundamentally must include practice with lesbians and gay men. Competence must be established through mastery of a knowledge base about practice with lesbians and gay men, having an exposure to LGBT clients during internship experiences, and investing in exploring one's own homophobia, biphobia, transphobia, stereotypes, and personal beliefs and biases.

Thus, content regarding the historic and current life experiences of LGBT persons should be an essential component of professional education. It is beyond the scope of this chapter to delineate the knowledge requisite to achieve competent practice with persons who are LGBT, but key components include the following:

- Individual human development, including the androgynous, dual gender characteristics of all persons
- Developmental milestones for LGBT persons, such as the coming-out experience, and the essential characteristics of lesbian and gay identity development as evidenced through the life stories now available in print (Alyson, 1991; Desetta & Hefner, 2002; Due, 1995; Heron, 1994; Kay, Estepa, & Desetta, 1996; Mallon, 1997; Miranda, 1996; Monette, 1992)
- The extensive literature regarding the source of sexual orientation, including genetics (see LeVay, 1991)

- The extensive literature regarding the source of gender orientation (see Burgess, 1999; Mallon, 1999; Mallon & DeCrecenzo, 2006; McPhail, 2004)
- Typical concerns of lesbian and gay couples (see McVinney and Dodd/Booker's chapters in this collection) and developmental cycles of lesbian and gay families
- The struggle for human rights by the LGBT communities (see Vaid, 1995)
- The study of and opportunity to apply assessment and intervention strategies for practice with LGBT clients and their families (see Mallon, Chapter 11 in this collection; Cooper, 1999)
- The study of and opportunity to apply knowledge about exemplary programs for members of the LGBT communities

A strength of social work education is the opportunity to test theory in supervised practice. These authors propose that all students should have the opportunity to practice with LGBT clients. It is anticipated that issues will arise related to students' heterocentrism and self-disclosure. Some students will struggle in practice and gain extensively from such a learning opportunity. In some instances, this opportunity will result in a better understanding of a student's appropriateness for the profession. To illustrate, a first-year student in a large social work MSW program in the western part of the United States was unwilling to provide counseling to a gay couple as a part of his field practicum. He refused to do so based upon his religious beliefs, which defined any gay sexual behavior as sinful. After lengthy discussions, this student was asked to leave the school because it was decided that he was not suited for the profession of social work. The authors concur that a student's refusal to practice in any way with lesbian and gay clients is deeply inconsistent with the value base of the profession. It is recognized that students will grow and develop in the learning process; however, a basic willingness to work fully with clients of both genders, multiple races and ethnicities, and differing gender and sexual orientations is a necessary condition for entry into the profession.

IDENTIFYING, ANALYZING, AND RESOLVING ETHICALLY CHALLENGING PRACTICE PROBLEMS AND DILEMMAS

Although in most situations the core values and related ethical principles identified in the profession's code of ethics are sufficient to shape and direct practice decisions, in some situations ethical dilemmas or conflicts emerge. The professional literature provides numerous discussions of these, and in many agencies and settings ethics committees have been established to provide guidance to professionals confronting such dilemmas. Several resources include guidelines for ethical decision making and are highly recommended. These include *Social Work Values and Ethics* (Reamer, 1995), *Ethical Decisions for Social Work Practice* (Lowenberg & Dolgoff, 1996), and *Ethical Dilemmas in Social Work Practice* (Rhodes, 1986).

CONCLUSION

Social work practice with persons who are LGBT must be infused with the core set of professional values and shaped by ethical principles. Given social work's commitment to serve oppressed populations, this area of practice is central to the profession. A set of core values and ethical principles has been explicated in this essay, providing one approach to developing practice that is sensitive to issues of sexual and gender orientation.

REFERENCES

Alyson, S. (1991). *Young, gay and proud.* Boston: Alyson Publications.

Burgess, C. (1999). Internal and external stress factors associated with the identity development of transgendered youth. *Journal of Gay & Lesbian Social Services, 10,* 35-47.

Cooper, K. (1999). Practice with transgendered youth and their families. *Journal of Gay & Lesbian Social Services, 10,* 111-129.

Council on Social Work Education (1992). *Curriculum policy statement for master's degree programs in social work education.* Alexandria, VA: Author.

Council on Social Work Education Commission on Accreditation (1994). *Handbook of accreditation standards and procedures* (4th ed.). Alexandria, VA: Author.

Davidson, J. R., & Davidson, T. (1996). Confidentiality and managed care: Ethical and legal concerns. *Health and Social Work, 21,* 2QH-215.

Desetta, A., & Hefner, K. (Eds.) (2002). *In the life: Narratives of lesbian and gay youth in foster care.* New York: New Youth Communications.

Due, L. (1995). *Joining the tribe: Growing up gay and lesbian in the 90s.* New York: Anchor Books.

Hartman, A. (1993). Out of the closet: Revolution and backlash. *Social Work, 38,* 245-246, 360.

Hartman, A., & Laird, J. (1998). Moral and ethical issues in working with lesbians and gay men. *Families in Society, 79,* 263-276.

Heron, A. (Ed.) (1994). *Two teenagers in 20.* Boston: Alyson Publications.

Hess, P. M., & Jackson, H. (1995). Practice with and on behalf of families. In C. Meyer & M. Mattaini (Eds.), *The foundations of social work practice* (pp. 126-155). Washington, DC: National Association of Social Workers.

Kay, P., Estepa, A., & Desetta, A. (Eds.) (1996). *Out with it: Gay and straight teens write about homosexuality.* New York: Youth Communications.

LeVay, S. (1991). A difference in hypothalamic structure between heterosexual and homosexual men. *Science, 253*(5023), 1034-1037.

Lowenberg, P. M., & Dolgoff, R. (1996). *Ethical decisions for social work practice* (4th ed.). Itasca, IL: F.E. Peacock.

Mallon, G. P. (1997). Entering into a collaborative search for meaning with gay and lesbian youths in out-of-home care: An empowerment-based model for training child welfare professionals. *Child and Adolescent Social Work Journal, 14,* 427-444.

Mallon, G. P. (Ed.) (1999). *Social services with transgendered youth.* Binghamton, NY: The Haworth Press.

Mallon, G. P., & DeCrescenzo, T. (2006). Transgender children and youth: A child welfare practice perspective. *Child Welfare, 85,* 215-241.

McPhail, B. A. (2004). Questioning gender and sexuality binaries: What queer theorists, transgendered individuals, and sex researchers can teach social work. *Journal of Gay & Lesbian Social Services, 17,* 3-21.

Miranda, D. (1996). I hated myself. In P. Kay, A. Estepa, & A. Desetta (Eds.), *Out with it: Gay and straight teens write about homosexuality* (pp. 34-39). New York: Youth Communications.

Monette, P. (1992). *Becoming a man: Half a life story.* New York: Harcourt Brace Jovanovich.

National Association of Social Workers (1996). *Code of ethics.* Washington, DC: NASW Press.

National Association of Social Workers (2003). *Social work speaks: NASW Policy statements 2003-2006.* Washington, DC: NASW Press.

Reamer, F. (1995). *Social work values and ethics.* New York: Columbia University Press.

Rhodes, M. (1986). *Ethical dilemmas in social work practice.* Boston: Routledge and Kegan Paul.

Sands, A. (Producer) (1986). *We are family.* Boston: WGBH.

Vaid, U. (1995). *Virtual equality: The mainstreaming of gay and lesbian liberation.* New York: Anchor Books.

Chapter 3

Lesbians, Gays, Bisexuals, and Transgender People of Color: Reconciling Divided Selves and Communities

Karina L. Walters
Roy L. Old Person Jr.

I used to wonder why I have so often felt preoccupied with issues of boundary and identity. Why am I still startled when someone asks, yet again . . . are you a woman first or a person of color/Asian American first? . . . [or] if this is a lesbian group, why do you keep talking about race? We are all women here. . . . How does one negotiate a multiple-situated identity if race, gender, and sexual orientation are taken for granted as so separate and boundaried?

Karen Maeda Allman (1996, p. 277)

The successful development of healthy group and self-identities among members of oppressed groups involves the ability to reconcile competing demands from the dominant society and the individual's ethnic, racial, or the lesbian, gay, bisexual, and transgender (LGBT) communities. Research has demonstrated that positive LGBT self and group identities as well as a positive racial or ethnic identity are integrally connected to psychological well-being (Bradford, 2004, 2006; Crawford, Allison, Zamboni, & Soto, 2002; Helms, 1989; Phinney, 1990; Sue, 1992; Walters & Simoni, 1993). Despite the recognition that ethnic or LGBT identity is important in mental health functioning, little research has investigated the multiple oppressed statuses and the interactions of these statuses in psychosocial functioning

Social Work Practice with LGBT People

among LGBT persons of color (LGBTOC). For LGBTOCs, the integration of a consolidated racial and LGBT identity are even more complex, involving negotiations of conflicting allegiances to the LGBT communities and their ethnic community. Despite the importance of understanding the complex interactions among racism, sexism, and heterosexism that LGBTOCs must negotiate, the social work practice literature remains inadequate in providing any practice guidelines that incorporate these issues. This chapter explores how racial and LGBT identities moderate life stressors associated with a double or triple oppressed group status and the conflicts in allegiances that arise as a result of these life stressors. At the end of the chapter, implications for individual and community social work practice will be discussed from an ecological life-modeled perspective (Germain & Gitterman, 1996).

To simply cluster all LGBTOCs into a homogeneous category is misleading. LGBTOCs come from very diverse backgrounds (e.g., American Indian, African American, Latino/a, and Asian American) and, as a result, there is greater diversity within groups than there is between groups (Sue, 1992). In addition, we recognize that there are a myriad of self- and community-designated terms for sexual and gender identity and expressions (e.g., queer or two-spirit). We also acknowledge the fluidity of gender and sexual identities and constructs in the postmodern era, and, as a result, whatever terminology we use will inadvertently essentialize that particular identity process in unintended ways. As a result, we use LGBTOC as a placeholder, a designated space for the insertion of culturally specific terms and understandings of sexual and gender identities (e.g., "two-spirit" in the case of American Indian communities or "ambiente" among Latinos or "same gender loving" among African Americans).

In addition, it is imperative that practitioners who use this chapter as a guide to practice with diverse communities should properly assess terminology and associated cultural and spiritual meanings for the individual and groups they are working with and utilize culturally specific understanding to frame interventions and community building. For the purposes of this work, the term LGBTOC refers to those individuals who self-identify primarily monoracially (e.g., African American) and as gay, lesbian, bisexual, or transgender (inclusive of queer or two-spirit identifications). Although the issues facing two-spirits, bisexuals, and transgender persons of color, as well as multiracial gays and lesbians, will be discussed in an effort to include all diverse constituents, a further explication of specific issues facing these groups is even more complex and deserves greater in-depth examination that is beyond the scope of this chapter. For an excellent preliminary discussion of these issues, see Allman (1996); Balsam, Huang, Fieland,

Simoni, and Walters (2004); Bockting, Huang, Ding, Robinson, and Rosser (2005); Bridges, Selvidge, and Matthews (2003); Diaz, Ayala, and Bein (2004); Greene (1993); Harper, Jernewall, and Zea (2004); Kich (1996); Nemoto, Operario, and Keatley (2005); Parks, Hughes, and Matthews (2004); Root (1996); Rosario, Scrimshaw, and Hunter (2004); Vidal-Ortiz (2002); Walters, Evans-Campbell, Simoni, Ronquillo, and Bhuyan (2006); Walters, Longres, Han, and Icard (2004); and Warner (2004).

In most mental health research, one of two dialectic frameworks frequently prevail: the universalist approach (etic) or a cultural-relativist approach (emic). The epistemological presentation of issues facing LGBTOCs is a fusion of these approaches. The focus of this chapter will be on identifying the universal processes involved in negotiating conflicts in allegiances across racial groups and highlighting culture-specific manifestations of the universal process for specific racial groups. Although the thrust of this chapter is on identifying universal processes, it is important that practitioners utilize this perspective only as a guide, integrating universal processes with the LGBTOC's culture-specific experience. Identifying only universal processes neglects the specificity of the LGBTOC's sociohistorical-cultural experience.

PREVIOUS RESEARCH ON RACIAL IDENTITY, LGBT IDENTITY, AND LGBTOC IDENTITY

First, it is important to note that the power of "naming" in identity construction, especially for LGBTOC, is a major issue. In fact, as an act of resistance, some LGBTOC refuse to self-identify as LGBT to counter white middle class LGBT majority hegemonic identity politics (Walters et al., 2006). Frequently, this label refusal is misnamed by dominant groups as "internalized homophobia." The in-depth discussion of how communities create names for themselves is beyond the scope of this chapter. Nevertheless, there is evidence that a parallel process of racial, ethnic, and sexual/gender-orientation identity development exists for oppressed populations, involving movement from internalized negative attitudes about self and group to an integrated identity (Cross, 1978; Heims, 1990; Parham & Helms, 1985a,b; Lev, 2004; Mallon, 1999; Phinney, 1990). Previous research suggests that mental health outcomes such as depression and self-esteem are moderated by one's positive or negative group and self-identity attitudes (Walters, 1995; Walters & Simoni, 1993). Although prior research has focused on how identity attitudes moderate various mental health outcomes, it is assumed here that a parallel process occurs, whereby LGBTOC identity attitudes moderate the relationship between conflicts in allegiances and mental health outcomes (e.g., anxiety or depression).

Collapsing the different ethnic/racial identity stage models, a progression emerges that stands as a standard framework in which identity-attitude processes evolve (Atkinson, Morten, & Sue, 1983; Cross, 1978; Parham & Helms, 1985a,b; Phinney, 1990; Sue, 1992; Walters, 1995). For example, the urban American Indian identity (UAII) model (Walters, 1995), like other racial identity models, consists of four stages (i.e., internalization, marginalization, externalization, and actualization) that tap into a process of identity development from internalized oppression and self/group deprecation to a positive, integrated self- and group identity (Walters, 1995). According to the UAII model, identity attitudes are formed in the context of the person (self-identity), the person's group (group identity), the person's social environment (urban environment), and the historical relationship with the dominant society (dominant group environment and institutional responses).

Research on gay men and lesbians of color and their concurrent identity development have been conducted on small samples of African Americans (Hendin, 1969; Icard, 1986; Johnson, 1982; Loiacano, 1989), Mexican Americans (Espin, 1987; Morales, 1989), and Asian Americans (Chan, 1989; Poon, 2000, 2004; Wooden, Kawaksaki, & Mayeda, 1983). Researchers (Walters, 1997) studying LGBTOC identity generally combine the racial and ethnic identity attitude models (i.e., Atkinson et al., 1983; Cross, 1978; Helms, 1990; Parham & Helms, 1985a,b; Phinney, 1990; Sue, 1992) with Cass's (1984) gay and lesbian identity model. Identity research on bisexual and transgender persons of color is very sparse. For preliminary discussions, see Nemoto et al. (2005), Ochs (1996), and Rust (1996).

The gay and lesbian of color (i.e., LGBTOC) identity research describes two orthogonal processes that occur simultaneously, one in terms of racial identity and the other in terms of the acquisition of a self-identity via the coming out process (Walters, 1997). The racial identity models focus on group identity and the corresponding attitudes that one has toward one's own group, whereas the "coming out" models focus on the awareness of self-identity and coming to terms with the realization of being gay. For example, Morales (1989) proposed a five-stage model of ethnic gay and lesbian identity that consists of

1. a denial of conflicts in allegiances;
2. coming out as bisexual versus gay/lesbian;
3. conflicts in allegiances;

4. establishing priorities in allegiances; and
5. integration of identities.

It is important to note that the "coming out" mental health literature presupposes that verbal disclosure is most desirable for good mental health. Moreover, this literature does not reflect other forms of nonverbal disclosure that many racial communities might gauge as more salient than verbal disclosure (Walters et al., 2006). As Walters et al. (2006, p. 135) note, for two-spirit American Indian communities, "coming out to self and others might be better thought of as becoming out in the sense that this process of identity acquisition is really a process of becoming who they were meant to be—a process of coming home or coming-in, as opposed to coming our [sic] or leaving an old identity behind to embrace a new one." None of the LGBTOC identity models addresses ethnic gay or lesbian identity as it changes over time throughout adulthood (i.e., post-"coming out" as gay or lesbian), nor do they examine the psychological attitudes that LGBTOCs have toward gays and lesbians as a group (i.e., group identity attitudes [Walters, 1997]). The trend in identity research suggests that a multilevel, multidimensional approach must explore self- and group identity attitudes across both LGBT group membership as well as racial group membership. LGBTOC's identity must be understood within this multilevel context.

In this chapter, the LGBTOC identity attitudes matrix model expands upon the earlier racial and gay identity models and the model proposed by Walters (1997) for gay and lesbian American Indians (i.e., the GLAI model) and serves as a means to demonstrate the identity adaptation of LGBTOCs; second, the authors present a stress-coping paradigm and discusses its implications for practice. Both conceptual models are needed for effective practice with LGBTOCs. Finally, in an effort to be inclusive, the author includes content on bisexuals and trans persons of color when appropriate and when evidence exists in the research and the professional literature.

APPLYING THE LIFE MODEL:
THE STRESS-COPING PROCESS REVISITED

Life-modeled practice is derived in part from Lazarus's (1980) stress-coping paradigm. This work expands on the traditional understanding of the stress-coping process, adding a moderating factor that strengthens positive coping responses for LGBTOCs. Germain and Gitterman (1996) point out that external life stressors and their corresponding internal stress are manifestations of negative transactions between the person and the environment. Life stressors are externally generated (e.g., racism) and can become internalized (e.g., internalized racism). In addition, life stressors can take the form of anticipated rejection by others or potential loss. The consequences of these life stressors can then be experienced as an internal stressor affecting emotional and psychological well-being (Germain & Gitterman, 1996). At times, stress can become immobilizing or become expressed as hopelessness, helplessness, powerlessness, anxiety, guilt, ambivalence, or despair (Germain & Gitterman, 1996).

A critical task that LGBTOCs face is to reconcile the conflicts in allegiances that arise as the result of being a member of two oppressed groups (i.e., gay men of color) or three oppressed groups (i.e., as women, lesbians, and persons of color and trans persons of color; Chan, 1989; Greene, 1994; Hendin, 1969; Icard, 1986; Johnson, 1982; Loiacano, 1989; Morales, 1989). LGBTOCs participate in disparate social worlds, which include their gay, lesbian, bisexual, and transgender communities, their community of color, and the dominant culture (i.e., heterosexuals and white Americans [Walters, 1996]). To walk in multiple worlds requires the ability to traverse many social and cultural boundaries and multiple social roles and expectations and, as a result, involves encountering multiple levels of stressors. Thus, LGBTOCs experience discrimination within their own culture (i.e., sexism and heterocentrism as a gay or lesbian person, bi/transphobia as a bisexual or trans person); within the LGBT communities (racism as a racial minority); and within the dominant group (heterosexism and racism as both a bisexual or gay male and as an ethnic person; or heterosexism and racism and sexism as an ethnic person, a bisexual or trans person, woman, and a lesbian).

Paradigm of the Stress Process

Dinges and Joos (1988) expanded upon a prior model of stress and coping to include antecedents of stressful life events in the conceptualization of client process (Dohrenwend & Dohrenwend, 1981). In their modified model, they identified environmental contexts and person factors as the antecedents of stressful life events, which lead to varying states of stress (Dinges & Joos, 1988). Positive, neutral, or negative wellness outcomes depend upon the interaction of internal factors (e.g., identity attitudes) with the state of stress. In addition, the vulnerability hypothesis posits that associations between life events and adverse health/mental health changes are moderated by preexisting personal dispositions (e.g., identity attitudes) that function as buffers, making individuals psychologically and emotionally strong (Dinges & Joos, 1988). Dinges and Joos found this model to be the most effective for depicting stress, coping, and health/mental health relationships for Indian populations and expect that this model can be generalized to other oppressed populations.

This work incorporates a heuristic model that examines how LGBTOC identity attitudes moderate (i.e., have an interactive effect upon) the relation between life stressors (i.e., heterosexism, sexism, and racism in creating conflicts in allegiances) and mental health outcomes for LGBTOCs. Morales (1989) reports that difficulties in integrating conflicts in allegiances may lead to heightened feelings of anxiety, tension, depression, isolation, anger, and problems in integrating aspects of self. Moreover, the potential rejection or perceived loss of support from one's own ethnic community compromises one's much needed social support, coping assistance, and survival skills. Identification of this process will assist social work practitioners in facilitating healthy LGBTOCs coping in response to the demands of their various communities.

HETEROSEXISM, RACISM, AND SEXISM: CREATING CONFLICTS IN ALLEGIANCES

Similar to multiracial individuals, LGBTOCs challenge preconceived notions of group membership and assumptions associated with racial and sexual orientation status. For example, Root (1996) states that race is socially constructed in terms of the perspective of the power holder, generally forcing blended individuals (e.g., LGBTOCs) to artificially pick which "side" they belong to. Moreover, Root (1996) notes:

> These experiences are not solely imposed by European-descended individuals; they are imposed from all sides in a manner that can choke the blended individual with a squeeze of oppression in the form of "authenticity tests," forced choices, or unwarranted assumptions about one's identity. (p. 20)

Although the functions and processes of both racism and heterosexism begin with those in power, the process can be internalized by oppressed groups and is manifested in the insistence on singular racial or sexual orientation loyalties (Root, 1996). For example, Audre Lorde (1984) writes:

> Differences between ourselves as black women are also being misnamed and used to separate us from one another. As a black lesbian

feminist comfortable with the many different ingredients of my identity, and as a woman committed to racial and sexual freedom from oppression, I find I am constantly being encouraged to pluck out some
one aspect of myself and present this as a meaningful whole, eclips-
ing or denying the other parts of self. But this is a destructive and frag-
menting way to live. (p. 63)

Thus, similar to multiracial individuals, LGBTOCs are constantly confronted with questions about their allegiances and forced to side with one
group or the other. In essence, LGBTOCs deconstruct and challenge by their
very presence the traditional assumptions of unilateral oppressed group
membership.

Tests of Group Loyalty

Root (1996) points out that tests of loyalty and group membership legitimacy are always power struggles reflecting the internalization of colonized
group thinking. Audre Lorde (1984) reminds us that as a tool of social control, oppressed groups are socialized to recognize only one aspect of their
experience as salient for the survival of the group. Moreover, Lorde notes
that we live in a society in which there is an institutionalized and socialized
rejection of within-group differences. Our refusal to recognize our within-
group differences and to investigate the distortions that arise from our misnaming these differences results in oppressive conditions for individuals with
multiple-situated identities (e.g., LGBTOCs [Lorde, 1984]).

The Root of Conflicts in Allegiances: Pressures for Unity via Homogeneity

Lorde states that often members of oppressed groups identify by only one
dimension of being oppressed and generalize that one dimension as being
the only salient category of oppression for the entire group. As a result, many
who experience one form of oppression as primary forget that members of
"their" group may be experiencing multiple oppressed statuses and that they
themselves might be oppressors to these individuals (Lorde, 1984). Thus,
there is an intense pressure for homogeneity within groups that is confused
with the need for group unity for survival purposes (i.e., for the fight against
racism and genocide [Lorde, 1984]). As a result, group unity is confounded
with group homogeneity. The result of this misnaming is the internalized
divide-and-conquer mentality. A colonized mentality assumes that individuals who embrace their multiple identities and fight corresponding inter-

locking oppressions are dangerous to the group's unity and survival. Owing to the continuous battle against genocide, the disavowal to recognize and name the within-group oppressions such as sexism, heterosexism, bi/transphobia causes them to become the status quo (Lorde, 1984), and, in fact, they are sometimes mislabeled as "cultural" norms. This internalized, colonized oppression often becomes the criterion within communities of color by which gender roles and group survival can be authenticated and measured (Lorde, 1984). Thus, hostility and oppression against LGBTOCs is practiced not only by white society and white LGBT persons, but by heterosexual communities of color as well. Moreover, just as LGBTOCs struggle to create terms to describe their identity free of white-dominated LGBT language, LGBTOCs also encounter rigid models of LGBT compulsory homonormativity (Walters et al., 2006). Compulsory homonormativity is manifested in expectations to conform to white-dominated LGBT values and rituals (such as getting one's first "dyke" haircut) or verbally disclosing one's sexual orientation (Walters et al., 2006).

Racism in the LGBT Communities

Historically, strong institutional ties (e.g., National Gay and Lesbian Task Force) and businesses (e.g., bars, social clubs) of LGBT communities tend to be white male dominated (Garnets & Kimmel, 1991). Moreover, researchers have documented the negative effects of the underrepresentation of LGBTOCs in positions of power in LGBT communities (Currah & Minter, 2000; Icard, 1986; Mallon, 1999). The unchecked power and privilege of the white LGBT communities to influence LGBT communities' experience and institutions has led to racial discrimination toward LGBTOCs (Harper & Schneider, 2003). Discrimination has taken many forms. For example, Asian Americans report being stereotyped as "erotic" or simply remain unacknowledged, invisible, or sexually "neutered" in LGBT communities (Chan, 1989). Similar to Asian Americans, African Americans, Latinos/as, and American Indians also have had to contend with being romanticized, objectified, and eroticized (Icard, 1986; Firestein, 1996; Jaimes & Halsey, 1992; Poon, 2000; Walters et al., 2006). Greene (1993) describes this objectification process of LGBTOCs by white lesbians and gay men as "ethnosexual stereotyping." She identifies ethnosexual stereotyping as the combination of racism and sexism as manifested in the sexual objectification of LGBTOCs according to racial stereotypes (e.g., Asian men depicted as geishas or African men depicted pictorially as huge, muscular men in chains in gay magazines). Moreover, she highlights the need for practitioners to be aware of how LGBTOCs might internalize the ethnosexual stereotype of their own ethnic group. Greene's findings can be extrapolated to include similar objectification toward bisexuals and trans persons.

Racism is further demonstrated in the discrimination toward LGBTOCs in admittance to gay/lesbian/trans bars (e.g., having to provide two or more pieces of identification to get into bars compared with a white, gay counterpart where one or no identification is requested [Icard, 1986]). Moreover, dealing with invisibility in LGBT community settings via being ignored at LGBT social events (Chan, 1989; Greene, 1993; Walters et al., 2006) leads to considerable feelings of social isolation and disempowerment. Frequently, LGBTOCs do know why they have been targeted or which aspect of their identities has disturbed the attacker (Walters et al., 2006). One two-spirit woman captures this experience:

> . . . when people insult me . . . I go through this thing in my head: Is it because I'm Indian? Is it because I'm poor? Is it because I'm a dyke? . . . I've been called a fucking dyke and a fucking squaw . . . don't know sometimes why I'm being attacked. I just know that I'm wrong to a lot of people. . . . I think there's a lot of hostility to the combination of things I am. (Walters et al., 2006, p. 144)

Among white lesbians, Allman (1996) notes that there is generally an assumption of "normative whiteness" within the term "lesbian." This is similar to the term "American" being implicitly reserved for white Americans or others who are expected to conform or assimilate to white American values and identity. For example, at many lesbian events the term "lesbian" is reserved for white lesbians, as evidenced by book readings by "lesbians" versus book readings by women of color or "lesbians of color" (Allman, 1996). Moreover, Allman (1996, p. 288) notes that "lesbian events may completely ignore nonwhite or mixed-race lesbians or selectively use our perspectives only as they support a 'normative' white lesbian experience or agenda." Similarly, bisexual, two-spirit, and trans persons of color face invisibility on multiple levels. In sum, although LGBTOCs may experience, to some degree, much needed LGBT community support and refuge from societal heterosexism, and bi/transphobia, the strength of that support and the stressors associated with racism diminish the full range of support for LGBTOCs that is otherwise available to white LGBT persons. The primary conflict in allegiance that arises as the result of racism in the white LGBT community structure is whether it is worth jeopardizing ethnic community priorities and ties to connect with a community that is wrought with racism. Although there is tremendous need for support to deal with the heterosexism, and bi/transphobia in one's own community of color, the potential loss of support from one's own ethnic community is a price too great to pay for many LGBTOCs who seek refuge in their own ethnic community to combat racist oppression. The stressors associated with picking one community over the other are tremendous.

Heterosexism in Communities of Color

In addition to being discriminated against by LGBT communities, LGBTOCs similarly experience rejection, stigmatization, heterosexism, and bi/transphobia within their own communities of color. However, even though the process parallels the discrimination of white LGBT persons toward LGBTOCs, it is not to be mistaken for the same process. The within-group prejudices must be understood as manifestations of internalized, colonized processes within a system of white heterosexual institutionalized systems of power. In other words, the group that ultimately benefits from within-group oppressions is white heterosexual men and to some degree white heterosexual women. Thus, white LGBT persons reinforce their power as members of white society by being racist, whereas heterosexuals of color do not benefit communities of color by being heterosexist. Having said this, I will explore further the stressors associated with the within-group oppressions among communities of color.

First, LGBTOCs frequently face questioning of their racial identity if they openly identify as an LGBT person, since such open identification is at times interpreted as an abandonment of priorities in fighting racial or cultural oppression. For example, Moraga (1983), a mixed Chicana lesbian, states that she has been accused of contributing to the genocide of the Chicano people through her resistance to succumb to cultural gender roles. Thus, for lesbians of color, the interlocking oppressions of heterosexism and sexism may be used by one's community of color as a form of social control (to maintain the illusion of unity) in the fight against racism.

Second, expectations regarding expected cultural gender roles in the continuance and survival of one's race play a critical role in exacerbating conflicts in allegiances for LGBTOCs. For example, Wong (1992) noted that for Chinese-born American immigrants, compulsory heterosexual relationships in the new country symbolizes a healthy adjustment to the United States. In addition, displays of assertiveness (sexual or otherwise) in Chinese women are interpreted as emasculating to Chinese men and as leading to "unnatural" power imbalances between men and women (Wong, 1992). Thus, any deviation from cultural gender roles may be interpreted as an attack on the group's survival. Such a burden creates considerable stress and conflict for LGBTOCs.

Lesbians and trans women of color face tremendous pressure as both the child-rearing and childbearing roles are closely associated with the culture's continuity and survival. For example, the interactive effects of hetero-sexism, sexism, and racism for African-American women are demonstrated in the misinterpretation of the strength of African-American women as emasculating to African-American men. Greene (1993) notes that group internalization of such controlling images misnames African-American male oppression as the result of emasculating African-American women, as opposed to the external racist institutions. Such group internalizations structure sexist and heterosexist gender role expectations as commensurate with group survival (Greene, 1993). Pharr (1988) argues that the intersection of heterosexism (including compulsory heterosexuality), sexism, and racism work simultaneously to reinforce racist gender roles. Moreover, these hetero-centric, sexist gender roles function as forms of social control to establish group conformity to a unilateral definition of oppressed group membership and group survival. Patricia Hill Collins refers to these socially constructed images or illusions as "controlling images," which serve to reinforce the status quo both within and between groups. Moreover, the implicit assumption inherent in such imperatives is that LGBTOCs would have no interest in community survival, as being an LGBT person is (mis)associated with the rejection of childbearing or child-rearing roles. Such assumptions are simply unwarranted given that child bearing/rearing and being gay or lesbian are not mutually exclusive states of being (Greene, 1994). Nevertheless, the community internalization of such imperatives creates tremendous stress for LGBTOCs. In addition, the LGBTOC's internalization of such assumptions exacerbates anxiety and feelings of inauthenticity. LGBTOCs face additional criticism from their communities of color regarding the notion that gay, lesbian, bisexual, or transgender identity is a white problem or a pathological response to white racism. Moreover, heterosexual persons of color tend to see identification with another oppressed group as being an unnecessary burden on an already oppressed status. Hemphill (1992), the late African-American activist, asserts that communities of color need to contest black nationalist proclamations that LGBT identity is evidence of white inferiority or that black LGBT identity is the result of internalized racism. Hemphill argues that communities of color must defy linking compulsory heterosexuality, heterocentricity, or heterosexism with group survival or the battle against racist oppression. In a more contemporary discussion, Crawford and colleagues (2002) explored the influence of dual-identity development on the psychosocial functioning of African-American gay and bisexual men.

Finally, the issue of visibility also creates tremendous stress for LGBTOCs. LGBTOCs frequently receive double-bind messages from their families. LGBTOCs who choose to be visible or open are subject to having their loyalty to family/community questioned. However, a lesbian, gay, bisexual, or trans identity might be tolerated or accepted by the family or the community as long as it is not visible or spoken of. For example, in a study of thirteen Japanese gay men, Wooden et al. (1983) found that the respondents were primarily concerned about the potential loss and rejection by the Japanese community for being visibly active in the gay community. Other racial groups have also documented their hesitancy to be open and visible in LGBT communities for fear of the loss of important cultural support systems, rejection from their families, and ultimately, rejection from the community of color at large (Fox, 1995; Garnets & Kimmel, 1991; Klein, 1993; Loicano, 1989). For example, studies have shown that African-American lesbians more than white lesbians maintain strong family ties and depend on family for social, emotional, and financial support (Bell & Wienberg, 1978; Croom, 1993; Greene, 1993). The threat of loss or rejection of cultural support leaves LGBTOCs vulnerable, particularly since family and extended kin networks typically function as the primary refuge against racist oppression (Greene, 1993). For assessment purposes, stressors associated with visibility issues as they connect to potential conflicting allegiances need to be disentangled from cultural processes associated with valuing collectivity and more nonverbal, subtle forms of self-expression and identity disclosure (Walters et al., 2006). For example, directness and drawing attention to oneself are not values consistent with some collectivist oriented cultures, where humility, cooperation, and collectivism are more highly valued. Adherence to nonverbal forms of LGBTOC "visibility" might in fact be the optimum healthful form of expression for individuals who embody these cultural worldviews.

Conclusion

The Functions of Heterosexism, Sexism, and Racism

The function of the use and abuse of such controlling images is rooted in sexism, heterosexism, and racism for LGBTOCs and and is also evident as a form of social control for unilateral oppressed-group conformity. These controlling images (Collins, 1990) by both groups, heterosexuals of color and white LGBT persons, function to constrain the LGBTOC's options and to "perpetuate misinformation, and render invisible or exceptional those [LGBTOCs] that do not fit the negative controlling image" (Allman, 1996,

p. 247). The intersection of sexism and heterosexism within heterosexual communities of color and the intersection of racism and sexism from white LGBT communities both utilize these controlling images to keep the "other" part of the LGBTOCs self-silenced. Thus, gender and racial role expectations become boundaried by racial, gender, and heterosexual group mandates between and within groups (Allman, 1996), and conflicts in allegiances arise as a response to these life stressors.

As a result of the multiple conflicts in allegiances, many LGBTOCs feel that they do not completely belong to one group or the other, thereby creating difficulty in consolidating an identity as LGBTOC. Research results have yielded contradictory findings concerning which group the LGBTOC feels most comfortable with and with which group the LGBTOC most strongly identifies. Espin (1987) noted that Latina lesbians identified with a white lesbian community in one sample; Chan (1989) noted that Asian lesbians' identification varied depending on the needs of the individual and the context of the situation. However, many researchers have documented the preference of LGBTOCs to be accepted and acknowledged by both their ethnic communities and the gay and lesbian community. Poon (2000) explores interracial same-sex abuse and the vulnerability of gay men of Asian descent in relationships with Caucasian men. Nevertheless, achieving this integration has been difficult given the life stressors discussed earlier (Chan, 1989; Colon, 2001; Espin, 1987; Garnets & Kimmel, 1991).

There are several notes of caution in interpreting research results regarding which group LGBTOC feel most comfortable with and with which group LGBTOC most strongly identify. First, most of these studies do not include a sizable sample of bisexual or transgender persons of color, and, therefore, any generalizations from these studies' findings must be carefully interpreted. The majority of LGBTOC studies are based on self-identified gay men of color and do not always include men who have sex with men who do not identify as gay, bisexual men of color, or gay men who do not openly self-identify among their heterosexual communities of color (King, 2004). As a result, the perception of discrimination on the basis of race or sexual orientation or their strength of persons of color in identification with one community over the other may vary for these other groups. Despite research shortcomings, many researchers state that for many LGBTOCs, the ability not to "split" themselves into disparate social parts depends on the situational context, the safety of the situation (ranging from potential physical harm to potential emotional rejection and loss), and the strength of their positive LGBTOC identity attitudes (Walters, 1997).

THE LGBTOC IDENTITY ATTITUDES MATRIX MODEL

In developing a model of LGBTOC identity processes, it is important to note that this model is to be used as an initial assessment framework that is modifiable according to the cultural, sexual, and gender orientation of the individual. In addition, the LGBTOC identity matrix provides an initial assessment of potential areas of strength for further reinforcement and areas of vulnerability in need of possible intervention. Based on previous mental health research on LGBTOC identity models, it is presumed here that by identifying the self- and group identity attitudes across racial and sexual orientation dimensions, the practitioner is better equipped to identify and anticipate problem areas for the LGBTOC client in negotiating their conflicts in allegiances successfully.

Potential Identity Attitude Constellations

First, LGBTOC may be highly ethnically identified and highly LGBT identified simultaneously, although the two are not necessarily correlated (Walters, 1997). As Oetting and Beauvais (1990-1991) point out, cultural identification is an orthogonal process where identification with one culture does not necessarily mean a lesser identification with another culture. Thus, cultural identification consists of independent identities (LGBT and racial) where individuals can have a unicultural, bicultural, or multicultural identification simultaneously (Walters, 1997).

In the LGBTOC identity attitude matrix model (see Figure 3.1; note that we use Q to represent queer or LGBT category for ease in visualization) ra-

Self-Identity Attitudes

Self-Identity Attitudes	LGBT Positive +		LGBT Negative −	
Racial Positive +	Q+	R +	Q −	R +
Racial Negative −	Q+	R −	Q −	R −

Group Identity Attitudes

Group Identity Attitudes	LGBT Positive +		LGBT Negative −	
Racial Positive +	Q+	R +	Q −	R +
Racial Negative −	Q+	R −	Q −	R −

FIGURE 3.1. LGBTOC Identity Attitudes Matrix Model

cial identity attitudes and LGBT identity attitudes are assessed simultaneously to form a 2 × 2 matrix of potential identity attitude constellations,
specifically: combined positive identity attitudes (Queer+ Race+), mixed
positive and negative identity attitudes (Q+ and R− or Q− and R+) and
combined negative identity attitudes (Q− and R−). Practitioners can utilize the matrix to visually see the strengths and vulnerabilities that the
LGBTOC individual possesses across racial and sexual/gender orientation
dimensions simultaneously as well as to design culturally relevant interventions (especially cognitive restructuring) to address conflicting allegiances
associated with disequilibrium in identity structures. For example, an African-American lesbian could have positive attitudes toward African Americans as a group and toward the self as African American yet simultaneously
hold negative attitudes toward LGBTs as a group but have positive attitudes
toward herself as a lesbian. Utilizing the matrix, practitioners can draw in-
ferences regarding salient assessment and intervention points to assist
LGBTOCs in negotiating their conflicts in allegiances.

Combined Positive Identity Attitudes (Q+ R+)

Individuals who possess self- and group Q+ R+ identity attitudes are
likely to have identity attitudes that buffer against their conflicts in allegiances,
facilitating positive mental health outcomes. Moreover, their LGBTOC
identity attitudes interact with life stressors to facilitate positive coping
responses in successfully negotiating group tensions. Generally, these individuals will tend to externalize their conflicts in allegiances, placing the
problems of the groups' heterosexism or racism in proper perspective. Thus,
they will likely be able to confront the heterosexism or racism as an example of colonized group processes and not internalize it and take inappropriate responsibility for misperceived threats to group survival. Moreover,
LGBTOCs who have this identity constellation will not have identity attitudes as a core area for intervention in dealing with conflicts in allegiances.
Rather, the identity attitudes that facilitate healthy coping will be further
strengthened given the LGBTOCs' social and cultural contexts in which
conflicts arise.

Mixed Positive and Negative Identity Attitudes (Q+ R− or Q− R+)

The individual who presents with self- and group Q+ R− or Q− R+
identity attitudes is at greater risk for difficulties in consolidating a positive
LGBTOC identity and internalizing colonizing attitudes. The matrix, however, identifies areas of strength and vulnerability. Thus, if an LGBTOC

presents with $Q+$ $R-$ identity attitudes, then racial identity functions as an area for cognitive interventions while it also reinforces the strengths of the gay or lesbian identity at the same time.

Cognitive interventions and positive reframing are powerful tools to reconceptualize the conflicts in allegiances as arising from the competing demands of two oppressed groups for group survival. The key in dealing with this constellation is to assist the LGBTOC individual to externalize the internalized group thinking and reframe their experience as not being a threat to group survival. In addition, by identifying the $R+$ or $Q+$ strengths and positive coping, the LGBTOC individual can then translate those skills for their $R-$ or $Q-$ conflicts. Moreover, it is important to assist LGBTOCs with identifying and anticipating potential loss or rejection by others in either community. In addition, it is important to strengthen existing support systems that embrace their multiple-situated identities. Individuals with $Q+$ $R-$ or $Q-$ $R+$ identity attitudes may also experience tremendous emotional ambivalence given the social context, moving from identifying as primarily "gay" in gay settings to primarily "racial" in ethnic community settings, thereby splitting off salient aspects of self given different social contexts. One particular task, given the ambivalence, is to facilitate an integrated identity across multiple settings, although timing of this process is also dependent on the strength and salience of support systems from both communities. In addition, if the LGBTOC individual needs to remain as one primary dimension across both settings, then it is important to keep an eye on the potential internalization of colonized group thinking processes and gently challenge them. Finally, individuals with this constellation may be most receptive to support groups and contact with other LGBTOC groups that can facilitate positive integrated role-modeled behaviors for negotiating ongoing conflicts in group allegiances.

Combined Negative Identity Attitudes ($Q-$ $R-$)

LGBTOC individuals who have self- and group $Q-$ and $R-$ identity attitudes are the most likely to experience tremendous difficulty in dealing with group conflicts. Moreover, they are likely to be socially isolated since they hold negative attitudes toward both racial and LGBT groups as well as their own sense of self as an ethnic and LGBT person. As a result, their ability to reconcile multiple life stressors will be compromised since they will not have many group survival skills to assist them in coping with group conflicts. These individuals will tend to minimize their LGBT status and their racial status as significant aspects of their lives (this of course is due to their internalization of negative dominant group attitudes, not their sense of self-group actualization). Moreover, they will try to distance themselves from either group and try to "pass" as "just a person" and identify with a dominant white heterosexual society. They will also hold very negative attitudes toward other gays or lesbians as well as people of color. LGBTOCs experiencing both negative self- and group identity attitudes will not perceive conflicts in allegiances as a stressor until they are confronted with either coming-out to others or by members of the gay or lesbian community or their ethnic community regarding their group loyalties.

These LGBTOCs will have tremendous difficulty negotiating multiple levels of internalized negative attitudes about themselves as persons of color who are gay or lesbian. It is important to focus initially on gently confronting negative stereotypes internalized by the LGBTOC, facilitating connections with other positive LGBTOC role models, and anticipating potential loss or rejection by others. Moreover, the primary issue for LGBTOCs experiencing such conflicts, given this identity matrix constellation, is that they are anticipating a perceived loss or rejection by one community or the other. It is imperative that one assess how the LGBTOC has coped with loss previously while simultaneously translating the strengths acquired in previous experiences coping with the current stressor. One form of coping may be to split off the self, given the social context for LGBTOCs at this stage (similar to individuals possessing mixed positive and negative group and self-identity attitudes discussed previously). This may be a necessary first step, but it must be made thoughtfully with the practitioner remaining cognizant of potential internalization of negative group messages. For example, the LGBTOC individual may choose to come out to someone from their ethnic community but choose to remain closeted within the larger ethnic community. This can be seen as an important step toward integration and consolidation of self- and group identity.

Although these three primary constellations are not exhaustive (there are sixteen possible combinations of self- and group identity and racial and LGBT identity attitudes that are beyond the scope of this chapter), the practitioner can utilize the above matrix to identify areas of strength and vulnerability in assessing LGBTOC identity attitudes and LGBTOCs' coping abilities in negotiating the conflicts in allegiances. Moreover, the matrices will highlight how the identity attitudes may be moderating the effects of conflicting allegiances on psychological wellness. For example, if individuals have both negative self- and group LGBTOC identity attitudes, then practitioners can identify the ways in which these identity attitudes effectively and negatively interact with the LGBTOCs' conflicts in allegiances and their corresponding anxiety or depression (i.e., mental health outcomes).

It is important to keep in mind that LGBTOCs may pass through different combinations of self- and group identity attitudes throughout their lifetime and may "spiral" back through earlier constellations at higher levels, experiencing early constellation/matrix traits if external impingements and sociohistorical circumstances exacerbate life stressors and increase feelings of isolation and powerlessness (Walters & Simoni, 1993).

Social Work Practice Issues

In addition to the assessment of the client's identity attitude matrix, the LGBTOC client's experience of stressors associated with acculturation, cultural value conflicts, and immigration status must also be assessed. These four factors (identity attitudes, acculturation level, cultural values, and immigration status) help the social work practitioner identify areas of vulnerability in need of intervention and strengthening.

Acculturative Stress: Cultural Values and Conflicts

Several empirical studies are now beginning to suggest that one could be highly acculturated while simultaneously being highly ethnically identified and vice versa (Hutnik, 1985; Kemnitzer, 1978; Zak, 1976). However, despite the promise of research highlighting the multidimensionality of acculturation processes, many LGBTOCs, like other oppressed populations, experience intense pressure to relinquish their own ethnic community cultural values and replace them with the dominant (in this case, white LGBT values) culture's values. For LGBTOCs, the acculturative stress that results from the pressures to acculturate is manifested in the assumptions from the LGBT community's cultural value to "come out" to others as a mental health and political imperative. However, as noted earlier, for many LGBTOCs "coming out" may at times conflict with their own cultural values. For example, among some populations, coming-out is a value that is dissonant with the cultural value of anonymity, where drawing attention to one's own needs is contrary to the collectivist nature of the culture. The individualism implicit in coming out may be seen as an affront to the higher value (in some cultures) placed on the sense of self in relation to the collective (see Walters et al., 2006, for further details).

Another acculturative stressor that LGBTOCs must contend with is the different acculturation levels of their families and community-kin networks in relation to their own acculturation levels. Any difference in acculturation levels creates further stress in reconciling one's own values and the values of one's culture and family. Thus, LGBTOC assessment should also identify the cultural values that are still held intact by the LGBTOC and his or her kin networks. This includes words and phrases regarding LGBT persons in the culture of the LGBTOC and the meaning of being an LGBT person from the cultural perspective (Espin, 1987). For example, identifying traditional ways in which the LGBTOC has a role that is specific to his or her culture may be helpful (especially for two-spirit or gay/lesbian American Indians [Walters, 1996]). Moreover, the worker should assess the possibility of incorporating other members of the client's family network, LGBTOC culture-specific community members, or traditional healers/medicine persons to help the client integrate a positive LGBTOC identity (Walters, 1997). In New York City the Gender Identity Project (GIP) openly represents the greater transgender and gender variant communities, proudly encompassing the diversity of gender expression. GIP participants include individuals who identify utilizing hundreds of different descriptors of gender. Importantly, 50 percent of the GIP's clients identify as people of color (accessed September 9, 2006, http://www.gaycenter.org/program_folders/gip/gip-more). Ultimately, acculturative stress may affect LGBTOCs' attitudes toward identifying with other LGBTOCs. For example, if an assimilationist ideology is internalized within a particular cultural group and is rooted in heterocentric biases from the dominant society, then the probability for contacting other LGBTOCs from one's own culture is diminished. In addition, there is an increased chance of isolation (Berry, Kirn, Minde, & Mok, 1987; Cornell, 1988; Kraus & Buffler, 1979) from important LGBTOC cultural supports, positive within-group LGBTOC role models, and LGBTOC survival strategies. To deal with conflicting allegiances associated with acculturative stress, LaFromboise (1988) and Moncher, Holden, and Trimble (1990) advocate the development of a "bicultural competence repertoire." They state that such a repertoire assists Indian youth in developing adaptive coping responses to the interaction between their tribal culture and that of the majority culture. Similarly, LGBTOCs could benefit from developing a bicultural competence repertoire in assisting them in successfully negotiating conflicts in allegiances—both between groups (i.e., with white LGBT communities) and within groups (i.e., different acculturation levels across self, family, and kin networks). For example, LGBTOC bicultural competence would assist LGBTOCs in integrating positive aspects of both cultures (gay/lesbian/ bisexual/transgender and racial/cultural) without losing their own cultural values or internalizing heterosexist biases (Rodriguez, 1998).

Immigration Issues

Immigration status is also a critical factor affecting LGBTOCs' successful negotiation of conflicts in allegiances. Espin (1987) notes that the time and reasons for immigrating to the United States are factors in shaping how LGBTOCs perceive and experience conflicts in allegiances. For example, even though immigration might be voluntary, LGBTOCs still experience significant losses of familial support systems upon arrival to the United States, even if they were leaving their country of origin to seek a more gay-affirmative environment. In addition, if immigration is recent, the LGBTOC might lose significant economic support from his or her family and become dependent on the extended family in the United States or on other ethnic community members (Espin, 1987). The interdependence on ethnic community financial and emotional supports makes it even more difficult to come out to one's ethnic community or consolidate one's multiple-situated identities (Greene, 1993).

In sum, level of acculturation (including the generation level) and corresponding acculturative stress, immigration status, and internalization of cultural values and frameworks are important factors that must be incorporated into LGBTOC assessment. They can provide information as to the appropriate areas of intervention, whether it is within the individual in terms of helping the LGBTOC client integrate both identities or whether it is external (i.e., fighting heterosexism or racism at the community level) (Walters, 1996).

Social Work Practice Skills

Empowerment-Oriented Reframing

In line with the ecological model of practice (Germain & Gitterman, 1996), a positive reframing of the stressors associated with multiple-situated identities assists LGBTOCs with negotiating a "border" status (Anzaldua, 1987). Anzaldua suggests that multiple-status individuals can bridge both communities by having both feet solidly planted in both worlds. This positive reframe suggests that LGBTOCs have the right to not fractionalize their allegiances and can integrate multiple perspectives and statuses simultaneously (Anzaldua, 1987; Root, 1996; Williams, 1996). Anzaldua states that to develop a new "border" consciousness we need to affirm the marginalized parts of self (whether racial, gender, or sexual orientation) and integrate them to heal the conflicts in allegiances within one's self. This act reflects healthy resistance to internalized oppression.

Another opportunity for a positive reframe is to challenge the notion that to be an LGBTOC means that one is "caught" or "stuck" between worlds and communities. As a practitioner, one can reframe this intermediary position not as a problem, but, rather, as an opportunity to have a unique vantage point, from which an analysis of conflicting allegiances, LGBTOC marginalization, and assumptions of community legitimacy are possible (Kich, 1996; hooks, 1981). Kich notes that "both insider and outsider positions can be reframed as a source of positive learning for marginalized peoples" (p. 271). Thus, the practitioner's task is to reframe the marginalization (which is the result of the internalization of group imperatives rooted in heterosexism, racism, and sexism) as an opportunity to achieve new insight into the assumptions of community legitimacy and ultimately challenge such assumptions when they are oppressive to community members (Kich, 1996). By embracing the position of a multiple-situated identity, LGBTOCs can challenge the status quo of both the LGBT communities and their respective communities of color.

Assisting LGBTOCs with positive reframing of the conflicts in allegiances that naturally arise when oppressed groups attempt to survive requires considerable cognitive flexibility in regard to both of the conflicts in allegiances that are identified in the LGBTOC identity attitudes matrix model.

Social work practitioners should be aware of the interplay between intrapsychic problems and external, systemic factors such as heterosexism and racism in individual LGBTOC functioning and in community functioning (Walters, 1996; Walters & Simoni, 1993). Practitioner effectiveness will be dependent on the ability to differentiate among these systemic factors (Trimble, 1981; Trimble & LaFromboise, 1985). Understanding the multidimensionality of the LGBTOC experience and the corresponding factors that contribute to identity attitude development; maintenance of within-group heterosexism, racism, and sexism; and the resulting conflicts in allegiances assists practitioners and program planners in developing culturally relevant treatment strategies and agency programs (Walters, 1997). By better understanding the complexities of within- and between-group pressures that LGBTOCs face, administrators and practitioners may be able to identify preference for an LGBT clinician, a non-LGBT practitioner of color, or a practitioner who is also an LGBTOC (depending on the levels of LGBTOC identity attitudes [Walters, 1997]).

In terms of community-oriented empowerment practice, heterosexual communities of color and white LGBT communities must first recognize their role in marginalizing LGBTOCs. When members of one group intimidate others within their own group, their marginalizing power ultimately undermines group unity to fight oppression.

In addition, community-based practice involves mild confrontation regarding racist and heterosexist community norms. One way to challenge community racism and heterosexism is to develop community relational competence (Kich, 1996). According to Kich, relational competence is defined as the "interest and capacity to stay emotionally present with, to enlarge or deepen the relational context to create enough 'space' for both or all people to express themselves, and to allow for possible conflict, tension and creative resolution" (p. 275). Flexibility of constructs, relational competence, and adaptability are the community-based social skills required for living with difference, without creating conflicts in allegiances within and between communities and, ultimately, within and between LGBTOCs' sense of self.

FUTURE RESEARCH

In terms of future research, the role of religion in LGBTOCs' community life needs to be further explored. Moreover, the LGBTOC identity attitude matrix model needs to be empirically validated. In addition, the stress/identity/mental wellness paradigm needs to be empirically tested. Furthermore, the issues of men who have sex with men but who do not identify as gay, as well as bisexuals and transgender persons of color, and also biracial or multiracial LGBTOCs need to be examined in future discussions.

Finally, Audre Lorde (1984) reminds us that in order to support healthy, integrated LGBTOC individuals and communities, we must recognize multiple identities and allegiances, examine multiple and simultaneous oppressions, and dismantle within- and between-group oppressive hierarchies.

REFERENCES

Allman, K. M. (1996). (Un)Natural boundaries: Mixed race, gender, and sexuality. In M. P. P. Root (Ed.), *The multiracial experience: Racial borders and the new frontier* (pp. 275-290). Thousand Oaks, CA: Sage Publications.

Anzaldua, G. (1987). *Borderlands/LaFrontera: The new Mestizo.* San Francisco: Spinsters/Aunt Lute Foundation.

Atkinson, D., Morten, G., & Sue, D. (1983). *Counseling American minorities.* Dubuque, IA: W. C. Brown.

Balsam, K. F., Huang, B., Fieland, K. C., Simoni, J. M., & Walters, K. L. (2004). Culture, trauma, and wellness: A comparison of heterosexual and lesbian, gay bisexual, and two-spirit Native Americans. *Cultural Diversity and Ethnic Minority Psychology, 10*(3), 287-301.

Bell, A., & Weinberg, M. (1978). *Homosexualities: A study of human diversity among men and women*. New York: Simon and Schuster.

Berry, J., Kirn, U., Minde, T., & Mok, D. (1987). Comparative studies of acculturative stress. *International Migration Review, 21,* 491-511.

Bockting, W., Huang, C. Y., Ding, H., Robinson, B., & Rosser, S. (2005). Are transgender persons at higher risk for HIV than other sexual minorities? *International Journal of Transgenderism, 8*(2/3), 123-131.

Bradford, M. (2004). The bisexual experience: Living in a dichotomous culture. *Journal of Bisexuality, 4*(1/2), 7-23.

Bradford, M. (2006). Affirmative psychotherapy with bisexual women. *Journal of Bisexuality, 6*(1/2), 13-25.

Bridges, S. K., Selvidge, M. M. D., & Matthews, C. R. (2003). Lesbian women of color: Therapeutic issues and challenges. *Journal of Multicultural Counseling and Development, 31,* 113-130.

Cass, V. C. (1984). Homosexual identity formation: Testing a theoretical model. *Journal of Sex Research, 20,* 143-167.

Chan, C. (1989). Issues of identity development among Asian-American lesbians and gay men. *Journal of Counseling and Development, 68*(1), 16-20.

Collins, P. M. (1990). Homophobia and black lesbians. In P. H. Collins (Ed.), *Black feminist thought: Knowledge, consciousness, and the politics of empowerment* (pp. 192-196). Boston: Unwin Hyman.

Colon, E. (2001). An ethnographic study of six Latino gay and bisexual men. *Journal of Gay & Lesbian Social Services, 12*(3/4), 77-99.

Cornell, S. (1988). The transformations of tribe: Organization and self-concept in Native American ethnicities. *Ethnic and Racial Studies, II,* 27-47.

Crawford, I., Allison, K. W., Zamboni, B. D., & Soto, T. (2002). The influence of dual-identity development on the psychosocial functioning of African American gay and bisexual men. *Journal of Sex Research, 39*(3), 179-181.

Croom, G. (1993). *The effects of a consolidated versus non-consolidated identity on expectations of African-American lesbians selecting mates: A pilot study.* Unpublished doctoral dissertation, Illinois School of Professional Psychology, Chicago, IL.

Cross, W. (1978). The Thomas and Cross models of psychological nigrescence: A literature review. *Journal of Black Psychology, 4,* 13-31.

Currah, P., & Minter, S. (2000). *Transgender equality: A handbook for activists and policymakers.* New York and San Francisco: The Policy Institute of the National Gay & Lesbian Task Force and The National Center for Lesbian Rights.

Diaz, R. M., Ayala, G., & Bein, E. (2004). Sexual risk as an outcome of social oppression: Data from a probability sample of Latino gay men in three U.S. cities. *Cultural Diversity and Ethnic Minority Psychology, 10*(3), 255-267.

Dinges, N. G., & Joos, S. K. (1988). Stress, coping, and health: Models of interaction for Indian and Native populations in behavioral health issues among American Indians and Alaska Natives, In S.M. Manson & N.G. Dinges, (Eds.), *Behavioral health issues among American Indians and Alaska Natives: Explorations on the frontiers of biobehavioral sciences. American Indian and Alaska Native mental health research.* Vol 1, monograph 1 (pp. 8-64). Denver, CO: National Center for American Indian and Alaska Native Mental Health Research, University of Colorado Health Sciences Center.

Dohrenwend, B. S., & Dohrenwend, B. P. (Eds.) (1981). *Stressful life events and their contexts.* New York: Neale Watson Academic Publications.

Espin, C. X. (1987). Issues of identity in the psychology of Latina lesbians. In Boston Lesbian Psychologies Collective (Ed.), *Lesbian psychologies: Explorations and challenges* (pp.35-5l). Urbana, IL: University of Illinois Press.

Firestein, B. A. (Ed.) (1996). *Bisexuality: The psychology and politics of an invisible minority.* Thousand Oaks, CA: Sage Publications.

Fox, R. C. (1995). Bisexual identities. In A. R. D'Augelli & C. J. Patterson (Eds.), *Lesbian, gay, and bisexual identities over the lifespan* (pp. 122-142). New York: Oxford University Press.

Garnets, L., & Kimmel, D. (1991). Lesbian and gay male dimensions in the psychological study of human diversity. In J. D. Goodchilds (Ed.), *Psychological perspectives on human diversity: Master lecture series* (pp. 143-189). Washington, DC: American Psychological Association.

Germain, C. B., & Gitterman, A. (1996). *The life model of social work practice: Advances in theory and practice* (2nd ed.). New York: Columbia University Press.

Greene, B. (1993). Stereotypes of African American sexuality: A commentary. In S. Rathus, J. Nevid, & L. Rathus-Fichner (Eds.), *Human sexuality in a world of diversity* (p. 257). Boston: Allyn and Bacon.

Greene, B. (1994). Lesbian women of color: Triple jeopardy. In L. Comas-Diaz & B. Greene (Eds.), *Women of color: Integrating ethnic and gender identities in psychotherapy* (pp. 339-427). New York: The Guilford Press.

Harper, G. W., Jernewall, N., & Zea, M. C. (2004). Giving voice to emerging science and theory for lesbian, gay and bisexual people of color. *Cultural Diversity and Ethnic Minority Psychology, 10*(3), 187-199.

Harper, G. W., & Schneider, M. (2003). Oppression and discrimination among lesbian, gay, bisexual, and transgendered people and communities: A challenge for community psychology. *American Journal of Community Psychology, 31* (34), 243-252.

Heims, J. (1990). *Black and white racial identity attitudes: Theory, practice, and research.* New York: Greenwood Press.

Helms, J. E. (1989). Considering some methodological issues in racial identity research. *The Counseling Psychologist, 17*(2), 227-252.

Hemphill, E. (1992). *Ceremonies: Prose and poetry.* New York: Plume/Penguin.

Hendin, H. (1969). *Black suicide.* New York: Basic Books.

hooks, b. (1981). *Ain't I a woman: Black women and feminism.* Boston: South End Press.

Hutnik, N. (1985). Aspects of identity in a multi-ethnic society. *New Community, 12,* 298-309.

Icard, L. (1986). Black gay men and conflicting social identities: Sexual orientation versus racial identity. In J. Gripton & M. Valentieh (Eds.), *Journal of Social*

Work and Human Sexuality: Social Work Practice in Sexual Problems [Special Issue], *4*(1/2), 83-93.

Jaimes, M. A., & Halsey, T. (1992). American Indian women: At the center of indigenous resistance in North America. In M. A. Jaimes (Ed.), *The state of Native America: Genocide, colonization, and resistance* (pp. 311-344). Boston: South End Press.

Johnson, L. (1982). The influence of assimilation on the psycho/social adjustment of black homosexual men. Unpublished dissertation, California School of Professional Psychology, Berkeley, CA.

Kemnitzer, L. S. (1978). Adjustment and value conflict in urbanizing Dakota Indians measured by Q-Sort technique. *American Anthropologist, 75,* 687-707.

King, J. L. (2004). *On the down low: A journey into the lives of "straight" black men who sleep with men.* New York: Harlem Moon/Random House Press.

Kich, G. K. (1996). In the margins of sex and race: Difference, marginality, and flexibility. In M. P. P. Root (Ed.), *The multiracial experience: Racial borders as the new frontier* (pp. 263-274). Thousand Oaks, CA: Sage Publications.

Klein, F. (1993). *The bisexual option.* Binghamton, NY: The Haworth Press.

Kraus, R. F., & Buffler, P. A. (1979). Sociocultural stress and the American Native in Alaska: An analysis of changing patterns of psychiatric illness and alcohol abuse among Alaska Natives. *Culture, Medicine and Psychiatry, 3,* 111-151.

LaFromboise, T. D. (1988). American Indian mental health policy. *American Psychologist, 43,* 388-397.

Lazarus, R. (1980). The stress and coping paradigm. In L. Bond & J. Rosen (Eds.), *Competence and coping during adulthood* (pp. 28-74). Hanover, NH: University Press of New England.

Lev, A. I. (2004). *Transgender emergence: Therapeutic guidelines for working with gender-variant people and their families.* Binghamton, NY: The Haworth Press.

Loiacano, D. K. (1989). Gay identity issues among Black Americans: Racism, homophobia, and the need for validation. *Journal of Counseling and Development, 68,* 21-25.

Lorde, A. (1984). Our difference is our strength. *Ms. Magazine* (1996), *VII*(1), 61-64. Reprinted from Age, race, class, and sex: Women redefining difference. In A. Lorde (Ed.), *Sister outsider* (pp. 64-71) Freedom, CA: The Crossing Press.

Mallon, G. P. (1999). Knowledge for practice with transgendered persons. *Journal of Gay & Lesbian Social Services, 10*(3/4), 1-18.

Moncher, M., Holden, G. W., & Trimble, J. E. (1990). Substance abuse among Native American youth. *Journal of Counseling and Clinical Psychology, 58,* 408-415.

Moraga, C. (1983). *Loving in the war years.* Boston: South End Press.

Morales. E. S. (1989). Ethnic minority families and minority gays and lesbians. *Marriage and Family Review, 14,* 217-239.

Nemoto, T., Operario, D., & Keatley, J. G. (2005). Health and services for male-to-female transgender persons of color in San Francisco. *International Journal of Transgenderism, 8*(2/3), 5-19.

Ochs, R. (1996). Biphobia: It goes more than two ways. In B. A. Firestein (Ed.), *Bisexuality: The psychology and politics of an invisible minority* (pp. 217-239). Thousand Oaks, CA: Sage Publications.

Oetting, E. R., & Beauvais, F. (1990-1991). Orthogonal cultural identification theory: The cultural identification of minority adolescents. *The International Journal of the Addictions, 25*(5A, 6A), 655-685.

Parham, T., & Helms, J. (1985a). Attitudes of racial identity and self-esteem of black students: An exploratory investigation. *Journal of College Student Personnel, 26*, 143-147.

Parham, T., & Helms, J. (1985b). Relation of racial identity attitudes to self-actualization and affective states of black students. *Journal of Counseling Psychology, 32*, 431-440.

Parks, C. A., Hughes, T. H., & Matthews, A. K. (2004). Race/ethnicity and sexual orientation: Intersecting identities. *Cultural Diversity and Ethnic Minority Psychology, 10*(3), 241-254.

Pharr, S. (1988). *Homophobia: A weapon of sexism.* Little Rock, AR: Chardon Press.

Phinney, J. (1990). Ethnic identity in adolescents and adults: Review of research. *Psychological Bulletin, 108*(3), 499-514.

Poon, M. K. (2000). Inter-racial same-sex abuse: The vulnerability of gay men of Asian descent in relationships with Caucasian men. *Journal of Gay & Lesbian Social Services, 11*(4), 39-68.

Poon, M. K. (2004). A missing voice: Asians in contemporary gay and lesbian social service literature. *Journal of Gay & Lesbian Social Services, 17*(3), 87-106.

Rodriquez, R. A. (1998). Clinical and practical considerations in private practice with lesbians and gay men of color. *Journal of Gay & Lesbian Social Services, 8*(4), 59-76.

Root, M. P. P. (Ed.) (1996). *The multiracial experience: Racial borders as the new frontier.* Thousand Oaks, CA: Sage Publications.

Rosario, M., Schrimshaw, E. W., & Hunter, J. (2004). Ethnic/racial differences in the coming-out process of lesbian, gay and bisexual youths: A comparison of sexual identity development overtime. *Cultural Diversity and Ethnic Minority Psychology, 10*(3), 215-228.

Rust, P.C. (1996). Managing multiple identities: Diversity among bisexual women and men. In B. A. Firestein (Ed.), *Bisexuality: The psychology and politics of an invisible minority* (pp. 53-83). Thousand Oaks, CA: Sage Publications.

Sue, S. (1992). Ethnicity and culture in psychological research and practice. In J. D. Goodchilds (Ed.), *Psychological perspectives on human diversity in America: Master lecture series* (pp. 51-85). Washington, DC: American Psychological Association.

Trimble, J. E. (1981). Value differentials and their importance in counseling American Indians. In P. B. Pederson, J. G. Draguns, W, J. Lonner, & J. E. Trimble (Eds.), *Counseling across cultures.* Honolulu, HI: University of Hawaii Press.

Trimble, J. E., & LaFrornboise, T. (1985). American Indians and the counseling process: Culture, adaptation, and style. In P. B. Pederson (Ed.), *Handbook of cross-cultural counseling and therapy* (pp. 127-134). Westport, CT: Greenwood Press.

Vidal-Ortiz, S. (2002). Queering sexuality and doing gender: Transgender men's identification with gender and sexuality. *Gender Sexualities, 6,* 181-233.

Walters, K. E. (1997). Urban lesbian and gay American Indian identity: Implications for mental health social service delivery. *Journal of Gay & Lesbian Social Services, 6*(2), 192-206.

Walters, K. L. (1995). *Urban American Indian identity and psychological wellness.* Unpublished doctoral dissertation, University of California, Los Angeles.

Walters, K. L., Evans-Campbell, T., Simoni, J. M., Ronquillo, T., & Bhuyan, R. (2006). "My spirit in my heart": Identity experiences and challenges among American Indian two-spirit women. *Journal of Lesbian Studies, 10*(1/2), 125-149.

Walters, K. L., Longress, J. F., & Han, Chong-Suk (2004). Cultural competence with gay and lesbian persons of color. In D. Lum (Ed.), *Culturally competent practice: A framework for understanding diverse groups and justice issues* (pp. 310-342). Belmont, CA: Wadsworth Publishing.

Walters, K. L. (1996). Mental health among elderly Native Americans [book review]. *American Indian Culture and Research Journal, 20* (4), 228-232.

Walters, K. L., & Simoni, J. M. (1993). Lesbian and gay male group identity attitudes and self-esteem: Implications for counseling. *The Journal of Counseling Psychology, 40,* 94-99.

Warner, D. N. (2004). Towards a queer research methodology. *Qualitative Research in Psychology, 1,* 321-337.

Williams, T. K. (1996). Race as process: Reassessing the "What are you" encounters of biracial individuals. In the margins of sex and race: Difference, marginality, and flexibility. In M. P. P. Root (Ed.), *The multiracial experience: Racial borders as the new frontier* (pp. 191-210). Thousand Oaks, CA: Sage Publications.

Wooden, W. S., Kawaksaki, H., & Mayeda, R. (1983). Lifestyles and identity maintenance among gay Japanese-American males. *Alternative Lifestyles, 5,* 236-243.

Wong, S. C. (1992). Ethnicizing gender, gendering ethnicity. In S. G. Lim & A. Ling (Eds.), *Reading the literatures of Asian America* (pp. 111-129). Philadelphia: Temple University Press.

Zak, I. (1976). Structure of ethnic identity of Arab-Israeli students. *Psychological Reports, 38,* 239-246.

Chapter 4

Social Work Practice with Bisexual People

Geordana Weber
Kathy T. Heffern

Bisexuality is a concept that is often misunderstood because we live in a culture of dichotomies, either/or thinking, where one is *either* straight *or* gay. This binary understanding of sexual orientation is also common in social work literature. Therefore, it is possible that most social workers may not fully understand what it means to be bisexual. This chapter is written as a social work primer for those interested in enhancing their knowledge and skills about working with a bisexual population.

DEFINITION OF BISEXUALITY

Firestein (1996) defines bisexuality as "erotic, emotional, and sexual attraction to persons of more than one gender" (p. xix). In order to understand bisexuality, it is helpful to look more closely at sexual orientation. Klein (1993) developed a definition of sexual orientation that took multiple factors into account. In this multidimensional definition, sexual orientation had seven components. "These components included sexual attraction, sexual behavior, sexual fantasies, emotional preference (which gender one prefers to be emotionally or romantically involved with), social preference (which gender one prefers to socialize with), heterosexual↔homosexual lifestyle (whether one participates more in the heterosexual or gay/lesbian community), and self-identification (how a person describes his or her sexual orientation)" (p. 16).

Social Work Practice with LGBT People

It is important to recognize that sexual orientation is not static but rather what Klein referred to as an "ongoing, dynamic process" (p. 19). A person's sexual orientation may change or evolve over time. For some clients, bisexuality is just a temporary stage in the transition from one sexual orientation to another, either from heterosexual to gay/lesbian, or from gay/lesbian to heterosexual. Other clients, however, identify as bisexual throughout their lives.

Bisexual persons are a diverse group who have different combinations of what Klein calls the seven components of sexual orientation. For example, one bisexual woman might have fantasies about sex with women, but be in a monogamous, long-term relationship with a man. Another bisexual woman might date and have sex with women and transgender men. It is vital that social workers do not assume that all bisexual people share similar experiences, relationships, and sexual practices.*

WHY BISEXUALITY MATTERS TO SOCIAL WORKERS

According to the National Association of Social Workers' *Code of Ethics,* "Social workers should have a knowledge base of their clients' cultures and be able to demonstrate competence in the provision of services that are sensitive to clients' cultures and to differences among people and cultural groups" (NASW, 1996, 1.05). Social workers have an ethical responsibility toward their clients to educate themselves about diverse clients and cultures, including clients with various sexual orientations. In order to be culturally competent in their work with bisexual clients, social workers should learn about bisexuality and the issues that bisexual clients may be dealing with. As with any clients, bisexual clients should not be expected to teach their social workers about their sexual orientations.

MYTHS AND TRUTHS ABOUT BISEXUAL PEOPLE

Bisexual people are often misunderstood as a result of society developing, using, and reusing myths about what it means to be bisexual. As social workers are part of larger society and may have learned these myths, it is

---

A note on language: We want to be affirming to transgender people and other people whose genders are not represented by the overly simplistic male/female gender binary. Therefore, we will discuss "multiple genders" instead of "both genders" and replace the phrase "opposite-gender" with "other-gender."

important to identify what they are, and replace them with accurate information. This will assist the social worker's development of a broader knowledge base and enhanced empathy with their bisexual clients. Sumpter identifies some of the following myths at www.bitheway.org.

Myth: Bisexual People Are Promiscuous

Truth: Bisexual people display myriad sexual behaviors that reflect their diversity as individuals. Some bisexual people are monogamous, some have multiple partners, and some do not seek out relationships. Some spend periods of their lives in relationships, and at other times remain single. There is nothing about bisexual orientation that makes bisexual people more likely to be promiscuous. It is also important to remember that, as with all orientations, the ability to feel attraction toward a person does not mean that attraction will exist automatically; if it does exist, it does not mean that the attraction will be acted upon.

Myth: Bisexual People Are Incapable of Monogamous Relationships; They Always Need to Have Partners of Each Gender

Truth: Bisexuality is an orientation, and orientations describe whom one might be attracted to; it does not imply one particular relationship style (monogamy, bigamy, polyamory, etc.). Bisexual people are as capable as anyone of maintaining long-term relationships with one partner, regardless of gender.

Myth: Bisexual People Are Confused About Their Sexuality

Truth: It is common for people of all orientations—particularly for gays, lesbians, and bisexuals—to go through periods of questioning about their identity. The lack of acceptance from multiple communities makes it likely that many bisexual people will feel discomfort at the mere act of questioning. However, being attracted to more than one gender does not equate confusion. Once they have accepted themselves as bisexual, many bisexual people are not confused at all about their sexuality. In addition, we must remember that sexuality and identity are quite fluid; bisexual people may shift their identity, behavior, attraction, etc., through different times in their lives similar to people of other orientations.

Myth: Bisexual People Can Pass for Straight or Choose to Be Straight

Truth: Some bisexual people may be mistaken for heterosexual. This is because a person's appearance simply does not indicate their orientation. In addition, if a bisexual person is currently dating someone who appears to be of their opposite gender, that couple portrays the same gender dichotomy as a heterosexual couple. However, the process of passing as straight can be painful and isolating for bisexual people because they are not seen for who they truly are. (We will discuss invisibility and passing later in the chapter.) Bisexual people cannot choose to be straight, the same way heterosexual people cannot choose to be bisexual or gay/lesbian.

Myth: Bisexual People Spread Sexually Transmitted Infections (STIs) and HIV/AIDS to Heterosexuals and Lesbians

Truth: This myth has been a particularly strong catalyst for discrimination against bisexual people. Transmission occurs between two people of any gender. STI and HIV transmission is a cause for concern for people of all orientations—gay/lesbian, straight, bisexual, and other—because everyone is at risk. Bisexual people are no more likely to transmit infection than people of other orientations.

In sum, it is helpful to remember that stereotypes are never truths about an entire group of people. Bisexual people run the gamut of sexual behaviors, expressions of their identity, and lived interpretations of their experience.

CLINICAL ISSUES THAT ARISE FOR BISEXUAL CLIENTS

Many bisexual clients may come to therapy for reasons that may have nothing to do with their bisexuality. In other cases, they may have issues having to do with bisexuality which will be the focus of therapy. This chapter will address the latter.

Coming-Out

Coming-out refers to both discovering one's own sexual identity and disclosing that identity to others. Coming-out is a different process for bisexual clients than for lesbian and gay clients (Fox, 1995). Although there are some similarities, bisexual people face unique issues during their coming-out processes.

Bradford (2004) conceptualized bisexual identity development as a four-stage process. These stages include questioning reality, inventing identity, maintaining identity, and transforming adversity. In the first stage, *questioning reality*, a person begins to recognize her or his same-gender and other-gender attractions and struggles to value her or his reality in a culture that offers only two options: gay or straight. In the second stage, *inventing identity*, a person has already accepted her or his same- and other-gender attractions. The tasks of this stage are establishing a sexual identity and searching for language and labels that reflect one's experience. In the third stage, *maintaining identity*, a person works to preserve her or his bisexual identity even when faced with invisibility, isolation, and biphobia. This stage is lifelong for bisexual people. While some bisexual people remain at the maintaining identity stage, others move on to *transforming adversity*. In this stage, a person takes social action by creating a bisexual community or by being a leader and role model for others.

Bradford (2006) explains that a person who comes out as bisexual may be met with "discomfort, confusion, fear, condemnation, invalidation, or outright denial of the existence of bisexuality" (p. 18). Bisexual people are faced with a difficult decision each time they consider coming out as bisexual, having to choose between risking these reactions or remaining closeted. Coming out may be more difficult for bisexual people than for lesbian and gay people because bisexual people often do not have a visible bisexual community into which to come out.

Invisibility and Passing

Bisexual invisibility is the internal feeling of bisexual people that they are not seen. It is also the external reality of not being included, discussed, and legitimized by society. Much of the literature that focuses on gay and lesbian clients excludes a focus on bisexual clients. Only recently has the voice of a bisexual "community" begun to emerge, and in its nascence, it is far from cohesive. When bisexual people choose not to come out as bisexual or when their partner is of a particular gender, they are likely to feel invisible.

Ochs (1996) suggests that some people who identify as bisexual only do so privately, lest they provoke the rejection, conflict, and alienation from the heterosexual and gay/lesbian communities. In public, they may identify as lesbian, gay, or straight. This serves to protect them from some of the negative reactions about bisexuality from society, but may subject them to the negative psychological consequences of staying in the closet. Also, coming out as gay or lesbian when one actually feels bisexual further hides bisexuality from society and adds to its political invisibility.

When in same-gender relationships, bisexual people often appear to be gay or lesbian. When in opposite-gender (other gender) relationships, they often appear to be heterosexual. In this way, bisexual people "pass" as straight or "pass" as gay/lesbian. Passing for bisexuals is when they are successfully believed to be of one orientation or another that is different from their orientation as bisexual. The term *passing* often connotes a state of acceptance, something to be desired. However, bisexual people do not always want to pass. Passing can cause stress in regard to the individual's sense of self because one's identity goes invalidated. It can exacerbate feelings of isolation. It is common for bisexual people to experience both guilt and relief at passing. Passing as straight may lead them to feel that they are betraying their true identity and also betraying the gay/lesbian community. Passing as gay/lesbian, they may feel that an essential part of themselves is ignored. Passing may bring relief, which is a common emotional response when one avoids violence and discrimination, and is also a common response when one feels accepted and part of a community. It is possible, though, that feeling relief at passing will bring on feelings of guilt or shame and thus an emotional cycle may ensue.

Note on bisexual visibility: Ochs (1996) points out that bisexuality is invisible except at points of complication or conflict, which adds to its negative associations. If made public, issues in bisexual relationships become sensationalized and highly contested. Celebrities who date various genders at different times in their career; adolescents involved in the coining of a heteroflexible fad (Morris, 2006); and men who have sex with men on the down-low (King, 2004) are just some of the recent examples where bisexuality has been viewed as fickle, transitional, or lacking in value. The negative response of the media makes it even more important that bisexual clients feel acknowledged and supported.

Biphobia

Biphobia may be one of the most relevant factors in the lives of bisexual people. Hamilton (2000) defined biphobia as "the oppression or mistreatment of bisexuals, either by heterosexuals (often called homophobia if it does not target bisexuals separately from lesbians and gay men), or by lesbians or gay men" (p. 112). Biphobia stems from the discomfort that heterosexual, gay, and lesbian people feel with bisexuality and bisexual people. Klein (1993) explained that bisexual people can be threatening because "to most heterosexuals and homosexuals, the bisexual is an alien being whose dual sexuality opens up the possibility of their own sexual ambiguity" (p. 11).

Therefore, acknowledging the existence of bisexuality and bisexuals creates inner conflicts in heterosexuals and homosexuals.

The main components of biphobia are discrimination, hostility, and the denial that bisexual people exist. Firestein (1996) elaborated: "Biphobia may manifest in negative stereotyping of bisexuals, in acting to exclude bisexuals from the social and political organizations of lesbians and gay men, in interpersonal fear and distrust, or in angry or hostile verbalizations directed at people who identify as bisexual" (p. 275).

Bisexual people experience biphobia from both heterosexual people and gay or lesbian people. Heterosexual people may be biphobic because they believe that bisexual people are amoral and oversexed, that bisexual people spread disease, and that they break up families. These views may be caused in part by the negative portrayals of bisexual people in the media. Heterosexual people often have little contact with bisexual people who are out, so they may not have any real life experience with bisexuality to counteract these negative media portrayals. In addition to biphobia, bisexual people also experience homophobia from heterosexuals.

Many bisexual people report that biphobia from heterosexual people is somewhat unsurprising. However, biphobia from the lesbian, gay, and trans (LGT) communities is often particularly painful for bisexual people. LGT persons may be biphobic for a variety of reasons: the belief that bisexuality is only a phase in the process of coming-out, as exemplified by the saying "bi now, gay later"; the belief that bisexual people are actually lesbian or gay, but are reluctant to give up their heterosexual privilege; the belief that bisexuals have more privilege because they have the option to only have other-gender relationships; and the belief that bisexual people are not as committed to the lesbian and gay community. Biphobia from the LGT communities is manifested in various ways. First, LGT people may deny that bisexuality exists and therefore refuse to take bisexual people seriously. Second, the LGT community may accept bisexual people when they are in same-gender relationships, only to reject them when they are in other-gender relationships. Third, the LGT community may exclude bisexual people from the community either socially or politically.

Internalized Oppression

When bisexual people experience their own biphobia and believe the myths of bisexuality, they are internalizing their oppression and losing their sense of self and legitimacy. The Bisexual Resource Center (2000, p. 5) states that "*internalized oppression* is the set of feelings and misinformation that individuals carry about themselves and other members of their own group. It is the turning inward of, and adopting as true, the misinformation that is directed toward oppressed people by the external oppression, and it is any way in which we treat other members of our group as if these things were true of them." Some examples of socially constructed negative ideas that bisexual people might internalize are

1. bisexuality does not exist;
2. bisexuals are "fence-sitters"; they cannot make up their minds, and they are greedy because they "want it all";
3. bisexuals are really gay/lesbian but they are hiding behind heterosexual privilege;
4. when bisexuals are in relationships other than same-sex relationships (those that appear to be heterosexual), they are traitors to the gay and lesbian community;
5. bisexuals cannot build "true friendships" because sex can potentially interfere in all of their relationships;
6. bisexuals deserve to be isolated from both the straight and gay/lesbian communities because they belong nowhere.

These are only some of the biphobic ideas that bisexual people may internalize. Each person may have their own long list, depending on the specific messages they have received about bisexual orientation in their community. To combat internalized oppression, bisexual people can learn to recognize these thought patterns for what they are: impositions from societal oppression. Some bisexual people (as well as other groups who are oppressed) find power through activism. Fighting against societal oppression may help alleviate the tendency to internalize negative thoughts. Fox (1995, p. 126) suggests that bisexual people should seek out "autobiographical evidence" from other bisexuals who have successfully come out and lived well in society. The Bisexual Resource Center (2000) also suggests building allies with other bisexual people, as well as gay, lesbian, and heterosexual people who can help create "safe space" to talk about bisexual internalized oppression.

Relationships

Bisexual clients experience unique issues in finding and maintaining romantic relationships. Many people, whether they are heterosexual, gay, lesbian, or transgender may be uncomfortable with bisexuals and unwilling to date bisexual people. Bisexual people may also find that some people fetishize them for their bisexuality. In these situations, fetishizers of bisexuality are attracted to bisexual people specifically for their bisexuality instead of appreciating all the aspects of their personalities. These fetishizers often assume that bisexual people are hypersexual and will want to fulfill their sexual fantasies, particularly for group sex encounters.

Once bisexual clients are in relationships, they are faced with the dilemma of when they should come out to their partners. They may decide to disclose their bisexuality on the first date, as the relationship deepens, or whenever they feel it is appropriate. Bisexual clients may worry about their partners' reactions to their coming out.

Bisexual people have different experiences when they are in same-gender relationships than when they are in other-gender relationships. In same-gender relationships, bisexual people experience the invisibility of their bisexuality, pressure from others to identify as gay or lesbian, and homophobia. In other-gender relationships, bisexual people experience the invisibility of their identity, pressure from others to identify as heterosexual, lack of support from the lesbian and gay community, and struggling with the heterosexual privilege they have as a result of their relationships. The following vignette illustrates several of the challenges that bisexuals may face within relationships.

Nina's Dilemma

Nina is a thirty-six-year-old Latina bisexual. Nina is a successful professor in a community college in a large city in the Midwest. She has close relationships and support from her family and has been out about her bisexuality to her parents and siblings for the past ten years.

Nina has in her past dated men and women, though never at the same time. For the past five years, Nina has dated Beth; they have not lived together, but share many of the same interests, and have a committed relationship. Beth also identifies as a bisexual, but has many close friends in the lesbian community in their city and belongs to a women's group. Beth and Nina are both welcome at women's events and feel accepted as a couple in that group. Six months ago, Beth and Nina chose to end their relationship; they had several long-standing issues in their lives that could not be resolved and amicably chose to end their relationship.

Three months after ending her relationship with Beth, Nina begins to date Doug, a man whom she met at her gym. Doug identifies as a heterosexual man, and is comfortable with Nina's bisexual identification. Nina told Doug on their first date that she identified as bisexual, so this has not been an issue in their relationship. Nina is somewhat troubled that people see her relationship with Doug as "more normal" than her relationship with Beth. She feels guilty that her bisexuality is invisible while dating a man, but when dating Beth was quite obvious. Recently while out on a dinner date, Nina and Doug ran into some of her friends from her women's group. When Nina introduced

Doug as her boyfriend, several of the women from her group abruptly ended their conversation and bid a hasty good-bye. Nina felt very upset and marginalized by her friends, and when she confronted them with these feelings later that night by phone, one of the women said, "Well, what do you expect? I guess if you're dating a guy you're not one of us anymore!" Nina feels that she doesn't fit in anywhere—she is rejected by heterosexuals as not being straight enough, and similarly rejected by lesbian women as not being gay enough. She feels caught somewhere in the middle.

Polyamory is a relationship pattern for some bisexual people. Weitzman (2006) defined polyamory as "a lifestyle in which a person may pursue simultaneous romantic relationships, with the blessing and consent of each of their partners" (p. 139). In a study of 217 bisexual people, Page (2004) found that 54 percent of the participants stated that they preferred polyamorous relationships, while 33 percent reported that they preferred monogamous relationships. Particular issues arise for people who are bisexual and polyamorous. These issues include coming out as polyamorous to oneself, family and friends, and one's partner, dealing with discrimination because of one's polyamory, one's partner's interest level in polyamory, and negotiating multiple romantic relationships.

Some bisexual people realize their bisexuality when they are already in a long-term, committed relationship. Bradford (2006) explained that these situations can be particularly painful because "the bisexual [person] is confronted with the risk of wounding or losing her partner, or the sacrifice of forgoing the exploration and experience of a vital part of her sexual and relational self" (p. 20).

Cultural Factors

As with any clinical issue, it's important to examine how cultural factors affect bisexuality. Bisexuality is affected by culture in a variety of ways. First, sexual identity is a culturally specific concept. Some cultures do not perceive sexual or gender orientation as a source of identity. For clients from these cultures, development of sexual identity may not be a goal. Second, different cultures provide different ways to interpret sexual feelings and behaviors. People from certain cultures with same- and other-gender attractions will not consider themselves "bisexual," but rather interpret their sexuality in other ways.

Unique issues arise for clients whose bisexual identities intersect with other marginalized identities, such as race, class, ethnicity, and religion. For those who have lived a relatively privileged life, coming out as bisexual might be their first personal experience with marginalization, discrimination, and oppression. However, as Rust (1996) pointed out, "For other individuals who are already marginalized for racial, ethnic, religious, or economic reasons, the discovery that they are bisexual compounds their marginalization and produces particular problems of identity integration and community building" (p. 54). Multiple marginalization particularly affects the decision to come out as bisexual. Bisexual people from marginalized groups might be discouraged from coming out by other members of their communities, who view bisexuality as a challenge to the culture, a sign of assimilation, or a "white"/"Western" phenomenon. Another factor in the decision to come out is that bisexual people from racial and ethnic minorities have less to gain by coming out because of racism in the mainstream, predominantly white, LGBT community. Finally, bisexual people with another marginalized identity might be hesitant to come out, because they may view their bisexuality as another strike against them, or a further marginalization. When working with bisexual clients with other marginalized identities, it is important keep in mind that bisexual people or groups of people with the same constellation of racial, ethnic, and sexual identities can be a helpful resource.

IMPLICATIONS FOR SOCIAL WORK PRACTICE

Developing practice that is culturally competent will aid social work with all clients. We suggest some specific practice guidelines for working with bisexual clients.

Develop one's own self-awareness. Social workers should recognize their own attitudes and beliefs, their own gender and sexual orientation, their valuing of heterosexuality as a normative orientation and their fear of working with someone different from themselves (if they themselves do not identify as bisexual). Self-awareness will help the social workers flag feelings of discomfort and should diminish their likelihood to pathologize their bisexual clients (Van Den Bergh & Crisp, 2004).

Acknowledge one's own homophobia, biphobia, and transphobia. As is the case with all isms, homophobia, biphobia, and transphobia are fears and actions that are culturally learned and sanctioned. Almost everyone in society can believe the myths about bisexual clients if they do not have exposure to accurate information about this population. Social workers can identify their own fears and stereotypes and learn to transform them into affirming and supportive work with bisexual clients (Bradford, 2006).

Make no assumptions about sexual or gender identity. Remember that one's sexual or gender orientation cannot always be determined simply by looking at the person or—by extension—by looking at the person's partner. Do not assume that your client is heterosexual, gay, lesbian, trans, bisexual, or other. Once a rapport has been established, talk to your client in the way he or she identifies and use the language and idioms that the client uses. Meeting clients where they are is a time-honored social work principle and encompasses this skill; do not attempt to convince clients of a different identity from what they present (Bradford, 2006).

Allow the client to define the presenting problem. Bisexual clients may seek social work services that have everything, little, or nothing to do with their sexual identity. Being bisexual is not in itself a problem; as Bradford (2006) reminds us, it is the intolerant and hostile environment created by biphobia that causes undue hardship and a propensity toward isolation for bisexual clients. Bisexual clients will experience the same breadth of problems as heterosexual and gay/lesbian clients.

Facilitate groups for bisexual clients. Models of group work are valued for alleviating social and emotional isolation for group members of all orientations and demographics. The bisexual client's propensity toward isolation and a lack of community makes him or her a great candidate for a group work intervention.

Seek out resources and training specific to bisexuality. Unfortunately, many resources that claim to include information on working with lesbian, gay, bisexual, and transgender people are often heavy on the lesbian and gay components while offering almost no explicit information on practice with bisexual people and transgender people. While the transgender community is organizing itself to address their invisibility, bisexual people are not formally organized into a community with which to combat their invisibility. Social workers can first seek out any bisexual-specific literature (such as the online *Journal of Bisexuality*) and also make demands on gay and lesbian affirming academic journals to be bisexual affirming.

Engage the bisexual specific resources that currently exist. Utilize the reference list at the end of this chapter to further your knowledge on bisexual clients and the issues they face. Using activities purposefully will assist social workers in their work with bisexual clients. Whitman and Boyd (2003) suggest several activities in *The Therapist's Notebook for Lesbian, Gay, and Bisexual Clients: Homework, Handouts, and Activities for Use in Psychotherapy* in the following chapters:

1. "To Pass or Not to Pass: Exploration of Conflict Splits for Bisexual-Identified Clients"
2. "Overcoming Biphobia"

3. "Creating a Cultural and Sexual Genogram"
4. "Creating a Thicker Description: Understanding Identity in Mixed-Identity Relationships"
5. "Enhancing Relationships: Sex-Role Values of Lesbian and Bisexual Women"
6. "Making Connections: Parallel Process in Lesbian and Bisexual Women's Recovery from Addiction and Healing from Homophobia"
7. "Examining Links Between Drug or Alcohol Use and Experiences of Homophobia/Biphobia and Coming Out."

REFERENCES

Bisexual Resource Center (2000). *Bisexual internalized oppression.* Retrieved February 27, 2006, from http://www.biresource.org/pamphlets/internalized.html.

Bi the way. Myths and truths. Retrieved February 27, 2006, from http://bitheway.org/Bi/Myths.htm.

Bradford, M. (2004). The bisexual experience: Living in a dichotomous culture. *Journal of Bisexuality, 4*(1/2), 7-23.

Bradford, M. (2006). Affirmative psychotherapy with bisexual women. *Journal of Bisexuality, 6*(1/2), 13-25.

Firestein, B. A. (Ed.) (1996). *Bisexuality: The psychology and politics of an invisible minority.* Thousand Oaks, CA: Sage Publications.

Fox, R. C. (1995). Bisexual identities. In A. R. D'Augelli & C. J. Patterson (Eds.), *Lesbian, gay, and bisexual identities over the lifespan* (pp. 122-142). New York: Oxford University Press.

Hamilton, A. (2000). *LesBiGay and transgender glossary.* Retrieved April 14, 2006, from http://www.biresource.org/pamphlets/ glossary.html.

King, J. L. (2004). *On the down low: A journey into the lives of "straight" black men who sleep with men.* New York: Harlem Moon/Random House Press.

Klein, F. (1993). *The bisexual option* (2nd ed.). Binghamton, NY: The Haworth Press.

Morris, A. (2006, February 6). The cuddle pool of Stuyvesant High School. *New York Magazine.* Retrieved April 16, 2006, from http://newyorkmetro.com/news/features/15589/index1. html.

National Association of Social Workers (1996). *Code of ethics.* Washington, DC: NASW Press. Retrieved February 27, 2006, from http://www.socialworkers.org.

Ochs, R. (1996). Biphobia: It goes more than two ways. In B. A. Firestein (Ed.), *Bisexuality: The psychology and politics of an invisible minority* (pp. 217-239). Thousand Oaks, CA: Sage Publications.

Page, E. H. (2004). Mental health services experiences of bisexual women and men: An empirical study. *Journal of Bisexuality, 3*(3/4), 138-160.

Rust, P. C. (1996). Managing multiple identities: Diversity among bisexual women and men. In B. A. Firestein (Ed.), *Bisexuality: The psychology and politics of an invisible minority* (pp. 53-83). Thousand Oaks, CA: Sage Publications.

Van Den Berg, N., & Crisp, C. (2004). Defining culturally competent practice with sexual minorities: Implications for social work education and practice. *Journal of Social Work Education, 40* (2), 221-251.

Weitzman, G. (2006). Therapy with clients who are bisexual and polyamorous. *Journal of Bisexuality, 6*(1/2), 137-164.

Whitman, J. S., & Boyd, C. J. (2003). *The therapist's notebook for lesbian, gay, and bisexual clients: Homework, handouts, and activities for use in psychotherapy.* Binghamton, NY: The Haworth Press.

Chapter 5

Social Work Practice with Transgender and Gender Nonconforming People

Carrie Davis

In the real world, gender theory isn't academic: It's about listening to the voices of the transgender communities.

A COMMON LANGUAGE

This chapter reviews the knowledge and practice that social workers need to establish beginning competency in working with transgender and gender nonconforming persons. The concepts, variables, and change logic to be explored require a common language. Because clinical language can often be "out of step" with the language of the trans communities themselves, whenever possible, this chapter emphasizes the language, terminology, and vocabulary of trans culture rather than the language or terminology used by social services and health care providers.

Language is a critical component in the recognition of subjugated knowledge (Anderson, 2000; Aranda & Street, 2001; Hartman, 1990, 1992; Holbrook, 1995). The trans communities have developed an inventive, expressive, and diverse language of preferred identities, terms, knowledge, and even pronouns. The clinical language that originates in the context of global knowledge is laden with hierarchy and is often in conflict with the language of trans communities, making translation of ideas and concepts necessary.

This is an evolutionary vocabulary. Both transvestite and transexual were first assigned global meaning in a medical and historical context during the first quarter of the twentieth century. The clinical distinction that developed between transvestite and transexual further enhanced the perception of these as psychopathological identities.

In the light of this pathology, trans people have begun to utilize their voices to make claim to, or reclaim, these terminologies (Terry & Davis, 2002). The creation and use of the word "transgender" in the 1960s is but one example. All-gender pronouns addressing aspects of sexism and the complexity of identity are another.

In seeking to understand our own subjugated knowledge, we must remain aware this knowledge is also produced and later interpreted under the oppressive influence of the prevailing and dominant global knowledge (Kondrat, 1995)—one steeped in an irrational fear of gender difference or cultural transphobia, as well as sexism, racism, classism, bigenderism, and so forth.

As such, it is not uncommon for the trans communities themselves to also use subjugating language. We routinely hear references to "real," "genetic," and/or "bio(logical)" men or women. Clearly these conflict with both the knowledge trans people have about their own lives, and our developing understanding of gender. Every individual, trans or nontrans, is real, genetic, and biological. When misused, terms such as these create a double standard applied by nontrans people and also by trans people themselves and enforce the existing cultural hierarchy which classifies and subjugates trans people as being less real and less natural than nontrans people.

Given the dichotomy between a subjugating knowledge such as that authored outside the trans communities and the knowledge derived from trans individuals, it is not surprising that relations between the trans communities and nontrans communities have often been uncertain, and frequently suspicious. In this manner, clinical service providers and researchers focusing their efforts on trans people for much of the last century have exacerbated the contradictory and uneasy power association in the marginalization of trans people by nontrans people.

DEFINITIONS

This might be the right place to take a moment to share or review some basics of this knowledge, a quick Trans 101 review. To that end, we begin with a discussion of gender, which is comprised of many different elements.

- *Sex* refers to biological, anatomical, or organic sexual markers such as vagina, ovaries, eggs, estrogen levels, and menstruation for females and penis, testis, sperm, and testosterone levels for males. We tend to think of these as very clear distinctions, yet the truth is more fluid. Variations in our sex include chromosomal variations, changing hormonal levels as we age, biological changes due to illness (such as hysterectomy, mastectomy), changes related to choice, and the varied anatomical differences faced by intersex individuals who are born with characteristics of both sexes (typically forced to undergo genital surgery at birth to make them "normal," long before they have the opportunity to confirm their own gender).

- *Gender role* can be defined as the social and perceived expectations of gendered acts or expressions; examples include cultural notions that boys play with trucks, girls play with dolls, boys wear pants, girls wear skirts, boys date girls, girls date boys. This changes over time and from cultural subgroup to cultural subgroup.

Gender had been conceived of as distinct from sex, or sexual identity, as early as the 1860s, but it is only relatively recently that a lucid conception of gender identity as distinct from understandings of sexual identity and sexual orientation has begun to evolve. This was articulated as a private, inner sense of maleness or femaleness (Hogan & Hudson, 1998) and coincided with the emergence of a gay civil rights movement. Money (1987) further developed an understanding of gender that suggests gender is a complex combination of many factors including variations and combinations of organic and nonorganic markers, such as chromosomal gender, gonadal gender, prenatal hormonal gender, prenatal and neonatal brain hormonalization, internal accessory organs, external genital appearance, pubertal hormonal gender, assigned gender, and gender identity. Despite this, transgender-identified persons would be conflated with the identities of those identified as lesbian and gay, within what was termed a "gay movement."

- *Gender identity* can be understood as the *self*-conception of one's gender; it's about how I see myself, how I feel about my gender identity, and myself, and may or may not have an organic component. We are still learning more about this.

All three of these, *sex + gender role + gender identity* combine to create one's *gender*. Although gender has typically been thought of as a binary construct, as man or woman, an alternative paradigm understands gender as a continuum—as an infinite series of individually defined genders, one for each living person.

Transgender

Though the term "transgender" was not created or used until the late 1970s, transgender-identified people have been present in all cultures and at all times (Feinberg, 2001). When the modern conception of differing sexual orientations began to emerge in the 1860s, people who were seen to express their gender differently were bundled into Karoly Maria Kertbeny's evolving definition of homosexuality (Hogan & Hudson, 1998). This has been an awkward fit, as people of transgender experience have historically sought out a variety of sexual partners, including those of the same or differing sexes.

What others have written on this subject and what I am suggesting here is clearly a modern and evolutionary language. The terms "transvestite" and "transsexual" were first assigned meaning in a medical context by Magnus Hirschfeld. Transsexual was later given prominence in both Cauldwell's (1949) "Psychopathia transexualis" and Benjamin's (1954) "Transsexualism and Transvestism as Psycho-Somatic and Somato-Psychic Syndromes." The clinical distinction made at this time between transvestite and transsexual further enhances the perception of these as psychopathological identities.

In light of this, trans people have begun to speak out to make claim to, or reclaim, these terminologies. The reconfiguration by some trans people of the word most commonly read as "transsexual" to read as "transexual" (with a single "s") is a poignant example of the reclamation of trans identities by trans people. Riki Ann Wilchins (1997), one of the founders of the Transexual Menace, notes:

> This . . . seemed a way of asserting some small amount of control over a naming process that has always been entirely out of my hands—a kind of quiet mini-rebellion of my own. I think transactivist Dallas Denny captured the spirit of the whole enterprise; "Yeah, we'll change it to one 's' until they all start using it. Then we'll go back to two, or maybe to three." (p. 15)

Popularized by Virginia Prince in the late 1970s, "transgender" (or "transgenderist") originally referred to someone who did not desire gender-confirming medical intervention and/or who considered that they fell between genders. Prince and others conceived transgender as a challenge to older terms that hinted at pathology or medicalized identity, such as the terms "transsexual" and "transvestite."

Transgender, created by people with trans histories to refer to trans people, is now generally considered an umbrella term encompassing many different identities. It is commonly used to describe an individual who is seen as gender-different. Outside the transgender communities, people identified as transgender are usually perceived through a dichotomous lens and are commonly described as transgressing gender norms, gender variant, or gender deviant. This traditional misreading is predicated in a conception of transgender within a pathologically oriented perspective framed in a language layered in heterosexist, sexist, bigenderist, and transphobic context and meaning.

In this definition, gender difference is not regulated. People who are identified or self-identify as transgender may or may not live full-time in a sex different from the sex that they were assigned at birth—sometimes referred to as the "opposite sex." Being seen as transgender may not have anything to do with whether they have had any sort of gender-confirming surgery (GCS), also commonly known as "sex-reassignment" surgery (SRS). Individuals who are seen as gender-different or gender-questioning may or may not personally identify themselves as transgender.

Therefore, care needs to be taken not to label or identify as transgender those who do not perceive themselves that way. By using the words "transgender" and/or "trans," this chapter looks for a common language, describing communities and purposes, and is not seeking to erase any of the diverse identities of those individuals who identify themselves and/or are seen as androgyne, bigendered, butch queen, CD, cross-dresser, drag king, drag queen, female-to-male, femme queen, FTM, gender bender, gender blender, gender challenged, gender fucked, gender gifted, gender nonconforming, gender-queer, male-to-female, MTF, new man, woman, non-op, non-operative transexual, passing man, passing woman, phallic woman, post-op, postoperative transexual, pre-op, pre-operative transexual, sex-change, she-male, stone butch, TG, third sex, trannie/tranny, trannie-fag, trans, trans butch, transexual/transsexual, transgender, transgenderist, transie, trans man, trans person, transexed, transexed man, transexed woman, transexual, transexual man, transexual woman, transvestic fetishist, transvestite, trans woman, tryke, TS, two-spirit, and the like. The framework provided by transgender as an umbrella term then serves as a transitory and common idiom, useful to connect communities and purposes.

DEVELOPMENT

Imagine if some nontrans children were randomly reared in a gender role opposite to that of their sexual identity—boys as girls, girls as boys. For many children, that event would be highly troubling and traumatic. The public, as well as mental health care providers, would most certainly consider this an abuse perpetrated by these children's caretakers. Yet, on some level, this is what all transgender-identified children and adults encounter until they finally muster the reserves to express their actual gender identity.

Coming-out for trans persons begins with an increasing awareness that one is different, the sense that how one sees oneself in terms of gender and how others perceive them does not match up. In these early stages, trans-individuals may be forced to compartmentalize their lives, to hide the true parts of themselves, to remain closeted at all costs—to manage their gender. Coming-out is a continuous process. While it begins with acknowledging the truth about one's identity to oneself, trans individuals find themselves continually confronted with the risks and possibilities of coming out to family, friends, religious groups, teachers and classmates, employers and co-workers, and medical and mental health professionals.

Certainly, it seems reasonable to recognize that perceiving one's identity as nonnormative and being restricted from expressing it, having to repress or being unable to recognize one's gender in childhood, as well as adolescence and adulthood, is, by itself, traumatic, and possibly abusive.

This would then posit the first, and perhaps most overlooked, abuse trans people experience, which is often at the hands of loving parents and caregivers in childhood. Many, if not most, trans people struggle consciously or unconsciously as children with the understanding that their gender identities are considered socially and parentally inappropriate or deviant. As children who display differing gender roles and identities are usually punished harshly and rarely have their differing gender roles parentally reinforced, the bonds of attachment and trust between these children and their caregivers are sure to be affected.

Trans youth are consciously or unconsciously aware that gender different behavior rarely brings about a nurturing and caretaking response from parents and other caregivers. This can elicit a pattern of blame and guilt. Related as a protective dissociation, this could be seen as one of the first adaptive tools trans people might utilize to endure the trauma of being unable to actualize their gender identity.

Gender Management

To survive this form of gender trauma, trans people typically employ adaptive and maladaptive strategies of gender management. These are usually functional, though often only temporary, and can engender acute confusion, anxiety, and despair, often characterized as depression. Family members may overtly or covertly participate in this process of negotiation and denial. Gender management can include the following:

- *Repression or erasure of gender identity* by consciously or subconsciously deciding to pass quietly and invisibly in the birth assigned gender and sex. This may involve extensive defenses, often aspects of sublimation.
- *Negation of gender identity and gender reconstruction* by consciously or subconsciously denying one's gender and adopting behavior and expression that confirms the gender assumptions made by others about one's identity and birth assigned gender and sex. This often includes admission to gender polarized groups and engaging in what is coded as hyper-gendered behavior such as joining the military, parenting children, and so forth.
- *Modify gender identity* to fit within cultural norms where possible—adopting "moderately" masculine- or feminine-vectored behavior so as to express an aspect of one's gender but still be able to fit in as much as possible.

Imagine having to manage, rather than explore, your gender identity, through childhood, adolescence, and adulthood. Imagine the absence of control and feelings of helplessness this might engender. This is the context most trans people must negotiate at some point in their lives.

Transition

Lesbian, gay, and bisexual (LGB) persons sometimes have the ability to "pass," but many trans-identified individuals do not have that privilege. Coming-out for trans individuals calls forth tremendous personal resources—maintaining one's own sense of identity in the face of invisibility, oppression, and discrimination challenges inner strength and determination. At the same time, we can never underestimate the stress of the closet. Having to hide always takes a toll spiritually, emotionally, socially, and sometimes physically.

Transitioning brings its own stresses and emerging strengths. Think for a minute about the challenges of shifting identities. Put yourself in the place of a trans person; consider how you might manage a transition of this magnitude. Imagine the struggle you might endure, even now, as an adult, with all the resources you have at your disposal; imagine the loss of privilege.

Now consider the same situation at age fifteen. What forces would confront you? How would your family and friends respond? What about your school and your place of worship? What about money and economic influence? Consider how all these forces and more would seek to erase who you are and deny your sense of self. Now consider how you might respond.

It is clear that gender difference and gender transition have the power to lead to disconnection from the trans person's own family and from the family of origin due to ignorance and lack of acceptance. Trans youth can find themselves disconnected from family affirmation and supports.

Although we know identification with one's cultural group is a significant component in the development of an individual's self-concept, many trans people delay in developing a trans self-concept—a devastating disconnection.

Trans youth lack suitable and positive trans role models. In the dominant culture, positive trans role models are rare. Trans people, when visible are typically portrayed in a pejorative sense. In addition, some trans-identified people may have never met another trans person.

In addition, peer networks can be tenuous for most trans people. Peer rejection and/or isolation is one of the most dangerous aspects of a trans identity.

While trans people often experience multiple disconnects from community, trans people of color experience even greater disconnects, often feeling cut off from their racial/ethnic communities or forced to choose between their ethnic communities and whatever trans community they have begun to connect with.

TRANSGENDER SPACE

Transgender and gender nonconforming individuals typically pose a challenge to public space and how it is made available via the use and misuse of gender (Namaste, 2000). In this way, transgender individuals are at risk within ordinary public space, which refuses to overtly incorporate what could be termed trans space. Trans people soon come to understand that trans spaces, and the trans communities that inhabit these spaces, are difficult to discover, are exceedingly fragile, and are often migratory. Those who do uncover some element of trans space, whether it be social, physical, online/electronic, or temporal, are always aware of the invisible borders, as well as the extremely hostile territory, that surround them at all times.

Anzaldua (1987) describes space such as this as a "borderland." As borderlands, these are resonant cultural zones of conflict and exchange populated by border citizens living both on the threshold and within the threshold of that space—the borderland. Such "borderlands are physically present whenever two or more cultures edge each other, where people of different races occupy the same territory, where under, lower, middle, and upper classes touch, where space between two individuals shrinks with intimacy" (Anzaldua, 1999, p. 19). In this way, the search for enduring trans space becomes a search for an enduring trans community.

Trans space may not be readily visible. Social spaces may include clubs and bars, performance spaces, and outdoor spaces such as parks or sex-work strolls. As there is a dearth in safe public trans space, providers who serve trans communities often become de facto trans spaces, whether or not they are equipped for social or community purposes. Some trans space may be electronic and reside online—in Web sites, message boards, or chat rooms. Trans space may also be perceived as temporal, varying with the day of the week and the hours of the day. Trans space is often subjected to police scrutiny and may close or shift its boundaries without warning. Like much of Western culture, trans spaces are usually segregated by gender (where trans men and trans women often occupy different space), class, race and ethnicity, and age.

> The sense of commonality with others and the individual ethnic meaning that people develop as a result of their experiences have implications far beyond those of shared religion, national origin, geography, or race . . . [although] societal definition and assigned value, among other factors, help determine whether . . . meaning for a given group or individual becomes positive, ambivalent, or negative. (Pinderhughes, 1988, p. 39)

The fissured sense of community that most trans people experience is often a barrier to service provision and may prevent a more uniform understanding of these communities and the diverse ethnicities that trans people understand and experience.

Sexual Identity

In adolescence, puberty is distinguished by physical growth and maturation, and the elaboration of the secondary sexual characteristics. As undeniable as these biological changes are, they are still subject to interpretation and assigned cultural meanings. Developmental theorists often make a strong connection between physical or biological developmental theory and psychosocial concerns. Legislators, clergy, physicians, researchers, and other clinicians have created various methods to quantify and value the sexes. However, these imposed markers of sexual identity are often incongruent with each other. Legislated sex can vary not only on the basis of the actual physical constitution of a trans body, but may also have a geopolitical component related to what state, city, or country a trans person may happen to enter, visit, or reside in, and what borders they might cross (Currah & Minter, 2000). In this framework, an understanding of one's biology as a social construction is reasoned, and sexual identity is understood as a social, not organic, construction (Butler, 1993). Despite this, organic markers have traditionally been used to categorize individuals as either male or female, though other individuals may also be considered intersex at birth. Sexual identity and an understanding of biological sex are replaced here with an understanding of the sex that the participants had been identified as at birth (assigned sex—typically based on genital appearance and gender of rearing), the sex that individuals understand themselves to be, and the legal sex that individuals currently understand themselves as being.

Transition

Transition refers to the place in which individuals perceive themselves to be in the process or vector, from living and being perceived as identified at birth (either male or female) to living and being perceived as the trans individuals they understand themselves to be. This often includes assessment of transition milestones sometimes described as living part-time, full-time, doing "drags," and so forth. This assessment also considers access to gender confirming surgery, described as operative or surgical status (nonoperative, preoperative, postoperative, partly operative); and access to gender confirming hormones (endogenous, cross-gender hormones), described as hormonal status (pre-hormones, using hormones).

Sexual Orientation

The language used to describe sexual orientation (sexual, affectional, or romantic attraction) is sometimes elusive when perceived in the context of the trans communities. Terms like straight, gay, lesbian, and bisexual/pansexual/omnisexual traditionally require agreement about individual conceptions of gender, as well as sexual identity, and are frequently framed around understandings of genitalia. Within the trans communities these choices and language are also valued often as independent of transition milestones such as access to gender confirming hormones or surgery.

In this phraseology, trans women attracted to men and trans men attracted to women may identify as straight, while trans women attracted to women identify as lesbian, and trans men attracted to men identify as gay, irrespective of genital configuration and/or access to gender-confirming surgeries. This further develops the significance of viewing people with transgender histories as sexual minorities. Other choices can include queer, asexual, pansexual, omnisexual, and questioning.

In addition, there are few, if any, affirming and representative terms for individuals who prefer and are attracted to trans people, commonly referred to in the trans women's communities with pejorative terms such as "trannie-chaser." The dearth of representative terminology can confound clinicians, researchers, social scientists, and others who seek to "bag and tag" the trans communities and who attempt to label trans partners as straight, lesbian, gay, and bisexual against their will, ignoring the complexities of gender and of representative identities.

Race/Ethnicity

Like the dominant, nontrans culture, the trans communities are ethnically heterogeneous. The experiences and histories of trans women of color are noticeably different from the experiences and histories of white trans women (see Chapter 3). The construction of an African-American or Latino/a person's experiences of, and struggle against, multiple oppressions need to be considered within the context of the possible construction of the existence of the trans person of color as irreconcilable with the struggle against racism, sexism, and heterosexism. In this model, the power of stereotypical images of trans people as prostitutes, as mentally ill, as men-in-dresses and women-in-suits, and as confused gay or lesbian people, cannot be discounted. The resulting erasure of the identities of trans people of color and the silencing of their voices often precludes the consideration and inclusion of their concerns.

Somatic Characteristics

Somatic characteristics may play a role in the provision and access to services especially those related to "passability." Passing refers to the ability to be perceived and identified as a nontransgender person. The ability to pass as nontrans is seen as directly related to economic and social privilege. Aspects of passing for trans persons include facial features, height, weight, body morphology, surgical status, hand and foot size, hair, body and facial hair, and so forth. In this regard, the trans communities are very heterogeneous, with some members passing very easily as nontrans people, and others being seen routinely as trans people. Jessica Xavier (1999, p. 98) describes passing, passing privilege, and its significance to the transgender communities:

> Passing affords all [trans-people] physical safety in public spaces, and for those of us living full-time, job security and access to the social, economic and professional pathways of the nontransgendered. Thus the vast majority of MTFs [male-to-female] and many if not most FTMs [female-to-male] become careful observers of those with birth privilege in their chosen genders.

Age

The impact of age on access to services as well as related concerns such as education, financial means, and social support is a primary consideration in this chapter. Minors encounter unique barriers to care that are presumed to end when one achieves majority status—typically age eighteen. Despite this, barriers to care are perceived to extend to trans individuals in early adulthood. Education may also play a factor in barriers to care. As such the ability to stay in school, financial means, type of schooling, and so forth are considered. Financial means are factors in all health care and include income, health insurance, and so forth. Aspects of support impact access to and efficacy of care. Support comprises parental consent as well as levels of support from family, community, trans families and friends, positive role models, and so forth.

INSTITUTIONALLY ESTABLISHED BARRIERS TO CARE

Age

Transgender youth typically confront minimal age requirement barriers for access to services, requirements for parental consent, and medical ethics issues. It is generally acknowledged that "the effectiveness of a health care intervention may best be measured in terms of the quality of life of the patient" (Wren, 2000, p. 33). Early hormonal treatment, and/or gender confirmation surgery has been shown to significantly improve the lives of trans adolescents, avoiding the sometimes immutable physical changes that are the result of a puberty associated with individuals' presumed biological sex, not their identified gender. In addition, trans youth who are able to access medical care to resolve some of their intense gender concerns may be better able to complete some of the developmental tasks of adolescence, enter into satisfying peer and interpersonal relationships, and continue in school similar to other youth their age (Cohen-Kettenis & van Goozen, 1997; Gooren & Delemarre-van de Waal, 1996; Wren, 2000).

Despite the value of the early affirmation of self-identity and respect for self-determination that intervention can offer, minor children typically cannot access medical care without parental consent. The instances where they can are usually narrowly defined, such as in the case of sexually transmitted diseases, pregnancy, and substance abuse treatment. In addition, emancipated minor status is not universal, subject to interpretation, and difficult for youth to easily accomplish (Russo, 1999; Swann & Herbert, 1999). As a consequence of this, Haynes (1998, p. 15) notes:

> Few medical providers are adequately trained in the proper hormonal treatment of transgender people, and those that are rarely provide care to minors without parental consent. Since parental consent is not the norm, especially for those who are homeless or otherwise detached from their families, many young people legitimately requiring hormonal therapy go without until they reach the age of majority.

Ethics

Professional ethical concerns also play a role in determining treatment for trans youth. The unique situations presented by trans and gender nonconforming people often do not neatly fit into ethical codes. Ethical codes for organizations such as the American Academy of Child Psychiatry (AACP), the American Psychological Association, and the National Association of Social Workers (NASW) either place responsibility for youth with their respective parents or guardians, are ambiguous, or are silent on the matter (Swann & Herbert, 1999). Though NASW recently published a policy position supporting the needs of the trans communities, the issues and concerns of trans youth were conspicuously absent (Lev & Moore, 2000). Medical providers and clinics are often cautious when working with trans youth. "'Every day, I feel torn between wanting to empower my patients and wanting to be sure not to harm them,' says Jayne Jordan, a physician's assistant in the [Michael Callen-Audre Lorde Community Health] Center's transgender medicine program" (Russo, 1999, p. 89). In addition, not all youth that identify as transgender, gender-different, and gender-questioning during adolescence will continue to identify themselves as transgender or transexual in adulthood (American Psychiatric Association, 1997; Cohen-Kettenis & van Goozen, 1997). The legal ramifications of providing such care to minors in a litigious society are not well understood yet. So, although research may indicate the value of early medical treatment and care for trans youth, legal and ethical concerns and possible conflicts may erect potent barriers to that care. The role of social workers and other mental health providers can be integral to the interdisciplinary provision of services in these instances. Social workers may be able to offer information and support to youth, parents, and providers in these cases and often ameliorate legal concerns.

Absence of Services

Trans people confront a critical shortage of services. In most areas this includes a near total absence of trans-positive providers offering medical and mental health care, substance abuse therapy, shelter from domestic violence, treatment for HIV/AIDS, hormone confirming therapy, trans-masculine-specific, and social services. In addition, trans people encounter few transgender-identified service providers. A scarcity of services in rural, suburban, or nonurban areas serves as a barrier as well as a factor exacerbating the isolation of trans people (Lombardi, 2001; Pazos, 1999).

The impact of harm reduction should also be examined in these situations. Many trans youth are acutely aware of the physical and social problems they will later face by undergoing the masculinizing or feminizing puberty that is associated with their presumed birth or biological sex. When faced with barriers to treatment, trans youth may seek hormones from nonmedical or discreditable medical providers, who provide them with injectable and noninjectable "street" medications. The actual consistency of these preparations is unknown to the end user and they are rarely taken under medical supervision and monitoring. In addition to the typical physical and mental health risks associated with any form of hormone confirming therapy, trans people who self-medicate using these substances may be subject to many of the same health risks as intravenous drug users (Denny, 1994, 1995, 2002; Haymes, 1998; Israel & Tarver, 1997; Lombardi, 2001; Russo, 1999).

Transgender As a Pathology

Identity concerns obscure the identities of trans youth and their partners. Baker's 1969 *American Journal of Psychiatry* article, "Transsexualism: Problems in Treatment" (as cited in Vitale, 1996), reports:

> We also find in the literature such terms and phrases as "psychotic," "delusional confection," "psychopath," "delusional quest," "masters

of the art of self-deception and of deceiving others," "psychopathic personality," "paranoid," "neurotic," "schizophrenic," "borderline psychoasthenics," "intricate suicidal dynamics," and "so-called transsexuals," all of which amounts to little more than psychiatric name calling and contributes little to our understanding. . . . My experience leads me to believe that the literature is actually quite constrained in its expression of disdain for these persons. Visits to medical, surgical, and psychiatric wards on which these individuals have been evaluated and treated have demonstrated clearly to me how physicians and nurses alike hold them up to ridicule. Is one paranoid in a delusional sense when he is in fact treated with ridicule, contempt, disdain and sometimes overt hatred by those from whom he seeks assistance, as well as being harassed by society in general? (pp. 1415-1416)

Sadly, echoes of Baker's words act as powerful barriers to care nearly forty years later. Despite an increasing awareness of the harmful role that transphobic, judgmental, and discriminatory behavior by health care providers plays in the relationship between care providers and transgender-identified people, this behavior is still prevalent. Zevin reports "appalling stories of discrimination in medical settings" (2000), while Dean et al. (2000) note, "Prejudice against transgendered individuals is pervasive within American medicine. . . . Most U.S. medical providers and researchers, as well as the public at large, believe that transgendered behavior is pathological. This in itself constitutes one of the most significant barriers to care" (p. 127).

In addition, trans people often encounter hostile stares and comments, as well as stigmatizing, pathologizing, and insensitive treatment from staff at all levels of the medical and social services systems. Colucciello (1999, p. 299) reports that nurses typically are unaware of the complexity of trans identities, making pejorative and dehumanizing comments such as, "'Why are they doing this?' and 'I do not know how to address them.'" Grimshaw (1998, p. 75) warns of nurses who do not use the client's pronoun of choice, refer to clients as "it" or "avoiding talking to them by always being busy."

In some instances, barriers to service have deadly consequences. The case of Tyra Hunter falls into this purview. Tyra, a woman who worked as a hairstylist, was struck by a car on a Washington, DC, street on August 7, 1995. Eyewitness reports indicated that, as the emergency medical technicians tended to her and cut her clothes off, they discovered that she was a trans woman and suspended care. As onlookers gathered, and Tyra lay bleeding, the technicians made scornful jokes and comments about her. They resumed care only under pressure from the assembled onlookers and witnesses. Though Tyra's family later won a wrongful death lawsuit against the fire department and the hospital, Tyra died in the hospital emergency room shortly upon arrival (Cope & Darke, 1999; Feinberg, 2001; Gay and Lesbian Medical Association and LGBT Health Experts, 2001).

Disclosing one's trans identity has many risks including institutionalization, violence and abuse, harassment and, possibly, homelessness. The therapy or counseling that trans people encounter is often reparative in intent or designed to obstruct or discourage the client's stated goals and self-determination. As such, the problems that transgender youth face are similar to those faced by LGB and gender-questioning youth, where much of the oppression that is casually related to homophobia is actually a fear of gender nonconformity, or genderphobia. In many instances, discrimination and oppression based on sexual orientation is often indistinguishable from that based on gender or gender identity (Mallon, 1999a,b). In addition, gender identity disorder in children is still used to institutionalize gender different youth—most of who will eventually identify as lesbian, gay, bisexual, and/or transgender (Minter, 2000; National Gay and Lesbian Task Force, 1996).

The Board of Trustees of the American Psychiatric Association's vote to "cure" a previously defined mental illness by removing the diagnosis of "homosexuality" from it's *Diagnostic and Statistical Manual of Mental Disorders,* Second Edition (DSM-II) in 1973 signaled the invigoration of the gay civil rights movement. Conversely, the American Psychological Association has resisted the removal or reform of gender dysphoria (first appearing in the DSM-III in 1980), later remodeled in the DSM-IV in 1994 as gender identity disorder (GID): transvestic fetishism (302.3), gender identity disorder in children (302.6), gender identity disorder not otherwise specified (302.6), and gender identity disorder in adolescents or adults (302.85) (American Psychiatric Association, 1994). The importance of depathologizing homosexuality has been considered critical in understanding lesbian and gay development (Dean et al., 2000).

An understanding of a normative transgender identity may not be possible until that identity is uncoupled from its pathological underpinnings. Today much of the focus on the pathologies exhibited by lesbian and gay people is formally directed toward the developmental concerns, stigmatization, and fear they encounter in an unaccepting and dominant culture. A similar, clinical focus toward the concerns of transgender people may also seem appropriate. Despite this, the belief that "homosexuality is a treatable, pathological condition is still widely held" (Olsen & Mann, 1997, p. 153) by medical students and can be assumed to translate to similar attitudes about transgender-identified people, affecting the care available to both communities. The social worker is not innocent in this discourse and the resistance to GID reform marks a major challenge for social work practice within the transgender communities. These diagnoses continue to stigmatize trans individuals and the trans communities as suffering from mental illness as well as severely hindering transgender civil rights efforts (Lombardi, 2001; Minter, 2000; National Gay and Lesbian Task Force, 1996; Wilchins, 1997). Blumenstein, Davis, Walker, and Warren (2000) note that "for many transgender people, societal stigma and the tendency of mental health professionals to still pathologize the trans experience, results in secrecy, shame, depression and fear" (p. 183).

Identity Erasure

Few screening, intake, and assessment procedures recognize trans identities. The subsequent erasure of the consumer's trans identity renders trans people and their unique concerns invisible, making the connection between trans identity and health needs obscure. In addition, the diversity and complexity inherent in the identities that trans people inhabit, many of which challenge clinical definition, may constitute a factor in care, as well as an access concern. Zevin (2000) notes that request to "transgender somewhat in between, as the patient would define where they want to be. And to some doctors that's been very disturbing" (p. 122).

As of this writing, many in the health care communities use the phrase "transsexual women" to refer to female-to-male individuals, while the reverse is true in the trans communities themselves where such people are referred to as transexual men, or as trans men. Similarly, many care providers commonly use the phrase "transsexual men" to refer to male-to-female individuals while the trans communities refer to these people as transexual women, or as trans women. The creation and use of the word "transgender," by people with trans histories, to refer to trans people, is another example of this friction. Nonclinical identities like transgender continue to make some in the psychiatric and medical communities, as well as the industries they are a part of, uncomfortable.

Ignorance of transgender identities may also confuse erstwhile allies. While the concerns of lesbian, gay, bisexual, and transgender youth overlap, many clinicians and other providers continue to stigmatize transgender, gender questioning, and gender different youth as "gender deviant" and "provocative." They seek to explain away their existence as victims of "cultures with rigidly drawn distinctions between male and female behavior" (Hetrick & Martin, 1987, p. 218) and not as having a unique and different identity in their own right. Russo (1999, p. 91) observes:

> Gay and lesbian advocates . . . often find it troubling to think that [some] people may choose transsexualism as an alternative to being gay. As a lesbian, Jayne Jordan [of the Michael Callen-Audre Lorde Community Health Center] says, "it crosses my mind a lot that some of my patients may choose sex changes out of internalized homophobia." (p. 122)

Comments that refuse to acknowledge the validity of trans identities, like those made by Hetrick and Martin, and Jordan, are the results of barely concealed transphobia. The consequence of these phobic attitudes is the consistent erasure of the identities of transgender individuals. The challenge then is to recognize that adolescence is not too early for youth to identify or be identified, as either trans women or trans men. Dean et al. (2000) report that "within the health care system, transgendered youth probably encounter ignorance and prejudice similar to and greater than that experienced by lesbian and gay youth" (p. 14). To this end, Haynes (1998) notes that "it is ironic that while the medical profession has advanced to the point of being able to effectively and appropriately treat transgender individuals, there is an internalized system-wide [trans]phobia that prohibits it from embracing the challenge" (p. 15).

PERSONALLY ESTABLISHED BARRIERS

The Economic Barriers of Oppression

The oppressions that trans people face have severe economic repercussions. Trans people are said to look different, or abnormal, leading to a lack of recognition of a trans-morphology (Wilchins, 1997). In this way, trans people can be "spotted," isolated, and separated from nontrans people. The violence, harassment, and discrimination associated with perceiving trans people as a form of deviance, or as pathology, can deprive them of legally sanctioned employment. The resulting underemployment or unemployment, poverty, homelessness, and diminished educational opportunities create severe economic hardship.

Adolescents are the most uninsured and underinsured of all groups (Gay and Lesbian Medical Association and LGBT health experts, 2001). Yet economic barriers to care exist even when trans youth are covered by health insurance. Almost all health insurance explicitly excludes coverage for any and all transgender related mental and medical care on the arbitrary premise that such treatment is experimental in nature. In contrast, psychiatric diagnosis of GID conveys little formal disability protection and is specifically excluded from the protection of the Americans with Disabilities Act (ADA).

In this context of economic and societal marginalization, sex-work and its derivations—exhibition and entertainment—have been the only historical employment opportunities permissible for many trans women, especially trans youth. This includes working as prostitutes, escorts, strippers, lap dancers, streetwalkers, telephone sex workers, showgirls, performers, and as models or actresses for masturbatory oriented print, film, and video materials (Dean et al., 2000). Scant parental support combined with absence of insurance coverage often converge and lead trans youth to sex-work to pay for the exigencies of gender transition.

Despite the risk, few trans youth can fund their medical and living costs without engaging in prostitution, stripping, or other forms of sex-work. In addition, "the economics of sex work puts youth at risk for HIV/AIDS and STDs, exploitation and violence, and chemical dependency" (Haynes, 1998, p. 14). Haynes continues:

> Few transgender youth are medically insured, privately or publicly. Coverage for hormone treatment, even for those with insurance, is not always immediate. In the age of managed care, few health centers or private physicians are prepared or able to provide the intensive medical and case management services needed to appropriately care for transgender youth. The economic realities of this situation strongly contribute to transgender youth engaging in sex work and being exposed to the potentially negative health outcomes resulting from it. There is no simple answer. The economic, ethical, racial, class, and access issues involved are complicated. Even health care systems designed for the underserved are not often designed to be able to meet the specific needs of transgender individuals. (p. 15)

Isolation

Social isolation may be considered one of the most significant, and dangerous aspects of a trans identity (Israel & Tarver, 1997). "Isolation keeps most transgendered youth from seeking essential health and medical care until crises occur" (Dean et al., 2000, p. 162).

James (1994) notes that "children's traumatizing experiences, particularly when chronic, can compromise all areas of childhood development" (p. 165). Many trans youth quickly understand that gender different behavior rarely "elicits adult caring" (p. 162) and the resulting attachment problem, especially the lifelong guilt and blame that trans people experience, most closely fits the pattern that James delineated as "Attachment Trauma." One might go further and consider whether the inability to live out one's gender role in childhood is, in itself, a childhood trauma. This is what almost all transgender-identified youth typically encounter until they are finally able to express and seek support for their actual gender identity—typically during their postadolescent development.

Identification with one's cultural group is a significant component in the development of an individual's self-concept. Despite the importance of this, peer networks can be tenuous for most trans youth. While support services and groups for lesbian, gay, bisexual, and gender-questioning youth appear with increasing regularity in schools and community centers, the stigma associated with expressing a trans identity prevents most trans youth from accessing these groups and resources. Rogers (2000) comments:

> In the young person's pursuit of an alternative gender identity there are few supports. When is the last time you saw a billboard with a happy, smiling, crossdressed or transsexual person advertising Coca Cola, counseling services or anything at all? . . . Which library carries the history books about the accomplishments of people who have crossed, blurred, or blended the gender line? Where is the visibility; where are the role models for these young people in search of a future? (p. 13)

In the dominant culture, positive trans role models are rare. Many trans-youth have never met another trans person. When trans people do appear in the media it is often in a pejorative sense. These portrayals usually depict trans people as sex workers, mentally ill, freaks, self-mutilators, cripples, criminals, and as unlovable. In this context, trans people

1. are sought out and regularly appear on daytime talk "shock" television shows;
2. are often used to jar the conventional viewer's sensibilities in advertising, news, and films;
3. appear with increasing frequency on street corners and sex-work strolls (Mallon, 1999), as well as in jails and prisons nationwide;
4. appear in the classified advertising sections of local newspapers, and in pornographic films and magazines (Rogers, 2000);
5. appear in anti-trans writings and rhetoric and labeled as male saboteurs by some vocal personages in the radical lesbian feminist movement, or

appear in pro-trans writings and rhetoric and labeled as heroic gender crusaders by some vocal personages in the post-modern feminist movement (Stone, 1994). The absence of trans peers and a trans social network can reinforce the maladaptive behavior that most trans youth utilize to erase or reconstruct their identities.

Riki Wilchins (1997) described the frustration trans people have confronted in the struggle to become the arbiters of their own identities and communities:

> Academics, shrinks, and feminist theorists have traveled through our lives and problems like tourists on a junket. Picnicking on our identities like flies at a free lunch, they have selected the tastiest tidbits with which to illustrate a theory or push a book. The fact that we are a community under fire, a people at risk, is irrelevant to them. They pursue Science and Theory, and what they produce by mining our lives is neither addressed to us nor recycled within our community. (p. 22)

Clearly social work practice with trans people requires a critical rereading of the relationship between the typically oppressive sources of global knowledge and the subjugated knowledge of the trans communities. The process by which trans-identified individuals and the trans communities recognize and value knowledge lies at social work's core of valuing the "dignity and worth of the person" and the individual's right to "self-determination" (National Association of Social Workers, 1999, pp. 4-5).

In this context, very little has been written about actual social work practice with the transgender communities. Yet praxis demands knowledge. Other than Mallon's useful *Social Services with Transgendered Youth* (1999a), Lev's *Transgender Emergence: Therapeutic Guidelines for Working with Gender-Variant People and Their Families* (2004), and various program descriptions, what is available is either dated or very limited in scope (Blumenstein et al., 2000).

Mallon (1999), Dietz (2000) and others indicate practice wisdom is primarily borrowed from a variety of sources, including sociology, psychology, medicine, ethnography, and so forth. The potent role the client plays in the creation of practice knowledge is typically minimalized (Imre, 1984, 1991).

> In this model, the vast majority of the knowledge addressing the lives and concerns of people of transgender experience has been collected and authored by non-transgender-identified clinicians and academics, organizations and providers, often raising concerns about the exploi-

tation of trans-identities as phenomena. This contrasts with a more primary resource: the spoken, written, electronic and performed voices, literature and material available from within the trans-communities, by trans-identified people themselves. (Imre, 1991, p. 199)

Knowledge provided by those who could traditionally be considered consumers of trans health services is generally self-reporting, anecdotal, autobiographical in nature, and narrative in intent. Despite this, the value of storytelling of this kind should not be underestimated. The words and works of trans feminists, trans theorists, trans performers, trans artists, trans activists, trans autobiographers, and trans biographers, all speaking about their existence, bodies, futures, and histories contrast vividly with the nature of the words that emanate from outside these communities.

INTERVENTION

The trans adolescence model then offers us a powerful tool for intervention—to understand and address problems and concerns related to trans development, family, and social relationships by seeing trans adolescence as normative and employing concepts of positive development. As such, we need to help trans youth maximize self-acceptance, learning, social competence, and healthy development while understanding and confronting the complex social realities they face.

We can offer or create positive role models and community to help ease the isolation and stigma of gender-difference so trans youth have more opportunities to thrive in their school and social settings. Education is a critical need and trans youth will need assistance to remain in school, reenter school, or continue in higher education.

Harm reduction needs to include a focus on high-risk sex, an understanding of the role sex-work may play in the trans community as well as the power affirmation sex may play in gender-confirmation. The significance of hormone and silicone use cannot be explained away by restricting access. Services must instead address these needs credibly and overtly. Medical policy must be reformulated to take the expressed needs of trans youth into account.

Work with trans youth may involve collaboration with other parties including parents or guardians, foster care agencies, therapists and counselors, medical care providers, and the legal system. A provider may need to create interdisciplinary collaborations, mediate concerns between parties, and educate where needed.

Interventions that seek to assemble the knowledge and power of trans people and community are a powerful place to begin. Personal narrative in the form of written, oral, performance and, more recently, film, video, and multimedia presentation combines to construct what Balsamo (1990) characterizes as a history of the present that values the everyday and personal experiences of those made invisible by dominant historical discourse. A narrative approach is seen to have value as a healing force as well as a tool for the development and promulgation of self-knowledge over medical knowledge.

There is a vast and developing wealth of written, electronic, and performed literature and material available from within the trans communities, by trans-identified people themselves. These narrative sources from within the trans communities offer a potent and underutilized resource. bell hooks (1989) recognized the power of emerging narratives as a process of development in this context and wrote, "Moving from silence into speech is for the oppressed, the colonized, the exploited, and those who stand and struggle side by side a gesture of defiance that heals, that makes new life and growth possible" (p. 9).

Groups and community forums widen the narrative process by assigning the role of interpreter to other individuals or the group itself. This is an active partnership, with the listener or reader translating the words strung together by the writer to form images and then meaning, which finally communicate stories of human lives. The social listener is critical to healing, confirmation, and may also serve as a silent partner (Coare & Jones, 1996; Frank, 1995; Kazemek & Logas, 2000; Kazemek, Wellik, & Zimmerman, 2002).

At the macro level, social workers can also seek to insert the narrative voice of the trans communities into the knowledge paradigm needed to affect policy (Davis, 2000; Marsh, 2002a,b). Knowledge maps of dominant needs typically ignore the needs of nondominant cultures. A social or cultural countermap that recognizes and, by extension, normalizes culture, space, policy, power, and language is a powerful intervention. This landscape can also include narrative countermaps of behavior, development, and identity, acting as a powerful tool in the development and recognition of the subjugated knowledge of the trans communities.

As such, the narratives of trans and gender nonconforming people contribute to the drawing of a countermap of trans experiences as normative. When seen as normative, the adaptive strengths that trans people accumulate, the communities they create, and their different sense of fit, become valued components in a cohesive sense of identity. Recognition of subjugated knowledge is integral to supporting this as a normative identity (Davis, 2002).

Intervention Models

Many urban areas such as New York City, Washington, DC, Boston, Philadelphia, Los Angeles, San Francisco, Seattle and so forth are devoting resources to develop peer-driven intervention within the trans communities. These have the power to foster the healthy development of transgender and gender nonconforming people, partners, family and community. Through the delivery of a range of transgender-driven supportive services, advocacy, outreach, education, and capacity-building, these programs seek to create safe and productive atmospheres for community-building, wellness and self-care, and leadership development. As such, these programs play a role in the normalization of transgender identities, working to help define and strengthen trans space using the knowledge generated by those communities and allowing trans people to access services through those same identities.

The knowledge trans people have of themselves and their lived bodies is a potent and underutilized resource for community development, as well as for the development of practice knowledge available to community members, the public at large, and practitioners who offer services to our communities. The active development and sharing of self-knowledge brings about the creation and discovery of meaningful ways for the trans communities to proclaim, "I am real."

In the seventeen years since New York City's Gender Identity Project (GIP) was conceived, the GIP has worked to recognize, formalize, and transfer a body of transgender generated practice knowledge relevant to individual, group, and community level interventions. In this process, the GIP has distilled a series of "practice goals" for delivering health care and prevention services within the transgender communities.

To these ends the GIP has developed three trans community-centered intervention models. The first, individual interventions, uses a peer education format to develop peer providers and advocates. Counseling is then provided by peer para-professionals, peer-professionals, and professional allies. A consequence of this is leadership development and the identification of an extensive referral network to refer participants to doctors, social service providers, and other professionals who have experience working with trans people and who will be sensitive to trans needs. Two forms of group intervention have been developed, peer-driven supportive groups and advocacy groups. Community interventions include hybrid community-focused forums, actions, and celebrations where members of the transgender communities share their experiences and life stories with peer-community members, providers, and allies, and hybrid-clinical events to bring providers and members of the transgender communities together to share best clinical practices. The GIP also recognizes the structural limitations inherent is its model and offers extensive capacity-building assistance for individual practitioners and organizations, as well as state and city organizations. This takes the form of: advocacy, technical assistance, and planning in partnership with providers or government agencies; trainings and forums directed toward providers; and national support where the GIP provides technical assistance, consultation, and support nationally to other LGBT organizations and transgender community groups and individuals.

Providers

To this end, the trans communities need nurturing, fully accepting, non-discriminatory providers. They require counselors who are willing to own their cultural knowledge gaps and then do something about it rather than expecting their clients to educate them. Trans people require providers who are willing to stand with them as trans allies as well as providers who are committed to working with partners, children, parents, and siblings of trans people so that transgender persons are no longer forced to choose between their families and their lives.

Finally, trans people need providers who acknowledge GID for what it is—a stigmatizing, pathologizing diagnosis by the traditional mental health system that seeks to control and dictate the lives of gender-different persons. These providers must recognize that disorders and diagnoses have the power to deliberately "mystify" our lived experiences, reconfiguring them as pathology, and refuse to be influenced by the social and cultural sources of this oppression. They must refuse to structure the adaptive strengths of trans people as deficits, as well as refusing to reinforce the already pervasive oppression trans people encounter and normalize the oppression itself.

Speaking the truth by naming the power and inequity of these relationships is essential to healing. Rather than colluding with the oppression, we need to focus our energies on the true culprits rather than those who are scapegoated by our culture as the visible aggressors.

The cultural violence that the binary nature of gender supports affects all of us in some way or another—trans people and nontrans people. Social workers seeking to work with transgender and gender nonconforming people must be ready to listen to more than details—more than facts. They will need to look inside themselves and at their personal relationship to these controlling images. They will need to consider how others might be affected by, or feel compelled to act on them. To this end, strength and healing must lie in growth, in seeking life through relationships, rather than through disconnections.

The social worker must be able to listen and to speak out, to do as Baraka (1971, p. 218) remarked, "I am real, and I can't say who I am. Ask me if I know, I'll say yes, I might say no. Still, ask."

A significant challenge for social workers is to participate in the collection of data necessary to assess the needs of the emerging trans communities. Competition for limited resources results in tacit acknowledgment of a hierarchical identity structure, but the scarcity of useful and verifiable trans-specific research has far reaching consequences for access to services. Scientific research specifically relating to trans people is generally minimal and often funder-driven, rather than being driven by the needs of the trans-communities themselves. In addition, most studies conflate the transgender communities, making it difficult to single out their specific concerns.

REFERENCES

American Psychiatric Association (1980). *Diagnostic and statistical manual of mental disorders* (3rd ed.). Washington, DC: American Psychiatric Association.

American Psychiatric Association (1994). *Diagnostic and statistical manual of mental disorders* (4th ed.). Washington, DC: American Psychiatric Association.

Anderson, J. M. (2000). Writing in subjugated knowledges: Towards a transformative agenda in nursing research and practice. *Nursing Inquiry, 7,* 145.

Anzaldua, G. (1987). *Borderlands/LaFrontera: The new Mestizo.* San Francisco: Spinsters/Aunt Lute Foundation.

Aranda, S., & Street, A. (2001). From individual to group: Use of narratives in a participatory research process. *Journal of Advanced Nursing, 33*(6), 791-797.

Baker, H. J. (1969). Transsexualism: Problems in treatment. *American Journal of Psychiatry, 125*(2), 1412-1418.

Balsamo, A. (1990). Reading the body in contemporary culture: An annotated bibliography. *Women & Language, 13*(1), 64.

Baraka, I. A. (1971). Numbers, letters. In D. Randall (Ed.), *The black poets* (p. 218). New York: Bantam Books.

Benjamin, H. (1954). Transsexualism and transvestism as psycho-somatic and somato-psychic syndromes. *American Journal of Psychotherapy, 8,* 219-230.

Blumenstein, R., Davis, C., Walker, L., & Warren, B. (2000). New York City Gender Identity Project: A model community-based program. In T. O'Keefe (Ed.), *Sex, gender & sexuality: 21st century transformations* (p. 183). London: Extraordinary People Press.

Cauldwell, D. (1949). Psychopathia transexualis. *Sexology, 16,* 274-280.

Coare, P., & Jones, L. (1996). Inside-outside. *Adults Learning, 7*(5), 105-106.

Cohen-Kettenis, P. T., & van Goozen, S. H. M. (1997). Sex reassignment of adolescent transsexuals: A follow-up study. *Journal of the American Academy of Child and Adolescent Psychiatry, 36,* 263-271.

Colucciello, M. T. (1999). Relationship between critical thinking, dispositions, and learning styles. *Journal of Professional Nursing, 15*(5), 294-301.

Cope, A., & Darke, J. (1999). *Making women's shelters accessible to transgendered women.* Ontario, Canada: Ministry of Education and Training.

Currah, P., & Minter, S. (2000). *Transgender equality: A handbook for activists and policymakers.* New York and San Francisco: The Policy Institute of the National Gay & Lesbian Task Force and The National Center for Lesbian Rights.

Davis, C. (2000). Do some bodies matter more than others? The emergence of the health care concerns of the transgender communities. Unpublished manuscript, Hunter College School of Social Work.

Davis, C. (2002, October). *The other voice: Group work with the trans-communities.* Paper presented at the 24th International Symposium for the Advancement on Social Work with Groups, New York.

Dean, L., Meyer, I., Robinson, K., Sell, R., Sember, R., Silenzio, V., et al. (2000). Lesbian, gay, bisexual, and transgender health: Findings and concerns. *Journal of the Gay and Lesbian Medical Association, 4*(3), 105-151.

Denny, D. (1994). *Gender dysphoria: A guide to research.* New York: Garland Publishing.

Denny, D. (1995). Transgendered youth at risk for exploitation, HIV, hate crimes. *Healing Well.* Retrieved October 9, 2001, from http://www.gender.org/aegis/index.html.

Denny, D. (2002). The politics of a diagnosis and a diagnosis of politics: The university-affiliated gender clinics, and how they failed to meet the needs of transsexual people. *Transgender Tapestry, 98, The Journal, 2*(3), 3-8.

Dietz, C. (2000). Responding to oppression and abuse: A feminist challenge to clinical social work. *Affilia, 15*(3), 369-389.

Feinberg, L. (2001). Trans health crisis: For us it's life or death. *American Journal of Public Health, 91,* 897-900.

Frank, A. (1995). *The wounded storyteller: Body, illness, and ethics.* Chicago: University of Chicago Press.

Gay and Lesbian Medical Association and LGBT Health Experts (2001, April). *Companion document for lesbian, gay, bisexual, and transgender (LGBT) Health.* San Francisco: Gay and Lesbian Medical Association. Retrieved October 8, 2001, from http://www.glma.org/policy/hp2010/index.html.

Gooren, L. J. G., & Delemarre-van de Waal, H. (1996). Memo on the feasibility of endocrine interventions in juvenile transsexuals. *Journal of Psychology & Human Sexuality, 8,* 69-74.

Grimshaw, J. (1998). Closing the gap between nursing research and practice. *Evidenced Based Nursing, 1*(3), 71-74.

Hartman, A. (1990). Many ways of knowing [Editorial]. *Social Work, 35*(1), 3-4.

Hartman, A. (1992, November). In search of subjugated knowledge [Editorial]. *Social Work, 37*(6), 483-484.

Haynes, R. (1998). Towards healthier transgender youth. *Crossroads: The newsletter of the National Youth Advocacy Coalition, 6,* 14-15.

Hetrick, E., & Martin, A. D. (1987). Developmental issues and their resolution for gay and lesbian adolescents. *Journal of Homosexuality, 13*(4), 25-43.

Hogan. S., & Hudson, L. (1998). *Completely queer: The gay and lesbian encyclopedia*. New York: Henry Holt & Co.

Holbrook, T. (1995). Finding subjugated knowledge: Personal document research. *Social Work, 40*(6), 746-751.

hooks, b. (1989). *Talking back: Thinking feminist, thinking black*. Boston: Southend Press.

Imre, R. W. (1984). The nature of social work. *Social Work, 29,* 41-45.

Imre, R. W. (1991). What do we need to know for good practice? [Editorial], *Social Work, 36*(3), 198-200.

Israel, G., & Tarver, D. (1997). *Transgender care: Recommended guidelines, practical information and personal accounts*. Philadelphia: Temple University Press.

James, B. (1994). *Handbook for treatment of attachment: Trauma problems in children*. New York: Lexington.

Kazemek, F. E., & Logas, B. (2000). Spiders, kid curlers, and white shoes: Telling and writing stories across generations. *The Reading Teacher, 53*(6), 446-451.

Kazemek, F. E., Wellik, J., & Zimmerman, P. (2002). Across the generations. *Journal of Adolescent & Adult Literacy, 45*(7).

Kondrat, M. E. (1995). Concept, act, and interest in professional practice: Implications of an empowerment perspective. *Social Service Review, 69*(3), 405-428.

Lev, A. I. (2004). *Transgender emergence: Therapeutic guidelines for working with gender-variant people and their families*. Binghamton, NY: The Haworth Press.

Lombardi, E. (2001). Enhancing transgender health care. *American Journal of Public Health, 91*(6), 869-972.

Mallon, G. P. (Ed.) (1999a). *Social services with transgendered youth*. Binghamton, NY: The Haworth Press.

Mallon, G. P. (1999b). Knowledge for practice with transgendered persons. *Journal of Gay & Lesbian Social Services, 10*(3/4), 1-18. Co-published simultaneously in G. P. Mallon (Ed.), *Social services with transgendered youth*. Binghamton, NY: The Haworth Press.

Marsh, J. C. (2002a). Using knowledge about knowledge utilization. *Social Work, 47*(2), 101-104.

Marsh, J. C. (2002b). What knowledge is relevant to social work practice? The case of TANF reauthorization. *Social Work, 37*(3), 489-494.

Minter, S. (2000). *Representing transsexual clients: An overview of selected legal issues*. San Francisco: National Center for Lesbian Rights, Retrieved December 10, 2001, from http://www.nclrights.org/publications/pubs_tgclients.html.

Namaste, V. K. (2000). *Invisible lives*. Chicago: University of Chicago Press.

National Association of Social Workers (1999). *Code of ethics*. Washington, DC: National Association of Social Workers.

National Gay and Lesbian Task Force (1996, December 13). *Statement on gender identity disorder*. Washington, DC. National Gay and Lesbian Task Force. Retrieved December 10, 2001.

Olsen, C. G., & Mann, B. L. (1997). Medical student attitudes on homosexuality and implications for health care. *Journal of the Gay Lesbian Medical Association, 1,* 149-154.

Pazos, S. (1999). Social work with female to male transgendered youth. In G.P. Mallon (Ed.), *Social services for transgendered youth* (pp. 65-82). Binghamton, NY: The Haworth Press.

Pinderhughes, E. (1988). *Understanding race, ethnicity, and power.* New York: Free Press.

Rogers, J. (2000). Getting real at ISU: A campus transition. In K. Howard & A. Stevens, (Eds.), *Out and about on campus: Personal accounts by lesbian, gay, bisexual, and transgendered college students* (pp. 12-18). Los Angeles: Alyson.

Russo, M. (1999). *Teen transsexuals: When do children have a right to decide their gender?* Retrieved on May 4, 2007, from www.salon.com/health/sex/urge/ 1999/08/28/transsexualteens/index.html.

Stone, S. (1994). "The empire strikes back: A posttranssexual manifesto" (3rd version). Retrieved March 24, 2001, from http://www.actlab.utexas.edu/~sandy. 1st version available in J. Epstein & K. Straub (Eds.), *Body Guards: The cultural politics of gender ambiguity.* New York: Routledge.

Swann, S., & Herbert, S. E. (1999). Ethical issues in the mental health treatment of gender dysphoric adolescents. In G.P. Mallon (Ed.), *Social services for transgendered youth* (pp. 19-34). Binghamton, NY: The Haworth Press.

Terry, C., & Davis, C. (Eds.) (2002). *Finding our voices: An anthology from the Gender Identity Project's writing groups.* Manuscript in progress.

Vitale, A. (1996, July 17). *Client/therapist conflict: How it started and some thoughts on how to resolve it. Notes on Gender Transition.* Retrieved November 10, 2001, from http://www.avitale.com/TvsClient.html.

Wilchins, R. A. (1997). *Read my lips: Sexual subversion and the end of gender.* Ithaca, NY: Firebrand Books.

Wren, B. (2000). Early physical intervention for young people with atypical gender identity disorder. *Clinical Psychology and Psychiatry, 5,* 220-231.

Xavier, J. (1999). *Passing as stigma management. Transsexual women's resource.* Retrieved May 4, 2007, from www.annelawrence.com/passing.

Zevin, B. (Speaker). (2000). Demographics of the transgender clinic at San Francisco's Tom Waddell Health Center. *Proceedings of the Transgender Care Conference May 5, 2000.* San Francisco: HIV InSite, University of California San Francisco. Retrieved November 8, 2001, from http://hivinsite.ucsf.edu/InSite .jsp?doc=2098.4742.

Chapter 6

Social Work Practice with Lesbian Individuals

Sarah Jane Dodd
Laura C. Booker

Embarking on a chapter related to practice with lesbian women necessitates talking about lesbians as though they are somehow a homogenous group to which specific principles can be applied. However, this is clearly not the case, as lesbian women are unique and diverse. As Clarke (1981) eloquently identifies, "there is no one kind of lesbian, no one kind of lesbian behavior, and no one kind of lesbian relationship" (p. 129). While it is a relief not to be trying to talk about lesbian, gay, bisexual, transgender, and questioning (LGBTQ) individuals together as a group, as is often the case, talking specifically about lesbians still has its limitations, so what follows are some general principles to act as guides through social work practice. There are some common experiences—a history of marginalization, stigmatization, and discrimination—that form the social context for your work. However, as with any good social work practice, do not make assumptions, instead find out exactly who your client is and work from there.

Unlike gay men, lesbianism is hardly mentioned in history. "The Greeks had little to say about female homoerotic attractions, and we have very little historical evidence of the place of lesbian attraction in ancient times" (Westheimer & Lopater, 2002, pp. 285-286). Prior to the Stonewall riots of 1969, lesbians connoted images of very masculine women whose same-sex attractions were rooted in a deep pathology. Throughout the 1950s and 1960s, psychotherapy with lesbians and gay men was focused primarily on reparative therapy, that is, shifting sexual identity, or at least sexual behavior, from homosexual to heterosexual (Nicolosi, 1991).

Social Work Practice with LGBT People

Reflecting the social context in which they originated, traditional models of psychoanalysis and mental health systems have pathologized homosexuality and, therefore, by default lesbianism. Traditional psychoanalytic thought equates healthy development with heterosexuality and therefore considers homosexual behavior to be a form of developmental arrest, and in the case of women, a regression to a primitive attachment to the mother (Deutch, 1995). Women who had sex with other women were said to be suffering from a "masculinity complex" or a form of "penis envy" (Friedman & Downey, 2002). In the late 1960s and early 1970s, gay activists, recognizing the ways in which the medical and psychiatric establishment helped to maintain these cultural and systemic prejudices and oppression of gay and lesbian people, began to challenge the American Psychiatric Association to recall their "sickness theory" (Gould, 1995, p. 4). Consequently, in 1973, the American Psychiatric Association removed homosexuality from the *Diagnostic and Statistical Manual of Mental Disorders*. It is important to note that the decision for its removal was based, as most research has been historically, on men. In 1975 the American Psychiatric Association adopted a resolution stating that "homosexuality per se implies no impairment in judgment, stability, reliability, or general social or vocational capabilities" (Conger, 1975, p. 620). In 1980 the American Psychological Association founded its Committee on Lesbian and Gay Concerns (CLGC), one of whose functions was to develop nomenclature guidelines, including "Avoiding Heterosexual Bias in Language" (American Psychological Association, 1991).

All of these positive changes were a result of activism by the Gay Rights Movement of the late 1960s and 1970s. These efforts led to psychotherapeutic treatment of gays and lesbians moving toward an affirmative model in which gays and lesbians are viewed as having a minority identity and the accompanying challenges of being a marginalized population (Cass, 1984; Fein & Nuehring, 1981). However, the historical and cultural perceptions of lesbianism as at worst abhorrent and at best undesirable run deep, and despite polls that suggest greater overall acceptance, many mental health professionals continue to stigmatize lesbianism (Berkeman & Zinberg, 1997; Heath, 2005).

WHO ARE LESBIANS?

Sexual identity and behavior evolves in fluid ways. A reclaiming of the term "queer" and an increase in the number of ways in which people label themselves is evidence of a dynamic social subculture that regularly reinvents itself. Women who might traditionally have been identified as lesbian may now choose to identify in any number of ways, including as queer, as a dyke, a boi, or a lesbian. However, a lesbian is usually defined as a woman who has an emotional-sexual relationship with another woman, and who defines herself as such. Mallon (2001) offered a comprehensive definition of a lesbian, noting that

> a lesbian is a woman whose homosexual orientation is self-defined, affirmed, or acknowledged as such. Lesbian also refers to female homosexually oriented ideas, communities, or varieties of cultural expression. The word lesbian historically refers to the island of Lesbos, where the poet Sappho and her female followers lived during the 6th Century BC. (p. 91)

Clarke (1981) also highlights self-identification in her definition, suggesting that lesbians are women who "engage in a range and variety of sexual-emotional relationships with women" noting "I, for one, identify a woman as a lesbian who says she is" (Clarke, 1981, p. 128).

Historically, common myth suggested that homosexuals make up 10 percent of the general population. The 1994 National Health and Social Life Survey (NHSLS) puts the percentage much lower, with 2.8 percent for males and 1.4 percent for females (Rubenstein, Sears, & Sockloskie, 2003). Unfortunately, census data do not refer to individual sexual orientation; however, the census data for the year 2000 do provide information related to same-sex couples. The data report 594,391 (0.56 percent) same-sex couples, including 293,365 (0.28 percent) female-female couples out of the 105,480,101 households reporting (Rubenstein et al., 2003). While these percentages are low, they still represent an enormous number of individuals and ones who are likely to require social work support (Razzano, Cook, Hamilton, Hughes, & Mathews, 2006; Roberts, Grindel, Patsdaughter, Reardon, & Tarmina, 2004).

Stereotypes around lesbians include notions of their having masculine characteristics, looking and behaving "butch," and being "tomboys." In reality, lesbians are a diverse group of women who differ by marital status, parental status, age, physical and mental ability, race, ethnicity, religion, socioeconomic status, geographic location, and physical appearance.

HETEROCENTRISM AND HOMOPHOBIA

Berkman and Zinberg (1997) describe a continuum of negative attitudes toward homosexuality ranging from heterosexism to homophobia. Heterosexual bias is the "belief that heterosexuality is normative and that non-heterosexuality is deviant and intrinsically less desirable" (Berkman & Zinberg, 1997, p. 320). Adrienne Rich (1983) highlighted the "bias of compulsory heterosexuality, through which lesbian experience is perceived on a scale ranging from deviant to abhorrent, or simply rendered invisible" (p. 178). Thus, homophobia emerges from this heterocentrist bias that is prevalent in society.

Originally defined narrowly as "the dread of being in close quarters with homosexuals" (Weinberg, 1972, p. 4), homophobia has also been referred to as "an irrational and distorted view of homosexuality or homosexual persons" (Gonsiorek, 1988, p. 115). Homophobia is always associated with negative attitudes and is often associated with discomfort, fear, anger, and disgust (Crisp, 2006; DiAngelo, 1997). Exploring the relationship between homophobia and heterosexism, DiAngelo (1997) defines homophobia as the "fear and/or hatred of gays, lesbians, and same-sex closeness, and heterosexism as the social and institutional power that supports homophobia and enforces heterosexual superiority" (p. 6). DiAngelo (1997) also acknowledges the "economic, political, and social privileges heterosexuals receive simply by virtue of those with whom they form their primary relationships," and warns that "these relationships create a very real power differential that invariably manifests, often subtly, in interactions with clients and co-workers" (p. 6).

Unfortunately, studies in Canada and the United States indicate that social workers and social work students are not immune to homophobia, heterosexism, and heterocentrism (Berkman & Zinberg, 1997; Brownlee et al., 2005; Krieglstein, 2003). One study found social work students to be more likely to hold positive attitudes toward gays and lesbians than nonsocial work majors, but that approximately 12 percent of the social work students indicated that they were "disgusted by homosexuality" (Cluse-Tolar, Lambert, Ventura, & Pasupuleti, 2004, p. 72).

Heterocentrism, a term derived from ethnocentrism, was first proposed in 1939 to offer an expansion of ethnocentrism, which refers to "in-group pride" (Mueller, 1939, p. 414) and the corollary derogatory attitude toward others. The first use was not associated with heterosexual bias; it in fact referred to peoples' propensity to be drawn to "the other." Recent uses of the term relate to assumptions of heterosexuality, which are reinforced socially and culturally (Mallon, 2001). Heterocentrism is favored over heterosexism as it focuses on all aspects of behavior and not just on sex.

Internalized homophobia occurs when a gay or lesbian individual incorporates the negative messages against homosexuals into their concept of self. The "negative feelings about a part of one's self (i.e., sexual orientation) may be overgeneralized to encompass the entire self" (Gonsiorek, 1988, p. 117) creating strong internalized negative feelings. The Gay, Lesbian, and Straight Education Network (GLSEN) (2001) National School Climate Survey (taken by 904 students representing forty-eight states) indicated that "84.3 percent of Lesbian, Gay, Bisexual, and Transgender (LGBT) students reported hearing homophobic remarks such as "faggot" or "dyke," frequently or often" (p. 21). Children see that gay and lesbian people are ridiculed, demonized, beaten, said to be "going to hell," and live in a country where their relationships and families are not protected or sanctioned by their government. Through repeated exposure, children absorb these negative attitudes and stereotypes of gay and lesbian people.

It is crucial for practitioners to be aware of heterosexual bias and any way in which heterosexual privilege may manifest (Di Angelo, 1997). Certainly, social workers need to be aware of their own homophobia, both overt and internalized, and take steps to work through it. It is important to note, however, that practicing without homophobia is not the same as a practice that is gay affirming (Crisp, 2006). Gay affirmative therapy is more proactive, requiring that "practitioners celebrate and validate the identities of gay men and lesbians" (Crisp, 2006, p. 116). It is gay affirming practice that we should strive to provide. Case Example 1 highlights how crucial affirming practice can be when a person's primary support system or family ties are suddenly strained or severed because of sexual orientation.

Case Example 1

Ana is a twenty-six year old Latina female who presented for therapy to deal with depression. Born in Guatemala, Ana moved with her family, including her mother, father, and five younger brothers to Los Angeles when Ana was eight years old. Raised devoutly Catholic, she attended both church and Catholic school throughout her childhood. When Ana was ten, her mother became chronically ill and Ana took on the primary role of raising her brothers. Although Ana recognized early on that she felt different from other girls, she did not really begin to question her sexual orientation until she felt attracted to a close friend of hers from church at age twenty-four. She began an emotional and sexual relationship with this woman, but felt deeply ashamed and kept the relationship a secret from friends and family for the first year. After a year, Ana decided to come out to her parents, a disclosure that they responded to with anger and hurt. Since that time Ana's contact with her parents has been less frequent and strained. She is beginning to feel ambivalent about her relationship and reports feeling depressed, unfocused, and isolated.

THERAPEUTIC RELATIONSHIP

What brings lesbians to therapy? Lesbians come to therapy for many of the same reasons as anyone else—relationship problems, depression, trauma, family difficulties, parenting, substance use—but what makes therapy different for lesbians is the lens through which they experience the world. Although being a lesbian is not in itself a therapeutic issue, it does serve as a context in which to understand the client's life experiences, both positive and negative. Some liberal-thinking therapists might be quick to say, "Oh, it doesn't matter that you're a lesbian. Relationships are relationships. We're all the same." However, therapists must navigate a fine balance between not viewing lesbianism as *the* issue at hand and acknowledging the unique and often difficult experiences of lesbians in our culture. It is not lesbianism itself that is problematic; it is the response to lesbianism that can exacerbate distress and a myriad of relationship and mental health problems.

A number of authors (Appleby & Anastas, 1998; Crisp, 2006; Hunter & Hickerson, 2003; Kingdon, 1979; Maylon, 1980; Morin & Charles, 1983) have proposed models and principles of gay and lesbian-affirmative therapy. Counselors who are affirming are not only able to see the dignity and worth of each individual, but also recognize that there is tremendous diversity among lesbians (Marion & Charles, 1983). Affirmative therapists are able to see lesbian issues as crucial and central in understanding clients. They recognize the ways in which their lesbian clients demonstrate tremendous courage and take tremendous risks all in the service of being their authentic and true selves in the world.

Therapists working with lesbian clients are in a unique position to provide those clients with a corrective experience. For some clients in the process of coming-out and later in their developmental process, the therapeutic relationship provides a context for risking authentic expression of themselves. A client may share part of herself, either directly or indirectly, that has been rejected or ignored by those close to her. The position of authority afforded to therapists based in their professional status gives the therapist's response great weight (Sophie, 1988). An affirming response, while still acknowledging the legitimate challenges faced, to a client's disclosure of same-sex feelings or attractions as well as her salient choices of partnering with a woman or possibly having children, is crucial in helping the client move towards self-acceptance. An affirmative approach will also create the sense of safety necessary to explore and challenge any negative self-perceptions or stereotypes that have been internalized. Sophie (1988) identified the following outcomes as indicative of successful treatment: comfort with self, able to form friendships and relationships with other lesbian women, respect and admiration for other lesbian, gay, and bisexual people, and feeling positive rather than shameful about self-disclosure.

Kohut (1971, 1977) writes in his theory of self-psychology that the therapeutic relationship serves three "self-object" functions for the client: a mirroring function, which reflects back to the client a sense of self-worth and value; an idealizing function, in which the client feels protected and safe; and sometimes a twinship function, in which the client sees that she is like others. All therapists can fulfill some of these functions by being affirming and creating an environment where clients feel safe to express themselves authentically. Lesbian therapists working with lesbian clients can also provide this twinship function, reducing a client's sense of isolation and possibly serving as a role model. Through the process of internalizing these functions, the client will experience higher self-esteem, a sense of being worthy, and the ability to regulate affect.

IDENTITY DEVELOPMENT AND COMING-OUT

Based on models of the development of positive racial identities, several theorists (Cass, 1979; Coleman, 1982; de Moteflores & Schultz, 1978; Lewis, 1984; Ponse, 1978; Sophie, 1985) have proposed models describing the development of a positive lesbian or gay identity. These models focus primarily on the process of coming-out and supportive interaction with one's environment as necessary to the achievement of a healthy self-concept and integrated identity. Cass (1979) developed a six-stage model in which a positive identity is developed through six stages: identity confusion ("Who am I?"), identity comparison ("I'm different"), identity tolerance ("I probably am gay"), identity acceptance ("I am gay"), identity pride ("I am proud to be gay"), and identity synthesis ("Being gay is one positive aspect of who I am"). Each stage requires the resolution of certain tasks, including struggling with the cognitive dissonance that occurs when a person holds the two conflicting ideas: "I am possibly gay," and "Being gay is bad." Certainly, not every gay or lesbian person succeeds in reaching the final stage of integration, and there is the possibility at each stage that a person may get stuck and go into "identity foreclosure," unable to develop any further (Cass, 1979).

Similarly, Coleman (1982) proposed a five-stage model of pre-coming-out, coming-out, exploration, first relationships, and culminating in identity integration. He emphasizes the importance of selecting carefully those to whom a person first comes out, noting that one of the purposes of coming-out is to begin moving toward self-acceptance. Early rejections from valued people may only serve to reinforce a person's conception of herself as bad. Although there are no guarantees about how a friend or family member may respond, the therapist can help the client make a decision about who is most likely to respond positively to the client's disclosure (Coleman, 1982). Woodman (1989, p. 56) suggests that therapists explore the following areas with a client in the process of coming-out:

> What is the worst thing that can happen if you come out?
> Can you accept those consequences and how can you handle them?
> What are some of the positive things that can come of coming out?

It is important to assist clients in exploring potential emotional and physical risks of coming-out (Will the person be in physical danger? Will her family kick her out? Will she be cut off financially or emotionally?) and make certain that the client, especially if she is reliant on others for meeting her basic needs, weighs the risks and makes plans accordingly. Coming-out is a very personal decision, a social worker should not insist or push a client to come out before she is ready. Rather, the social worker should provide a supportive environment in which to explore her desire or fears regarding coming-out, encouraging the client to come out at her own pace, initially to those who are most likely to respond positively. Case Example 2 illustrates the sometimes slow and difficult process that lesbians may encounter as they begin to integrate their sexual orientation into their current identity.

Case Example 2

Melanie is a thirty-four-year-old Caucasian female who came to therapy because she has recently found herself in a relationship with a woman. Although Melanie knew she was a lesbian from about age eleven, she has never acted on her attractions and feels uncomfortable with the idea of being a lesbian. Two years ago, she began to secretly date a woman she met at work, but called it off after several months, claiming, "I just couldn't deal with it. I was worried people would find out." Melanie has a social network of heterosexual friends, none of whom know about her relationship, and Melanie has not told her family either. Her father struggles with heart problems, and

Melanie is afraid of the stress that the disclosure might cause. Melanie has a difficult time both identifying and expressing her feelings, and her affect is extremely blunted, but her perceptions of lesbians are mostly negative.

Although some of these early models of development helped us to begin to understand some of the major challenges that gay and lesbian people face during the course of their development, these stage models perhaps do not accurately convey some of the complexity of the developmental process in that people do not always methodically move from one stage to the next. In fact, a person may be grappling with the tasks of several stages simultaneously or be stuck at one point in her development permanently (Coleman, 1982; Sophie, 1985).

Whereas Cass's (1979) and Coleman's (1982) models do not distinguish between the different experiences of gay men and lesbian women, a number of theorists have written about lesbians' unique experiences of development (de Moteflores & Schultz, 1978; Lewis, 1984; Parks, 1999; Ponse, 1978; Sophie, 1985). Sophie (1985) proposed a general model of development based specifically on lesbians' experiences. Her stage model included

1. first awareness of homosexual feelings;
2. testing and exploration;
3. identity acceptance;
4. identity integration.

Her model reflects the basic constructs of previously proposed models, but Sophie found that there was great variance in the manner in which the women in her study experienced each of the stages. For example, some lesbians identified as such before they had had much contact with other lesbians, whereas for others, lesbian identity followed contact with other lesbians. Further, disclosure to others occurred throughout the developmental process and could not be relegated to a certain period of time (Sophie, 1985).

Notably, Sophie (1985) also found in her sample that sexual identity was flexible over time (with some women even reincorporating an attraction to men into their identity) and that behavior was not always congruent with identity. It should be noted that her study was based solely on fourteen participants, all but one of whom were Caucasian, leaving a question about the generalizability of her model to lesbians of color (Sophie, 1985). Cass (1984) concurred that homosexuality is multidimensional and that "there is no such thing as a single homosexual identity. Rather, its nature may vary from person to person, from situation to situation, and from period to period" (p. 111).

As an integral part of the process of developing a positive lesbian identity, women may need to mourn aspects of their heterosexuality (Crespi, 1995). Heterosexuality is cast as both an ideal and as an imperative, and lesbians need to explore the loss associated with giving up or having to relinquish the status and the rites of passage (e.g., legal marriage, being able to make a baby with a person you love) that accompany being straight. Many lesbians have had satisfying sexual and loving relationships with men, and therefore may need to grieve for their unmet desire for physical or emotional closeness with men (Crespi, 1995).

MENTAL HEALTH

Some studies suggest that mood, anxiety, and substance abuse disorders are likely to be influenced by the effects of oppression and stigma (Dohrenwend, 2000; Markowtiz, 1998; Mazure & Druss, 1995). A study by Kessler, Mickelson, and Williams (1999) suggests that lesbian, gay, and bisexual people may be at greater risk for some psychological disorders specifically because of the effects of social stigma. Lesbian and bisexual women are more likely to experience generalized anxiety disorder than their heterosexual female counterparts (Cochran & Mays, 2000). Research suggests that lesbians are at greater risk for attempting and completing suicide than heterosexual women. One study of adults found that lesbians were significantly more likely to have considered suicide in the past than heterosexual women, with over half of the lesbians having contemplated suicide (51 percent), compared to 38 percent of heterosexual women (Hughes, Haas, Razzano, Cassidy, & Mathews, 2000). Similarly, the National Lesbian Health Care Survey (NLHCS) found that over half their sample had thought about suicide, with 18 percent having attempted suicide (Bradford, Ryan, & Rothblum, 1997). The Boston Lesbian Health Project II showed that 20 percent of their sample had made a suicide attempt (Roberts et al., 2004).

In light of these findings, how do we understand what is happening for lesbians on a sociocultural level that is contributing to higher rates of depression, suicidality, and anxiety? The overwhelmingly vast majority of children in our culture learn that being gay or lesbian is undesirable and are literally bombarded with antigay messages. For a child or adolescent who is aware of her difference or becoming aware of same-sex feelings, the internalization of these beliefs and attitudes and the identification with an antihomosexual culture (i.e., internalized homophobia) can lead to tremendous psychological distress, including depression, anxiety, and tremendous self-loathing and self-annihilation. Gay and lesbian people learn very early that this part of themselves is unacceptable and in order to be loved, be accepted, and sometimes even survive in their families, they must leave this aspect of themselves out of their relationships.

Relational-cultural theorists see these "disconnections" at the root of the problem. Disconnections occur when people feel unable to share parts of themselves within a relationship because of a lack of empathy and personal and systemic discrimination (Miller, 1988). Our cultural norms that lesbianism is a genetic or moral deficiency in which the sexual behavior, focus on emotional attachments to other women, and the "lifestyle" are seen as inadequate serve to reinforce these disconnections. Disconnections and the related inability to share aspects of one's self or experiences lead to a "depressive spiral" (Miller, 1988), where zest and vitality is diminished, disempowerment occurs as well as confusion, diminished self-worth, and isolation. Disconnections can lead to an internal sense of shame about one's self, including self-blame and a sense of being undeserving of connecting authentically with others (Jordan, 1997a,b).

SUBSTANCE ABUSE

Looking at drug and alcohol abuse among lesbian women means being knowledgeable about and incorporating the factors that are both pertinent to women as well as factors unique to being lesbian, while recognizing that there are tremendous differences among individuals. Although there is a commonly held belief that lesbians have a greater likelihood of alcohol and other drug use than heterosexual women, research findings reveal conflicted support of this belief (Bloomfield, 1993; Bradford & Ryan, 1988; Fifield, DeCresenzo, & Latham, 1975; Hughes, Johnson, & Wilsnack, 2001; Hughes & Wilsnack, 1997; Lewis, Saghir, & Robins, 1982; Lohrenz, Connelly, Coyne, & Spare, 1978; McKirnan & Peterson, 1989). Methodological weaknesses, including oversampling at lesbian bars, may have led to earlier studies reporting higher rates of alcohol use and alcoholism among lesbians than women in general (Fifield et al., 1975; Lewis et al., 1982; Lohrenz et al., 1978). However, improved methodology has not yielded consistent results. Some studies have found lesbian substance use to be consistent with the general public (Bradford & Ryan, 1988) or with a comparison group of heterosexual women (Bloomfield, 1993). McKirnan and Peterson (1989) found that though lesbians were no more likely to be heavy drinkers than heterosexuals, they were more likely to be moderate drinkers, and that fewer lesbians abstained from alcohol.

Lesbians may abuse drugs and alcohol for many of the same reasons as the general population: the desire to escape stress, to connect more easily with others, and to self-medicate difficult emotions like depression or anxiety. Reliance on gay bars and parties for socialization is also thought to contribute to increased alcohol use (Herbert, Hunt, & Dell, 1994; Hughes & Wilsnack, 1997). A more detailed analysis acknowledges that for lesbians alcohol initially "served a social function in the contexts of identity exploration and immersion" (Parks, 1999a, p. 149), but suggests that alcohol use subsides as identity emerges, bicultural competence increases, and connection within the community expands (Parks, 1999a,b). Family history of alcoholism or addiction may play a factor as it does with any person with a genetic predispostion to abuse substances. In working with lesbians with substance abuse issues, the function of each woman's use must be assessed. The connection between lesbians and substance use has often been understood as a response to the stress, stigma, and discrimination imposed by a homophobic society as well as a way to cope with the internalized homophobia that may result (Herbert et al., 1994). Together, the practitioner and client should determine for what purposes she is using alcohol. In what context—with partners, friends, family, in bars, alone—does use take place, and what is the significance of that context?

The role of oppression, being part of a marginalized population, and the importance women place on relationships are integral in understanding addiction among lesbian women. In the past thirty years, feminist thinkers have departed from traditional male-based models of development which emphasize autonomy to positing models of healthy female development, emphasizing the importance of relationships, noting that women experience themselves as selves-in-relation (Chodorow, 1978; Gilligan, 1982). Relational-cultural theorists from the Stone Center (Covington & Surrey, 2000) suggest that lesbians may begin using substances to facilitate making connections, to maintain connections, or to medicate depression, anxiety, and painful disconnections from others. The depressive spiral that occurs as a result of not being able to express oneself authentically (see mental health section) lays the foundation for substances to provide what relationships do not: an illusion of comfort, empathy, connectedness, and general sense of well-being. Using drugs or alcohol is an attempt to feel connected, energized, or loved when that is not generally the user's experience. However, as use progresses, the cycle of addiction is perpetuated as substances exacerbate the sense of isolation, alienation, and disconnection from others. Some lesbians (as well as other nonlesbians) use substances to deal with hurt and pain in relationships. As women tend to value relationships, women (and hence, lesbians) are more prone to substance use in the context of relationships with drug-using partners, as a way of feeling connected or to maintain the relationship through drug or alcohol use. Treatment interventions for lesbians need to include an emphasis on developing authentic connections with others that promote expression of the true self, examining both external and internal homophobia, including addressing shame or lack of self-acceptance (Covington & Jordan, 2000). Alcoholics Anonymous has specific meetings both for gays and lesbians as well as for women, and these meetings may serve as a setting to begin to develop healthy relationships with other sober lesbian and nonlesbian women.

TRAUMA

There is some evidence to suggest that the incidence of various types of trauma may be even higher for lesbian and bisexual women than for heterosexual women (Dodd, Savage, Rose, & Finklestein, 2004; Hughes et al., 2001; Hughes et al., 2000). The hate crimes reported to the FBI Uniform Crime Reporting Program indicate that 15.7 percent of the single bias incidents reported in 2004 were sexual orientation bias. Of those 1,197 bias crimes, 164 (13.7 percent) were specifically anti-lesbian (FBIUCR, 2004). The National Coalition of Anti-Violence Programs (NCAVP) reported that during 2005 there were 2,306 victims in 1,985 anti-LGBT bias incidents, with 28 percent (613) of those victims identified as female (NCAVP, 2006). It is not clear whether bias crimes against lesbians have decreased over the past several decades; certainly the reporting and documentation of such crimes has become more likely and more sophisticated, but they remain largely underreported or completely invisible (NCAVP, 2006). Self-report studies offer some insight into prevalence. An early study, the NLHCS, found that half of their sample ($n = 999$) had been verbally attacked for being gay, with 6 percent having been physically attacked (Bradford & Ryan, 1988). A study of 400 self-identified lesbians in San Francisco found that 84 percent had experienced verbal harassment, 40 percent had been threatened with violence, 27 percent had had objects thrown at them, and 12 percent had been punched, kicked, hit, or beaten (Von Schulthess, 1992). Herek, Gillis, and Cogan (1999) reported that 19 percent of lesbians had experienced at least one incident of physical victimization related to homophobia. Dodd, Savage, Rose, and Finklestein (2004) reported that in their sample of women with co-occurring disorders who had also experienced interpersonal violence, 22.8 percent of the lesbian and bisexual women had experienced a hate crime, compared with 13.2 percent of the heterosexual women.

Along with hate crimes, other trauma experiences appear to occur at higher rates in the lesbian community. For example, secondary data analysis of the NLHCS found that 32 percent of the sample reported having been raped (Descamps, Rothblum, Bradford, & Ryan, 2000). Several studies have indicated concern that rates of child sexual abuse (CSA) are higher in the lesbian population (Dodd et al., 2004; Hall, 1996; Hughes et al., 2000; Hughes et al., 2001). In a study of a community sample of 342 GLBT individuals 57.7 percent of the lesbians reported having been a victim of either child sexual abuse and/or adult sexual assault (Heidt, Marx, & Gold, 2005). An important clinical point to note is that lesbian and heterosexual women were both more likely to qualify for the definitional criteria of childhood sexual abuse than to self-identify as having experienced abuse (Hughes et al., 2001). This highlights the need for careful assessment of CSA with all clients.

HEALTH

The development of health care in the United States as a patriarchy resulted in women's health issues receiving less attention and less research funding than men's health care issues (Ehrenreich & English, 1973; Starr, 1982). Conversely, women's normal maturational processes, for example childbirth and menopause, were seen as diseases that needed physician care. Given the heterocentrist bias of the health care system (Steinhorn, 1998), it is not surprising that the negative health and mental health care experiences of women in general have been exacerbated for women who identify as lesbian or bisexual. As Peterson and Bricker-Jenkins (1996) suggest, for lesbians the experiences of women are compounded by the "homophobia and heterosexism that pervade the health care system and its sociocultural context" (p. 43). Indeed, historically, any deviation from heterosexuality was regarded as a medical illness that required treatment from a physician (Eliason, 1996). The invasive and dangerous treatments included "institutionalization, shock treatment, genital mutilation, aversion therapy, psychosurgery, hormonal injection, psychoanalysis and psychotropic chemotherapy" (Stevens & Hall, 1990, p. 24). It is not hard to assume, therefore, that women who identify as lesbian or bisexual may have some hesitation in accessing health and mental health service providers.

In an Iowa-based qualitative study of twenty-five self-identified predominantly Caucasian lesbians, 72 percent reported negative reactions from health care providers when their sexual orientation was known (Stevens & Hall, 1990). In fact, in a different study 84 percent of the lesbians reported a "general reluctance to seek health care" (Stevens & Hall, 1988, p. 73). The women in the study also feared withdrawal of treatment or increased identification of pathology if their sexual orientation was known. A follow-up study with a slightly larger and more diverse sample of forty-five lesbians in San Francisco supported these findings and suggested that the heterosexist structure of the health care system played a large role in the barriers (Stevens, 1995).

Despite the increase in lesbian-specific or lesbian sensitive health care centers (predominantly in metropolitan areas), these study findings support the notion that across the majority of the country "lesbians remain invisible within the health care system and have fewer contacts with health care providers" (Peterson & Bricker-Jenkins, 1996, p. 33). When lesbians do seek health care its effectiveness may be compromised because of the lack of recognition for her support system or "family" (Peterson & Bricker-Jenkins, 1996; Steinhorn, 1998). Social workers should be aware of the potential for discrimination within the health care system and should encourage their lesbian clients to prepare for such situations by completing durable power of attorney forms, living wills, and advanced directives for health care (Steinhorn, 1998).

LESBIANS AND THEIR FAMILIES OF ORIGIN

Media in our culture perpetuates a myth that lesbians are rejected and cut off from their families, whereas the reality is that most lesbians do maintain relationships with their families, and those relationships vary in degrees of closeness, conflict, and complexity similar to families without lesbian daughters (Kennedy & Davis, 1993; Kurdek & Schmitt, 1987; Laird, 1996; Levy, 1989). The nature of communication varies greatly, and although the process of coming-out can be painful for the entire family, it can also be a time of great personal growth and differentiation. Anger, confusion, grief, and concern are normal parts of the grieving process for parents who now must also deal with a stigmatized identity (having a lesbian daughter). For some lesbian daughters, coming-out is part of the process of becoming an adult and becoming an individual, and although lesbianism may be the means through which this happens, the process of differentiation is a developmental imperative (Laird, 1996). In fact, Lewin (1993) found in a study of lesbian mothers that the women sampled were likely to regard family members, particularly their parents, as the most reliable support. Some women had experienced cutoffs from their families, but for most of those women, the ruptures were amended over time.

How a family deals with a daughter's disclosure of her lesbianism is not necessarily as related to traditional cultural or religious values as we might expect. Conservative religiosity did not necessarily predict total estrangement, and family members employed a number of strategies, both healthy and unhealthy, to avoid cutoffs (Tremble, Schneider, & Appathurai, 1989). A number of factors play a part in the type of relationship maintained with family: cultural values about gender and sexuality, the importance placed on family and loyalty, and existing degrees of closeness and separation. Certainly, families with conservative religious beliefs may struggle with reconciling those teachings with their love for their child and the importance placed on family, but how a family responds to a daughter's disclosure is more related to historically prevailing patterns of organization and communication within the family (Laird, 1996). For example, a family that tends to be inflexible in terms of expectations placed on the children, or a family that resists a child's separation from the family, will probably have the most difficulty with a daughter's coming-out and subsequent lesbian identity. It may be that a lesbian daughter's patterns of connecting and separating with her family are similar to those of daughters in general, but her lesbianism becomes the catalyst for this negotiation (Laird, 1996).

LESBIAN MOTHERS

In the past ten years, we have seen the flourish of what has been named the lesbian baby boom. Increasingly, lesbians are opting to become mothers (see also Mallon's chapter on LGBT parenting in this volume). Until quite recently most lesbian mothers had conceived children within heterosexual relationships prior to their coming-out. Now the majority of lesbian mothers, both single and partnered, come out first and then have children either through adoption or artificial insemination, using either known or unknown (anonymous) sperm donors (Martin, 1993; Patterson, 1992). Currently in 2006, the gay rights movement is embattled in a local, state, and national struggle to ensure that families and partnerships are protected and acknowledged by law. Children have been removed from homes because a lesbian mother was deemed unfit. Gay and lesbian people are still denied the right to adopt in some states and only in Massachusetts is marriage legal. In 2005, twenty-six states introduced antigay marriage amendments, while President Bush continued his vocal support for an antigay constitutional amendment. This political context is extremely important in working with lesbian mothers because their families are deemed invisible and inadequate. Lesbian mothers, in addition to all of the everyday stresses that accompany parenting, have an additional set of worries and concerns: Will their children be teased or discriminated against because of having lesbian parents? Will their children be protected should a parent die or become ill (e.g., will the remaining parent be legally recognized as such in states where they have not been allowed to adopt as a "second-parent")? Will foster children be taken away from them? Will their children be accepted by each partner's family of origin? What is the psychological cost to both children and parents living in a society where their family is deemed unworthy and in some cases unacceptable?

Despite the abysmal political climate that lesbian mothers face, the fact that lesbian-headed families are thriving is a tribute to the tremendous resilience of the lesbian community. A number of studies have looked at the adjustment, separation-individuation, social development, sex roles, and cognitive and behavioral skills of children with lesbian parents (Flaks, Fischer, Masterpaqua, & Joseph, 1995; McCandlish, 1987; Patterson, 1996; Steckel, 1987). In each of these studies, children appeared normal in comparison to a nonclinical sample of children with two heterosexual parents. In fact, Flaks et al. (1995) found that lesbian couples had better parenting awareness skills than did heterosexual couples. Patterson (1996) studied thirty-seven lesbian-mother families and found that children of lesbian mothers reported greater stress reactions and also a greater sense of well-being (joyful, content, comfortable with themselves) than children of heterosexual mothers. This finding could be attributed to the possibility that children with lesbian mothers are actually under greater stress because of their marginalized status. However, it may also be that children of lesbian mothers are more aware of their emotions, having been socialized with two female parents, and are therefore more able to report both negative and positive feelings. She also found that household labor was divided more evenly in lesbian households and when child care in particular was shared more evenly, mothers were happier and children more well-adjusted (Patterson, 1996).

SPECIAL POPULATIONS

As we have already suggested, women who identify as lesbian are an incredibly diverse group. Although it is not possible to provide detailed information related to each of the many subgroups of lesbians a few warrant special mention. To this end this chapter also talks about lesbian youth, lesbians of color, lesbians with disabilities, and older lesbians.

Lesbian youth warrant extra attention because of the combined volatile experiences of adolescence and sexual identity development. LGBT youth are at particularly high risk for emotional distress including anxiety, depression, and suicide (Elze, 2002). Elze (2002) found that the gay, lesbian, and bisexual (GLB) adolescents in her study shared common risk factors with other adolescents but had additional "psychosocial challenges unique to their experience as members of a stigmatized group" (p. 96).

The second wave of the Boston Lesbian Health Project found lesbian youth to be at particular risk for both suicide attempts and eating disorders (Roberts et al., 2004). Twenty percent of their sample had made a suicide attempt, most of which had occurred during teenage years. Twenty percent of respondents also reported an eating disorder, which also tended to have teenage onset. It is important to note that for nearly half the respondents the eating disorder was overeating (Roberts et al., 2004). As most of the mental health concerns reported in the study had an onset during adolescence, the researchers concluded that "resources for lesbian adolescents are of special concern because they are a uniquely high risk population" (Roberts et al., 2004, p. 12).

As noted during the discussion of internalized homophobia, school environments can be especially hostile for LGBT youth. One small study using a nonrepresentative sample found that 60 percent of the students had experienced victimization in their school as a result of their sexual orientation, and 84 percent perceived GLB students as being verbally abused, while 41 percent stated that teachers told homophobic jokes (Elze, 2003). What was perhaps more troubling was the chronic pattern of victimization that occurred. Emotional distress is not surprising in light of such hostile environments. Social workers need to be proactive in developing and supporting gay/straight alliances within schools and community groups. Social workers also need to address discrimination and challenge school administrators to do the same. In addition, social workers need to develop interventions that enhance youths' comfort with their sexual identity and build supportive environments within the family, schools, peers, and community (Elze, 2002; Mallon, 2001).

The intersection of race and ethnicity with sexual orientation in a dominant white, heterocentrist, patriarchal culture creates a triply stigmatizing experience for lesbians of color. DeCrescenzo (1992), in writing about gay and lesbian youth of color, noted that "these young people live as a minority within a minority, often feel(ing) isolated, and afraid of losing their support system" (p. 8). Lesbians of color often have strong allegiance to their ethnic/racial communities, despite the acknowledged homophobia within these communities (Park, Hughes, & Mathews, 2004). As a result, "the integration of a consolidated racial and . . . lesbian identity is even more complex, involving negotiations of conflicting allegiances to the gay and lesbian community and their community of color" (Walters, 1998, p. 48; see also Chapter 3 in this text). Social workers need to be cognizant of the potential for such a struggle and provide room for clients to work toward integration of their racial and lesbian identity. Interestingly, learning skills for bicultural competence to negotiate the experience of oppression within their families of origin may be a point of resilience for lesbians of color. They "may more readily acknowledge an additional minority status and may feel better prepared or better equipped to meet the challenges associated with it" (Parks, Hughes, & Mathews, 2004, p. 251).

Social workers should provide an opportunity for lesbians of color to explore the potentially conflicting experiences of allegiance to both a racial/ethnic community and the lesbian community. Providing a supportive environment and gathering relevant resources associated with an increasing number of race and ethnicity specific LGBT groups might be helpful. In addition, as social workers we must continue to fight overt, covert, and institutional racism that continues to be pervasive within U.S. culture.

Over the past few years, there has been an increase in the amount of information and resources available regarding lesbians with disabilities and an academic literature is beginning to develop (Hunt, Mathews, Milsom, & Lammel, 2006; Whitney, 2006). Key points raised by the literature for social workers to keep in mind include not defining the individual by either sexual orientation or a disability. Hunt et al. (2006) recommend that "neither sexual orientation nor disability status should immediately be viewed as the defining characteristic for the client; rather it should be seen as one of the many relevant aspects of the client's life" (p. 172). It is also important not to assume that disabled clients are not sexually active, or that they do not want to be (Whitney, 2006). As with all other clients, sexuality should be explored as a natural part of your work together. It is also important to maintain an awareness that lesbians with a disability may feel like outsiders in each group. For example, among other lesbians they are the ones who have a disability, while among other people with disabilities, they are the lesbians. If your client is attending groups related to sexual orientation or physical disability it might be important to explore the group composition with her to discover how she feels about the demographics of the group and her place within it.

The graying of the baby boom generation is raising awareness of the needs of older adults in the United States. Once seen as lonely and isolated, older adults are now taking advantage of opportunities to engage within their communities or to create communities of their own. Lesbian older adults are no different. Meeting the demands of the estimated one to three million LGBT older adults in the United States (Allen, 2004), LGBT specific groups for older adults have formed in many urban areas and in cyberspace, including: Services and Advocacy for Gay, Lesbian, Bisexual, and Transgender Elders (formerly known as Senior Action in the Gay Environment [SAGE]) and Gays and Lesbians: Older and Wiser (GLOW). LGBT specific retirement communities are also beginning to form (Allen, 2004). Social workers should familiarize themselves with the resources available in their area both in person and online, and should be proactive in creating groups or social networking events where none exist.

Although greater opportunities do currently exist, it is important to remember that all older adults, regardless of sexual orientation, may be at risk for isolation as a result of physical limitations or the loss of friends or partners. LGBT older adults have been thought to be at greater risk because of the stigma and discrimination historically associated with sexual orientation, and the likelihood that older LGBT individuals have experienced a range of stigma and discrimination throughout their lifetime. Although some positive research evidence suggests that homosexual men and women are not more vulnerable to issues of depression and social support than heterosexual men and women (Dorfman et al., 1995), social workers should pay special attention to these issues when conducting assessments with all older adults.

One final comment on older lesbian clients relates to the reluctance on the part of social workers to admit that sexuality is a relevant clinical issue when working with older adults. In fact, one nursing article noted the compounding effect of ageism and the presumption of heterosexuality, leaving no room for LGBT older adults to explore their concerns regarding sexuality (*Nursing Standard,* 2005). Social work practitioners should strive to create an open environment and engage in positive dialogue around sexuality with older adult clients, taking the initiative to raise the subject as a normal part of a comprehensive assessment.

AGENCY ENVIRONMENT—
THE METAPHORICAL "WELCOME MAT"

Current debates regarding gay marriage, gay adoption, appropriateness of gay individuals to serve in the church, and a range of other sociopolitical issues offer sometimes daily attacks on LGBT individuals and their worth. Given this onslaught it is vital that social workers and social work agencies provide welcoming environments for LGBTQ clients, staff, and interns. Both the NASW *Code of Ethics* (1999) and the *NASW Standards for Cultural Competence* (2001) require that social workers respect the inherent dignity and worth of all persons, and work to fight social injustice. Specifically, "social workers should act to prevent and eliminate domination of, exploitation of, and discrimination against any person, group, or class on the basis of race, ethnicity, national origin, color, sex, sexual orientation, age, marital status, political belief, religion, or mental or physical disability" (NASW, 2001, p. 13). Given this mandate we need to ensure that we do everything we can to eliminate heterocentrist bias from our agency environments and our personal interactions.

It is important to avoid essentializing people. Do not assume that just because you know a person to be LGBTQ that you know who the person is; leave room for personal expression. Be careful not to make assumptions or, more preferably, test them out with clients to ensure that you are communicating effectively. Language is very powerful; it can convey the power of the dominant culture, it can convey understanding and respect, and it can convey misunderstanding and disrespect. It is important to understand the terminology used by your clients to describe themselves and their experiences. Language is dynamic; try to stay abreast of current terminology, but when you are unsure ask. It is better to ask for clarification than to make an incorrect assumption. Echo back the language the clients use; ask their preferred name and their preferred pronoun. Language is often about context. If a self-identified lesbian describes herself as a dyke it is different than if the term is yelled on the street late at night by a passerby. It is important to always use inclusive language, both in person and on written forms. For example, ask "Do you have a partner?" not "Are you married?" or "How long have you been together?" not "How long have you been married?"

Throughout this chapter we have emphasized how important it is to check yourself, your assumptions, your homophobia, and your heterocentrist bias. However, it is also essential to check the agencies within which we practice. Does the agency décor reflect a range of experiences through posters and pictures that are not just heterocentrist? Sometimes a small rainbow flag can be a wonderfully welcome symbol, especially for someone in a potentially hostile setting such as a school. Are there lesbian friendly magazines in the waiting room? As Poverny (2000) suggests, "unspoken observations are part of a program's organizational culture" (p. 79), so display LGBTQ materials prominently to provide a hospitable environment. Do intake forms and phone assessment protocols provide a neutral stance around gender and sexual orientation that will feel welcoming to a lesbian client? Does your referral list include LGBTQ agencies? Do you advertise in LGBTQ media, donate to LGBTQ organizations, and advocate for LGBTQ political causes? Take on the advocacy role; do not leave it to the LGBTQ-identified people associated with your agency to have to raise the concern. Oppression affects us all and social justice is a key ethical concept.

CONCLUSION

This chapter has noted some of the key issues to be aware of when practicing with lesbian clients. We have highlighted the potential for lesbian women to experience stigmatization and discrimination from a dominant heterocentrist culture. We have also indicated the potential for lesbians to be at risk for increased depression, anxiety, suicidality, eating disorders, substance abuse, and trauma. Paying special attention to these issues during the assessment phase of work with lesbian clients may be important. We have also noted the central role that relationships play in the lives of women, and therefore lesbians. Rather than pathologizing connection, as has previously been the case, we recommend nurturing women's ability for intimacy, facilitating the creation of healthy connections.

Finally, despite facing a political and cultural climate of stigmatization and oppression, lesbians are an incredibly resilient and creative community. Even facing tremendous challenges and adversity daily, many lesbians lead rich, fulfilling lives. It is often said that there are no models of relationships for lesbians. However, because lesbians, as cultural outsiders, are not bound in the same way to traditional paradigms and gender role expectations, there is the capacity to create, to envision, and to define families and partnerships. Social workers practicing with lesbian clients should focus on supporting this process, helping clients to create and live their visions.

REFERENCES

Allen, D. (2004). It takes a retirement village. *Advocate, 919*(7/20-8/3), 30-31.

American Psychological Association (1991). Avoiding heterosexual bias in language: Committee on Lesbian and Gay Concerns. *American Pychologist, 46*(9), 973-974.

Appleby, G., & Anastas, J. (1998). *Not just a passing phase: Social work with gay, lesbian, and bisexual people.* New York: Columbia University Press.

Berkman, C., & Zinberg, G. (1997). Homphobia and heterosexism in social workers. *Social Work, 42*(4), 319-332.

Bloomfield, K. (1993). A comparison of alcohol consumption between lesbians and heterosexual women in an urban population. *Drug and Alcohol Dependence, 33*(3), 257-269.

Bradford, J., & Ryan, C. (1988). *The national lesbian health care survey: Final report.* Washington, DC: National Lesbian and Gay Health Foundation.

Bradford, J., Ryan, C., & Rothblum, E. (1997). National lesbian health care survey: Implications for mental health care. *Journal of Lesbian Studies, 1*(2), 217-249.

Brownlee, K., Sparkes, A., Saini, M., O'Hare, R., Kortes-Miller, K., & Graham, J. (2005). Heterosexism among social work students. *Social Work Education, 24*(5), 485-494.

Cass, V. C. (1979). Homosexual identity formation. *Journal of Homosexuality, 4,* 219-236.

Cass, V. C. (1984). Homosexual identity: A concept in need of definition. *Journal of Homosexuality, 9*(2/3), 105-126.

Chodorow, N. (1978). *The reproduction of mothering.* Berkeley: University of California Press.

Clarke, C. (1981). Lesbianism an act of resistance. In C. Moraga & G. Anzaldua (Eds.), *This bridge called my back: Writings by radical women of color* (pp. 128-137). New York: Kitchen Table Women of Color Press.

Cluse-Tolar, T., Lambert, E., Ventura, L., & Pasupuleti, S. (2004). The views of social work students towards gay and lesbian persons: Are they different from other undergraduate students? *Journal of Gay & Lesbian Social Services, 17*(3), 59-85.

Cochran, S., & Mays, V. (2000). Relation between psychiatric syndromes and behaviorally defined sexual orientation in a sample of the US population. *American Journal of Epidemiology, 151*(5), 516-523.

Coleman, E. (1982). Developmental stages of the coming out process. *Journal of Homosexuality, 7*(2/3), 31-43.

Conger, J. (1975). Proceedings of the American Psychological Association, Incorporated, for the year 1974: Minutes of the annual meeting of the Council of Representatives. *American Psychologist, 30,* 620-651.

Covington, S., & Surrey, J. (2000). *The relational model of women's psychological development: Implications for substance abuse* (Work in Progress No. 91). Wellesley, MA: Stone Center Working Paper Series.

Crespi, L. (1995). Some thoughts on the role of mourning in the development of a positive lesbian identity. In T. Domenici & R. Lesser (Eds.), *Disorienting sexuality: Psychoanalytic reappraisals of sexual identities* (pp. 19-32). New York: Routledge.

Crisp, K. (2006). The gay affirmative practice scale (GAP): A new measure for assessing cultural competence with gay and lesbian clients. *Social Work, 51*(2), 115-126.

DeCrescenzo, T. (1992). The brave new world of gay and lesbian youth. In B. Berzon (Ed.), *Positively gay* (pp. 112-142) Menlo Park, CA: Celestial Arts.

De Monteflores, C., & Schultz, S. (1978). Coming out: Similarities and differences for lesbians and gay men. *Journal of Social Issues, 34*(3), 59-72.

Descamps, M. J., Rothblum, E., Bradford, J., & Ryan, C. (2000). Mental health impact of child sexual abuse, rape, intimate partner violence, and hate crimes in the national lesbian health care survey. *Journal of Gay & Lesbian Social Services, 11*(1), 27-56.

Deutch, L. (1995). Out of the closet and on to the couch: A psychoanalytic exploration of lesbian development. In J. Glassgold & S. Iasenza (Eds.), *Lesbians and psychoanalysis: Revolutions in theory and practice.* New York: The Free Press.

DiAngelo, R. (1997). Heterosexism: Addressing internalized dominance. *Journal of Progressive Human Service, 8*(1), 5-21.

Dodd, S. J., Savage, A., Rose, T., & Finkelstein, N. (2004, January). Self-report of trauma in women with co-occurring disorders and a history of interpersonal violence: Sexual orientation as a differentiating factor. The 8th Annual Conference of the Society for Social Work and Research, New Orleans, LA.

Dohrenwend, B. P. (2000). The role of adversity and stress in psychopathology: Some evidence and its implications for theory and research. *Journal of Health and Social Behavior, 41*(1), 1-19.

Dorfman, R., Walters, K., Burke, P., Hardin, L., Karanik, T., Raphael, J., & Silverstein, E. (1995). Old, sad and alone: The myth of the aging homosexual. *Journal of Gerontological Social Work, 24*(1/2), 29-44.

Ehrenreich, B., & English, D. (1973). *Complaints and disorders: The sexual politics of sickness.* New York: The Feminist Press.

Eliason, M. (1996). Caring for the lesbian, gay, or bisexual patient: Issues for critical care nurses. *Critical Care Nursing Quarterly, 19*(1), 65-72.

Elze, D. (2002). Risk factors for internalizing and externalizing problems among gay, lesbian and bisexual adolescents. *Social Work Research, 26*(2), 89-100.

Elze, D. (2003). Gay, lesbian, and bisexual youths' perceptions of their high school environments and comfort in school. *Children and Schools, 25*(4), 225-239.

Federal Bureau of Investigations. (2004). Uniform Crime Report. Retrieved from www.fbi.gov/ucr/hc2004/hctable1.htm.

Fein, S., & Nuehring, E. (1981). Intrapsychic effects of stigma: A process of breakdown and reconstruction of reality. *Journal of Homosexualtiy, 7*(1), 3-13.

Fifield, L., DeCresenzo, T., & Latham, J. D. (1975). *On my way to nowhere: Alienated, isolated, drunk.* Available from the Los Angeles Gay Community Services Center.

Flaks, D., Fischer, I., Masterpasqua, F., & Joseph, G. (1995). Lesbians choosing motherhood: A comparative study of lesbian and heterosexual parents and their children. *Developmental Psychology, 31,* 101-114.

Friedman, R., & Downey, J. (2002). *Sexual orientation and psychoanalysis.* New York: Columbia University Press.

Gilligan, C. (1982). *In a different voice: Psychological theory and women's development.* Cambridge, MA: Harvard University Press.

Gay, Lesbian, and Straight Education Network (GLSEN) (2001). *The GLSEN 2001 National School Climate Survey results.* New York: GLSEN.

Gonsiorek, J. (1988). Mental health issues of gay and lesbian adolescents. *Journal of Adolescent Health Care, 9*(2), 114-122.

Gould, D. (1995). A critical examination of the notion of pathology in psychoanalysis. In J. Glassgold & S. Iasenza (Eds.), *Lesbians and psychoanalysis: Revolutions in theory and practice* (pp. 112-132). New York: The Free Press.

Hall, J. M. (1996). Pervasive effects of childhood sexual abuse in lesbians' recovery from alcohol problems. *Substance Use & Misuse, 31*(2), 225-239.

Heath, K. (2005). Psychologists' attitudes and therapeutic approaches toward gay, lesbian, and bisexual issues continue to improve: An update. *Psychotherapy: Theory, Research, Practice, Training, 42*(3), 395-400.

Heidt, J., Marx, B., & Gold, S. (2005). Sexual revictimization among sexual minorities: A preliminary study. *Journal of Traumatic Stress, 18*(5), 533-540.

Herbert, J., Hunt, B., & Dell, G. (1994). Counseling gay men and lesbians with alcohol problems. *Journal of Rehabilitation, 60*(2), 52-60.

Herek, G. M., Gillis, J. R., & Cogan, J. C. (1999). Psychological sequelae of hate-crime victimization among lesbian, gay, and bisexual adults. *Journal of Consulting and Clinical Psychology, 67*(6), 945-951.

Hughes, T. L., Haas, A., Razzano, L., Matthews, A. K., & Cassidy, R. (2000). Comparing lesbians' and heterosexual women's mental health: Findings from a multi-site study. *Journal of Gay & Lesbian Social Services, 11,* 57-76.

Hughes, T. L., Johnson, T., & Wilsnack, S. C. (2001). Sexual assault and alcohol abuse: A comparison of lesbians and heterosexual women. *Journal of Substance Abuse, 13*(4), 515-532.

Hughes, T. L., & Wilsnack, S. C. (1997). Use of alcohol among lesbians: Research and clinical implications. *American Journal of Orthopsychiatry 64*(1), 20-37.

Hunt, B., Mathews, C., Milsom, A., & Lammel, J. (2006). Lesbians with physical disabilities: A qualitative study of their experiences with counseling. *Journal of Counseling & Development, 84,* 163-173.

Hunter, S., & Hickerson, J. (2003). *Affirmative practice: Understanding and working with lesbian, gay, bisexual, and transgender persons.* Washington, DC: NASW Press.

Jordan, J. (1997a). Introduction. In J. Jordan (Ed.), *Women's growth in diversity* (pp. 1-8). New York: The Guilford Press.

Jordan, J. (1997b). Relational development: Therapeutic implications of empathy and shame. In J. Jordan (Ed.), *Women's growth in diversity* (pp. 1-8). New York: The Guilford Press.

Kennedy, E. L., & Davis, M. D. (1993). *Boots of leather, slippers of gold: The history of a lesbian community.* New York: Routledge.

Kessler, R., Mickelson, K., & Williams, D. (1999). The prevalence, distribution, and mental health correlates of perceived discrimination in the United States. *Journal of Health and Social Behavior, 40,* 208-230.

Kingdon, M. A. (1979). Lesbians. *The Counseling Psychologist, 8*(1), 44-45.

Kohut, H. (1971). *The analysis of the self.* Madison, CT: International Universities Press.

Kohut, H. (1977). *The restoration of the self.* Madison, CT: International Universities Press.

Krieglstein, M. (2003). Heterosexism and social work: An ethical issue. *Journal of Human Behavior in the Social Environment, 8*(2/3), 75-91.

Kurdek, L., & Schmitt, J. P. (1987). Perceived emotional support from family and friends in members of homosexual, married, and heterosexual couples. *Journal of Homosexuality, 12*(2), 85-99.

Laird, J. (1996). Invisible ties: Lesbians and their families of origin. In J. Laird & R. J. Green (Eds.), *Lesbians and gays in couples and families* (pp. 89-122). San Francisco: Jossey-Bass Publishers.

Levy, E. (1989). Lesbian motherhood: Identity and social support. *Affilia, 4*(4), 40-53.

Lewin, E. (1993). *Lesbian mothers: Accounts of gender in American culture.* Ithaca, NY: Cornell University.

Lewis, C., Saghir, M., & Robins, E. (1982). Drinking patterns in homosexual and heterosexual women. *Journal of Clinical Psychiatry, 43*(7), 277-279.

Lewis, L. (1984). The coming out process for lesbians: Integrating a stable identity. *Social Work, 29,* 464-469.

Lohrenz, L., Connely, J., Coyne, L., & Spare, L. (1978). Alcohol problems in several midwest homosexual populations. *Journal of Studies on Alcohol, 39,* 1959-1963.

Mallon, G. P. (2001). *Lesbian and gay youth issues.* Washington, DC: CWLA Press.

Markowitz, F. E. (1998). The effects of stigma on the psychological well-being and life satisfaction of persons with mental illness. *Journal of Health and Social Behavior, 39*(4), 335-347.

Martin, A. (1993). *The gay and lesbian parenting handbook.* New York: Harper-Collins.

Maylon, A. (1980, September). *Toward a definition of gay-affirmative psychotherapy.* Paper presented at the annual convention of the American Psychological Association, Montreal.

Mazure, C. M., & Druss, B. G. (1995). A historical perspective on stress and psychiatric illness. In C. M. Mazure (Ed.), *Does stress cause psychiatric illness?* (pp. 1-41). Washington, DC: American Psychiatric Association.

McCandlish, B. (1987). Against all odds: Lesbian mother family dynamics. In F. W. Bozett (Ed.), *Gay and lesbian parents* (pp. 23-38). New York: Praeger.

McKirnan, D., & Peterson, P. (1989). Alcohol and drug use among homosexual men and women: Epidemiology and population characteristics. *Addictive Behaviors, 14*(5), 545-553.

Miller, J. B. (1988). *Connections, disconnections and violations* (Work in Progress No. 33). Wellesley, MA: Stone Center Working Paper Series.

Morin, S. F., & Charles, K. A. (1983). Heterosexual bias in psychotherapy. In J. Murray & P. Abramson (Eds.), *Bias in psychotherapy* (pp. 309-338). Binghamton, NY: The Haworth Press.

Mueller, J. (1939). Heterocentrism—Proposing a new term. *Social Forces, 17*(3), 414-415.

NASW (1999). *Code of ethics of the national association of social workers.* Washington, DC: NASW.

NASW (2001). *NASW standards for cultural competence in social work practice.* Washington, DC: NASW.

NCAVP (2006). *Anti-lesbian, gay, bisexual and transgender violence in 2005.* A report of the National Coalition of Anti-Violence Programs. 2006 release draft. New York: Author.

Nicolosi, J. (1991). *Reparative therapy of male homosexuality.* Northvale, NJ: Jason Aronson.

Nursing Standard (2005). The needs and concerns of older lesbians and gay men. *Nursing Standard, 19*(42), 18.

Parks, C. (1999a). Bicultural competence: A mediating factor affecting alcohol practices and problems among lesbian social drinkers. *Journal of Drug Issues, 29*(1), 135-154.

Parks, C. (1999b). Lesbian social drinking: The role of alcohol in growing up and living as lesbian. *Contemporary Drug Problems, 26,* 75-129.

Parks, C., Hughes, T., & Mathews, A. (2004). Race/ethnicity and sexual orientation: Intersecting identities. *Cultural Diversity and Ethnic Minority Psychology, 10*(3), 241-254.

Patterson, C. J. (1992). Children of lesbians and gay parents. *Child Development, 63,* 1025-1042.

Patterson, C. J. (1996). Lesbian mothers and their children. In J. Laird & R.-J. Green (Eds.), *Lesbians and gays in couples and families* (pp. 420-438). San Francisco: Jossey-Bass Publishers.

Peterson, K. J., & Bricker-Jenkins, M. (1996). Lesbians and the health care system. In K. J. Peterson (Ed.), *Health care for lesbians and gay men: Confronting homophobia and heterosexim* (pp 231-252). Binghamton, NY: The Haworth Press.

Ponse, B. (1978). *Identities in the lesbian world: The social construction of self.* Westport, CT: Greenwood Press.

Poverny, L. (2000). Employee assistance practice with sexual minorities. *Administration in Social Work, 23*(3/4), 69-91.

Razzano, L., Cook, J., Hamilton, M., Hughes, T., & Mathews, A. (2006). Predictors of mental health service use among lesbian and heterosexual women. *Psychiatric Rehabilitation Journal, 29*(4), 289-298.

Rich, A. (1983). Compulsory heterosexuality and lesbian existence. In A. Snitow, C. Stansell, & S. Thompson (Eds.), *Power of desire: The politics of sexuality* (pp. 177-205). New York: Monthly Review Press.

Roberts, S., Grindel, C., Patsdaughter, C., Reardon, K., & Tarmina, M. (2004). Mental health problems and use of services of lesbians: Results of the Boston Lesbian Health Project II. *Journal of Gay & Lesbian Social Services, 17*(4), 1-16.

Rubenstein, W., Sears, R., & Sockloskie, R. (2003). Some demographic characteristics of the gay community in the United States. The Williams Project, UCLA School of Law.

Sophie, J. (1985). A critical examination of stage theories of lesbian identity development. *Journal of Homosexuality, 12*(2), 39-51.

Sophie, J. (1988). Internalized homophobia and lesbian identity. In E. Coleman (Ed.), *Psychotherapy with homosexual men and women* (pp. 53-66). Binghamton, NY: The Haworth Press.

Starr, P. (1982). *The social transformation of American medicine: The rise of a sovereign profession and the making of a vast industry.* New York: Basic Books.

Steckel, A. (1987). Psychosocial development of children of lesbian mothers. In F. W. Bozett (Ed.), *Gay and lesbian parents* (pp. 75-85). New York: Praeger Publishers.

Steinhorn, A. (1998). Individual practice with lesbians. In G. Mallon (Ed.), *Foundations of social work practice with lesbian and gay persons* (pp. 105-129). Binghamton, NY: The Haworth Press.

Stevens, P. E. (1995). Structural and interpersonal impact of heterosexual assumptions on lesbian health care clients. *Nursing Research, 44*(1), 25-30.

Stevens, P. E., & Hall, J. M. (1988). Stigma, health beliefs and experiences with health care in lesbian women. *Journal of Nursing Scholarship, 20*(2), 69-73.

Stevens, P. E., & Hall, J. M. (1990). Abusive health care interactions experienced by lesbians: A case of institutional violence in the treatment of women. *Response to the Victimization of Women & Children, 13*(3), 23-27.

Tremble, B., Schneider, M., & Apparthurai, C. (1989). Growing up gay or lesbian in a multicultural context. In G. Herdt (Ed.), *Gay and lesbian youth* (pp. 253-264). Binghamton, NY: The Haworth Press.

Von Schulthess, B. (1992). Violence in the streets: Anti-lesbian assault and harassment in San Francisco. In G. M. Herek & K. T. Berrill (Eds.), *Hate crimes: Confronting violence against lesbians and gay men* (pp. 133-152). Newbury Park, CA: Sage Publications.

Walters, K. (1998). Negotiating conflicts in allegiances among lesbians and gays of color: Reconciling divided selves and communities. In G. Mallon (Ed), *Foundations of social work practice with lesbian and gay persons* (pp. 47-75). Binghamton, NY: The Haworth Press.

Weinberg, G. (1972). *Society and the healthy homosexual.* New York: Doubleday Anchor.

Westheimer, R., & Lopater, S. (2002). *Human sexuality: A psychosocial perspective.* Philadelphia, PA: Lippincott, Williams & Wilkins.

Whitney, C. (2006). Intersections in identity—Identity development among queer women with disabilities. *Sexuality & Disability, 242*(1), 39-52.

Woodman, N. J. (1989). Mental health issues of relevance to lesbian women and gay men. *Journal of Gay and Lesbian Psychotherapy, 1*(1), 53-64.

Chapter 7

Social Work Practice with Gay Individuals

Michael Shernoff

INTRODUCTION

Social workers preparing to do individual practice with men who have sex with men (MSM) need to understand that these clients present at any social service or health care agency or in private practice seeking direct or clinical social work services. MSM may be at any stage of the life cycle, and it is crucial that social workers do not make any assumptions about the nature of these clients or their presenting problems prior to doing a complete psychosocial assessment. In addition, it is important for social workers to understand that men who simply have sex with other men, repeatedly and over time, may never identify themselves as homosexual or gay (Kinsey, Pomeroy, & Martin, 1948). It cannot be stressed enough that for social workers to effectively engage with sexual minority clients they should not confuse sexual behaviors or even affectional preference with sexual identity.

An illustration of this is the attention men on the down-low have been receiving (Denizet-Lewis, 2003; King, 2004; Trebay, 2000). The expression "down-low," or "DL" refers to sexual relationships between men which are never discussed or openly acknowledged. "These men's unwillingness to address the fact that they may be gay or bisexual leads many to engage in unprotected sex when on the DL. To use a condom would be to acknowledge in some way what one is actually doing" (Williams, 2004, p. 6). Originally described only as a phenomenon within the African-American community, this behavior, albeit without the identity, occurs across all racial, ethnic, and class lines. In order to successfully intervene with a broad variety of men who have sex with men, social workers should familiarize themselves with the various stages of gay identity formation that homosexually active men may be at in the process of forming an identity as a gay man (Cass, 1979; Coleman, 1988; Isay, 1989).

Germain (1981) and Gitterman and Germain (1976) discuss social work practice in terms of understanding and being able to intervene at the ecological or environmental level as well as with the individual client, and his or her immediate system. Germain (1980) explains that "ecology seeks to understand the transactions that take place between environments and living systems and the consequence of these transactions for each" (p. 121). She then goes on to elaborate on how an ecological perspective is a useful lens through which to examine the social context of clinical social work. It is essential for social workers to incorporate an ecological perspective into their clinical work with clients from any marginalized population like racial, ethnic, or sexual minorities. It is only through utilizing this broad systems perspective that a worker will be able to understand and correctly reflect back to the client how the biases and assumptions of the mainstream culture have impacted upon them, and contributed to their unique psychodynamic and psychosocial realities. In the case of gay men, this means that an awareness on the worker's part of how the pervasiveness of both societal and internalized homophobia, as well as heterosexual bias, has effected the client's development, self-image, and current functioning, both adaptively and maladaptively. The material in this chapter is based on over thirty years of direct clinical practice with gay men, initially in agency work and private practice, and exclusively in private practice since 1983. In addition, the author draws on experiences supervising clinical social workers in practice with gay men.

DEFINITION

Gonsiorek and Rudolph (1991) state that developing a gay identity would be highly sensitive to cultural, class, socioeconomic, racial, and ethnic variation. Economic privilege provides middle class gay men with opportunities to experiment with forming gay identities that is lacking for economically disadvantaged men who must continue to live with families and rely upon them for concrete support. Therefore one area that will be tremendously useful to any social worker seeking to provide services to gay men is to develop cultural competency in order to have the sensitivity and skills necessary to work with men who come from various racial, cultural, religious, and economic backgrounds.

Beginning in the 1990s, sexual minority people began to adopt the use of the term "queer" to self-identify. Used in this context, "queer" refers to a flexible identity that's constantly in motion, constantly becoming, constantly transgressing in regard to gender and sexual orientation (Gunther, 2005). The assumption of the term "queer" was in direct response to the assimilationist politics and identities of many gay and lesbian individuals. In the early days of the American LGBT movement, the term "queer" explicitly asserted, an "in-your-face difference with an edge of defiant separatism: 'We're here, we're queer, get used to it' " (Gamson, 1998). With time the use of the term "queer" has moved beyond simple anti-assimilationism toward a more destabilizing rebellion against the formation of identities around fixed poles of gender or sexual orientation. To be proudly queer is a call to arms against fixed binary identities (Gunther, 2005). In addition, it took a negative expression and assumed ownership of it by making it a positive way to self-identify.

It is a mistake to make assumptions about who is and who is not gay simply on the basis of appearances. A client may in fact be gay who looks and initially presents as indistinguishable from a heterosexual man. Many men who have a current self-definition as gay went through periods of their lives when they attempted to hide their homosexual feelings from themselves and others. Some married and fathered children (Ross, 1983). Other men choose to remain married even after accepting and acting upon their homosexual feelings (Wyers, 1987). There are times that these men are reluctant to seek out services from openly gay clinicians out of fear of being pressured into coming-out or ending long-term marriages to women. With increasing frequency, openly gay men are choosing to adopt or actually father and raise children (Martin, 1993; Shernoff, 1996). Ultimately the only way a worker knows with certainty that a client is gay is when and if he chooses to disclose either his sexual behaviors or sexual orientation. It is never the goal of treatment to make the client feel that he must reveal his sexual orientation, or identify as homosexual, gay, bisexual, or queer. It is imperative that the worker tolerate his or her own discomfort with the ambiguity inherent in a client's unwillingness to label where he may be on the spectrum of sexual orientation or sexual identity.

In order to create a clinical environment where clients feel safe and not judged about how they express their sexuality, it is imperative that social workers not simply ask: "are you gay, bisexual, or homosexual?" This is not a useful question even when asked in a totally nonjudgmental manner. Instead, asking all clients early in the initial assessment: "Do you have sex with men, women, or both?" creates an environment where the client will feel comfortable about being accepted no matter what the response is. Similarly by asking "Are you now or have you ever been romantically involved with men, women, or both?" provides the worker with access to useful information about a client's behaviors and feelings without forcing an individual to fit himself into categories or identities that may not be relevant to his self image. After these questions have been asked, the worker can then ask "How do you feel about what you just shared with me?" Once this information has been assessed then the worker may choose to inquire "Do you identify as gay, bisexual, queer, or homosexual?" This helps the worker assess levels of homophobia, gay identity formation, and whether these same sex attractions and behaviors are ego syntonic or ego dystonic.

HETEROSEXUALLY MARRIED HOMOSEXUALLY ACTIVE MEN

Social workers need to be prepared to work with some heterosexually married male clients who are sexually active and even romantically involved with other men. Counseling these men is complex, and the clients will be alert to any indications of being judged by the worker. Bozett (1981) points out that these men often experience difficulty in achieving a positive gay identity, in part because of the perceived incongruity between the two identities of a heterosexually married father and a gay man. An empathic social worker can be helpful to the client in deconstructing any obstacles he has about being both gay and a father and even remaining married.

Wyers (1987) posits that formerly married gay men are likely to fall into two different groups. When the men have not fully acknowledged to themselves or to others that they are homosexual, the services they require are similar to the services needed by other gay men who are in the early process of coming-out. After resolving some or many of their personal problems with being homosexual, they may need assistance in working out relationships with their wives and children, and evaluating whether it is possible and desirable to remain married. Concerns about custody of, or at least access to, children is of prime importance to gay fathers. When a gay man has children who live with him at least part time, family therapy is very useful, especially if the client resides with a male lover and step-parenting concerns need to be addressed (Shernoff, 1984).

ETHNIC AND CULTURAL DIVERSITY

There are no stereotypes or generalizations which are universally relevant to all gay men. Differences exist in class, ethnicity, health status, rural or urban environment, and stage of gay identity formation. The skilled social worker must assess the impact of the above issues in addition to the individual's psychodynamics, ego strengths, and social supports. There is a frequent yet inaccurate stereotype that most gay men are affluent, yet as Hollibaugh (2001) describes, many gay men (as well as lesbians) are poor. These differences in socioeconomic realities will have a tremendous influence on the lives and issues that various men seek social work services for. A middle-class gay white man who lives in one of the large cities and who does not conceal his sexual orientation from family, friends, colleagues, or an employer may view being gay as his primary cultural identification of at least equal importance to his religious or ethnic background. In contrast, a poor inner city gay man of color often views his experience of being black or Latino as the primary way he relates to the world and to a social service agency or practitioner, even if the presenting problem is somehow associated with his homosexuality.

Commonly, African-American gay men feel torn between loyalties to homophobic black community institutions or families and racist gay white culture (Loiacano, 1989). The author's experience has been that successful professional gay African-American men in his practice have reported a significant degree of pain about not being accepted as total human beings within either of their two communities. The most self-actualized clients in this category found deep nurturance within the traditional institutions of the African-American community and at the same time developed a peer support group of other gay men of color, who functioned as additional family.

Understanding and responding to cultural differences becomes crucial when attempting to intervene with nonwhite gay men in such life threatening situations as AIDS prevention efforts. As noted by de la Vega (1995, p. 228), "it is difficult to speak of sexuality issues among Latinos in the U.S. as if they were just one homogeneous group of individuals." The worker must be alert to distinctive differences among clients of various Hispanic nationalities. For instance, a gay man from Argentina will not have many cultural identifications with a Mexican American or a Puerto Rican.

Carballo-Dieguez (1989) points out that when counseling gay Latino men, religion and folk beliefs must be considered. The impact of conservative Catholicism and its emphasis on traditional values (which strongly reject same-sex love or sexual expression) is a powerful influence for most Latino men. Although gay Latino men will generally refrain from discussing Santeria and Espiritismo (spiritualism) with non-Latino professionals out of fear that they will not be taken seriously, these widespread folk beliefs should be explored in counseling and therapy with gay Latino men (Carballo-Dieguez, 1989). Diaz (1998) suggests that "how an individual solves the integration between their Latino and gay identities, and at what stage of this process they are at a given time, will determine to a great extent who they interact with, what groups they will join, and how they will live and express their homosexual desires" (p. 136). Diaz also describes how either the rejection of gay sons or what he calls "sexual silence" around the issue of a son's homosexuality has a profound impact on the psychosocial health of Latino gay men. Many Latino men are more burdened by the shame that their being gay brings upon their family, than by their anger at their family's nonacceptance of them as openly gay men. Diaz (1998) also discusses how the convergence of being poor, brown, and gay has such a strong negative impact upon many Latino gay men both consciously and unconsciously, and how, despite their intentions to practice safer sex, large numbers of Latino gay men find themselves unable to be self-regulating about not taking sexual risks.

Similar issues arise when working with Native-American gay men. Tafoya and Rowell (1988, p. 65) write that "one must remember there is no such thing as 'the' American Indian; rather, there are literally hundreds of different tribes with different languages, customs and world views. Native American gay and lesbian clients often combine elements of common gay experiences with the uniqueness of their own ethnicity. To treat them only as gay and to ignore important cultural issues may bring therapy sessions to a quick end with little accomplished."

Chan (1989) explains that for Asian-American gay men identifying as gay may be perceived as a rejection of traditional family roles and Asian cultural values. However, to identify as Asian-American may require negating one's gay identity, at least within the family. Therefore Asian-American gay men often develop a dual identity that encompasses both facets of their cultural identification. It is also important for social workers to be aware that Asian-American gay men who were born in the United States will have many different issues from the Asian-American gay man who has immigrated to the United States.

RURAL GAY MEN

Little is known about the lives of rural gay men and the barriers they encounter when in need of social services (Gunter, 1988). Moses and Bucker

(1980) identified specific problem areas, such as the clients' isolation, fear of discovery of their homosexuality, and the effects of generalized anxiety on self-image. They go on to address issues that a professional should consider when providing services to rural gay men. These include clients' misconceptions and attitudes about being gay, lack of local resources and information systems, limited options and alternatives, and the need for the worker to assess the situation realistically.

Breeze (1985) discusses the need for legal assistance and networking services in order to intervene effectively with this population. He asserts that the professional must be prepared to become involved in some or all of the following activities in order to work productively with rural gay men: advocacy work, educating professionals and other service providers about problem areas, and actively enlisting support from other sympathetic professionals.

Gunter (1988) cautions against the assumption that the majority of gay men and lesbians are natives of the metropolitan and suburban environments in which they end up living. "Individuals who have successfully adapted to a gay lifestyle within a metropolitan area may have difficulties during visits home or when family and friends visit the city" (Gunter, 1988, p. 50).

In the same article, Gunter explains that confidentiality is a difficult issue in rural communities since many agencies utilize paraprofessionals and volunteers to provide services. There is a legitimate fear on the part of the gay individual seeking services that his or her sexual orientation will be disclosed to other members of a small community, resulting in ostracism or worse. This fear of exposure limits the gay individual's activities and prevents successful identification with other gay people.

The rest of this chapter will focus on individual clinical practice issues relevant to gay men.

ASSESSMENT

Gay men who seek social work services manifest all the symptoms and present the same variety of problems as do every other kind of client. In addition, they often have some unique issues arising from their sexual orientation, including: adaptation to their current stage of gay identity formation (Cass, 1979; Coleman, 1988); the impact of homophobia, which is defined as the "negative attitudes toward homosexual persons and homosexuality" (Herek, 1990, p. 552); social stigma; a sense of isolation and alienation; coming-out; rejection by families of origin; being victims of anti-gay violence; and the impact of AIDS on their own lives and the lives of their friends and lovers. When gay men are economically disadvantaged, their needs for social services like public assistance, food stamps, Medicare or housing if they are homeless, take precedence over issues related to sexual orientation.

SEXUAL CONVERSION THERAPY

In 1973, the American Psychiatric Association ceased to specify homosexual adjustment as psychopathological (Bayer, 1981). The American Psychiatric Association's official position is that "homosexuality itself is not considered a mental disorder" (American Psychiatric Association, 1987). Even today anti-gay prejudices exist among mental health professionals. There are groups like National Association for Research and Therapy of Homosexuals (NARTH) whose objectives are to train mental health professionals on how to do sexual conversion therapy and to advocate for trying to change a person's homosexual orientation (www.NARTH.COM, 2005); Exodus International which is an organization of Christian Counseling Groups that help people renounce the "gay lifestyle," and seek "freedom from homosexuality" (www.exodus-international.org, 2005); and Positive Alternatives to Homosexuality (PATH), which is a "coalition of organizations that help people with unwanted same-sex attractions to realize their personal goals for change" (www.pathinfo.org, 2005). These organizations continue to thrive despite hard empirical evidence that sexual orientation cannot be changed and attempts to do so results in harm to the individual (American Psychiatric Association, 1998, 2000; Schroeder & Shidlo, 2001; Shidlo & Schroeder, 2002; Shidlo, Schroeder, & Drescher, 2001). Numerous men have arrived in the author's private practice profoundly depressed and/or highly anxious as a direct result of failed psychotherapeutic attempts to change their sexual orientation. These clients need nurturance in the form of helping them understand that there is nothing intrinsically wrong with their sexual orientation, and that society's homophobia and intolerance is the cause of their distress. One way of accomplishing this is through the use of bibliotherapy, where gay affirmative readings are assigned and discussed during sessions. Sometimes just the assignment of going to a lesbian or gay book store and having the client browse will be a powerful initial healing intervention when the client sees so many titles that reflect the diversity of the gay community. Theoretically, this kind of intervention represents the kind of synthesis of both ego-psychology and the ecological social work perspective discussed by Germain (1978).

MENTAL HEALTH ISSUES

Smith (1988) states: "An understanding of the intrapsychic and psycho-social factors contributing to psychopathology in homosexually oriented persons requires a clear appreciation of the role of homophobia" (p. 62). As gay men do manifest psychiatric illness, social workers must be skilled in diagnosing any psychiatric symptoms in order to help clients as much as they can.

Clinical social workers need to be aware that gay men seeking treatment can present with indications of severe anxiety or depression, thought disor-der, persistent characterological problems, chemical dependency, neuropsy-chological impairment, psychosis, etc. These symptoms may be in addition to or instead of issues related to societal oppression and coming-out (Gonsiorek, 1982). "The coming out process by itself can produce in some individuals psychiatric symptomology that is reminiscent of serious under-lying psychopathology" (Gonsiorek, 1982, p. 11). In addition, many high functioning gay men seek therapy for help in improving the interpersonal areas of their lives. These men are men who are professionally successful and who have friends, and by all appearances live a self-actualized life, but are not happy about the lack of a satisfying primary romantic relationship.

Depression and Developmental Issues

Chronic low-grade depression is often the reason gay men seek therapeu-tic assistance. These symptoms can sometimes arise out of incomplete de-velopmental stages of gay identity formation in individuals experiencing a conflict between behaviors and values, when they have not as yet disclosed to important people in their lives about being gay (Smith, 1988). In other gay men, long-term symptoms of depression are masked by substance abuse and only emerge after the individual begins recovery from chemical depend-ency. Clinical social workers working with gay men must become skilled in diagnosing depression and urging clients to have consultations with a gay sensitive psychopharmacologist regarding beginning a treatment regime of anti-depressant medication.

For some depressed gay men, therapy needs to facilitate disclosure (when appropriate), and peer socialization. The sense of belonging to a commu-nity and the formation of a network of support among friends and family will protect against decompensation during times of stress. A decrease in social isolation, if present, must be a goal in psychotherapy (Smith, 1988).

Once again, using Germain's (1980) description of an environmental or ecological approach to clinical social work is a useful theoretical framework for making appropriate interventions with gay men that are actually within the realm of "milieu therapy," for example, introducing the concept of "homosocializing" (Isay, 1989) to a client. Often it is appropriate to explore the client's knowledge of gay social organizations and clubs where he might go to meet other men who have similar interests. In order to help facilitate the development of relationships with peers, social workers need to be aware of local resources for gay clients, and how to direct the client in that direction. Most large cities now have gay political, athletic, social, and religious groups that can provide clients with the opportunity to strengthen affiliations with other gay men.

Developmental Dysynchronicity

Many gay men do not accomplish the normal developmental tasks of adolescence, such as forming a peer group, exploring sexuality, experimenting with intimacy, and initial forays into love, when they are in their teens or twenties. Therefore, when experiencing some of the turbulence and emotionality of teenagers as adults in their twenties, thirties, or even older, there is a dissonance between chronological age and the developmental tasks they are struggling with. This discrepancy between age and developmental tasks is often the source of high anxiety and/or depression that is resolved as the man gains mastery over these new situations. There are frequently aspects of psychotherapy with gay men that are in fact counseling that consists of problem solving, rather than intrapsychic explorations of unresolved feelings. Very often the content of therapy sessions will focus on how to learn the various social skills necessary to meet and date other men, and similar issues relating to practical concerns like sexual risk reduction.

Feeling Different

During the course of therapy, most gay men will recall and discuss early childhood memories of feeling different and bad, which they connect to their homosexuality. These recollections are important to explore, yet the skilled clinician must also lead his or her client in an exploration of experiencing difference that has its etiology before feelings for members of the same sex began to emerge (Shernoff & Finnegan, 1991). Once explored, this early sense of being different can relate to family secrets like a parent's drinking, childhood sexual abuse, or simply to being the only one in a blue-collar family not interested in sports.

Social workers should also understand that growing up gay in a heterosexual family is, most often by its very nature, a dysfunctional process—unless the family is clearly, outwardly, verbally, and emotionally accepting when the child discloses his or her same-sex attractions (Shernoff & Finnegan, 1991). This is not to say that being gay is dysfunctional; rather, when people grow up in a family system where they cannot be or acknowledge who they truly are, they are placed in a system of dysfunction. A gay youth then must create a false self that he presents to his family in order to survive. Very often the gay adult is still maintaining a false self in some components of his life, whether it be work, family, or with nongay friends. The intrapsychic toll that this takes, and how it is manifested in either symptoms of depression or anxiety, are often the material of psychotherapeutic treatment with gay men. The toll of hiding one's true self must be identified and validated in order for the gay man to be able to move on and develop a positive gay image not based on shame and the need to hide (Shernoff & Finnegan, 1991). Even when working with gay men who are totally open about their sexual orientation, a skilled clinician must be alert to, and probe for, manifestations of internalized homophobia and notice how it can emerge and affect a client's feelings about himself. What is important to note is that a gay man's expressing homophobic feelings about himself, his relationship, his friends, or the gay community is not an indication that he wishes to change his sexual orientation, but merely a verbalization of internalized homophobia that provides fertile areas for therapeutic exploration.

Developmentally Disabled Gay Men

Mentally retarded gay men, like all others who are mentally handicapped, have sexual needs. If the retardation is not severe, and the individual is able to live independently, then he will likely find partners as part of his adjustment to adulthood. Social workers in agencies that serve this population must take the lead in developing interventions which teach safer sexual practices regarding preventing AIDS.

Smith (1988) explains that for those with a severe handicap, the attitudes of caregivers are important. Expressing a need for sexual release may be viewed as "acting out," rather than the expression of a legitimate need, especially if the sexual desires are for a person of the same sex. On the other hand, professionals who condone or facilitate sexual expression between gay clients may find themselves vulnerable to accusations of "condoning" homosexuality, which in fact they are.

Chronically Mentally Ill Gay Men

Gay men with severe psychopathology who have had multiple psychiatric hospitalizations are often clients in day treatment programs. Social workers in these settings need to be alert to gay clients, and how issues pertaining to their sexual orientation may exacerbate psychiatric symptoms. Ball (1994) discusses how these clients' psychosocial potential can be maximized in a group that addresses issues relating to their sexual orientation, including their double stigmatization as both mental patients and homosexuals. Ball also notes that psychiatrically disabled gay and lesbian clients must often leave their rehabilitation program to find support for their social and sexual needs. Yet in more mainstream settings within the gay community, these clients report feeling awkward because of their mental health history. Houston-Hamilton, Day, and Purnell (1989) discuss that, like all people, clients who are severely emotionally disturbed need education about AIDS that is customized for them.

SUBSTANCE ABUSE

The gay community has a long history of alcohol and drug abuse (Cabaj, 1992; McKirnan & Peterson, 1989; Morales & Graves, 1983; Stall & Wiley, 1988). Stall and Wiley (1988) report that gay men not only use drugs more often but use a greater variety of drugs than heterosexual men, while Shernoff (1983) reported incidence of injected drug use among middle-class gay white men. Despite the different geographic areas and sampling methods used in studies, there is strong evidence that gay men have more problems related to substance abuse than heterosexuals (McKirnan & Peterson, 1989). Explanations for this phenomenon include internalization of society's homophobia, nonacceptance of self, fear of coming-out, leading a double life, and low self-esteem (Finnegan & McNally, 2002; Kus, 1988; McKirnan & Peterson, 1989).

What is clear is that gay men use drugs in specific situations, such as during sex or during visits to specific "homosocial" venues like bars, clubs, sex parties, or bathhouses. Thus, a unique aspect of gay culture is that drug use is very often specifically connected to seeking or having sex. Purcell, Parsons, Halkitis, Mizuno, and Woods (2001) note that "the link between gay bars and substance use has a powerful history in the gay community, and many drugs have strong sexual meanings for MSM, meanings that may persist after people know that they are HIV-positive" (p. 186).

As the AIDS epidemic has continued, there is no uncertainty about the role that drugs and alcohol play in high-risk sexual behaviors. Many gay men have online profiles stating they are "chem friendly," want to "party," or "PNP" (which stands for party and play), all of which mean they seek to have sex while using one of the currently fashionable "party drugs" or "club drugs" like methamphetamine, GHB, ketamine, or Ecstasy (MDMA). Research documents that high-risk behaviors that spread HIV and other STDs occur more frequently among individuals who have poor impulse control, particularly if their sexual activity takes place under the influence of alcohol or drugs (Halkitis & Parsons, 2002; Halkitis, Parsons, & Stirratt, 2001; Halkitis, Parsons, & Wilton, 2003; Royce, Sena, Cates, & Cohen, 1997; Stall & Leigh, 1994; Stall, McKusick, Wiley, Coates, & Ostrow, 1986). As Woody et al. (1999) state, "Most studies now show a relationship between alcohol or drug use and increased sexual risk among MSM, but it is clear that these relationships are complex and difficult to evaluate" (p. 198).

The Crystal Methamphetamine Epidemic

Special attention needs to be given to crystal methamphetamine—referred to as crystal, Tina, meth, crank, or ice—a drug that has reached epidemic levels of use among gay men across America and has become the premium fuel for unsafe sex (Halkitis, Greene, & Mourgues, 2005). What is it about crystal that draws men to take it and precisely what is the connection between crystal and sexual risk taking? Guss (2000) gives the most succinct answer to this question in the title of an article, "Sex Like You Could Never Imagine." The particular properties of crystal leads users to abandon caution and regularly take sexual risks. Crystal methamphetamine more than poppers (amyl or butyl nitrate), cocaine, and alcohol, lowers inhibitions and heightens sensitivity to sensations, making it a desirable aphrodisiac among a growing number of gay men. One study of gay men revealed that crystal meth use is a serious problem for MSM because of its relationship with high-risk sexual behaviors (Halkitis et al., 2001). Guss (2000) suggests that when doing therapy with gay men who abuse crystal, it is wise to counsel them that sex will almost certainly never be as intense as it was while they were using drugs.

Treating Substance Abusers

Faltz (1988) notes that often gay men have sought treatment for relationship difficulties, depression, anxiety, compulsive behavior, or phobias and have never been asked about, nor have they mentioned, their drug or alcohol use. Thus social workers should be skilled at diagnosing substance abuse problems, and need to take an alcohol and drug use history of each gay client seeking clinical services. Finnegan and McNally (2002) described the stages of coming-out as lesbian or gay and how this experience affects chemically dependent behavior. Commonly, a client may be in one stage of denial about his chemical dependency and in another about being gay. To be effective the worker must assess both stages of denial in order to formulate an effective treatment plan. Ratner (1993) cautions that the clinician should be wary of clients who enter treatment claiming to be comfortable with their sexual orientation and therefore insist that talking about lifestyles is unnecessary.

Shernoff and Finnegan (1991) suggest that a client's chemical dependency is not always the only justifiable focus early in treatment. There are times when people's concerns about their sexual orientation may demand attention if they are to get or stay clean and sober. For instance, counselors need to recognize that sometimes it is very important to validate clients' bitter or pained assertions that homophobia has seriously contributed to their use of chemicals.

A worker in a detox unit or other substance abuse facility may encounter an individual who does not identify as gay or bisexual and who has trouble maintaining his sobriety. This kind of client has repeatedly relapsed into active use of chemicals even when attending AA meetings and ostensibly working his program. In an attempt to help the client make sense of why he is unable to remain sober, it can be helpful to explore with this client the possibility that he might be struggling with feelings or fantasies related to being attracted to other men, even if he has never acted on these feelings.

THE INTERNET

An entire online gay culture has blossomed in the last decade, transforming how gay and bisexual men meet one another. The Internet has streamlined the whole pickup and mating ritual. Men who in the past might have been too intimidated to even enter a gay bar, bookstore, or community center, or if they did find the courage to go into one of these establishments, might never have actually approached and initiated conversations, suddenly found that online they could be bold and forthright in their pursuit of partners, and fulfill their need to meet other men for socializing or realize their sexual fantasies.

An article from a national gay and lesbian news magazine referred to Internet chat rooms as "the new gay bars" (Fries, 1998). Cutting through the small talk, which helps to bypass many anxieties, accounts for a lot of the appeal of the Internet as a venue for meeting men. In addition, the Internet allows users a high degree of anonymity, which is highly appealing to those who are not out, or who are just coming-out, or who are questioning their sexual orientation. I remember years ago hearing patients talk about how they would drive past the gay bar again and again, trying to find the courage to go inside. Now, they can go to a virtual gay community online from the safety of their homes. Ross (2004) feels that the Internet's creating of the dynamic of "approximation" is like a one-way window into a gay bar that men who struggled with their same-sex sexual orientation prior to the development of the Internet did not have access to. Many of those men took years to find and then go into a gay bar, a struggle that the safe space of virtual reality provided by the Internet now ameliorates.

Psychologically, it may feel vastly safer for a man who is in a stage of pre-gay identity formation to test the waters by chatting online with men either to homosocialize or to arrange a sexual liaison, rather than having to actually brave going into a gay bar, club, or community center or having real-life sexual or social encounters, which were the only available options in the days prior to the Internet. Benotsch, Kalichman, and Cage (2002, p. 179) describe how "MSM individuals, in general have relatively few places to meet without fear of negative social consequences." Therefore, especially for bisexual men or those who are either experimenting with or questioning their sexual orientation, the Internet can be an "important gateway for those who may not immediately feel comfortable in an overtly gay environment, but are seeking social support form [*sic*] individuals with similar preferences" (MacMaster, Aquino, & Vail, 2003, p. 149).

It is not just anonymity, but also privacy that men can preserve as they explore their feelings about their queer attractions in virtual reality. Gay youth are using the Internet to explore gay culture and community even if they do not have access to the gay community where they live. They join chat rooms for GLBT youth and find online support groups, which greatly mitigate their feelings of isolation. A decade ago, the Gay and Lesbian Hotline was the main lifeline for these young people. Now, they can go to the library or log on at home and find moral support, answers to questions, and social affirmation.

The Internet is a relatively new venue for finding sex partners, but it has quickly become one of the most popular. Over the course of the past fifteen years, there has been a massive proliferation of online profiles. Researchers in the United Kingdom found that use of the Internet by gay men doubled between 1999 and 2001, and that in 2001, the Internet was the second most popular venue where men with a new partner had met in the previous year (Weatherburn, Hickson, & Reid, 2003). A San Francisco study published in 2001 found that gay men were more likely than heterosexual men or women to use the Internet to meet sexual partners (Kim, Kent, & McFarland, 2001).

Ross and Kauth (2002) estimated that in the United States the Internet is used most often for sexual purposes. They provide the following statistics regarding Internet use by people who visit sites specifically targeting gay men: "On any given weekday afternoon, there are approximately 10,000 people signed into sexual chat rooms on gay.com. The number participating during the evening hours and weekends is much higher" (Ross & Kauth, 2002, p. 4). These were only numbers cited from one popular gay cyber cruising site. When all the other gay-specific Web sites that gay men visit are considered (e.g., gaydar.com, manhunt.com, etc.), the number of visitors to gay sites rises dramatically. In addition, all of the major Internet service providers (AOL, MSN, etc.) have gay-specific chat rooms where men seek social, romantic, and sexual relationships. As of February 2005, Manhunt .net had close to 300,000 active members in the United States alone (Adelson, 2005). Several studies conducted both in the United States and Europe have shown that people who use the Internet to meet sexual partners are more likely to practice high-risk sexual behaviors (Elford, Bolding, & Sherr, 2001; Halkitis & Parsons, 2003; Kim et al., 2001; McFarlane, Bull, & Rietmeijer, 2000). Factors such as loneliness and depression contribute to "cyber cruising" (using the Internet to find sexual partners), and also seem to contribute to high-risk sex. Some men lack the sexual self-confidence to tolerate the host of anxieties that face-to-face cruising brings up, and the Internet provides a margin of safety and comfort for them. They may use their willingness to take sexual risks as a way of becoming more attractive to other men and feeling more sexually desirable. Some depressed clients have described not having the energy or self-confidence to go out and search for sexual partners. From the comfort of their own homes they can seek out sexual partners. Both the search for sex as well as the actual experience also frequently serve as ways of self-medicating themselves against their depression and isolation. Chatting with men online provides the illusion of connecting and being socially engaged.

DOMESTIC VIOLENCE

Social workers must be alert to instances where a gay client is either a victim or perpetrator of domestic violence. Walber (1988) discusses that no group within the gay community, regardless of race, class, ethnicity, age, ability, education, politics, religion, or lifestyle is exempt from domestic violence. Gay men can be battered or abused by a lover, ex-lover, roommate, or family member.

The worker may have difficulty identifying either a batterer/abuser or a survivor. Being abusive is not determined by a gay man's size, strength, or economic status. Gay men who batter or abuse can be friendly, physically unintimidating, sociable, and charming. Gay men who are battered or abused can be strong, capable, and dynamic (Walber, 1988). The issue in domestic violence, however, is control and it is this unequal power relationship that distinguishes battering from fighting. Reports from both batterers and survivors indicate that abuse and violence most often occur when the abusive individual is under the influence of alcohol and/or drugs (Pitt & Dolan-Soto, 2001).

It is important for the clinician to remember that it is usually no easier for a gay man to leave an abusive or violent relationship than for any other abused spouse to do so. Battering relationships are rarely *only* violent or abusive. Love, caring, and remorse are often part of the cyclical pattern of abuse. This cycle can cause a survivor to feel confused and ambivalent about the nature of the relationship (Walber, 1988).

ANTI-GAY VIOLENCE

Berrill (1992) reports that thousands of episodes—including defamation, harassment, intimidation, vandalism, assault, murder, and other abuse— have been reported to police departments and to local and national organizations (NGLTF Policy Institute, 1991), while countless more incidents have gone unreported. Statistics on incidences of anti-gay violence show them to be on the increase throughout the United States (NCAVP, 2005).Wertheimer (1992) notes that although lesbians and gay men are prone to a level of victimization that far exceeds that of the nongay population, existing crime victim service networks have largely failed to acknowledge gay victims of violent crime. He further contends that regardless of whether this failure has resulted from ignorance, neglect, or conscious hostility, its consequence is that gay people still frequently suffer the often devastating consequences of victimization in isolation and silence. As a result, the initial physical and psychological injuries that follow an assault are compounded. Wertheimer (1992) also asserts that most crime victim service providers remain unfamiliar with and insensitive to the needs of gay crime victims. Consequently, gay men who report crimes committed against them frequently must choose between hiding their sexual orientation from the service providers and disclosing it and risking ridicule and revictimization.

Social workers can offer invaluable assistance to gay victims of antigay violence in a number of concrete ways. After an assault, a gay client will be desperately in need of an ally who can assist during the period immediately following the attack. A social worker should be prepared to advocate for the client with both the local police precinct and prosecutor's offices, by accompanying the survivor to police stations and to interviews with prosecutors. This support helps ensure that officials treat the survivor with sensitivity and respect.

Gay victims of hate crimes need skilled professional assistance in working through their responses to the attack, turning the initial trauma into a potential growth experience (Garnets, Herek, & Levy, 1992). Helping the client transform his experience from that of a victim to one of a survivor is key. Garnets et al. (1992, p. 223) suggest that the cognition that "Bad things happen because I'm gay" can be reformulated to "Bad things happen." They also discuss the need for mental health workers to help survivors of antigay sexual assault to separate the victimization from their experience of sexuality and intimacy.

AGING

Kertzner (1997) states, "The significance of being gay in the context of growing older varies greatly among gay men. Some men regard their homosexuality as largely irrelevant to their experiences of becoming older, while others view sexual orientation as a pervasive determinant of all life experiences, including aging" (p. 92). Berger (1984) states that older gays and lesbians are most vulnerable to social, economic, and psychological forces, and therefore are likely to come to the attention of social workers. Berger's research found that the social recluse did exist, but most of the older gay men in the study function in networks of friends, lovers, and family as well as social, civic, and religious organizations within the gay community. Grossman, D'Augelli, and O'Connell (2001) similarly discuss that most of the respondents in their study reported fairly high levels of self-esteem, but many experienced loneliness. Participants in this study averaged six people in their support networks, most of whom were close friends who knew that the individual was gay. Not surprisingly, those living with partners were less lonely than those living alone. Brown, Alley, Sarosy, Quarto, and Cook (2001) found that a majority of sixty-nine men from thirty-six to seventy-nine years old who were studied reported that they spent 50 percent or more of their time with gay friends within their own age cohorts.

Berger (1984) found that the majority of respondents were still sexually active, but not as frequently as in their youth. The men in Brown et al.'s study (2001) felt that HIV/AIDS has had a devastating impact on older gay men, interrupting the normal aging process for those who have contracted it, and prematurely aging those who care for them. The author's personal experience and that of numerous men he has seen as clients is that many older gay men have outlived friends and partners who died from AIDS, and in some cases are the sole survivor of a friendship group that had been a family. More than one man has told the author, "I have literally buried all the men I came out and hung out with as a young man. These were the men I had expected to grow old with, take care of one another and move through life with." Survivors need recognition of their losses as well as support and encouragement to build new friendship networks. In some cases, these men suffer from post-traumatic stress disorder. The men who have been able to meet new people and begin new friendships or romances report a higher level of emotional satisfaction with their lives than those who have not been able to or willing to replenish their social networks. Social workers serving the elderly must learn about existing resources for older gay men and en-courage clients to seek services from them.

The urban gay men's community is often not inappropriately character-ized as being youth oriented. A glance at most of the advertisements in any gay publication quickly reinforces this concept by the dearth of middle-aged or older gay men pictured. If, as he ages, a gay man remains committed to socializing in clubs and bars largely populated by younger gay men, and judges his attractiveness by an ability to meet younger gay men for sex or relationships, then he is setting the stage for creating a very fragile sense of self-esteem and self-worth. Ageism is rampant within the gay men's com-munity, and becomes psychologically dangerous when it becomes internal-ized by a gay man who fears growing older. One-third of the men surveyed by Brown et al. (2001) had experienced discrimination within the gay com-munity based on age or ethnicity.

My clinical experience is that men who age with the least amount of stress about growing older do so because they are not invested in trying to fit in to the youth culture of the gay community in the same way that they did earlier in their lives. Like most people, gay men need to learn that in order to grow old gracefully they have to allow themselves and their interests to evolve and grow so that they no longer crave doing the same things socially and recreationally at thirty, forty, fifty, sixty years of age, or older that they did when they were younger. Having a group of friends that includes at least some people at the same developmental stage of life is a necessity in order to feel better able to cope with the inevitable indignities that accompany aging and the corresponding health challenges. However, as already mentioned, the peer groups of many gay men have been decimated by AIDS.

Older gay people need the same services as all older people (Berger, 1984). Berger and Kelly (2001) found that older gay men reported less depression and fewer psychosomatic symptoms than younger gay men. Older men in the midst of a transition to a newly acquired gay identity may seek out counseling for help with this passage (Berger, 1984). Kertzner (1997) suggests, "Clinicians should carefully consider the difficulties in defining what constitutes psychological well-being in gay men as they age" (p. 93). Social workers may also be of assistance in responding to an older gay client's request for a gay visitor from the friendly visiting service. Social workers in nursing homes can be helpful to elderly gay clients by trying to facilitate that roommates be other gay residents if so desired, or providing counseling to the male couple when one member is placed in a nursing home. Clinicians may also be called upon to provide bereavement counseling for the surviving partner of a gay couple.

DEATH AND DYING

Doka (1989) explains the concept of *disenfranchised grief* which occurs when (1) the relationship is not recognized, (2) the loss is not recognized, and (3) the griever is not recognized. These are ordinary experiences for many gay men mourning a friend, lover, or in the darkest days of the AIDS epidemic, a community. As Dworkin and Kaufer (1995) correctly note, "all of these factors must be taken into account in redefining the process of grieving and identifying the coping mechanisms and interventions appropriate for responding to the needs of today's gay men" (p. 43).

Following the death of his lover, the surviving partner may not receive condolences from family or co-workers who do not view a gay relationship as the equivalent of a marriage. This absence of understanding and support only increases the pain and anger surrounding his loss (Shernoff, 1998). Social workers doing individual counseling must be aware of these additional issues which have an impact upon a gay man's grieving process, and find ways to elicit feelings of anger and shame that may surface in the absence of appropriate support while also actively consoling the grieving partner.

AIDS

By the beginning of 1997, combination therapy with more than one class of antiretroviral drugs had become the standard of care for HIV-infected individuals, although no clear-cut consensus has emerged about the best time to initiate therapy. This decision must be based on balancing a variety of factors, including the length of time since initial infection, current CD4 cell count and viral load, clinical prognosis, side effect profile, and the individual's psychological readiness and motivation to begin and adhere to treatment.

Today combination therapy is known as highly advanced antiretroviral therapy (HAART). Though many are still dying from HIV-related illness, overall rates of illness and death in the developed world have dramatically decreased, largely due to HAART (Palella et al., 1998), and the rates at which people progress from being HIV-positive to being full-blown AIDS patients has slowed down dramatically. HAART, in combination with prophylaxis drugs that prevent many of the opportunistic infections associated with AIDS, has resulted in increasing numbers of people with HIV now living longer. In developed countries, HIV disease has become a chronic and manageable illness for more than a small minority of those infected. For many men living with HIV and AIDS, HAART and weight training (in combination with testosterone, human growth hormone, and steroids) have had a major impact on their appearance and robustness (Halkitis, 2000; Shernoff, 2002), so that most people living with HIV and AIDS are no longer emaciated and ill looking.

Yet, combination therapies have not yet achieved the most optimistic goals set by scientists. In particular, the complete elimination, or eradication, of HIV from an infected individual has never been achieved, and perhaps may never be achieved because HIV has the capacity to remain dormant in certain cells of the body. The introduction of HAART is among the most important advances in the treatment of HIV/AIDS. Large numbers of people with AIDS are "long-term survivors" which is defined as an individual who has been diagnosed as having AIDS and has had a good quality of life for at least three years (Cao, Qin, Zhang, Safrit, & Ho, 1995). About 5 percent of people living with HIV are now known as long-term nonprogressors (Levy, 2005, as cited in Pogash, 2005). Dr. Anthony Fauci, Director of the National Institute of Allergy and Infectious Diseases, defines nonprogressors as treatment naïve individuals who have a confirmed exposure to HIV for at least ten years, and who have so little virus in their blood that it cannot be detected (Pogash, 2005).

The changes brought about by combination therapy have created unique challenges for social workers in two different areas. The first relates to the rapidly changing knowledge base with which mental health and social service professionals must feel comfortable in order to help their clients handle the medical issues they face. The second is the need to become familiar with the psychosocial issues created by HAART.

In order to help men living with HIV and AIDS handle the range of treatment options available, social workers need to understand some basic concepts related to medical treatment, side effects, and treatment decision making (Shernoff & Smith, 2000). Topics include the use of various laboratory tests to assess the client's stage of illness, the importance of adherence to complex treatment regimens, and the side effects of the new therapies. Social workers have a potential role to play in helping clients make decisions about treatment, assuring that their clients are knowledgeable about the medications they are considering, assessing the limitations of the medications' effects, helping clients explore the implications for choosing or not choosing to use them, and managing adherence issues and side effects. The best way that social workers can keep their knowledge base up to date regarding the rapidly changing medical and corresponding psychosocial realities of HIV care is through the Internet (see the appendix at the end of this chapter).

Supporting clients in obtaining information from their medical providers and other sources, and coaching them on strategies to manage the doctor-patient relationship is also an important role for social workers. It is not essential that a nonmedical mental health professional fully comprehend all of these complex issues, but he or she should take an active role in urging clients to question their medical care providers in enough detail so that they have a sense of being partners in their medical treatment. Social workers need to be alert to the reality that the need to "coach" clients to approach and consult with their medical team is not going to be a one-time phenomenon, and will need to be revisited repeatedly. For instance the social worker might hear a client talk about being afraid to be honest with his doctor about not taking the medications exactly as prescribed, for fear of being labeled a "bad patient." In situations like this, first probing the motivating factors as to why the client is reluctant to be honest with the doctor and then giving some role playing and assertiveness training during counseling sessions can go a long way to prepare the client to be more authentic in the relationships he has with the other members of their health care team. Social workers can also be useful in helping individuals develop strategies for adhering to difficult medication schedules, again by coaching clients to be honest about their own limitations when faced with the need to adjust their lifestyles in order to accommodate a medication that the physician is suggesting they begin.

Since the onset of the epidemic, social workers counseling clients infected and affected by HIV have been experimenting with new therapeutic approaches in order to meet client needs. The paradigm of what constitutes "good mental health treatment" for this client population has most often been an eclectic approach that actively addresses interpersonal, systemic, and intrapsychic issues and dynamics. There have been, and remain, times when a primary therapist may function as a case manager or counselor, rather than as a safely distant and objective clinician. Even with the arrival of combination therapy there remains a need for social workers to understand when it is appropriate to add counseling or case management to the process of intrapsychic exploration that has been the hallmark of classic psychotherapy.

In addition to helping clients with AIDS obtain needed services and benefits, social workers have an important role to play in providing psychosocial support to those living with AIDS and their loved ones (Gambe & Getzel, 1989; Getzel, 1991; Shernoff, 1990). A key component of providing psychotherapy to this population is to help clients manage the anxiety disorders, which are probably the most frequent psychiatric complications of HIV disease, in both those who are uninfected and yet at high risk and those symptomatic of HIV disease (Dilley & Boccellari, 1989). Depression in people with AIDS and symptomatic HIV disease is common (Dilley & Boccellari, 1989); clinicians must be alert to the possibility that the depression can be organic in origin and usually responds well to psychotropic medication. Helping clients balance hope with the realities of living with a life threatening illness is another essential component of counseling. For people who are responding well to HAART, exploring quality of life issues associated with the constant uncertainty regarding how long the treatment will remain effective provides fertile areas for therapeutic exploration.

Barriers to HAART's Being Successful

Combination antiretroviral therapy continues to be effective over time, yet between 10 and 30 percent of people who undertake combination therapy either fail to respond or experience viral breakthrough (Waldholz, 1996). One of the biggest drawbacks experienced by people taking HAART is side effects, which are actions caused by a drug other than that which was intended. Each drug in the HAART armamentarium comes with a number of side effects that can cause a significant amount of discomfort and, quite possibly, prevent continued use. The range of possible side effects from combination therapy is broad, and includes nausea, vomiting, diarrhea, skin rashes, headaches, fever, chills, peripheral neuropathy (painful tingling of the hands and feet), and depression. Another unusual side effect associated with combination therapies is lipodystrophy, or the redistribution of body fat from the extremities to the torso, a loss of subcutaneous fat on a person's face as well as elevated levels of fat or cholesterol in the bloodstream, posing a risk for, and sometimes actually causing, heart attacks and strokes.

Although these symptoms can sometimes be treated, their impact on quality of life can be significant when they limit mobility or otherwise prevent people from going about their normal routines. Some side effects can be effectively treated with antidiarrheal and antiemetic medications. Nonetheless, for many people, side effects may be perceived as the primary effects of the medications, and in the short term they may seem more serious than HIV infection. When serious, side effects can be a valid reason for an individual to discuss altering the course of a medication regimen.

Adherence Issues

Medication adherence, of key importance in fending off drug resistance, remains a major issue for people living with HIV/AIDS, and is frequently a topic discussed by men living with HIV/AIDS with social workers. Taking medications as prescribed has long been recognized as problematic for nearly all types of conditions and treatments. Adherence is generally at its most challenging when the regimen is complex, intrusive, and of long duration, exact characteristics of the anti-HIV therapies. Adherence is also difficult when the treatment is for chronic conditions which are often asymptomatic, as opposed to acute, symptomatic conditions; again, the case with many people with HIV. Compared with the finality of an all-out cure, the prospect of long-term adherence to a complex regimen of combination therapy is disheartening and confusing. Nonetheless, the simple reality is that if an individual cannot adhere to the strict dosing schedule and food requirements, the therapy is destined to fail because of the growth of insufficiently suppressed viral strains. Similarly, adherent patients unable to absorb the drug, due to diarrhea or gastrointestinal problems (including those caused by the drugs themselves) are also likely to find that treatment fails them. Diarrhea can flush out medications before they are fully absorbed into the body. Thus, in entering the age of combination therapies, we have entered the era of complex and uncertain resistance-based treatment choices. The extremely high costs of these new medications are another significant barrier for many individuals with HIV disease (Gay-Stolberg, 1997a,b). The average annual cost of HIV antiretroviral therapy alone is about $15,000, and this is not including any of the other drugs that people with HIV or AIDS are routinely prescribed (Doyle, Jeffreys, & Schamber, 1999).

Psychologically, people taking HAART are living with what many have called "cautious optimism," as no one can say how long the drugs will be effective or whether they will interact with the various organ systems of the body as people with HIV/AIDS age. This author once said to a *New York Times* reporter that those of us on HAART are the largest uncontrolled clinical study in the history of the world. Living with this uncertainty has the potential to create a very potent anxiety that clinicians need to be alert to in working with people who are long-term survivors of HIV.

Sexual Safety and Sex Without Condoms

Sex without condoms never stopped happening, even when AIDS was at its most lethal. During the first wave of the AIDS epidemic, sexually active gay men began using condoms during anal intercourse (Martin, 1987), but many are returning to the ways of sex before the onset of AIDS, such as having unprotected anal intercourse (UAI). The term for gay men having UAI is generally known as barebacking, but is also known as raw sex or natural sex. Sexual behavior that poses a risk for transmitting HIV is on the rise among men from all racial groups who have sex with men (Centers for Disease Control and Prevention [CDC], 2002b). At the 2003 National HIV Prevention Conference, the CDC reported that the number of gay and bisexual men diagnosed with HIV during 1999-2002 increased 17 percent (CDC, 2003).

Men of all ages are engaging in barebacking. Middle-aged gay men who were sexually active prior to the onset of the AIDS crisis are foregoing the use of condoms (Bonnel, Weatherburn, & Hickson, 2000). Men who practiced safer sex for years and even decades reported experiencing safer sex fatigue or burnout as a reason for returning to sex without condoms (Halkitis et al., 2003). In-school sex education, increased availability of condoms, knowledge of HIV and safer sex all helped educate younger people about how to avoid HIV infection and other STDs (Rotheram-Borus et al., 2001), yet HIV infection among the young remains high (Koblin et al., 2000), especially among young gay men of color (CDC, 2002a).

The definition that social scientists have given to barebacking for both HIV-negative and HIV-positive men is "intentional anal sex without a condom with men who are not a primary partner (i.e., not someone the individual lives with or sees often and toward whom the individual feels a special emotional commitment)" (Mansergh et al., 2002, p. 653). Evidence suggests that barebacking is the relatively infrequent act of a relatively large number of gay men (rather than the very frequent acts of a few), and is often moderated by relationship status as well as HIV status (Coxon & McManus, 2000).

Having high-risk sex is sometimes connected to the advent of HAART (Vanable, Ostrow, McKirnan, Taywaditep, & Hope, 2000). Antiretroviral therapies provide gay men with a misplaced sense of complacency. Many believe that contracting HIV is not a big deal anymore—certainly not a risk to life. It is incumbent upon social workers to use psychoeducational interventions to ensure clients understand that, regarding HIV infection, a chronic illness is not the same as a mild or unimportant medical condition.

A major factor contributing to barebacking is the Internet. A majority of men of all racial groups cited the Internet as a major factor in the rise of the phenomenon. Halkitis and Parsons (2003) found that gay men overwhelmingly stated that it is easy to find sex partners who want to bareback on the Internet. They explained that because the Internet is anonymous, men are more likely to find other men into barebacking since online profiles often state HIV status which removes the difficulties of needing to disclose or ask about HIV status.

Mansergh (2002) discusses that some men intentionally put themselves and/or others at risk of HIV and STD to meet important human needs (e.g., physical stimulation, emotional connection) other than physical health. It would be simplistic to adduce a single issue or dynamic as the "reason" for an individual's engagement in unsafe sex. Usually a complex combination of factors underlies such behavior, some of which are understandable and adaptive for that particular individual.

Ron Stall is a leading AIDS researcher who was formerly the director of the CDC's Prevention Research Branch at the National Center for HIV, STD, and TB Prevention. Speaking about gay men taking sexual risks, Stall identified four significant epidemics co-occurring in gay communities, interacting to make the others worse, which influence gay men's willingness to take sexual risks. These are depression, partner violence, substance abuse, and HIV. Stall refers to this phenomenon as "syndemics"—a syndrome of interacting epidemics. Speaking of the nearly three thousand men in one study, he said, "The higher the number of the epidemics that any particular man experienced, the more likely he was to have risky sex and to test positive for HIV" (quoted in Specter, 2005, p. 44).

It is important to differentiate between having high-risk sex that places the individual at risk for transmitting HIV and unprotected sex. "Men in mutually monogamous, HIV-negative concordant relationships are not at high risk for transmission of HIV if they only have sex with each other— even if they have unprotected anal intercourse" (Hoff et al., 1997, p. 75). For committed couples who are not having protected anal intercourse, the increase in intimacy, closeness, and spontaneity may outweigh any potential risks of HIV infection or superinfection.

It is all too easy and reductionistic to pathologize sexual risk-takers as self-destructive, suicidal, damaged individuals or to believe that "for some gay men danger is a permanent fetish" (Savage, 1999, p. 62). Pinkerton and Abramson (1992) found that "for certain individuals, under certain circumstances, risky sexual behavior may indeed be rational, in the sense that the perceived physical, emotional and psychological benefits of sex outweigh the threat of acquiring HIV" (p. 561). Cheuvront (2002) reminds all mental health professionals working with gay men who bareback that "the meanings of sexual risk-taking are as varied as our patients" (p. 15). It is the task of clinical social workers to help an individual articulate the particular meanings of his high-risk behaviors. It is vital that social workers make every effort to elicit the variety and profundity of needs that condomless sex meets for each man who is barebacking in order to try and provide the opportunity for each individual to begin to explore these highly fraught issues in a safe and nonjudgmental environment. Cheuvront suggests that for many gay men self-care may indeed include taking risks, which, in the context of barebacking, means that the benefits derived from condomless sex in the present vastly outweigh any long-term potential risk to their health.

There is no single, obvious therapeutic goal when working with gay men who are not having safer sex. The therapist must help each individual evaluate whether he feels having safer sex is adaptive for him, even if the therapist strongly differs with the position taken by the patient. This is noted by Rofes (1996) and confirmed by my clinical observations that, despite knowing the risks of certain sexual behaviors, some gay men consciously prefer to prioritize pleasure over possible longevity.

Harm Reduction and Barebacking

Assuming that the only goal of AIDS prevention or therapeutic work is for every gay man to only have safer sex every time he is sexually active is analogous to maintaining that the only goal for an individual who has a problematic relationship with substances should be to abstain from the use of alcohol and drugs. Harm reduction is an especially useful and practical strategy in dealing with individuals who are wrestling with substance use and/or high-risk sex. Harm reduction was first developed to prevent and reduce the spread of HIV among active intravenous drug users (Springer, 1991). It is a philosophy and set of practical and effective strategies originally developed for helping drug users reduce the attendant risks and harms that accrue from using drugs when the individual has no desire for abstention. Harm reduction is now expanding into a therapeutic modality employed with individuals engaging in any kind of potentially self-destructive behavior they are reluctant to stop, such as barebacking (Tatarsky, 2002). The primary goal of harm reduction is to reduce potential harm while encouraging safer behaviors. This makes it an ideal clinical approach for gay men who bareback.

The vast majority of men who are having sex without condoms are not looking to get infected or to infect another individual, and can in fact reduce their risk of spreading or getting HIV by making small alterations to their behaviors. Social scientists studying this phenomena have reported on, and in some cases provided labels for, the behavioral modifications that men who are having UAI make in order to reduce the risk of transmitting HIV. These include the following:

- "Negotiated safety" is an agreement between two gay men in a HIV-negative seroconcordant relationship to go through the process of getting ready to stop using condoms when they have anal sex.
- "Serosorting" refers to the practice of men having UAI with other men of the same HIV status (Pinkerton & Abramson, 1992; Hoff et al., 1997).
- "Strategic positioning," used by both HIV-positive and HIV-negative gay and bisexual men, refers to the practice of infected men adopting the receptive role during UAI with HIV-negative men (Van de Ven et al., 2005; Wolitski & Bailey, 2005).
- "Dipping" refers to anal insertion for just one or two strokes without wearing a condom (Parsons et al., 2005).
- Withdrawal prior to ejaculation.
- Using information that they or a partner have an undetectable viral load to make decisions about whether or not to bareback.
- Substituting unprotected oral sex for UAI.

Negotiated safety (Kippax, Crawford, Davis, Rodden, & Dowsett, 1993; Prestage et al., 1995) is a harm reduction strategy for HIV-negative men in a monogamous relationship, which is an agreement between two gay men in a relationship to begin a process of getting ready to stop using condoms when they have anal sex. The basis of this agreement is an explicit understanding that both know each other's HIV status and are both uninfected. The only time that both partners do not use condoms is when they have sex with each other, making this an acceptable safer sex option. There must be no unprotected sex outside the relationship; if either partner does so, then he must immediately inform his partner prior to their having sex again. They resume using condoms until subsequent HIV tests prove that the partner who had unprotected sex is still negative (freedoms.org, 2002). A useful tool for helping a couple decide whether negotiated safety will be viable for them is an agreement developed by an organization in England that the author either distributes to couples or asks them to download, complete, and then come to sessions to discuss.

SUMMARY

Individual practice with MSM as well as gay- or queer-identified men is a rich and challenging clinical specialty. State-of-the-art interventions with this population in the twenty-first century need to challenge traditional models of therapeutic intervention. Whereas traditional psychotherapy is often still appropriate treatment, the skilled practitioner must be knowledgeable about and ready to employ a variety of case work, counseling, crisis intervention, and advocacy skills, in addition to intrapsychic exploration and a systems approach. By being eclectic in working with gay men, services are customized to meet diversified client needs. Gay men seeking clinical social work services often discuss issues that have the potential to bewilder and overwhelm the most skilled clinician.

The political and social climate in the United States is illustrated by the ascendancy of the religious right and the Bush administration's global, domestic, and environmental policies. People who were disenfranchised previously are only more so now, both within the United States as well as abroad. Within a political climate where a women's right to choose is threatened, where the teaching of evolution in schools is being challenged, where federally funded sex education teaches "abstinence only," and where, under pressure from religious conservatives, any mention that condoms can help prevent HIV is removed from the CDC's Web site, honest conversations about sex and the balance between sexual freedom and sexual responsibility will not be encouraged as part of official, government-approved AIDS prevention programs. These conversations have the potential to occur during clinical work with gay-affirmative social workers. They are not only clinically appropriate, but potentially life saving. Epstein (2001) suggests that change results neither from people getting rid of their problems, nor from their going into them more deeply. It comes from helping them to accept what is true about themselves and working from there. He also proposes that good psychotherapy consists of helping individuals to find their own meaning in their lives as well in the interaction with the therapist, as opposed to being fed interpretations. These thoughts seem particularly relevant for therapists working with gay men today. Contemporary practice with this population brings with it demands and challenges that reenforce the basic social work tenets of the need for regular ongoing supervision, training, and supportive self-examination to help enable the practitioner to continue to make a skillful and disciplined use of his or her self in a sustainable fashion.

APPENDIX: INTERNET RESOURCES
FOR HIV/AIDS INFORMATION

The science of AIDS therapies is a rapidly evolving field, and it is difficult enough even for physicians in full-time AIDS practice to keep up completely with the latest developments. Just as it is not a client's responsibility to educate his or her therapist or counselor about sexual orientation or cultural diversity issues, people living with HIV and AIDS should not need to educate their providers about AIDS care, treatments, and side effects. Although social workers do not need to become completely versed in the hard science of HIV and AIDS, ongoing continuing education will be a tremendous asset in working with people with HIV and AIDS. The following is a list of just a few of the major HIV/AIDS Web sites where the latest information about treatments and psychosocial issues is available.

AEGIS (AIDS Education Global Information System)—one of the largest and most comprehensive AIDS sites on the Internet, at http://www.aegis.com

AIDS.org—quality HIV/AIDS information and resources world wide including online CME courses in HIV care and hosting *AIDS Treatment News,* at www.AIDS.org

Community Research Initiative (CRIA)—a nonprofit community-based organization which studies new treatments for HIV and AIDS-related diseases, at http:// www.criany.org

Project Inform—offers comprehensive information on treatments for HIV/AIDS, at http://www.projectinform.org

The Body.com—the world's largest and most comprehensive HIV/AIDS Web site, at http://www.thebody.com

Treatment Action Group—the very latest in the rapidly changing world of AIDS treatment research, at http://www.ATDN.org

REFERENCES

Adelson, S. (2005, February 28). A gay cruising site defends itself: The manager of Manhunt.net on the HIV superstrain, unsafe sex, crystal meth and corporate and personal responsibility. *New York Magazine,* p. 12.

American Psychiatric Association (1987). *Diagnostic and statistical manual of mental disorders* (3rd ed., Revised). Washington, DC: American Psychiatric Press.

American Psychiatric Association (1998). *Position statement on psychiatric treatment and sexual orientation.* Retrieved April 26, 2007, from www.psych.org/news_stand/reptherapy.cfm.

American Psychiatric Association (2000). *COPP position statement on therapies focused on attempts to change sexual orientation (reparative or conversion therapies).* Retrieved April 26, 2007 from www.psych.org/psych/htdocs/practofpsych/copptherapyaddendum83100.html.

Ball, S. (1994). A group model for gay and lesbian clients with chronic mental illness. *Social Work, 39,* 109-115.

Bayer, R. (1981). *Homosexuality and American psychiatry.* New York: Basic Books.

Benotsch, E., Kalichman, S., & Cage, M. (2002). Men who have met sex partners via the Internet: Prevalence, predictors and implications for HIV prevention. *Archives of Sexual Behavior, 31,* 177-183.

Berger, R. (1984). Realities of gay and lesbian aging. *Social Work, 29,* 57-62.

Berger, R., & Kelly, J. (2001). What are older gay men like? An impossible question. *Journal of Gay & Lesbian Social Services, 13,* 55-64.

Berrill, K. (1992). Anti-gay violence and victimization in the United States: An overview. In G. Herek & K. Berrill (Eds.), *Hate crimes* (pp. 19-45). Newbury Park, CA: Sage Publications.

Bonnel, C., Weatherburn, P., & Hickson, F. (2000). Sexually transmitted infection as a risk factor for homosexual HIV transmission: A systemic review of epidemiological studies. *International Journal of STD and AIDS, 11,* 697-700.

Bozett, R. (1981). Gay fathers: Evolution of the gay-father identity. *American Journal of Orthopsychiatry, 51,* 552-559.

Breeze (1985). Social service needs and resources in rural communities. In H. Hidalgo, T. Peterson, & N. Woodman (Eds.), *Lesbian and gay issues: A resource manual for social workers* (pp. 43-48). Silver Spring, MD: National Association of Social Workers.

Brown, L., Alley, G., Sarosy, S., Quarto, G., & Cook, T. (2001). Gay men: Aging well! *Journal of Gay & Lesbian Social Services, 13,* 41-54.

Cabaj, R. P. (1992). Substance abuse in the gay and lesbian community. In J. Lowenson, P. Ruiz, R. Millman (Eds.), *Substance abuse: A comprehensive textbook* (2nd ed., pp. 852-860). Baltimore: Williams & Wilkins.

Cao, Y., Qin, L., Zhang, L., Safrit, J., & Ho, D. (1995). Virologic and immunologic characterization of long term survivors of human immunodeficiency virus type 1 Infection. *New England Journal of Medicine, 332,* 201-208.

Carballo-Dieguez, A. (1989). Hispanic culture, gay male culture, and AIDS: Counseling implications. *Journal of Counseling & Development, 68,* 26-30.

Cass, V. (1979). Homosexual identity formation: A theoretical model. *Journal of Homosexuality, 4,* 219-235.

Centers for Disease Control and Prevention (2002a). Unrecognized HIV infection, risk behaviors, and perceptions of risk among young black men who have sex with men: Six U.S. cities, 1994-1998. *Morbidity and Mortality Weekly Report, 51,* 733-736.

Centers for Disease Control and Prevention (2002b). Incorporating HIV prevention into the medical care of persons living with HIV: Recommendations of Centers for and Prevention, the Health Resources and Services Administration, the National Institutes of Health, and the HIV Medicine Association of the Infectious Diseases Society of America. *Morbidity and Mortality Weekly Report, 52*(RR-12), 1-24.

Centers for Disease Control and Prevention (2003). Increases in HIV Diagnoses— 29 States, 1999-2002. *Morbidity and Mortality Weekly Report, 52,* 1145-1148.

Chan, C. (1989). Issues of identity development among Asian-American lesbians and gay men. *Journal of Counseling & Development, 68,* 16-20.

Cheuvront, J. P. (2002). High-risk sexual behavior in the treatment of HIV-negative patients. *Journal of Gay & Lesbian Psychotherapy, 6,* 7-26.

Coleman, E. (1988). Assessment of sexual orientation. In E. Coleman (Ed.), *Integrated identity for gay men and lesbians: Psychotherapeutic approaches for emotional well-being* (pp. 9-24). Binghamton, NY: The Haworth Press.

Coxon, A. P. M., & McManus, T. J. (2000). How many account for how much? Concentration of high-risk sexual behaviour among gay men. *Journal of Sex Research, 37,* 1-7.

de la Vega, E. (1995). Considerations for presenting HIV/AIDS information to U.S. Latino populations. In W. Odets & M. Shernoff (Eds.), *The second decade of AIDS: A mental health practice handbook* (pp. 255-274). New York: Hatherleigh Press.

Denizet-Lewis, B. (2003, August 3). Living (and dying) on the down low. *New York Times Magazine,* pp. 28-33 & 48, 52-53.

Diaz, R. (1998). *Latino gay men and HIV: Culture, sexuality and risk behavior.* New York: Routledge.

Dilley, J., & Boccellari, A. (1989). Neuropsychiatric complications of HIV infection. In J. Dilley, C. Pies, & M. Helquist (Eds.), *Face to face: A guide to AIDS counseling* (pp. 138-151). Berkeley, CA: Celestial Arts.

Doka, K. (1989). *Disenfranchised grief: Recognizing hidden sorrow.* Lexington, MA: Lexington Books.

Doyle, R., Jeffreys, J. K., & Schamber, S. (1999, March). *National ADAP Monitoring Project, Annual Report.* National Alliance of State and Territorial AIDS Directors and the AIDS Treatment Data Network. Washington, DC: Author.

Dworkin, J., & Kaufer, D. (1995). Social services and bereavement in the gay and lesbian community. In G. Lloyd & M. A. Kuszelewicz (Eds.), *HIV disease: Les-*

bians, gays and the social services (pp. 41-60). Binghamton, NY: The Haworth Press.

Elford, J., Bolding, G., & Sherr, L. (2001). Seeking sex on the Internet and sexual risk behaviour among gay men using London gyms. *AIDS, 15,* 1409-1415.

Epstein, M. (2001). *Going on being: Buddhism and the way of change—A positive psychology for the West.* New York: Broadway Books.

Exodus-International (2005). www.exodus-international.org.

Faltz, B. (1988). Substance abuse and the lesbian & gay community: Assessment and intervention. In M. Shernoff & W. Scott (Eds.), *The sourcebook on lesbian/ gay health care* (2nd ed., pp. 151-161). Washington, DC: National Lesbian/Gay Health Foundation.

Finnegan, D., & McNally, E. (2002). *Counseling lesbian, gay, bisexual and trans- gender substance abusers: Dual identities.* Binghamton, NY: The Haworth Press.

Freedoms.org.uk (2002). http://www.freedoms.org.uk/advice/air/air02.htm.

Fries, S. (1998). A place where no one knows your name. *The Advocate: The National Gay & Lesbian Newsmagazine, 752,* 24-31.

Gambe, R., & Getzel, G. (1989). Group work with gay men with AIDS. *Social Casework, 70,* 172-179.

Gamson, J. (1998). Must identity movements self-destruct? In P. Nardi & B. Schneider (Eds.), *Social perspectives in lesbian and gay studies* (pp. 114-132). New York: Routledge.

Garnets, L., Herek, G., & Levy, B. (1992). Violence and victimization of lesbians and gay men: Mental health consequences. In G. Herek & K. Berrill (Eds.), *Hate crimes* (pp. 207-226). Newbury Park, CA: Sage Publications.

Gay-Stolberg, S. (1997a, August 22). Despite new AIDS drugs, many still lose the battle. *New York Times,* p. A1.

Gay-Stolberg, S. (1997b, October 14). AIDS drugs elude the grasp of many thou- sands of poor. *New York Times,* p. A1.

Germain, C. B. (1978). General-systems theory and ego psychology: An ecological perspective. *Social Service Review, 62,* 535-550.

Germain, C. B. (1980). Social context of clinical social work. *Social Work, 45,* 483-488.

Germain, C. B. (1981). The ecological approach to people-environment transac- tions. *Social Casework 62,* 323-331.

Gitterman, A., & Germain, C. B. (1976). Social work practice: A life model. *Social Service Review, 60,* 601-610.

Getzel, G. (1991). Survival modes for people with AIDS in groups. *Social Work, 36,* 7-11.

Gonsiorek, J. (1982). The use of diagnostic concepts in working with gay and lesbian populations. *Journal of Homosexuality, 7,* 9-20.

Gonsiorek, J., & Rudolph, J. (1991). Homosexual identity: Coming out and other developmental events. In J. Gonsiorek & J. Weinrich (Eds.), *Homosexuality: Re- search implications for public policy* (pp. 161-176). Newbury Park, CA: Sage Publications.

Grossman, A., D'Augelli, A., & O'Connell, T. (2001). Being lesbian, gay, bisexual and 60 or older in North America. *Journal of Gay & Lesbian Social Services, 13,* 23-40.

Gunter, P. (1988). Rural gay men and lesbians in need of services and understanding. In M. Shernoff & W. Scott (Eds.), *The sourcebook on lesbian/gay health care* (2nd ed., pp. 49-53). Washington, DC: National Lesbian/Gay Health Foundation.

Gunther, S. (2005). Alors, are we queer yet? *The Gay and Lesbian Review, Worldwide, XII,* 23-25.

Guss, J. R. (2000). Sex like you can't even imagine: "Crystal," crack, and gay men. *Journal of Gay & Lesbian Psychotherapy, 3,* 105-122.

Halkitis, P. N. (2000). Masculinity in the Age of AIDS: HIV-seropositive gay men and the "Buff Agenda." In P. Nardi (Ed.), *Gay masculinities* (pp. 130-151). Thousand Oaks, CA: Sage Publications.

Halkitis, P. N., Greene, K., & Mourgues, P. (2005). Patterns, contexts, and risks associated with methamphetamine use among gay and bisexual men in New York City: Findings from Project BUMPS. *Journal of Urban Health, 82,* 18-25.

Halkitis, P. N., & Parsons, J. T. (2002). Recreational drug use and HIV risk sexual behavior among men frequenting urban gay venues. *Journal of Gay & Lesbian Social Services, 14,* 19-38.

Halkitis, P. N., & Parsons, J. T. (2003). Intentional unsafe sex (barebacking) among gay men who seek sexual partners on the Internet. *AIDS Care, 15,* 367-378.

Halkitis, P. N., Parsons, J. T., & Stirratt, M. (2001). A double epidemic: Crystal methamphetemine use and its relation to HIV prevention among gay men. *Journal of Homosexuality, 41,* 17-35.

Halkitis, P., Parsons, J. T., & Wilton, L. (2003). An exploratory study of contextual and situational factors related to methamphetamine use among gay and bisexual men in New York City. *Journal of Drug Issues, 33,* 413-432.

Herek, G. M. (1990). Homophobia. In W. R. Dynes (Ed.), *Encyclopedia of homosexuality* (pp. 552-554). New York: Garland.

Hoff, C., Stall, R. D., Paul, J., Acree, M., Daigle, D., Phillips, K., et al. (1997). Differences in sexual behavior among HIV discordant and concordant gay men in primary relationships. *Journal of AIDS and Human Retrovirology, 14,* 72-78.

Hollobaugh, A. (2001, June 26). Queers without money. *The Village Voice,* pp. 47-49.

Houston-Hamilton, A., Day, N., & Purnell, P. (1989). Educating chronic psychiatric patients about AIDS. In J. Dilley, C. Pies, & M. Helquist (Eds.), *Face to face: A guide to AIDS counseling* (pp. 199-209). Berkeley, CA: Celestial Arts.

Isay, R. (1989). *Being homosexual: Gay men and their development.* New York: Avon Books.

Kertzner, R. (1997). Entering midlife: Gay men, HIV and the future. *Journal of the Gay and Lesbian Medical Association, 1,* 87-95.

Kim, A., Kent, C., & McFarland, W. (2001). Cruising on the Internet highway. *Journal of Acquired Immune Deficiency Syndromes, 28,* 89-93.

King, J. (2004). *On the down low: A journey into the lives of "straight" black men who sleep with men.* New York: Broadway Books.

Kinsey, A., Pomeroy, W. B., & Martin, C. E. (1948). *Sexual behavior in the human male.* Philadelphia: W. B. Saunders.

Kippax, S., Crawford, J., Davis, M., Rodden, P., & Dowsett, G. (1993). Sustaining safe sex: A longitudinal study of a sample of homosexual men. *AIDS, 7,* 257-263.

Koblin, B. A., Torian, L. V., Gulin, V., Ren, L., MacKellar, D. A., & Valleroy, L. A. (2000). High prevalence of HIV infection among young men who have sex with men in New York City. *AIDS, 14,* 1793-1800.

Kus, R. (1988). Alcoholism and non-acceptance of gay self: The critical link. *The Journal of Homosexuality, 15,* 25-41.

Loiacano, D. (1989). Gay identity issues among black Americans: Racism, homophobia, and the need for validation. *Journal of Counseling & Development, 68,* 21-25.

MacMaster, S., Aquino, R., & Vail, K. (2003). Providing HIV education and outreach via Internet chat rooms to men who have sex with men. *Journal of Human Behavior in the Social Environment, 8,* 145-151.

Mansergh, G. (2002). The paradigm shift for HIV prevention in the US. *AIDScience, 2*(10), 653-659.

Mansergh, G., Marks, G., Colfax, G., Guzman, R., Rader, M., & Buchbinder, S. (2002). Barebacking in a diverse sample of men who have sex with men. *AIDS, 16,* 653-659.

Martin, A. (1993). *The lesbian and gay parenting handbook.* New York: Harper Collins.

Martin, J. (1987). The impact of AIDS on gay male sexual behavior patterns in New York City. *American Journal of Public Health, 77,* 578-581.

McFarlane, M., Bull, S. S., & Rietmeijer, C. A. (2000). The Internet as a newly emerging risk environment for sexually transmitted diseases. *Journal of the American Medical Association, 284,* 443-446.

McKirnan, D., & Peterson, P. (1989). Alcohol and drug use among homosexual men and women. *Addictive Behaviors, 14,* 545-553.

Morales, J., & Graves, M. (1983). *Substance abuse patterns and barriers to treatment for gay men and lesbians in San Francisco.* San Francisco: Department of Public Health.

Moses, A., & Bucker, J. (1980). The special problems of rural gay clients. *Human Services in the Rural Environment, 5,* 22-27.

NARTH (2005). www.NARTH.com.

National Coalition of Antiviolence Programs (NCAVP) (2005). *National information from the 2004 Report on anti-lesbian, gay and transgender & bisexual violence.* Retrieved April 26, 2007, online from www.ncavp.org.

National Gay & Lesbian Task Force Policy Institute (1991). *Anti-gay/lesbian violence, victimization and defamation in 1991.* Washington, DC: National Lesbian/Gay Task Force.

Palella, F. J., Delaney, K. M., Moorman, A. C., Loveless, M.O., Fuhrer, J., Satten, G.A., et al. (1998). Declining morbidity and mortality among patients with advanced human immunodeficiency virus infection. *New England Journal of Medicine, 338,* 853-860.

Parsons, J., Schrimshaw, E., Wolitski, R., Halikitis, P., Purcell, D., Hoff, C., et al. (2005). Sexual harm reduction practices of HIV-seropositive gay and bisexual men: Serosorting, strategic positioning, and withdrawal before ejaculation. *AIDS, 19*(Suppl. 1), S13-S26.

PATH (2005). www.pathinfo.org.

Pinkerton, S., & Abramson, P. (1992). Is risky sex rational? *The Journal of Sex Research, 29,* 561-568.

Pitt, E., & Dolan-Soto, D. (2001). Clinical considerations in working with victims of same-sex domestic violence. *Journal of the Gay and Lesbian Medical Association, 5,* 163-169.

Pogash, C. (2005, May 3). The inexplicable survivors of a widespread epidemic. *The New York Times,* pp. F6, F10.

Prestage, G., Noble, J., Kippax, S., Crawford, J., Baxter, D., & Cooper, D. (1995). *Methods and sample in a study of homosexually active men in Sydney, Australia.* Sydney, Australia: National Centre in HIV Social Research, University of New South Wales.

Purcell, D., Parsons, J., Halkitis, P., Mizuno, Y., & Woods, W. (2001). Substance use and sexual transmission risk history of HIV-positive men who have sex with men. *Journal of Substance Abuse, 13,* 185-200.

Ratner, E. (1993). Treatment issues for chemically dependent lesbians & gay men. In L. Garnets & D. Kimmel (Eds.), *Psychological perspectives on lesbian & gay male experiences* (pp. 567-578). New York: Columbia University Press.

Rofes, E. (1996). *Reviving the tribe: Regenerating gay men's sexuality and culture in the ongoing epidemic.* Binghamton, NY: Harrington Park Press.

Ross, M. (1983). *The married homosexual man: A psychological study.* London: Routledge & Kegan Paul.

Ross, M. (2004, December 14). Personal e-mail communication.

Ross, M., & Kauth, M. (2002). Men who have sex with men, and the Internet: Emerging clinical issues and their management. In A. Cooper (Ed.), *Sex & the Internet: A guide for clinicians* (pp. 47-69). New York: Brunner-Routledge.

Rotheram-Borus, M. J., Lee, M., Zhou, S., O'Hara, P., Birnbaum, J. M., Swendeman, D., et al. (2001). Variations in health and risk behavior among youth living with HIV. *AIDS Education and Prevention, 13,* 42-54.

Royce, R. A., Sena, A., Cates, W., Jr., & Cohen, M. S. (1997). Current concepts: Sexual transmission of HIV. *New England Journal of Medicine, 336,* 1072-1079.

Savage, D. (1999, March). The thrill of living dangerously. *Out Magazine,* pp. 62, 64, 118.

Schroeder, M., & Shidlo, A. (2001). Ethical issues in sexual orientation conversion therapies: An empirical study of consumers. *Journal of Gay & Lesbian Psychotherapy, 5,* 131-166.

Shernoff, M. (1983, October 10-23). Nice boys and needles. *New York Native,* pp. 7-8.

Shernoff, M. (1984). Family therapy for lesbian and gay clients. *Social Work, 29,* 393-396.

Shernoff, M. (1990). Why every social worker should be challenged by AIDS. *Social Work, 35,* 5-8.

Shernoff, M. (1996). Gay men choosing to be fathers. In M. Shernoff (Ed.), *Human services for gay people: Clinical and community practice* (pp. 41-54). Binghamton, NY: The Haworth Press.

Shernoff, M. (1998). Gay widowers: Grieving in relation to trauma and social support. *Journal of the Gay & Lesbian Medical Association, 2,* 224-266.

Shernoff, M. (2002). Body image, working out and therapy. *Journal of Gay & Lesbian Social Services, 14,* 89-94.

Shernoff, M., & Finnegan, D. (1991). Family treatment with chemically dependent gay men and lesbians. *Journal of Chemical Dependency Treatment, 4,* 121-135.

Shernoff, M., & Smith, R. (2000). *HIV treatment: Mental health aspects of antiviral therapy.* San Francisco: UCSF AIDS Health Project.

Shidlo, A., & Schroeder, M. (2002). Changing sexual orientation: A consumer's report. *Professional Psychology: Research and Practice, 33,* 249-259.

Shidlo, A., Schroeder, M., & Drescher, J. (2001). *Sexual conversion therapy: Ethical, clinical and research perspectives.* Binghamton, NY: The Haworth Press.

Smith, J. (1988). Psychopathology, homosexuality and homophobia. In M. Ross (Ed.), *Psychopathology and psychotherapy in homosexuality* (pp. 59-74). Binghamton, NY: The Haworth Press.

Specter, M. (2005, May 23). Higher risk: Crystal meth, the Internet and dangerous choices about AIDS. *The New Yorker,* pp. 38-45.

Springer, E. (1991). Effective AIDS prevention with active drug users: The harm reduction model. In M. Shernoff (Ed.), *Counseling chemically dependent people with HIV illness* (pp. 141-158). Binghamton, NY: The Haworth Press.

Stall, R., McKusick, L., Wiley, J., Coates, T., & Ostrow, D. (1986). Alcohol and drug use during sexual activity and compliance with safe sex guidelines for AIDS: Behavioral research project. *Health Education Quarterly, 13,* 359-371.

Stall, R., & Wiley, J. (1988). A comparison of alcohol and drug use patterns of homosexual and heterosexual men. *Drug & Alcohol Dependence, 22,* 63-73.

Stall, R. D., & Leigh, B. (1994). Understanding the relationship between drug or alcohol use and high-risk sexual activity for HIV transmission: Where do we go from here? *Addiction, 89,* 131-134.

Tafoya, T., & Rowell, R. (1988). Counseling gay and lesbian native Americans. In M. Shernoff & W. Scott (Eds.), *The sourcebook on lesbian/gay health care* (2nd ed., pp. 63-67). Washington, DC: National Lesbian/Gay Health Foundation.

Tatarsky, A. (Ed.) (2002). *Harm reduction psychotherapy: A new treatment for drug and alcohol problems.* New Brunswick, NJ: Jason Aronson Inc.

Trebay, G. (2000, February 8). Homo thugz blow up the spot. *The Village Voice,* pp. 44-49.

Vanable, P. A., Ostrow, D. G., McKirnan, D. J., Taywaditep, K. J., & Hope, B. A. (2000). Impact of combination therapies on HIV risk perceptions and sexual risk taking among HIV-positive and HIV-negative gay and bisexual men. *Health Psychology, 19,* 134-145.

Van de Ven, P., Mao, L., Crawford, J., Prestage, G., Grulich, A., Kaldor, J., & Kippax, S. (2005). Willingness to participate in HIV vaccine trials among HIV-negative gay men in Sydney, Australia. *International Journal of STD & AIDS, 16,* 314-317.

Walber, E. (1988). Behind closed doors: Battering and abuse in the lesbian & gay communities. In M. Shernoff & W. Scott (Eds.), *The sourcebook on lesbian/gay healthcare* (2nd ed., pp. 250-258). Washington, DC: National Lesbian/Gay Health Foundation.

Waldholz, M. (1996, October 10). Some AIDS cases defy new drug cocktails. *Wall Street Journal,* p. B1.

Weatherburn, P., Hickson, F., & Reid, D. (2003). Net benefits: Gay men's use of the Internet and other settings where HIV prevention occurs. *Sigma Research, London.* Retrieved April 26, 2007, from http://www.sigmaresearch.org.uk/down loads/report03b.

Wertheimer, D. (1992). Treatment and service interventions for lesbian and gay male crime victims. In. G. Herek & K. Berrill (Eds.), *Hate crimes* (pp. 19-45). Newbury Park: Sage Publications.

Williams, J. (2004). The low-down on the down low. *The Gay & Lesbian Review Worldwide,* p. 6.

Wolitski, R. J., & Bailey, C. J. (2005). It takes two to tango: HIV-positive gay and bisexual men's beliefs about their responsibility to protect others from HIV infection. In P. N. Halkitis, C. A.Gómez, & R. J. Wolitski (Eds.), *HIV + Sex: The Psychological and Interpersonal Dynamics of HIV-Seropositive Gay and Bisexual Men's Relationships* (pp. 147-162). Washington, DC: American Psychological Association.

Woody, G. E., Donnekk, D., Seage, G. R., Metzger, D., Marmor, M., Koblin, B. A., et al. (1999). Non-injection substance use correlates with risky sex among men having sex with men: Data from HIVNET. *Drug and Alcohol Dependence, 53,* 197-205.

Wyers, N. (1987). Homosexuality in the family: Lesbian and gay spouses. *Social Work, 32,* 143-148.

Chapter 8

Social Work Practice with Lesbian Couples

Laura C. Booker
Sarah Jane Dodd

The historical and political climate in the United States has made researchers reluctant to study effective treatment methods for same-sex couples, and research funding in the area has been relatively scarce (Spitalnick & McNair, 2005). As a result, current therapeutic techniques have been developed for heterosexual couples and then applied to lesbian (or gay) couples. Certainly, same sex couples struggle with many of the same issues as heterosexual couples and therefore, treatment is similar for both types of couples (Decker, 1984; Martell & Prince, 2005; van Wormer, Wells, & Boes, 2000). In fact, Decker (1984) noted that "many of the relationship problems can be traced to the same developmental issues and family scripts that cause problems for heterosexual couples" (p. 40). However, there are differences, so although lesbian couples may face similar challenges to heterosexual couples seeking treatment, there are key variables that distinguish lesbian relationships: (1) both partners are women and have been socialized as such; (2) the relationship is stigmatized and not afforded legitimacy by our social institutions; and (3) a healthy lesbian relationship requires that each partner accepts her stigmatized identity (Roth, 1989). Therefore, social work practice with lesbian couples builds on standard couples practice but considers the political, social, and legal factors that may be involved in the presenting problem (Spitalnick & McNair, 2005).

Social Work Practice with LGBT People

TRADITIONAL PSYCHOANALYTIC NOTIONS
OF LESBIAN COUPLES

Much of the literature written about lesbian relationships focuses on the issue of closeness and distance regulation, a common problem for all couples, gay or straight (Feldman, 1979; van Wormer et al., 2000). Traditional psychoanalytic theories and models of human development have been authored primarily by white men, and, consequently, these models directly reflect their experience and interests (Jordan, 1997). Autonomy and separation-individuation have commonly been identified as hallmarks of healthy development that are achieved as an infant incrementally and progressively disengages from a symbiotic merger with his mother (Erikson, 1968; Mahler, 1975; Fairbairn, 1952). According to Chodorow (1978), the different socialization of boys and girls informs the degree to which each learn to connect with others. In order to actualize "maleness," boys must defend against attachment (or they will be too feminine and dependent), while girls can achieve their "femaleness" while staying more attached to the mother. Therefore, men have greater skill in separating and women have greater skill in connecting (Chodorow, 1978).

In a heterosexual relationship, it is the man who defends against regression to a complete merger, whereas with two women there is no one to create the defense. So, according to psychoanalytic theory, their relationship will regress toward symbiosis, a regression that is always viewed as pathological or immature. For example, Kernberg (1976) views "mature love" as relationships that have moments of merger, but which always return to a state of separation or autonomy. In Erikson's (1968) stages of development, he proposes that identity must be achieved before intimacy, implying that healthy development entails developing a sense of separateness before being able to develop connection. Each of these theories emphasizes the primacy of separation over connection. Therefore intense relational connection or fusion is seen as a developmental regression, where the individual is unable to symbolically separate from the mother-infant dyad.

Rooted in these traditional psychoanalytic theories, the majority of professional literature about lesbian couples pathologizes them as overly merged or fused (Mencher, 1997). Bowen (1978) originated the term "fusion" to represent "excessive emotional reactivity in which family members' responses to one another have a reflexive, predetermined quality" (Green, Bettinger, & Zachs, 1996). There is not full agreement about what fusion actually is, and it is often used synonymous with codependence, merger, and enmeshment. However, there is agreement that when related to couples "fusion" represents an intense level of connectedness, and it has been defined as "the process by which the boundaries and emotional distance between each partner become blurred to the point where there tends to be an extreme form of emotional closeness" (Spitalnick & McNair, 2005, p. 49). Often one partner's needs become dominant while the other partner's needs become submerged. The creation of one dominant and one submissive partner prevents each member of the couple from having her authentic self in the relationship (Green et al., 1996).

The Notion of Fusion in Lesbian Relationships: The U-Haul Factor

Who hasn't heard the joke: What does a lesbian take on a second date? A U-Haul. This joke offers a play on the belief that lesbians tend to move too fast when it comes to relationships. As we have noted, reflecting theoretical traditions dominated by men, the literature about lesbian relationships still utilize standards of separation and autonomy as markers of health, and hence have pathologized the connection or intimacy that many lesbian couples report. Therefore, fusion or "enmeshment" is presented as a problem in lesbian couples. Consequently, clinicians are often prone to emphasize the need for more separation and autonomy (Mencher, 1997).

The existing literature on lesbian relationships names the following patterns or characteristics as fusion and, hence, problematic: lesbians' placing high value on connection and intimacy, identification, mutual understanding, and shared beliefs and goals; conflict is avoided or unresolved; lesbians put partners' needs before their own; identities become blurred; individual development seen as contingent on remaining in relationship; and being mutually dependent on each other (Mencher, 1997). In terms of behavior, lesbians are seen to be in frequent contact, spend all their time together, and share possessions, friends, and clothes (Kaufman, Harrison, & Hyde, 1984). These examples are frequently used to represent merger to the unit at the expense of the individuated self.

FEMINIST PSYCHOLOGY: DEBUNKING TRADITIONAL PSYCHOANALYTIC NOTIONS OF LESBIAN COUPLES

In a reaction against traditional psychoanalytic thought, and the sexist and heterocentrist bias it represents, feminist psychologists and writers began to challenge some of these accepted models of human development, and began to look specifically at the unique aspects of female development, and the implications for lesbian relationships (Chodorow, 1978; Gilligan, 1982; Miller,

1976). Counter to male-focused models of development, relational-cultural theorists out of the Stone Center emphasize that women grow through connection, rather than through separation and autonomy. In this model, the goal of development is participation in "mutually-growth fostering" relationships and that the individual self grows in relation to others (Jordan, 1986).

These female models of development have tremendous implications for working with lesbian couples. Viewing lesbian relationships from a feminist lens allows us to see the emphasis on connection as desirable and healthy, and as a sign of progression not regression. Therefore, in contrast to traditional theorists we would argue that since fusion and intimacy represent points along a continuum of connection, and "judgments about what is too much or not enough closeness are fraught with personal bias" (Nichols, 2004, p. 365), then what may be perceived as intimacy by one person may be perceived as fusion by another.

Whereas historically theoretical literature draws a picture of lesbians as overly dependent and blurred, empirical data suggest that the presence of dynamics that are labeled fusion are not inherently dysfunctional or problematic (Blumstein & Schwartz, 1983; Eldridge & Gilbert, 1990; Loulan, 1988; McCandlish, 1982; Vetere, 1982). In fact, studies found that lesbians prioritize empathic identification; they focus on emotional closeness, have high degrees of self-disclosure, and emphasize the quality of the relationship as extremely important to them (Blumstein & Schwartz, 1983; Eldridge & Gilbert, 1990; Loulan, 1988; McCandlish, 1982; Vetere, 1982). So whereas previous literature measures lesbian couples against heterosexual couples and defines these attributes as problematic, lesbians in these studies identify them as extremely desirable. Mencher's (1984) dissertation, as cited in Mencher (1990), studied high-functioning lesbian couples who had been together six to eight years. The subjects saw intimacy, closeness, and the prioritizing of the relationship in their lives as *advantages* of being in a lesbian relationship. They believed that as a result of intimacy, they felt more trusting, were more able to take risks, and consequently were more self-actualized. Similarly, Berzoff (1990) studied female friendships among heterosexual women. Contrary to theoretical suggestions that merger represents regression, she found that the women who had experienced a sense of fusion also tested highest in ego development, meaning that they were emotionally the healthiest. Given these results, feminist psychologists have argued that, in fact, fusion might be a sign of relational strength (Mencher, 1997).

When working with lesbian couples, clinicians should be wary of pathologizing high degrees of closeness, instead seeing this fusion as normative and satisfying for many couples. Clients may feel pressure to "individuate" or even leave the relationship (as in Case Example 1). In fact, in some instances the pressure to "separate and individuate" may cause unnecessary stress to the couple. However, lesbian couples are a distinctly heterogeneous group, so for some lesbian couples, the emphasis on connectedness and prioritizing the relationship may be seen as a strength in congruence with normal female development, while for others separation and individuation may be more comfortable. Surrey (1985) suggests that it need not be an either-or situation, as lesbian partners might be both extremely close and highly differentiated, representing a kind of "individuation-in-relation." Occasionally, high degrees of interpersonal connection can have a negative impact on the relationship leading to intrusiveness, including high separation anxiety, possessiveness, and jealousy (Green & Werner, 1996). The job of the clinician is to assess the characteristics of the connection and determine whether from the client's perspective it appears to be problematic, rather than starting from an assumption that intense connection is pathological.

Case Example 1

Karen, age forty-five, has been with her partner, Sylvia, age forty-eight, for the past twenty-three years. In the past few years, since her retirement, Sylvia's drinking has become problematic, and thus far, her attempts to get sober have failed. Karen and Sylvia have come to therapy because Karen is angry and frustrated by Sylvia's active alcoholism and the toll it is taking on their relationship. Karen's siblings and friends have encouraged her to leave Sylvia but she wants to stay in the relationship. She says, "Sylvia is my family. She is all I have; I could never abandon her." She feels confused and uncertain about what to do. Karen was especially reluctant to come to therapy as she did not want to be told to leave the relationship (which she had been told in previous individual treatment encounters).

Although psychoanalysts may understand the tendency for lesbian couples to be highly identified with one another as related to women's greater skill at connection (Chodorow, 1978), other factors may be involved. Homophobia and stigmatization of lesbian relationships may also contribute to the fusion some couples experience. Intense connection may be an attempt to insulate the relationship in defense against oppression, lack of support from family, or lack of legal validation (Krestan & Bepko, 1980; Nichols, 2004; Spitalnick & McNair, 2005). So, along with assessing the couples' comfort and satisfaction with their level of closeness, the social worker should also assess the function that the closeness is serving for the couple. It may be that it provides insulation against an actual or perceived hostile social environment, in which case developing other social supports with the couple may be a key piece of your work.

Certainly, problems between partners can arise when each partner has different expectations and varying degrees of comfort with closeness, intimacy, and separation. Social workers treating lesbian couples should carefully assess the couples' satisfaction with their connection or separation and identify whether it is mutually agreeable for each member of the couple. Problems with fusion may not be about closeness or distance; they may be about differing expectations within the couple. If problems are related to dissatisfaction with levels of closeness or dependence, it is possible that the excessive dependence of one partner creates unmet needs for the other partner. Social workers should help clients to achieve more equal power within the relationship to recalibrate the balance of power (van Wormer et al., 2000).

TRIANGULATION AS A SYMPTOM OF FUSION

Although nonclinical samples of lesbians report satisfaction with high levels of cohesion within the relationship, couples presenting in therapy are experiencing some difficulty, which may be related to regulating their levels of closeness and distance. Bowen (1978) identifies triangulation as one of the potential responses to fusion (in addition to emotional distance, unresolved conflicts, and physical or mental dysfunction) (Green et al., 1996). Therefore, while triangulation may occur in any relationship, it may be especially prevalent in lesbian relationships. Triangulation provides the individual with a way of defending against fusion, a reaction against the fear of loss of self, a way of regulating distance between partners (Decker, 1984), and creating a demand-withdrawal interaction pattern within the relationship (Martell & Prince, 2005). A range of people may be triangled into the relationship including children, friends, family members, sexual partners, and work associates (Decker, 1984; Green et al., 1996). In some cases, something other than a person may be triangled in, for example, alcoholism, a job or a pet. The third person (or object) serves to provide relief from the stress of the overwhelming, all-consuming connection. It is an attempt to create distance and reclaim autonomy. Although triangulation can occur in all relationships it may be more common for lesbians because the boundaries of the relationship are not as clearly delineated by society, and so are often more diffuse. Without the respect of society for the couple's relationship it becomes easier for a third person to get pulled in. Within heterosexual marriage, social recognition of the couple's boundary is intact. Case Example 2 illustrates a case where triangulation is the symptom of the presenting problem.

Case Example 2

Andrea, twenty-nine, and Sam, twenty-seven, have come to couples therapy because "we are just not getting along like we used to." Andrea and Sam met in the military and they have been living together for five years. This first serious relationship for both has been generally satisfying and positive, with both women enjoying their connection and spending much of their time together. They believe that both their families know about the relationship although it has never been directly spoken about. In the first session, Sam reveals that she is incredibly angry about the friendship Andrea has recently developed with another woman at work. Andrea claims that she is not having an affair but is also unwilling to terminate the friendship with this woman.

DEVELOPMENT OF THE RELATIONSHIP:
WHAT IS A HEALTHY LESBIAN RELATIONSHIP?

As lesbian relationships have historically been invisible and invalidated, there are few models as to what a healthy lesbian relationship looks like. The absence of social markers such as marriage, gender role expectations, and expectations of having children bring richness, creativity, and challenges to lesbian relationships (Slater & Mencher, 1991). As there are few role models, lesbian couples generally improvise and develop their own normative relationship dynamics (Decker, 1984; Spitalnick & McNair, 2005). Because there are not many predetermined roles in the couple and parenting relationship, there is more freedom to create a relationship that works for that particular couple.

Lesbians couples have been portrayed historically in media and literature as needing to ascribe to "butch/femme" roles in order to complement each other (Laird, 1993). Peplau (1991) found that rigid power differentials and the contrast of masculine and feminine roles were actually not the norm in most lesbian couples. Not only do lesbian relationships tend to be more egalitarian and report more sex role undifferentiated behavior (Blumstein & Schwartz, 1983; Peplau, 1991; Spitalnick & McNair, 2005; Sue & Sue, 2003), women in egalitarian relationships tend to report higher levels of satisfaction (Peplau, Padesky, & Hamilton, 1982). Lesbians and gay men also demonstrate more flexibility around gender roles than heterosexuals, and lesbians report more satisfaction with flexibility (Green et al., 1996). Using a measure of overall closeness, lesbians also reported the highest levels of cohesion compared to heterosexual and gay male couples (Green et al., 1996).

However, with more role ambiguity and freedom can also come some confusion. In working with lesbian couples, the worker will want to help each partner share her fantasies and expectations about the relationship, as each partner may have very different ideas as to what the relationship will look like. There may also be some confusion or ambiguity about how to define the relationship. Heterosexual couples have marriage to signify each person's commitment to the relationship, whereas lesbian and gay couples may use a number of different events, such as moving in together or merging finances, to signify varying degrees of seriousness (Laird, 1993). Mencher and Slater (1993) note the importance of ritual in successfully navigating the life cycle, and that the absence of these rituals, at least publicly, can result in a sense of illegitimacy. As the relationship is not sanctioned in the same way as heterosexual relationships, there may be some difficulty in defining the rules. As lesbian couples do not always undergo the same social rituals to signify their movement from dating to marriage (Krestan & Bepko, 1980), the worker may need to help them verbalize their feelings about their commitment to one another and how they wish to acknowledge it. It may be that a couple has different symbols of commitment over time, for example, moving in together, then a large joint purchase (e.g., a couch), then a joint checking account, then a property purchase, and then creating a family. It may be that they choose to have a ceremony to acknowledge their relationship to their friends and family or that they choose to acknowledge these markers only to themselves. Either way, the therapist can provide a safe space for the couple to explore their desires around commitment and may act as a witness for the couple to validate their experience.

In response to a paucity of material illustrating developmental patterns of lesbian relationships, Slater (1995) proposed a five-stage model of the lesbian family life cycle, incorporating developmental tasks and stage-related issues. Clunis and Green (1988) also offer a six-stage model of lesbian relationships that can provide some structure or guidelines for couples desiring a deeper understanding of their relationship life cycle. The models incorporate those issues, transitions, and tasks faced by any long-term couple while also addressing the added components of the stress related to coming-out and seeking external validation for the couplehood.

Lesbian couples have generally been free to create relationships that are devoid of patriarchal power structures and generally experience greater gender role flexibility.

However, as the gay rights movement fights for the right to marry and to parent, some lesbian couples, at least in urban areas, are beginning to experience more pressure and expectations from within the community to "marry" and have children (Glazer, personal communication, 2006). As parenting becomes more expected and accessible, lesbians may start to experience some of the same conflicts as heterosexual women, for example, giving up financial autonomy or their career to parent, or feeling that parenting is a developmental imperative (Glazer, 2001). Parenting may inevitably lead to necessary shifts in the division of labor, and more traditional, highly defined roles within the partnership (e.g., "breadwinner" versus "stay-at-home mom").

Identity Development and Partnership

Case Example 3

Jenny, twenty-three, and Tanisha, twenty-six, came to couples therapy because Tanisha is frustrated that Jenny will not come out to her parents. They have been in a relationship for three-and-a-half years, and living together for the past two. Both Jenny and Tanisha report overall satisfaction with the relationship, but acknowledge that Jenny's lack of disclosure to her family is a major source of conflict. Tanisha is unhappy because she feels that Jenny is ashamed of her and their relationship, and she feels discounted when she is left out of the stories that Jenny tells her family and friends on the phone. The situation intensifies and conflict increases when Jenny's parents visit town. Furniture and photographs have to be moved to "de-gay" the apartment, and Tanisha finds the stress of it all overwhelming. Tanisha says that she is very much in love with Jenny but is not willing to continue to put herself in this position.

Although certainly every couple has its own developmental path, each individual is in the midst of her own individual developmental process as well. In lesbian couples, it is not unusual for partners to be at different stages of development, particularly around coming-out, and there are implications of an individual's development on the couple's overall function and happiness (as in Case Example 3). The degree to which a person is "out" will affect her interactions with her family, support network, and other relevant systems and have consequences for the relationship. When one partner feels particularly shameful about being a lesbian or when one partner is not out to significant people in her life, the relationship may feel stunted and stressful, leaving partners feeling invisible and undervalued (Sue & Sue, 2003). In fact, being out to family is related to higher levels of relationship satisfaction (Berger, 1990), while higher levels of support from friends and family are related to healthier psychological adjustment and better relationship quality (Kurdek & Schmitt, 1987).

There are often tremendous legal and social incentives for heterosexual couples to stay together. However, for lesbians, without legal and social support, the relationship may be prone to dissolution (Decker, 1984). The opposite reaction may also occur when the relationship does not have support of friends and family; it may cause partners to turn inward in response to oppression, resulting in added pressure on the partners to maintain the relationship on their own. Similarly, when a relationship does end, grieving the relationship can be complicated since the relationship was not valued in the first place.

After the U-Haul: Lesbian Bed Death!

Following rapidly after the U-Haul joke mentioned earlier is usually one about lesbian bed death: the notion that sex leaves lesbian relationships after a relatively short period. However, there is uneven evidence as to whether this notion is true. Some reports indicate that sexual activity decreases earlier in lesbian relationships than in gay or heterosexual relationships (Spitalnick & McNair, 2005). However, whereas Nichols (2004) found that women having sex with women had sex slightly less than women having sex with men, they did report having sex about once a week, which, as she notes, hardly represents being "sexually abstinent" (p. 368).

As with all things, women have a range of different experiences, with some couples having very active sex lives and others choosing other types of intimate connection. To the extent that there are lower levels of sexual activity in lesbian couples, several factors may be at work. One factor contributing to reduced sexual activity in lesbian couples is associated with the degree of fusion within the relationship. It is suggested that a key function of sex within relationships is to create intimacy. With such a high degree of connection already present within female relationships, it is argued that sex is less necessary and may even be redundant (Nichols, 1990). In fact, it has even been suggested that the closeness in lesbian relationships is so intense that it feels familial or sisterly, and therefore sex might feel incestuous.

A second factor contributing to reduced sexual expression in lesbian couples may be internalized homophobia, which can generate feelings of shame and guilt about being gay (Downey & Friedman, 1995). Internalized homophobia can generate feelings of self-hatred, which may serve to block sexual expression or promote the belief that they are unworthy of sexual pleasure.

A third factor in the reduced frequency of sexual activity in lesbian couples may be related to the fact that assertiveness is not socially sanctioned for women. Peplau (2003) noted that in general women reported lower rates of sexual activity, lower libido, and less sexual assertiveness than men. Therefore, it makes logical sense that when two women are coupled the lack of a male with a higher sex drive and greater assertiveness reduces the frequency of sexual contact. Since women are socialized to be less assertive than men (Spitalnick & McNair, 2005), lesbian sexuality may be reduced because of an inability on the part of one or both partners to initiate otherwise desired sexual activity (Blumstein & Schwartz, 1983).

In cases in which a lesbian couple reports dissatisfaction with the frequency of sexual encounters it may be important to work on issues of assertiveness and to encourage one or both partners to work on being comfortable with initiating sexual contact. It is also important not to confuse quantity of activity with quality of activity and with sexual satisfaction. As Nichols (2004) notes, "lesbian sexual activity may exemplify sex that is more tailored to women's sexual needs—longer in duration, including nongenital as well as genitally focused acts, more varied sexual acts, and more reliably resulting in orgasm" (p. 369). Therefore, workers should explore the couples' satisfaction with both the quantity and quality of their sexual encounters.

Although evidence does suggest that women in general and lesbians in particular have reduced levels of sexual activity when compared with men, social trends in younger generations toward greater sexual fluidity and sexual freedom are being played out within the lesbian community as well (Nichols, 2004). Sex clubs for lesbians have emerged, along with lesbian-run or lesbian-friendly sex shops in a number of cities and online (e.g., the Pleasure Chest and Toys in Babeland). In addition, there has been an increase in the number of lesbian erotica books that have been published, and those which have been written specifically about lesbian sex in an effort to demystify and desensitize the subject (see the Alyson Books list of lesbian erotica and the Good Vibrations sex guides). It is important for the therapist working with lesbians either individually or as a couple to become familiar with some of these resources, so that they can be explored and recommended to clients. Conveying gay-affirming sex-positive messages plays an important role in creating a safe and open space for clients to explore their sexual concerns. Therapists should work with couples to address internalized homophobia, explore new role possibilities, and expand their sexual repertoires.

CO-MOTHERING

Case Example 4

After four years together, Linda and Cynthia, both Asian, decided to have a baby via artificial insemination. When Cynthia was four months pregnant, Linda decided to tell her family that they were having a baby. Despite having appeared somewhat tolerant of their partnership, Linda's mother became outraged at the idea of two women parenting a baby together, telling Linda, "that baby will be no grandchild of mine. I am ashamed of you and what you've become." Since the birth of the baby, Linda and Cynthia have gotten tremendous support from friends, but have had no communication from Linda's family. Although she is extremely happy to be a mother, she feels tremendous sadness and grief about her mother's rejection.

Increasingly, lesbian couples are making decisions to raise children together. Prior to the 1990s, most children raised in lesbian-headed households had been born into heterosexual marriages before their mothers divorced and came out. Although the reported desire to have children is the same for lesbians as it is for heterosexual women (Kirkpatrick, Smith, & Roy, 1981), in the past fifteen years, we have seen the progression of the "lesbian baby boom," as more lesbians see childbearing and child rearing *within lesbian relationships* (or as single parents) as viable options.

Lesbian couples coming to therapy may be struggling with a number of challenges related to deciding whether or not to have children. Even when both partners want to have a child, therapists ought to encourage them both to talk about their expectations and fears. As with heterosexual couples, the partners may feel differently about having a child and need to work hard to understand each other's feelings and desires. If a partner decides to forgo having a child in order to maintain the relationship, she will have to grieve that loss (Martin, 1993). Embedded in a patriarchal culture, psychoanalytic theory suggests that mentally stable and "mature" women naturally want to have children, and conversely, women who do not want to have children or be pregnant are developmentally stunted. On the contrary, we would argue that choosing not to parent (as opposed to being excluded from the option) is a courageous decision running against social pressure. Therefore, lesbian-affirmative therapists need to support a woman's decision not to have children or not to be pregnant.

For lesbian couples that decide to have a child, there are a number of decisions, each loaded with its own implications and meanings, which lesbian couples have to make that differ from heterosexual couples. Will they adopt or will one of the partners become pregnant through artificial insemination?

If so, how do they decide who will carry the baby? Will they use a known donor or an anonymous donor, and what are the implications of each on the family structure they envision? If they choose a donor whose identity is known, to what extent, if any, do they want that person to be involved in the child's life?

Most lesbian couples deciding to have a child will grapple with what it means to raise a child who may be teased or ostracized because of having gay parents. Although it is true that children of gay and lesbian parents are often teased by peers, the same is true for children who come from any type of family that can be labeled as "different": poor, disabled, and racially mixed (Lewis, 1980). Most major cities have support groups for lesbian moms, lesbians who want to be parents, and children of gay and lesbian parents (such as Children of Lesbians and Gays Everywhere [COLAGE]), and certainly these support groups, along with multiple online communities, can allow couples and families to feel supported.

Just like all families, lesbian-headed families may struggle with issues of parenting, and the strain of raising children can have an impact on the relationship. When a baby enters the picture, the family structure shifts from dyadic to triadic (or greater), complicating interpersonal dynamics (Crespi, 2001). Like all new parents, each partner may feel slightly abandoned, as they have less attention and energy for each other. When one mother is doing the bulk of the nurturing (perhaps staying at home or breastfeeding), the other parent may feel left out. Most families struggle with meeting the needs of all three people in the triangle (Martin, 1993). In blended families, there will be questions about how to integrate a new partner (and perhaps children from a previous relationship) into the family and what "step-parenting" role will that partner have?

However, there are a number of unique dynamics and additional stressors to be considered when working with lesbian-headed families. Whereas a couple may have been selective about when and to whom to come out, depending on how emotionally and physically safe they felt, coming-out has different implications once children are present. Parents may lose control of when to come out, as children indiscriminately yell for two mommies in public (Newfield, 2006). It may also force extended family to come out—if they want to acknowledge their new relative. In some cases, as in Case Example 4, the addition of children may make a daughter's lesbian orientation or partner more difficult to overlook, causing friction or even rejection. Martin (1993) suggests that being open about being lesbian parents will ease the degree of stress for all family members and that denying sexual orientation may send a message to children that their family is something to be ashamed about.

Lesbian and gay families also have to contend with a number of legal concerns that are cause for anxiety and stress. Only eight states recognize second-parent adoption where the nonbiological mother is afforded the same rights and responsibilities as the biological parent. A further eighteen states have had second-parent adoption rulings or county-specific recognition. In states without second-parent adoptions, the nonbiological parent has very few rights and she is not perceived as being the "real" mother. In some states, lesbians can still be denied custody, adoption, or foster parenting because of their sexual orientation. Progress has been made in this area, particularly in the area of fostering and adopting, but lesbian and gay families are still not afforded the legitimacy necessary to ensure the protection of their children (Martin, 1993; Newfield, 2006).

In addition to coming-out and legal concerns, lesbian-headed families also experience additional stress because of the lack of role models and support. Despite evidence to the contrary, the social power of negative myths attributed to gay and lesbian parents (e.g., children will be damaged by growing up in a gay home, lesbians and gays molest children) place additional pressure on these women to prove they can be good parents (Patterson, 1992).

Whereas some heterosexual people become parents more passively because that is what is expected of them, lesbians wanting to be parents have to put tremendous effort and intention into their decision. Their persistence and dedication to create a family that is congruent with their internal sense of self and identity is reflective of strengths that can be drawn upon throughout therapy.

IMPACT OF SEXUAL ABUSE ON LESBIAN COUPLES

Case Example 5

Tanya and Margie are both African-American women in their mid-thirties who have been together for one and a half years. Tanya has a history of incest by her uncle and consequently finds it difficult to be sexual with her partner. She masturbates frequently but experiences disturbing flashbacks when her partner touches her in certain ways. Margie is at a loss as to what to do since she wants to have empathy and patience for her partner's experience and healing, yet feels guilty about having her own sexual needs which are not being met. When Margie voices her desire for sexual intimacy, Tanya feels pressured and withdraws.

As women are more likely to be victims of sexual abuse and sexual assault, and both partners of a lesbian relationship are by definition women, it is likely that at least one of the partners may bring to the relationship a history of sexual trauma. Estimates vary but suggest that between 20 and 38 percent of women have experienced childhood sexual abuse, and 3 to 44 percent have experienced sexual violence (Hall, 1996; Hughes, Johnson, & Wilsnack, 2001). For lesbians, the prevalence may be even higher as two comparison studies found significantly higher rates of childhood sexual abuse in lesbians than in heterosexual women (Hughes, Haas, Razzano, Cassidy, & Mathews, 2000; Hughes et al., 2001). In a national sample, 29 percent of lesbians reported having been sexually abused as children (Descamps, Rothblum, Bradford, & Ryan, 2000).

Dealing with the impact of sexual abuse on an adult relationship can be challenging for all couples, however, there are again some factors that are unique to addressing a history of abuse in lesbian couples. First, common lore often suggests that childhood sexual abuse by a male perpetrator is what causes lesbianism, a conjecture that pathologizes sexual orientation as being rooted in trauma. However, evidence does suggest that there is a connection between identity and trauma, but that being lesbian, and, perhaps more significantly, not adhering to traditional female gender presentation, may make both children and adults more susceptible to verbal, physical, sexual, and emotional abuse (Hetrick & Martin, 1987).

Many survivors of sexual abuse deal with issues of trust, sexual intimacy, shame, secrecy, guilt, and isolation. For women whose lesbian identity is also associated with issues of shame and secrecy, these issues may be magnified. Survivors of abuse are forced by family members to disavow part of their experiences and their selves in much the same way that lesbian and gay people are. Particularly if the client believes that her identity was formed as a result of the trauma, the degree of internalized homophobia and resulting shame may be exacerbated (Kerewsky & Miller, 1995).

Kerewsky and Miller (1995) suggest that conceptualizing the trauma as the third point of the triangulation with a couple can be helpful as a means of externalizing the problem and also acknowledging a "third presence" in the relationship. Much like heterosexual couples, sexual intimacy may be an issue in the relationship. Extremes of sexual aversion or sexual compulsion are often viewed as a person's means of addressing the sexual abuse (whether conscious or unconscious) (Bass & Davis, 1994). As women are socialized to believe that their sexual needs are not important and are not taught to give voice to their sexual interests, lesbian couples may have particular difficulty in discussing the ways in which the sexual abuse of one or both partners is interfering in their sexual connection (Hall, 1999; Kerewsky & Miller,

1995). A further complication that workers may also need to be aware of are the ways in which the partner who has experienced abuse may project feelings of either being re-perpetrated against or unprotected to her partner (Kerewsky & Miller, 1995). Such projected feelings can create very difficult dynamics within the couple's sexual relationship that need careful exploration in session.

DOMESTIC VIOLENCE IN LESBIAN COUPLES

Domestic violence within lesbian couples has been a difficult topic to address for a number of reasons. First, feminists who posed the argument that domestic violence was created by power, privilege, and patriarchy in order to raise awareness of it were afraid that incidences of abuse between two women would threaten their premise and weaken their argument (Morrow & Maxhurst, 1989). Second, lesbians are reluctant to acknowledge the presence of abuse for fear of drawing negative attention to relationships that are already viewed as dysfunctional (van Wormer et al., 2000). Third, the lesbian community will not relinquish its idealized view of lesbian relationships (Morrow & Maxhurst, 1989), and, fourth, there is a belief that women are not violent because they have been socialized to be less aggressive than men (Morrow & Maxhurst, 1989; Steinhorn, 1998).

Despite the reluctance to acknowledge domestic violence within the lesbian community, a beginning literature and research is establishing definitions and illustrating the scope of the problem (Elliot, 1996; Farley, 1996; Helfrich & Simpson, 2006; Lobel, 1986; Morrow & Maxhurst, 1989; Peterman & Dixon, 2003; Steinhorn, 1998; van Wormer et al., 2000). An oft-cited definition of lesbian battering established by Hart (1986) is "that pattern of violent and coercive behaviors whereby a lesbian seeks to control the thought, beliefs or conduct of her intimate partner or to punish the intimate for resisting the perpetrator's control over her" (p. 173).

As with all domestic violence, the private nature of the event and the reluctance of the abused to come forward results in underreporting and a limited understanding of the scope of the problem. However, the problem is exacerbated by fear of homophobia for the lesbian who has been abused. Although research suggests that heterosexual men are more likely to be abusive than lesbians, reports indicate that between 22 and 46 percent of all lesbians or between 25 and 33 percent of all same-sex relationships have been involved in domestic violence (Elliott, 1996; Peterman & Dixon,

2003). Such evidence suggests that social workers should carefully assess issues of power and control within the couple and be aware of symptoms that reflect post-traumatic stress disorder (PTSD) in one of the partners (Steinhorn, 1998). A thorough history for abuse in family relationships is also important, as strong links have been found between female perpetrators of domestic violence and a history of physical and sexual abuse (Farley, 1996).

Silence about domestic violence within lesbian couples has perpetuated feelings of isolation, guilt, and shame for the survivors. The silence has also kept services limited and prevented women from receiving the help that they need. Social workers can play a vital role in raising awareness and in developing lesbian sensitive trauma services, including support groups and shelters. (For suggestions and resources, see Helfrich & Simpson, 2006.)

CONCLUSION

Since there is not one set of uniform federal rights that apply to lesbian couples, it is important for social workers to become familiar with any applicable federal or state laws which may affect their clients. The social worker should become familiar with laws surrounding health benefits, health care proxies, advanced directives, living wills, inheritance, adoption, second-parent adoption, immigration, and property purchase. Working with couples to create legal protection for their relationship, their family, and their property can be a very validating experience for the couple. Advocating for state and federal policy changes to create laws providing greater protection for lesbian couples and their families is also a crucial intervention that social workers can provide.

We have presented both the traditional psychoanalytic understanding of lesbian couples and the feminist reaction to those models. We have emphasized the importance of allowing the couple to identify the presenting problem from their perspective rather than immediately rushing to pathologize dynamics which may be associated with dysfunction in some circumstances, but may represent satisfying connection in others. Lesbian couples do not have socially sanctioned milestones to navigate, providing room for creativity on the one hand but confusion on the other. Helping couples to define their milestones and providing an outside validation for their relationship are the important roles of the social worker.

REFERENCES

Bass, E., & Davis, L. (1994). *The courage to heal* (3rd ed.). New York: Harper Collins.

Berger, R. (1990). Passing: Impact on the quality of same-sex relationships. *Social Work, 35*(4), 328-332.

Berzoff, J. (1990). Fusion and women's friendships: Implications for expanding our adult development theories. *Women and Therapy, 8,* 93-107.

Blumstein, P., & Schwartz, P. (1983). *American couples: Money, work, sex.* New York: William Morrow.

Bowen, M. (1978). *Family therapy in clinical practice.* Northvale, NJ: Aronson.

Chodorow, N. (1978). *The reproduction of mothering: Psychoanalysis and the sociology of gender.* Berkeley, CA: University of California Press.

Clunis, D., & Green, G. (1988). *Lesbian couples.* Seattle: Seal Press.

Crespi, L. (2001). And baby makes three: A dynamic look at development and conflict in lesbian families. In D. Glazer & J. Drescher (Eds.), *Gay and lesbian parenting* (pp. 131-151). Binghamton, NY: The Haworth Press.

Decker, B. (1984). Counseling gay and lesbian couples. *Homosexuality and Social Work, 2*(2-3), 39-52.

Descamps, M., Rothblum, E., Bradford, J., & Ryan, C. (2000). Mental health impact of child sexual abuse, rape, intimate partner violence, and hate crimes in the national lesbian health care survey. *Journal of Gay and Lesbian Social Services, 11*(1), pp.27-56.

Downey, J., & Friedman, R. (1995). Internalized homophobia in lesbian relationships. *Journal of the American Academy of Psychoanalysis, 23,* 435-447.

Eldridge, N., & Gilbert, L. (1990). Correlates of relationship satisfaction in lesbian couples. *Psychology of Women Quarterly, 14,* 43-62.

Elliott, P. (1996). Shattering illusions: Same-sex domestic violence. *Journal of Gay and Lesbian Social Services, 4*(1), 1-8.

Erikson, E. (1968). *Identity: Youth and crisis.* New York: Norton.

Fairbairn, W. R. D. (1952). *Object relations theory of personality.* London: Tavistock.

Farley, N. (1996). A survey of factors contributing to gay and lesbian domestic violence. *Journal of Gay and Lesbian Social services, 4,* 35-42.

Feldman, L. (1979). Marital conflict and marital intimacy: An integrative psychodynamic-behavioral-systemic model. *Family Process, 18*(1), 69-78.

Gilligan, C. (1982). *In a different voice: Psychological theory and women's development.* Cambridge, MA: Harvard University Press.

Glazer, D. (2001). Lesbian motherhood: Restorative choice or developmental imperative. In D. F. Glazer & J. Drescher (Eds.), *Gay and lesbian parenting* (pp. 221-242). Binghamton, NY: The Haworth Press.

Green, R.-J., & Werner, P. (1996). Intrusiveness and closeness-caregiving: Rethinking the concept of family "enmeshment." *Family Process, 35*(2), 115-136.

Green, R.-J., Bettinger, M., & Zacks, E. (1996). Are lesbian couples fused and gay male couples disengaged? In J. Laird & R. J. Green (Eds.), *Lesbians and gays in couples and families: A handbook for therapists* (pp. 185-230). San Francisco: Jossey-Bass.

Hall, J. (1999). An exploration of the sexual and relationship experiences of lesbian survivors of childhood sexual abuse. *Sexual and Marital Therapy, 14*(1), 61-70.

Hall, J. M. (1996). Pervasive effects of childhood sexual abuse in lesbians' recovery from alcohol problems. *Substance Use & Misuse, 31*(2), 225-239.

Hart, B. (1986). Lesbian battering: An examination. In K. Lobel (Ed.), *Naming the violence: Speaking out about lesbian battering* (pp. 173-189). Seattle: Seal Press.

Helfrich, C., & Simpson, E. (2006). Improving services for lesbian clients: What do domestic violence agencies need to do? *Health Care for Women International, 27*(4), 344-361.

Hetrick, E., & Martin, A. (1987). Developmental issues and their resolution for gay and lesbian adolescents. *Journal of Homosexuality, 14,* 25-43.

Hughes, T., Johnson, T., & Wilsnack, S. (2001). Sexual assault and alcohol abuse: A comparison of lesbians and heterosexual women. *Journal of Substance Abuse, 13*(4), 515-532.

Hughes, T. L., Haas, A. P., Razzano, L., Cassidy, R., & Matthews, A. (2000). Comparing lesbians' and heterosexual women's mental health: A multi-site survey. *Journal of Gay and Lesbian Social Services, 11*(1), 57-76.

Jordan, J. (1986). *The meaning of mutuality* (Work in Progress No. 23). Wellesley, MA: Stone Center Working Paper Series.

Jordan, J. (1997). A relational perspective for understanding women's development. In J. Jordan (Ed.), *Women's growth in diversity* (pp. 142-161). New York: The Guilford Press.

Kaufman, P., Harrison, E., & Hyde, M. (1984). Distancing for intimacy in lesbian relationships. *American Journal of Psychiatry, 141,* 530-533.

Kerewsky, S. D., & Miller, D. (1995). Lesbian couples and childhood trauma: Guidelines for therapists. In J. Laird & R. J. Green (Eds.), *Lesbians and gays in couples and families: A handbook for therapists* (pp. 185-230). San Francisco: Jossey-Bass.

Kernberg, O. (1976). *Object-relations theory and clinical psychoanalysis.* New York: Jason Aronson.

Kirkpatrick, M., Smith, C., & Roy, R. (1981). Lesbian mothers and their children: A comparative survey. *American Journal of Orthopsychiatry, 51,* 545-551.

Krestan, J., & Bepko, C. (1980). The problem of fusion in the lesbian relationship. *Family Process, 19,* 277-289.

Kurdek, L., & Schmitt, J. (1987). Perceived emotional support from family and friends in members of homosexual, married, and heterosexual cohabiting couples. *Journal of Homosexuality, 14,* 57-68.

Laird, J. (1993). Lesbian and gay families. In F. Walsh (Ed.), *Normal family processes* (2nd ed., pp. 282-230). New York: Guilford Press.

Laird, J., & Green, R.-J. (1996). *Lesbians and gays in couples and families: A handbook for therapists.* San Francisco: Jossey-Bass.

Lewis, K. (1980). Children of lesbians: Their point of view. *Social Work, 25*(3), 203.

Lobel, K. (1986). *Naming the violence: Speaking out about lesbian battering.* Seattle: Seal Press.

Loulan, J. (1988). Research on the sex practices of 1,566 lesbians and the clinical applications. *Women and Therapy, 7,* 221-234.

Mahler, M. (1975). *The psychological birth of the human infant: Symbiosis and individuation.* New York: Basic Books.

Martell, C., & Prince, S. (2005). Treating infidelity in same-sex couples. *Journal of Clinical Psychology/In Session, 61*(11), 1429-1438.

Martin, A. (1993). *The lesbian and gay parenting handbook: Creating and raising our families.* New York: HarperCollins.

McCandlish, B. M. (1982). Therapeutic issues with lesbian couples. *Journal of Homosexuality, 7*(2/3), 71-78.

Mencher, J. (1990). *Intimacy in lesbian relationships: A critical re-examination of fusion* (Stone Center Working Paper Series, No. 42). Wellesley, MA: Wellesley College Stone Center for Women's Development.

Mencher, J. (1997). Intimacy in lesbian relationships: A critical re-examination of fusion. In J. Jordan (Ed.), *Women's growth in diversity* (pp. 221-237). New York: The Guilford Press.

Miller, J. B. (1976). *Toward a new psychology of women.* Boston: Beacon Press.

Morrow, S., & Maxhurst, D. (1989). Lesbian partner abuse: Implications for therapists. *Journal of Counseling and Development, 68,* 58-62.

Newfield, N. A. (2006.) The second coming out. *Social Work Today, 6*(3), 8-9.

Nichols, M. (1990). Lesbian relationships: Implications for the study of sexuality and gender. In D. McWhirter, S. Sanders, & J Reinisch (Eds.), *Homosexuality/ heterosexuality: Concepts of sexual orientation* (pp. 351-363). London: Oxford University Press.

Nichols, M. (2004). Lesbian sexuality/female sexuality: Rethinking "lesbian bed death." *Sexual and Relationship Therapy, 19*(4), 363-371.

Patterson, C. (1992). Children of lesbian and gay parents. *Child Development, 63,* 1025-1042.

Peplau, L. (1991). Lesbian and gay relationships. In J. C. Gonsiorek & J. D. Weinrich (Eds.), *Homosexuality: Research implications for public policy* (pp. 177-196). Newbury Park, CA: Sage publications.

Peplau, L. (2003). Human sexuality: How do men and women differ? *Current Directions in Psychological Science, 12*(2), 37-40.

Peplau, L., Padesky, C., & Hamilton, M. (1982). Satisfaction in lesbian relationships. *Journal of Homosexuality, 7*(2), 23-37.

Peterman, L., & Dixon, C. (2003). Domestic violence between same-sex partners: Implications for counseling. *Journal of Counseling and Development, 81*(1), 40-48.

Roth, S. (1989). Psychotherapy with lesbian couples: Individual issues, female socialization and the social context. In M. McGoldrick, C. Anderson, & F. Walsh (Eds.), *Women in families: A framework for family therapy* (pp. 286-305). New York: W.W. Norton & Company, Inc.

Slater, S. (1995). *The lesbian family life cycle.* New York: The Free Press.

Slater, S., & Mencher, J. (1991). The lesbian family life cycle: A contextual approach. *American Journal of Orthopsychiatry, 61*(3), 372-382.

Spitalnick, J. S., & McNair, L. D. (2005). Couples therapy with gay and lesbian clients: An analysis of important clinical issues. *Journal of Sex & Marital Therapy, 31,* 43-56.

Steinhorn, A. (1998). Individual practice with lesbians. In G. Mallon (Ed.), *Foundations of social work practice with lesbian and gay persons* (p. 129). Binghamton, NY: The Haworth Press.

Sue, D. W., & Sue, D. (2003). *Counseling the culturally diverse: Theory and practice* (4th ed.). New York: John Wiley & Sons, Inc.

Surrey, J. (1985). *Self-in-relation: A theory of women's development* (Work in Progress No. 13). Wellesley, MA: Stone Center Working Paper Series.

Van Wormer, K., Wells, J., & Boes, M. (2000). *Social work with lesbians, gays and bisexuals*. Boston: Allyn & Bacon.

Vetere, V. (1982). The role of friendship in the development and maintenance of lesbian love relationships. *Journal of Homosexuality, 8*(2), 51-65.

Chapter 9

Social Work Practice with Gay Couples

L. Donald McVinney

Gay male couples are highly diverse. Various social and historical conditions combine with constructs of eroticism, gender, and intimate relationships to create the rich constellations of gay male couples. These include, but are not restricted to, variations of ethnicity, race, class, models of coupling (such as exclusivity versus nonexclusivity; see LaSala, 2001, 2002, 2004a,b), heterosexually married gay men with extramarital gay relationships, and noncohabiting partnerships (Kurdek, 1998, 2006), longitudinal stage of development, age discrepancies, and a cohort of gay identity and coupling formation (Kurdek, 2004). Thus, gay male couples must be conceptualized as subcategories within a broader frame of social relations and are not identical to heterosexual couples in structure or form.

Just as it becomes difficult to make unifying statements about gay male couples without stereotyping, generalized descriptions of the difficulties that motivate gay male couples to seek social work services is also problematic. Gay male couples may engage in couples counseling for as many reasons as any other subgroup (Bepko & Johnson, 2000). However, it may be hypothesized that, similar to their heterosexual counterparts, the majority of gay male couples initiate couples therapy to reduce relational conflict and stabilize the coupling system.

Although tentative, some preliminary remarks can be offered concerning content issues that are expressed by gay male couples requesting social work intervention. These content issues may be influenced by process dynamics inherent in partnerships of two people of the same masculine gender embedded within a nongay culture (McWhirter & Mattison, 1984, 1985, 1998;

Social Work Practice with LGBT People

McVinney, 1998). Common issues of gay male couples involved in couples work may include the following:

1. Conflicts associated with differences in stage levels of being "out" about their gay identity
2. HIV health status concerns
3. Conflicts associated with internalized homophobia
4. Conflicts associated with differences in extended family involvement
5. Conflicts associated with differences in constructions and expectations of coupling
6. Conflicts associated with differences in age
7. Conflicts associated with differences in expectations of sexual exclusivity/nonexclusivity
8. Conflicts associated with perceived inequalities of power and difficulty in negotiating
9. Conflicts associated with chemical use, chemical dependency, and recovery
10. Conflicts associated with finances and financial disparity

An understanding of presenting issues for gay male couples is greatly enhanced by the social worker's attention to interactions of (1) gay male clients' experience of social oppression, (2) issues of male gender role socialization, and (3) the gay male coupling structure. This chapter will address process dynamics and structural variations as they apply to the issues of internalized homophobia, heterosexism, and gay identity development in gay male couples. Through an exploration of these factors, it is hoped that social workers can be assisted in formulating interventions that are specific to gay male couples.

Social work practice with gay male couples is an outgrowth of a family systems perspective (Carl, 1990; Goldenberg & Goldenberg, 1990; Rothberg & Weinstein, 1996). However, family systems theory has limitations. Besides the theoretical tendency to focus on larger systems and less on the two-person system, McGoldrick (1996) notes that most family systems theory and family systems practitioners have traditionally been heterocentric. There is a paucity of attention to gay male couples in the literature, or including gay male couples within the definition of a family, until very recently.

Although gay male practitioners with large numbers of gay male clients have always provided services to gay male couples, the emerging literature among family systems theorists has arisen less because of their own spontaneous enlightenment than because of the increasing empowerment of gay male couples. As consumers, gay male couples are demanding equal rights to access mental health services. In their efforts to define the dominant meaning of "family," the radical right and conservative, fundamentalist Christian movement's interjection into national political discourse of definitions of a family in an effort to redefine "traditional family values" has resulted in an oppositional discourse by gay and lesbian families, including gay male couples, who have become more political in advocating for their needs (Hartman, 1996). The increasing insistence that political movements hostile to gay men and lesbians will not define their partnering as anything less than equal to heterosexual couples has become a political issue that has moved increasingly into the legislative arena where, at the time of this writing, several states in the United States are considering the legal recognition of gay marriages. Although this larger political discussion is outside of the parameters of this article, it is helpful for social workers to remember that policy issues impact directly on the lives of the clients they serve and may be the underlying causal factor as to why clients seek services.

Gay male couples can be seen by social work providers in all health and mental health care settings in which there is a social work presence, such as

1. hospitals or outpatient clinics, either mainstream (public and private) or health clinics that are gay/lesbian/bisexual/transgender specific;
2. organizational or industrial settings;
3. private or independent practice offices;
4. social services agencies, for instance, those serving young people or senior citizens;
5. HIV/AIDS services organizations;
6. mainstream or gay/lesbian/bisexual/transgender community centers;
7. schools and academic settings;
8. counseling centers; or
9. chemical dependency treatment programs.

Although gay male clients are seen in all of these settings, their sexual identity may remain invisible unless attended to and supported by the social work provider (Butler, 2000; Rothberg & Weinstein, 1996). Initially, gay men may seek services as individuals and then the gay male partner may be introduced into the practice setting. Gay male couples may also directly present as a couple seeking counseling services. Unfortunately, the assessment of clients' needs may be largely determined by the setting—for instance, residential or community based, the mission of the agency or institution, the theoretical orientation of the supervisor or department head, or the license under which the agency operates (mental health or substance abuse)—rather than client generated. Intervention strategies and outcome goals will largely follow from the initial and ongoing assessment (Meyer, 1993).

INTERNALIZED HOMOPHOBIA, HETEROCENTRISM, AND GAY IDENTITY

Although the concepts of internalized homophobia, heterocentrism, and gay identity are covered elsewhere in this collection, the redundancy here is intentional as these concepts have particular bearing on and particular significance for the gay male couple. Homophobia can be defined as the irrational fear of gay/lesbian people. Internalized homophobia is defined as "the taking in or internalization of society's negative attitudes and assumptions about homosexuality by gays and lesbians" (Bozett & Sussman, 1990, pp. 337-338). Negative beliefs and attitudes about homosexuality and gay men are naturally absorbed in a heterosexist and homophobic culture by gay and straight people alike. For gay men, however, the effects of this internalization are particularly pernicious (Biery, 1990; Isensee, 1991; Malyon, 1985; Weinberg, 1972). Internalized homophobia has been implicated as the cause for significantly higher rates of chemical dependency in the gay/lesbian community (Eliason, 2000; Finlon, 2002; Finnegan & McNally, 1987, 2002), gay/lesbian adolescent suicide (D'Augelli et al., 2005; Savin-Williams, 1990), low self-esteem and social isolation, and difficulties in establishing or maintaining intimate relationships among gay men (LaSala, 2006).

Socially constructed negative attitudes and myths about gay men are easily identified and include the following:

1. Most gay men are effeminate.
2. Most gay males in relationships adopt passive/active sexual and gender roles.
3. All gay men are sexually promiscuous.
4. Gay men believe they are women trapped in men's bodies.
5. Most gay men would have a sex change operation if they could.
6. Most gay men are child molesters.
7. Most gay people are miserable, lonely, and psychologically disturbed.
8. Gay relationships never last.
9. Gay identity is unnatural.
10. Gay identity affects a minute segment of the population.

These stereotypes and negative attitudes must be shed by gay men before they can develop a sense of pride and positive self-image. While most prejudicial statements concerning "gayness" may be consciously rejected by those successfully formulating a gay identity, some are less consciously perceived. Unconscious beliefs of personal failure, unhappiness, relational impermanence, or unrecognized beliefs in heteronormative constructions of "natural" may be especially detrimental to gay male identity and coupling.

Problems regarding internalized homophobia are described by Forstein (1986, p. 114), who writes, "Although many gay people aspire to 'couple-hood,' their capacity to function and grow within the context of an intimate relationship is significantly determined by the degree to which a positive self-affirming gay identity has been formed." Isay (1989, p. 92) argues that gay men establishing intimate relationships have, at least in part, integrated a healthy gay identity. He writes, "The capacity [for gay men] to fall in love and to maintain a healthy relationship over time requires a high degree of self-esteem, or 'healthy narcissism'. . . . Only a man with a healthy sense of self-esteem can feel capable of being loved and of loving." It may be hypothesized that a minimal level of self-acceptance must exist before a gay man might even entertain the notion of same-sex relational involvement, but this does not imply that internalized homophobia is absent in even the healthiest of gay male relationships as a consequence of growing up within the dominant heterosexist culture.

Heterosexism may be defined as the blatant cultural disavowal of the validity of same-sex desire and coupling. While internalized homophobia describes the absorption of negative social attitudes, heterosexism creates the social structure of gay invisibility. Describing this phenomenon, Blumenfeld and Raymond (1988, p. 244) state:

> When parents automatically expect that their children will marry a person of the other sex at some future date and will rear children within this union; when the only possible and satisfying relationships portrayed by the media are heterosexual; when teachers presume all of their students are straight and teach only about the contributions of heterosexuals—these are examples of heterosexism. It takes the form of pity—when the dominant group looks upon sexual minorities as poor unfortunates who "can't help being the way they are."

Heterosexism is institutionalized in the United States through the lack of national legal protection for gay men and lesbians. Same-sex behavior in over half of the states remains illegal, and gay men and lesbians are predominantly excluded from protection regulating housing discrimination, fair employment practices, immigration, child custody rights, adoption, inheritance, security clearance, approved participation in the military, and police protection. Gay male relationships are not open to legal recognition, denying same-sex couples the economic advantages of marriage. Perhaps most profound, however, is the lack of rituals, models, sanctioned boundaries, and cultural support for gay coupling, making explicit society's view that gay male relationships are not "real," or equal to those of heterosexuals (Meyer, 1990).

The lack of societal support for gay male relationships is often painfully brought home through the intolerance or disrespect of family members toward a gay son's partner. Some parents and siblings may respond favorably to one's relationship. However, for almost all gay men, coming out to parents and relatives in regard to one's same-sex relationship is a time of significant stress. The importance of coming-out and being out to parents for gay male couples is documented by LaSala (2000). McWhirter and Mattison (1984), in their study of gay male couples, found that the majority of their subjects did not have full family support or participation. They reported:

> Many have a warm relationship with one set of parents and no relationship with the other. In other cases the families are unaware of or disregard their son's sexual orientation. These men return to their respective homes at holiday times and on other occasions of family celebrations without their partners. (p. 240)

A lack of familial support for gay relationships may weigh heavily upon the couple. Expectations of continuing family of origin involvement and the maintenance of prior family roles may persist, promoting relational conflict and stress. Family rejection may reinforce internalized homophobia and may also color perceptions of self and relational value. For others, family rejection may promote a profound sense of isolation.

COUPLING DYNAMICS

McWhirter and Mattison's (1984, 1985, 1988) monumental work on gay male couples presents a stage model that is longitudinal and is conceptualized as an aid in describing and understanding male couples formation. McWhirter and Mattison's work emphasizes stages of gay male coupling. "Stage One" dynamics are characterized by high limerance (compatibility) and cohesion. As the relationship becomes more reality-based and conflicts surface, the couple may begin to withdraw from each other. They suggest that fear of intimacy in "Stage One" couples may also promote emotional with-drawal. Should couples survive this process, "Stage Two" issues and themes occur. "Stage Two" is described as a period when passion declines and con-flict is based on differences in values and tastes. McWhirter and Mattison also suggest that "Stage Two" couples must begin to address the issue of ex-clusivity/nonexclusivity, and jealousy or possessiveness is common. Prob-lems in "Stage Three" center around increased needs for autonomy and the concomitant experience of loss of early romanticism, with independent functioning by one member of the couple often perceived as a threat gener-ating anxiety or anger. "Stage Four" is depicted as "a time of considerable distancing from each other." In "Stage Five," after ten to twenty years to-gether, "routine and monotony" become causes of distress for gay male couples. McWhirter and Mattison (1988, p. 250) write that the "tendency to become more fixed or rigid in personality characteristics while struggling to change each other can also plague men who have been together over ten years." Couples in "Stage Six" reportedly express feelings of "restlessness, sometimes withdrawal and feelings of aimlessness," often as a function of the attainment of both individual and coupling goals.

McWhirter and Mattison's stage theory of gay male coupling seems to overemphasize structural disengagement and open coupling dynamics for all but those engaged in early coupling formation. However, recognizing that gay male couples vary according to life transitions and understanding the different relational stages are both crucial to normalizing conflicts in gay couples, allowing for an appreciation of differences, conflicts, or dis-satisfactions to be more a function of stage sequence, rather than inherent to the relationship.

Whereas an assessment of stage development is essential to appropriate descriptions of gay male couples, it too must be linked to the effects of inter-nalized homophobia. Couple formation requires the creation and mainte-nance of boundaries (Johnson & Keren, 1996). The level of permeability of boundaries may be influenced by that which is perceived as threatening to the couple. Couples may react to anticipated or actual responses of familial rejection, peer indifference to the meaning of partnership, and/or internal-ized negativity by producing closed coupling systems as an attempt to ex-clude social hostility and fortify the "bonds of love." Thus, this style of coupling may be understood as an adaptive reaction to cultural conditions. The greater the level of perceived threat, the more closed a relationship may become. Yet closed coupling systems generate tremendous pressure on the couple, making partners feel responsible for fulfilling the majority of the other partner's needs. Without cultural sanctions against coupling dissolu-tion, or social support to reduce relational pressures, gay male couples may move from markedly enmeshed to disengaged to dissolved to newly formed and enmeshed relationships.

Alternatively, internalized homophobia may promote highly disengaged coupling styles as a consequence of the absorbed devaluing of same-sex intimacy. Gay male couples who adopt a "best friend" or "roommate" model of coupling may establish extremely loose relational boundaries (open relational style) as a manifestation of social/familial hostility, or internalized and unconscious attitudes concerning the "impossibility" of gay male relations. In extreme forms, the disconnectedness of highly open boundaries (closed relational style) makes relational involvement irrelevant, again potentiating coupling dissolution.

While neither open nor closed relational styles, in themselves, are indicative of future relational failure, the level of adaptability of these systems to respond to conflict becomes crucial. Both chaotic and rigid coupling styles may lack the skills to alter relational patterns in order to address conflicts arising from or occurring within extreme forms of open or closed systems. Again, coupling adaptability may be influenced by internalized homophobia. For those who once sought and anchored themselves to societal rules as a means of avoiding exposure, suppressing desire, or "fitting in," rigidity may become a way of life. Forstein (1986, p. 113) states, "The more conflicted a gay man is about his homosexuality, the more rigid and stereotyped his gender role identity is likely to be." For others, maintaining chaotic decision-making styles may allow for an avoidance of commitment, initiated by an earlier avoidance to commit to a gay identity and lifestyle. Although structural paradigms are always affected by parental modeling, this does not preclude the importance of homophobia in influencing structural dynamics in gay male couples.

Other theorists have focused on issues of sexuality and sexual dysfunction in gay male couples. Shernoff, in his notable work with gay male couples, presents a classification system in which he examines a variety of relationship styles (Shernoff, 1995). He develops five categories with which to define male couples:

1. The sexually exclusive couple
2. The sexually nonexclusive but unacknowledged open relationship
3. The primarily sexually exclusive relationship
4. The sexually nonexclusive and acknowledged open relationship
5. Nonsexual lovers

While Shernoff's model has grown out of his extensive work with gay men and gay male couples, this model may have limitations to a social work practitioner who has had fewer opportunities to work with gay male couples. Practitioners may find themselves, in using this model, which constructs gay male coupling around sexuality and sexual behaviors, unwittingly presuming that sex is the exclusive area around which gay men partner. To an unseasoned or nongay practitioner, this model may reproduce the stereotype about gay male identity and gay male coupling as defined primarily by their sexuality. For a more recent discussion of the topic of monogamous versus nonmonogamous relationships in gay male couples, see LaSala's (2001, 2004a,b) work. In another important contribution to the literature on gay male couples, George and Behrendt (1988) suggest that sexual dysfunction in one or both partners may produce stress on the couple, and they state that, anecdotally, many gay male couples are never asked about this. They hypothesize that this is due to a provider's lack of comfort with the subject or their misperception that gay male couples do not experience sexual dysfunction. They break out the concept of sexual dysfunction into three areas: (1) inhibited sexual desire, (2) inhibited male orgasm, and (3) inhibited sexual excitement. Inhibited sexual desire, they suggest, may be caused by either internalized cultural homophobia or a phobic aversion to sex in general. Inhibited orgasm may also be due to internal conflicts related to homophobia or sexual fantasies of aggression and the fear of loss of control. Finally, inhibited sexual excitement is considered a result of discrepant views of masculinity perpetuated by society, which results in the belief that their performance is being "graded" by their partner, leading to inhibition.

MALE GENDER ROLE SOCIALIZATION

It has been argued (Finnegan & McNally, 1987, 2002; Johnson & Keren, 1996; Mass, 1990) that gay men, like heterosexual men, are socialized to behave according to culturally determined gender patterns. Although some gay men may believe themselves to have rejected conditioning associated with socially determined masculine role norms, heterosexually prescribed masculine values are often latent. These values may include themes of power and control. Although any relationship, regardless of gender and sexual orientation, must address these issues, male socialization, in its emphasis on winning and competition, makes male intimacy especially problematic.

In addition to problems associated with masculine identity, any subgroup that has been culturally marginalized or disempowered is be more likely to act out their social repression through intimate relationships. This may be particularly salient in gay men, where attempts at self-control over one's same-sex desires in early stages of gay identity formation and fears of exposure are apparent. Cabaj (1991, p. 2), in regard to help seeking in gay men, states, "Since men, in general, and gay men who are struggling to accept their homosexuality, in particular, have difficulties with intimacy and sharing, they may seek help to learn how to communicate about and be comfortable with intimacy." Thus, the manifestation of power dynamics interrupting the potential for intimate relations in gay male couples may be more a function of internalized homophobia rather than, or exclusively, masculine gender socialization. This social hypothesis would also predict that the observation of issues of power and control in gay male couples may be more extreme in those less integrated in their gay male identities and community.

JOINING

Before couples counseling can become solution focused, the social worker must join with the couple in a therapeutic alliance. This requires that the social work practitioner is perceived as both nonjudgmental and supportive of the couple. For many gay male couples, suspicion on the part of helping professionals and the profession of social work in general due to homophobia may predict the delay or avoidance of initiating treatment. There is a history in the mental health profession of viewing homosexuality as psychopathological with curative therapies existing to treat the condition (Isay, 1989). According to George and Behrendt (1988, p. 78), "Homosexual men will seek therapy when they recognize they are having difficulties as a couple, provided that (1) identifying themselves as a couple is not precluded by discriminatory practices by the therapist, and (2) they are not treated as if their homosexuality were the cause of their conflict." Similar to other minority populations, gay male couples integrated into the gay male community may be more likely to turn to friends in times of crisis as opposed to social work practitioners because of fears of provider prejudice (Hines & Boyd-Franklin, 1982), as well as gender socialization concerning male attitudes of self-sufficiency and the rationalization of feelings (Isensee, 1990).

Should services be sought, however, gay male couples are often particularly sensitive to bias on the part of the social work provider. Many gay male couples will only contact gay or lesbian therapists to avoid potential insensitivity. For gay male clients engaging in treatment with someone unknown to the lesbian/gay community, direct questioning by the social worker about homosexuality and personal sexual orientation is common. Such questioning, however, could lead to initial engagement problems as an inquiry process by the therapist may cause stress for the clients who may feel resentful that they have had to "educate" the therapist about gay couples. In addition, some gay male couples may feel reluctant to question the therapist and, instead, maintain an initial suspension of trust. Without direct attention to issues of trust, sexual orientation, and respect for differences between heterosexual providers and gay male clients, treatment progress and, at the very least, the initial engagement process may be significantly impaired.

The issue of trust for gay male couples working with heterosexual providers is magnified for couples experiencing problems of internalized homophobia. Couples struggling with culturally absorbed negativity may project these attitudes onto the social work practitioner. However, it should be understood that initial defensive posturing may be expressed by any gay male couple engaging in the services of heterosexual or gay providers and would not reveal unusual coupling dynamics.

Self-disclosure by gay male social work practitioners is essential in counseling gay male couples due to role modeling and self-empowerment (Kooden, 1991). Gay male couples who seek the services of a gay male practitioner who refuses to acknowledge his sexual orientation for reasons of professional "neutrality" may perceive the practitioner's decision as problematic and often as a homophobic practice in reproducing the psychosocial stressors of the closet.

ASSESSING PRESENTING CONCERNS

The assessment of presenting concerns by clients and social workers is filtered by both theory and unconscious assumptions. Social work practitioners working with gay male couples must continuously assess countertransferential dynamics influencing the perceptions of the couple, as well as interpretations and interventions. One must be particularly careful about attributing coupling dynamics to internal dysfunctioning, rather than attending to the social and systemic conditions influencing relational patterns. Normalizing and refraining coupling conflict through attributions of stage level, heterosexism, internalized homophobia, structural paradigm, and gender socialization often provide gay male couples with an opportunity to avoid blaming the self and partner for problems. This will in turn provide the clients and the practitioner with a working alliance by the provider communicating that he or she understands the unique conditions affecting the gay male couple and is not interested in pathologizing them.

INTERVENTIONS

Systems theory and intervention act to reestablish relational homeostasis through conflict resolution without presenting dysfunctional symptoms. This requires an analysis of communication patterns, triangles, hierarchies, roles, and boundaries (Carl, 1990). Although systems theory makes irrelevant the sexual orientation of the couple, some systems providers may be biased in their approach to gay male couples. For example, therapists working with couples with one or both partners having HIV/AIDS may discourage multiple sexual contacts, regardless of the couple's valuing of nonexclusive sexual involvements. This may stem from a belief that nonexclusivity interferes with coupling intimacy, or as a reaction to fears of HIV transmission (Goldenberg & Goldenberg, 1990; Odets & Shernoff, 1995). A second example of provider bias is the devaluing of relational role definition by social workers imposing the personal values of role fluidity. These examples of provider bias reflect a superimposition of heteronormativity onto individual gay couples, rather than respecting a diversity of coupling styles. Given the dearth of information and training on systemic interventions with gay male couples, provider bias is somewhat understandable. However, it behooves social work practitioners to appreciate the values and uniqueness of any couple with whom one works.

Case Illustration

Tom and David were self-referred for couples work with presenting concerns of emotional disengagement on Tom's part, described by David, and Tom stating that he wasn't sure he was capable of "loving anyone." Through the assessment process, it was learned that Tom and David had been together for three years. According to McWhirter and Mattison's (1984) stage model, they were reacting within the context of the "Nesting Stage," with common difficulties of developing compatibility, and dealing with relational ambivalence after the initial "blending" period. They reported nonsexual relations for six months, and Tom heatedly reported finding David to be using Internet chat rooms and Webcam sites on the computer with increasing regularity. David felt sympathetic toward Tom, but was unsure if he could assure Tom that he could discontinue this behavior. David also reported that their initial sexual life together had been the best he had ever known, but over the past year he felt he had just "lost interest." This loss of coupling eroticism and sexuality appeared to be related to a period of significant stress and depression for David during a job change. It was at that time that David had become increasingly withdrawn.

David reported that his relationship with Tom was his first gay relationship, whereas Tom had had one prior partner of six years. Tom reported that the relationship had ended for many of the same reasons he felt David and himself were experiencing difficulties: lack of emotional and sexual contact, problems communicating, and the feeling that David "just didn't care." The latter issue was further reinforced by David's recent trip home for the holidays, leaving Tom behind because he was not "out" to his parents. Tom expressed some understanding of David's reluctance to come out to his parents who are devoutly religious, but with further exploration bitterly complained about David's disregard for his needs.

As the couple was informed of the normality of their conflicts as a function of coupling development, they visibly relaxed. However, when it was also suggested that both David and Tom were contributing to their relational problems, rather than David alone, Tom became increasingly anxious. Yet this also facilitated the exploration of Tom's occasionally demanding attitude and lack of empathy regarding David's emotional concerns, which in turn left David to fend for himself and led both partners to become increasingly angry and polarized.

Over time, it was discovered that David's sexual difficulty with Tom was largely a function of internalized homophobia. They both began to explore their histories of shame surrounding their desires and came to realize how both partners had a share in the problem of closeness. These discussions produced a depth of intimacy between them previously unrealized and soon they began, tentatively, to return to their prior sexual involvement. While Tom and David continue to address communication problems and a tendency to disengage when stressed, they have been able to solidify their partnership through support. Their acceptance of the social worker's interventions was founded upon the worker's respect for the couples' strengths, validation of their homoerotic and intimacy needs, and theoretical appreciation of both gay-specific and general systems dynamics impacting upon coupling development.

IMPLICATIONS FOR SOCIAL WORK PRACTICE

Ecologically oriented social workers who are interested in working with gay couples should be prepared to consider the following:

- As one undertakes an assessment process, the basis for the referral or the presenting problem must be prioritized and respected, rather than any predetermined agenda on the part of the social work provider (Compton & Galloway, 1989; Hepworth & Larsen, 1990; Meyer, 1993). It is important to remember that gay male couples may be somewhat reserved during an initial contact until it has been established that the provider is accepting of the couple's sexual orientation and non-judgmental with regard to their concerns.

- Environmental stressors often precipitate relational distress and can lead to maladaptive coping by one or by both members of the couple. Responses to environmental stressors need to be appreciated within the context of the unique strengths, histories, and needs of each member of any gay male partnership.
- In addition to assessing the unique characteristics of the couple, social work practitioners should be trained in general systems theory, gay male coupling, and gay male developmental dynamics, as well as becoming knowledgeable about social and cultural factors impacting upon gay men. Unless comfortable with this knowledge base, it is recommended that the provider make an appropriate referral.
- Practitioners need to address levels of internalized homophobia within each partner. Due to internalized homophobia, heterosexism, and negative media depictions of gay men, gay males in a couple may believe that relationships are difficult or impossible to sustain and may also believe that they should define their relationships around their sexual behavior, gender constructions, or cultural stereotypes rather than discovering the meaning of their own partnership. It is often very helpful to assist gay couples in analyzing these belief systems and how they may negatively affect their relationships.
- Practitioners should assess at what stage each partner and the relational system is in the coming-out process. George and Behrendt (1988) identify the coming-out process as unfolding in three ways: (1) acknowledgment of one's own self as gay (private admission); (2) acknowledging one's identity to other people and building a support system; and (3) acknowledging one's sexual orientation to co-workers, relatives, and heterosexual friends, which can be considered a high risk for rejection. All of these may produce significant stress for the couple.
- Practitioners need to assess the extent of social supports. Many gay male couples stop socializing within gay male communities, finding support from each other. During crises, they may experience social isolation. Gay male couples in crisis may need to expand social networks.
- Depending on prior negative experiences with people in positions of authority, including social service providers, homophobia may be anticipated and projected onto the provider. Unless these transferential issues are addressed, progress in treatment may be greatly compromised.

- HIV/AIDS and other sexually transmitted diseases have significantly affected gay men. Social work practitioners need to reassure clients about confidentiality and inquire about HIV fears, exposures, infection, diagnosis of AIDS, and problems related to HIV medications. Just as individual gay men will require interventions that are differentiated across the HIV continuum (HIV ignorance and ongoing high-risk behavior, HIV untested, HIV negative, HIV positive and asymptomatic, HIV symptomatic, diagnosed with AIDS, terminally ill and dying as a result of AIDS), so too will gay male couples require differentiated interventions depending upon each partner's HIV status. (Cadwell, Burnham, & Forstein, 1994; Carl, 1990; Livingston, 1995, 1996; Odets & Shernoff, 1995). Given the reported higher rates of chemical dependency among gay men, assessment of substance use, abuse, and dependency, and referrals to gay-affirmative treatment programs is essential (Finnegan & McNally, 1987, 2002; Faltz, 1988, 1992; Greene & Faltz, 1991; Neisen, 1997; Ratner, 1988; Weinberg, 1994).

CONCLUSION

Social work practice with gay male couples within an ecosystemic perspective has similarities to work with nongay couples as well as distinctions from heterocentric interventions and heterosexist treatment. Effective interventions with gay male couples requires an appreciation of the interactions among cultural oppression, coupling dynamics, and individual development. Most important, social work practice with gay male couples mandates a respect for intimate unions in any form.

REFERENCES

Bepko, C., & Johnson, T. (2000). Gay and lesbian couples in therapy: Perspectives of the contemporary therapist. *Journal of Marital and Family Therapy, 26*(4), 409-420.

Biery, R. E. (1990). *Understanding homosexuality. The pride and the prejudice.* Austin, TX: Edward-William Publishing Company.

Blumenfeld, W. J., & Raymond, D. (1988). *Looking at gay and lesbian life.* Boston: Beacon Press.

Bozett, R W., & Sussman, M. B. (Eds.) (1990). *Homosexuality and family relations.* Binghamton, NY: The Haworth Press.

Butler, A. C. (2000). Trends in same-gender sexual partnering, 1988-1998. *Journal of Sex Research, 37*(4), 333-343.

Cabaj, R. P. (1991, April). Counseling gay couples. *FOCUS: A Guide to AIDS Research and Counseling, 6*(5). San Francisco, CA: UCSF AIDS Health Project.

Cadwell, S. A., Burnham, R. A., & Forstein, M. (Eds.) (1994). *Therapists on the front line. Psychotherapy with gay men in the age of AIDS*. Washington, DC: American Psychiatric Press.

Carl, D. (1990). *Counseling same-sex couples*. New York and London: W.W. Norton and Company.

Compton, B. R., & Galloway, B. (1989). *Social work processes* (4th ed.). Belmont, CA: Wadsworth Publishing Company.

D'Augelli, A. R., Grossman, A. H., Salter, N. P., Vasey, J. J., Starks, M. T., & Sinclair K. O. (2005). Predicting the suicide attempts of lesbian, gay, and bisexual youth. *Suicide and Life-Threatening Behavior, 35*(6), 646-660.

Eliason, M. J. (2000). Substance abuse counselor's attitudes regarding lesbian, gay, bisexual, and transgendered clients. *Journal of Substance Abuse, 12*(4), 311-328.

Faltz, B. G. (1988). Substance abuse and the lesbian and gay community: Assessment and intervention. In M. Shernoff & W. Scott (Eds.), *The sourcebook on lesbian and gay health care* (2nd ed., pp. 151-161). Washington, DC: National Lesbian and Gay Health Foundation.

Faltz, B. G. (1992). Counseling chemically dependent lesbians and gay men. In S. H. Dworkin & F. J. Gutierrez (Eds.), *Counseling gay men and lesbians: Journey to the end of the rainbow* (pp. 245-258). Alexandria, VA: American Counseling Association.

Finlon, C. (2002). Substance abuse in lesbian, gay, bisexual, and transgender communities. *Journal of Gay & Lesbian Social Services, 14*(4), 109-123.

Finnegan, D. G., & McNally, E. B. (1987). *Dual identities: Counseling chemically dependent gay men and lesbians*. Center City, MN: Hazelden.

Finnegan, D. G., & McNally, E. B. (2002). *Counseling lesbian, gay, bisexual, and transgender substance abusers*. Binghamton, NY: The Haworth Press.

Forstein, M. (1986). Psychodynamic psychotherapy with gay male couples. In T. S. Stein & C. J. Cohen (Eds.), *Contemporary perspectives on psychotherapy with lesbians and gay men* (pp. 103-137). New York and London: Plenum Medical Book Company.

George, K. D., & Behrendt, A. E. (1988). Therapy for male couples experiencing relationship problems and sexual problems. In E. Coleman (Ed.), *Integrated identity for gay men and lesbians: Psychotherapeutic approaches for emotional well-being* (pp. 77-88). Binghamton, NY: The Haworth Press.

Goldenberg, H., & Goldenberg, I. (1990). *Counseling today's families*. Pacific Grove, CA: Brooks/Cole Publishing Company.

Greene, D., & Faltz, B. (1991). Chemical dependency and relapse in gay men with HIV infection: Issues and treatment. In M. Shernoff (Ed.), *Counseling chemically dependent people with HIV illness* (pp. 79-90). Binghamton, NY: The Haworth Press.

Hartman, A. (1996). Social policy as a context for lesbian and gay families: The political is personal. In J. Laird & R-J. Green (Eds.), *Lesbians and gays in couples and families: A handbook for therapists* (pp. 69-85). San Francisco: Jossey-Bass.

Hepworth, D. H., & Larsen, J. A. (1990). *Direct social work practice* (3rd ed.). Belmont, CA: Wadsworth Publishing Company.

Hines, P. M., & Boyd-Franklin, N. (1982). Black families. In M. McGoldrick, J. K. Pearce, & J. Giordano (Eds.), *Ethnicity and family therapy* (pp. 84-107). New York and London: Guilford Press.

Isay, R. A. (1989). *Being homosexual: Gay men and their development.* New York: Avon Books.

Isensee, R. (1990). *Love between men: Enhancing intimacy and keeping your relationship alive.* New York: Simon and Schuster.

Isensee, R. (1991). *Growing up gay in a dysfunctional family: A guide for gay men reclaiming their lives.* New York: Prentice Hall.

Johnson, T. W., & Keren, M. S. (1996). Creating and maintaining boundaries in male couples. In J. Laird & R.-J. Green (Eds.), *Lesbians and gays in couples and families: A handbook for therapists* (pp. 231-250). San Francisco, CA: Jossey-Bass.

Kooden, H. (1991). *Self-disclosure: The gay male therapist as agent of social change.* In C. Silverstein (Ed.), *Gays, lesbians, and their therapists* (pp. 143-154). New York: W.W. Norton.

Kurdek, L. A. (1998). Relationship outcomes and their predictors: Longitudinal evidence from heterosexual married, gay cohabiting, and lesbian cohabiting couples. *Journal of Marriage and Family, 60*(3), 553-568.

Kurdek, L. A. (2004). Are gay and lesbian cohabiting couples really different from heterosexual married couples? *Journal of Marriage and Family, 66*(4), 880-900.

Kurdek, L. A. (2006). Differences between partners from heterosexual, gay, and lesbian cohabiting couples. *Journal of Marriage and Family, 68*(2), 509-528.

LaSala, M. C. (2000). Gay male couples: The importance of coming out and being out to parents. *Journal of Homosexuality, 39*(2), 47-71.

LaSala, M. C. (2001). Monogamous or not: Understanding and counseling gay male couples. *Families in Society, 82*(6), 605-611.

LaSala, M. C. (2002). Walls and bridges: How coupled gay men and lesbians manage their intergenerational relationships. *Journal of Marital and Family Therapy, 28*(3), 327-339.

LaSala, M.C. (2004a). Extradyadic sex and gay male couples: Comparing monogamous and non-monogamous relationships. *Families in Society, 85*(3), 405-412.

LaSala, M. C. (2004b). Monogamy of the heart: Extradyadic sex and gay male couples. *Journal of Gay & Lesbian Social Services, 17*(3), 1-24.

LaSala, M. C. (2006). Cognitive and environmental interventions for gay males: Addressing stigma and its consequences. *Families in Society, 87*(2), 181-190.

Livingston, D. (1995). Group counseling for gay couples coping with AIDS. In W. Odets & M. Shernoff (Eds.), *The second decade of AIDS: A mental health practice handbook* (pp. 69-84). New York: Hatherleigh Press.

Livingston, D. (1996). A systems approach to AIDS counseling for gay couples. In M. Shernoff (Ed.), *Human services for gay people: Clinical and community practice* (pp. 83-93). Binghamton, NY: The Haworth Press.

Malyon, A. K. (1985). Psychotherapeutic implications of internalized homophobia in gay men. In J. C. Gonsiorek (Ed.), *A guide to psychotherapy with gay and lesbian clients* (pp. 59-690). Binghamton, NY: The Haworth Press.

Mass, L. D. (1990). *Homosexuality and sexuality: Dialogues of the sexual revolution* (Vol. 1). Binghamton, NY: The Haworth Press.

McGoldrick, M. (1996). Foreword. In J. Laird & R.-J. Green (Eds.), *Lesbians and gays in couples and families: A handbook for therapists* (pp. xi-xiv). San Francisco, CA: Jossey-Bass.

McVinney, L. D. (1998). Social work practice with gay male couples. In G. P. Mallon (Ed.), *Foundations of social work practice with lesbians and gay persons* (pp. 209-228). Binghamton, NY: The Haworth Press.

McWhirter, D. P., & Mattison, A. M. (1984). *The male couple: How relationships develop*. Englewood Cliffs, NJ: Prentice-Hall.

McWhirter, D. P., & Mattison, A. M. (1985). Psychotherapy for gay male couples. In J. C. Gonsiorek (Ed.), *A guide to psychotherapy with gay and lesbian clients* (pp. 79-91), Binghamton, NY: The Haworth Press.

McWhirter, D. P., & Mattison, A. M. (1988). Stage discrepancy in male couples. In E. Coleman (Ed.), *Integrated identity for gay men and lesbians: Psychotherapeutic approaches for emotional well-being* (pp. 89-99). Binghamton, NY: The Haworth Press.

Meyer, C. H. (1993). *Assessment in social work practice*. New York: Columbia University Press.

Meyer, J. (1990). Guess who's coming to dinner this time? A study of gay intimate relationships and the support for those relationships. In F. W. Bozeit & M. B. Sussman (Eds.), *Homosexuality and family relations* (pp. 59-82). Binghamton, NY: The Haworth Press.

Moses, A. E., & Hawkins, R. O., Jr. (1986). *Counseling lesbian women and gay men: A life-issues approach*. Columbus, OH: Merrill Publishing Company.

Neisen, J. H. (1997). An inpatient psychoeducational group model for gay men and lesbians with alcohol and drug abuse problems. In L. D. McVinney (Ed.), *Chemical dependency treatment: Innovative group approaches*. Binghamton, NY: The Haworth Press.

Odets, W., & Shernoff, M. (Eds.) (1995). *The second decade of AIDS: A menial health practice handbook*. New York: Hatherleigh Press.

Ratner, E. (1988). Treatment issues for chemically dependent lesbians and gay men. In M. Shernoff & W. Scott (Eds.), *The sourcebook on lesbian and gay health care* (2nd ed., pp. 162-168). Washington, DC: National Lesbian and Gay Health Foundation.

Rothberg, B., & Weinstein, D. L. (1996). A primer on lesbian and gay families. In M. Shernoff (Ed.), *Human services for gay people: Clinical and community practice* (pp. 55-68). Binghamton, NY: The Haworth Press.

Savin-Williams, R. C. (1990). *Gay and lesbian youth: Expressions of identity,* Washington, DC: Hemisphere.

Shernoff, M. (1995). Male couples and their relationship styles. *Journal of Gay & Lesbian Social Services, 2*(2), 43-57.

Weinberg, G. (1972). *Society and the healthy homosexual.* Garden City, NY: Anchor Press/Doubleday.

Weinberg, T. S. (1994). *Gay men, drinking, and alcoholism.* Carbondale and Edwardsville, IL: Southern Illinois University Press.

Chapter 10

Group Work Practice with LGBTQ People

Mitchell Rosenwald

Social group work is a very positive and optimistic way of working with people. It is truly empowering and affirming of people's strengths. In fact, the very act of forming a group is a statement of belief in people's strengths and in the contribution that each person can make to others' lives. In today's troubled world, effective group work is needed more than ever.

Kurland and Salmon (1998, p. ix)

This quote from Kurland and Salmon highlights the power of group work as well as the importance and relevance for social workers to conduct group work with clients within the communities social workers serve. For this chapter, the "community" references individuals who identify as lesbian, gay, bisexual, transgender, and/or questioning (LGBTQ). As LGBTQ individuals comprise a significant minority of the individuals we work with, it is essential to have a sense of the issues that this community faces and may be relevant in the particular members' lives. Group work as a modality in social work relies on the assumption that the nature of the group is a powerful tool that provides support and promotes change for the individuals who comprise it as well as the group as a whole. Therefore, combining group work practice with this population has the promise of empowering LGBTQ individuals, assisting them with working through challenges and problems, and celebrating their successes.

Social Work Practice with LGBT People

This chapter begins with a review of the current literature on the state of group work practice with individuals who are LGBTQ. Particular issues and diversity considerations relevant to specific populations are highlighted. It continues with a discussion of a central concept in group work—mutual aid—and mutual aid's ability to promote these groups. It concludes with two case vignettes that are relevant to the LGBTQ population and details sample exchanges among members, including commentary about mutual aid's dynamics within the interaction.

PERSPECTIVES ON GROUP WORK WITH LGBTQ INDIVIDUALS

Before we begin, it is important to distinguish between the LGB and the T and Q. Although there is some overlap between the two with respect to societal oppression, "LGB" relates to *sexual orientation* (including affective and sexual attraction, fantasy, and behavior components) while the "T" focuses on meaning and expressions of *gender identity*. "Q" can stand for the *questioning* which refers to individuals who are still exploring their sexual orientation or gender identity, as well as serving as an umbrella term of "queer," a term that has been reclaimed by some as a label of empowerment.

It is important to note that "intersex" (where a person is born with chromosomes and genitalia that are both male and female) and "two spirit" (a Native American conception wherein individuals are endowed spiritually with the attributes of female and male gender, though not necessarily gay or lesbian) are other components of gender diversity.

Whether social workers facilitate a group that is particularly for an identified LGBTQ population (or subpopulation) or are working with a different client group in which an individual identifies from within the LGBT community, familiarity with the issues that might emerge within the group is very important. Equally important is for the social worker to examine her or his own countertransference toward this population, identify where she or he is in regard to identity development with the varying subpopulations of this population, and work toward strengthening competencies. Finally, skill in general group work principles, including a solid working knowledge and skill in mutual aid (to be discussed), promises to promote success in conducting group work with individuals who are LGBTQ.

Although the place of group work in social work's history dates as far back as 1861 (Schwartz, 1985), the first groups for "homosexuals," in the mid-1950s to the early 1970s, focused on pathology and conversion (Conlin & Smith, 1982). In the early 1980s, groups that focused on empowering gay and lesbian individuals began to appear (Conlin & Smith, 1982), representing a paradigmatic shift. The authors share a model of helping gay men "come out" and advocate for its inclusion in mental health service delivery. Morston and McInnis (1986) describe a "coming out" group from the mid-1980s in which individuals gradually felt comfortable with their sexual orientation; these groups included exploring identity and providing resource information. Other early research on AIDS prevention groups was conducted in 1984 (Flowers et al., 1991).

It is heartwarming to know that more research has been conducted on the character of group work and the array of issues that emerge with LGBTQ populations since the time that Getzel (1998) wrote about group work with lesbians and gay men in the first edition of this text. Such group work with this population continues to occur in a variety of settings, including community settings, family service agencies, mental health clinics, and universities.

POTENTIAL ISSUES TO EXPLORE IN GROUP WORK

The following issues and challenges may emerge among clients in a group when working with the LGBTQ population. When clients join a group, the social worker should be familiar with these issues. This familiarity will assist the social worker in conducting group and individual assessment, contracting for group work, establishing the purpose of the group, the type of group that it will be (e.g., support, socialization, education, therapy, and growth [Toseland & Rivas, 2005]), and, as always, with preparation for relevant themes that might emerge in the exciting, yet at times unpredictable, nature of group work.

Identity Development and Coming-Out

Individuals from this population often have to struggle with understanding their gender identity or sexual orientation because being transgender or lesbian or bisexual or gay does not fit into neatly scripted social norms. In fact, much of identity work relates to how youth (and, frankly, all individuals) who are LGB manage their "adjustment to a socially stigmatized role" (Hetrick & Martin, 1987, p. 25). For transgender individuals, although the gender they may wish to identify with is acceptable to society, the very notion that they want to express themselves with a different expression is strongly stigmatized and manifests even with the continued appearance of "gender identity disorder" in the *Diagnostic and Statistical Manual of Mental Disor-*

ders of the American Psychiatric Association (2000). ("Homosexuality" was removed as a mental illness from this manual in 1973.) Therefore, as individuals explore their affective and sexual feelings, their fantasies, their behavior, and their self-image, and incorporate these into their identity formation as a member of the LGBTQ population, their identity begins to take shape and continues to form.

Interestingly, for this population developmental issues of identity do not always match chronological ages, because some individuals begin to come out when they feel safe to do so as adults, and the developmental tasks that include learning about romantic and sexual relationships which typically befall adolescents are new for those adults who recently came out. In describing the coming-out process to self, Isay (1996) discusses how individuals who are gay can embark on an empowering journey that ultimately may lead to feelings of freedom, as both internalized and institutional homophobia are confronted and managed. Groups such as National Youth Advocacy Coalition (NYAC), Human Rights Campaign (HRC), and Gay, Lesbian, Straight, Teachers Education Network (GLSTEN) all provide useful materials on identity and coming-out issues that can be utilized in groups. The National Association of Social Workers (NASW) has clear policy statements that support LGBTQ identity development and promote positive environments that include group work, to assist in the coming-out process (National Association of Social Workers, 2003).

Relationships

Group work is a perfect forum for individuals to explore the full domain of relationships in their lives (i.e., familial, romantic) and understand their own thoughts and feelings as well as the other members of the group. Family relationships for individuals who compose a sexual minority are challenging as families might have difficulty accepting the individual as gay or lesbian (Morrow, 1993). Parents, Families, and Friends of Lesbians and Gays (PFLAG) provides self-help groups that specifically focus on the adjustment process for family members and friends who need support in accepting and/ or supporting their loved one who is LGBTQ. In addition, members of groups, themselves, can provide each other with essential peer support and become friends. Dietz and Dettlaff (1997) describe members' appreciation of participating in a church-related group to meet others who are similar, learning about homosexuality, and creating mentoring relationships.

When the individuals are parents, group work is also a helpful way for them to sort out their thoughts and feelings about reconciling their status as an LGBTQ parent. Groups for gay parents are growing in number, yet there is room for additional growth to meet the needs of all members of the LGBTQ population. For example, Dunne's (1987) work with a support group of seven men "help[ed] them explore issues relating to coming out to their children" (p. 215). This group explored homophobia, including internalized homophobia, and used role plays and discussion to help men identify and understand these dynamics. Berger's (2000) focus groups revealed a "triple-stigmatiza[tion]" that can occur when gay and lesbian "parents" are stepparents.

Finally, many group members will discuss their thoughts and experiences with romantic relationships. Romantic relationships are important to virtually all individuals and negotiating them can be complex. For LGBTQ individuals, this complexity is compounded by the social stigma associated with entering into and maintaining them as well as the individuals' own varying levels of acceptance about romantic relationships. Many same sex couples have very healthy relationships, yet other couples' relationships are complicated by feelings of internalized homophobia and "coupling" in a climate that is increasingly supportive, albeit slowly. Johnson and Keren (1996) detail the legal obstacles, social stigma, few positive role models of couples, and homophobia (and transphobia) that challenge couples who are LGBTQ.

Health

HIV/AIDS

A fairly large literature focuses on support groups for men with HIV/AIDS. A major need exists for "information, support and affirmation" for individuals living with HIV/AIDS (Lewis, 1999, pp. 87-88). Peer support groups for gay men with HIV/AIDS are crucial for they get "understanding, information and friendship" (Sandstrom, 1996, p. 51) and can be life-renewing (Getzel, 1991; see also Dilley, McFarland, Sullivan, & Discepola, 1998; Sandstrom, 1996). In regard to lesbians, Richardson (2000) explores their thinking that they are immune from contracting AIDS. Foster, Stevens, and Hall (1994) advocate the use of long-term group work models with lesbians with HIV, and the continued need to incorporate ethnic/racial diversity and class into the groups.

With respect to safe sex, Roffman et al. (1998) evaluated a seventeen-session, cognitive-behavioral relapse prevention group for HIV prevention that resulted in more condom use. Distinguishing between populations, (Roffman et al., 1997), the authors found that cognitive-behavioral group counseling work that seeks to prevent HIV has better outcomes with gay men than bisexual men. Participating in a community-based support group for gay men with HIV was correlated with having less unprotected sex (Martin, Riopelle, Steckart, & Geshke, 2001). Kelly (2000) urges for more long-term, behaviorally-based AIDS prevention groups to address men who have sex with men (MSM) who are of other races than white and who are young. Finally, caregiver support groups are important to those who providing care for individuals with AIDS (Land, Hudson, & Stiefel, 2003).

Substance Abuse

Drug use remains a problem for a number of members of this population, as drugs are seen as avenues to temporarily escape painful stigma and depression and are constantly promoted as a major vehicle to have fun and conform within gay culture. "Party" drugs, such as methamphetamine, are used by a number of gay and bisexual men (Halkitis, Shrem, & Martin, 2005). There is also a correlation between men who have sex with men and drug use (e.g., Deren et al., 2001). A study by Rankow and Tessaro (1998) found that lesbian and bisexual women have higher rates of alcohol use as well as lower rates of being examined for breast cancer.

For those with addiction issues, experiential (group) therapy is useful and "incorporates group dynamic techniques through the use of sharing, role-playing, psychodrama, sculpturing, visualizations, touching/sensitivity exercises and mirroring to achieve a desired result" (Picucci, 1987, p. 121). Further, Ratner's (1993) observation of treating substance abuse by lesbians and gay men can be applied to group work; "[T]he therapist must assess a wide variety of factors, including (a) homophobia, (b) the coming-out experience, (c) social network, (d) spirituality and religion, (e) relationship with the family of origin, and (f) history of relationships and sexual behavior" (p. 571).

Mental Health

Mental health issues, apart from substance abuse and addiction, can confront LGBTQ individuals. For example, risk for suicide among this population is higher than in the general population (Rotheram-Boerus, Hunter, & Rosario, 1994; Savin-Williams, 1994), although Savin-Williams and Ream (2003) state that suicidal attempts are higher for a particular subgroup of gay, bisexual, and questioning adolescent males and not characteristic of this subpopulation as a whole. Depression and anxiety can occur for some individuals as responses to social stigma, physical threats, estranged relationships, and living with HIV/AIDS and other STDs. As a response to this, social support and finding meaning contribute to higher self-esteem and reduced anxiety for those living with HIV (Linn, Lewis, Cain, & Kimgrough, 1993). Group work has a powerful potential to address these mental health concerns.

DIVERSITY CONSIDERATIONS

Although much of group work has focused on gay and white male adults, literature on other populations exists that provides insight into issues that might be particularly relevant to these subpopulations. The following provides information that is useful for the social worker to consider when working with particular subpopulations within the LGBTQ community.

Lesbians

For women who identify as lesbian, having a group devoted to their particular needs and shared experience as lesbian can be quite useful, for example, an education and support group for adult lesbians focused on issues of identity development, homophobia and heterosexism, religious concerns, career concerns and family-of-origin concerns (Morrow, 1996). In a group for lesbians who batter, Margolies and Leeder (1995) describe how a new culture was created where the norm of violence can be challenged and members can learn anger management techniques. Facilitators can help lesbian survivors of incest adapt a strengths-based perspective on their response to the incest (Groves & Schondel, 1997/1998). When working with lesbian, as well as bisexual, female group members (in a mixed sexual orientation group), it is important for the therapist who facilitates the group to be committed to diversity, to feel comfortable with women of different sexual orientations, and still be able to focus on the commonalities of women's contribution to the group (Firestein, 1999). Cramer and Eldridge (1997) detailed the challenges and success associated with establishing with an interdisciplinary team a group that addressed milestones and other important issues for lesbian, bisexual, and questioning women in a conservative area.

Bisexual, Transgender, and Questioning Individuals

The literature continues to pay sparse attention to group work specific to bisexual, transgender, and questioning individuals. This may be because the "BTQ" is frequently subsumed in group work with gay and lesbian individuals, and their needs might receive short shrift in their own right as a few of the aforementioned articles do; however, each of these groups face unique issues that social workers are encouraged to continue to address in both creating groups for these individuals as needed and writing about these experiences.

With respect to bisexual individuals, one bisexual male support group occurred where topics addressed included the need for social support with other bisexual, married men, prejudice from straight and gay culture, and managing their sexuality in relation to their families (Wolfe, 1987). Group counseling worked better (with respect to HIV-prevention outcomes) for gay men than bisexual men (Roffman et al., 1997). Finally, though not in group work, more homophobia existed among bisexual than gay men according to one study (Stokes, Vanable, & McKirnan, 1997).

Less literature appeared on transgender support groups. One article discussed group work practice with sex workers who are transgender (Klein, 1999); there continues to be a need, however, for social workers to be attentive to practice with transgender individuals (Hartley & Whittle, 2003). Finally, no literature was found exclusively devoted to questioning individuals although, again, their issues may have been subsumed by broader groups focused on LGBT and Q.

Race and Ethnicity

Within the LGBTQ lies a broad diversity of race. As expected, group work with different racial groups focuses on how different racial and ethnicity norms respond to issues of alternative sexual orientation and gender identity. Group work literature on group practice with LGBTQ and race is growing but is still in its infancy. Masequesmay (2003) discusses the different identities that LGBT Vietnamese individuals juggle in a support group. Chan (1989) states issues of disclosure and discrimination are important to Asian-American lesbians and gay men. A group for Latino/a gay men and lesbians that took place in a mental health clinic focused on the challenging intersection of homophobia and Latino culture, combined with childhood sexual abuse and domestic violence that members had experienced (De Vidas, 1999). Although not speaking about groups per se, important issues that emerged for African-Americans, in a limited study, related to managing sexual orientation, race, and religion (Crisp, Priest, & Torgerson, 1998). Also, African-American queer youth use particular language to express their response to homophobia, ageism, and racism (Blackburn, 2005). Finally, Boykin's (2005) complex discussion of some African-American and other men's identification as "on the down low" (the traditional notion of men who engage with sex with other men but do not identify as "gay") is an issue that certainly could emerge with respect to identity and group work.

Age

In general, group work with individuals who are LGBTQ spans most of life's developmental stages with members ranging from adolescents to seniors. More literature has been written on issues pertaining to different age cohorts than other diversity variables. Particular literature that has been written on working with the two ends of the lifespan (youth, seniors) provides helpful information when conducting group work practice with this population.

Youth

The literature generally details group work for adolescents. This is likely because adolescents' developmental task associated with negotiating sexual orientation/gender identity occurs at this age (approximately twelve or thirteen and older). (Younger individuals might be part of a group if the group relates to children whose parents are same-sex or transgender, for example.) In adolescence, youth begin to fully explore the component of their identity that is their sexual/gender orientation for the first time, negotiate the meaning of this orientation and identity in their immediate social support network, assess their social support network, and develop romantic relationships.

Research on group work focuses on community-based and school-based groups. Peters (1997) found that themes when working with lesbian and gay youth in a group include coming-out, isolation, introduction to the community, and learning/relearning. Expanding the notion of group work practice to the youth community as a group itself, Hays, Rebochook and Kegeles (2003) describe positive results with the "Mpowerment Project," a community-based HIV prevention intervention that promotes safe sex for youth. The community-based gay-straight alliance that Snively (2004) studied is noteworthy, not just due to its mere existence, but because it expanded its membership to LGBT as well as queer and questioning individuals (Q) and it did so in a rural setting. These gay-straight alliances have significantly increased in number in the past decade and they remain pivotal because a lot of verbal harassment toward youth continues to exist in schools.

For young adults who attend college, group work has also expanded and more has been written about the school setting. For example, DeLois and Cohen (2000) describe an educational group for MSW students who identify as LGBT. The positive effects of a GLB student organization in a church-affiliated university are illustrated by Moore, Dietz, and Jenkins (1996). In addition, although not particularly citing group work per se, Lipton (1996) advocates the need for college counseling centers to meet the needs of this population, and group work is another useful intervention in this approach. Therefore, group practice with youth promotes identity development and is addressed through a variety of community and college settings.

Seniors

The literature on LGBT seniors (particularly gay and lesbian) has also grown in the past decade. As seniors understand their identity, coming out in a safer era than when they grew up, and gain insight into their relationships with families and romantic relationships, manage health issues, and conduct life review, group work can be an important intervention to assist them. Adelman's 1991 observation continues to be true: "Today, however, gay people no longer have to view themselves or each other as defiant or deficient, but can consider themselves members of an oppressed minority group. This new status brings gay people together and promotes self-esteem through self-affirmation (self-disclosure and identification with other gay people)" (p. 30).

Drumm (2004) details one support group that is provided on a weekly basis by Services and Advocacy for Gay, Lesbian, Bisexual, and Transgender Elders (formerly known as Senior Action in the Gay Environment [SAGE]). Telephone support groups for lesbian and senior elders who were caregivers to their partners with dementia are a viable group intervention as a useful alternative to traditional face-to-face groups (Moore, 2002). Using group work for evaluative purposes, Orel's (2004) findings from focus groups identified seven areas that LGB seniors had, including mental and physical health, spirituality, family, housing, social supports, and legal issues. Butler's (2004) insight into the challenges seniors face dealing with invisibility and difficulty in accessing health and other services provides a good reminder of other issues seniors may face that group work can attend to.

Ability

At the time of this writing, literature on group work with LGBT individuals with a physical/mental challenge still has room to grow substantially. Individuals with a "dual" stigma, that is of being perceived as "disabled" as well as "LGBT," face particular needs. For example, chronic mental illness can address sexual orientation and their illness (Ball, 1994). Only one article was found that described mental health clinics and the mental health services provided to LGBTQ groups (Medeiros, Seehaus, Elliott, & Melaney, 2004).

MUTUAL AID AND GROUP WORK
WITH THE LGBTQ POPULATION

Having outlined a number of issues and diversity considerations that can emerge in group work, it is time to get a snapshot or two on how a group might actually be conducted. Group work is ideal for five to seven individuals, with or without a co-facilitator, and can be support, growth, education, socialization, or therapy, or some combination, in purpose (Toseland & Rivas, 2005). Regardless of the type of group, "mutual aid" is a hallmark to the social work approach to group work. Mutual aid refers to the process by which individuals within a group, and the group itself, complementarily assist each other on working on group goals. Gitterman and Shulman (1994) and Shulman (2006) detail ten dynamics that contribute to mutual aid's creation and maintenance. They are: "sharing data," "the dialectical process," "the 'all-in the-same-boat' phenomenon" "discussing a taboo area," "developing a universal perspective," "the 'strength-in-numbers' phenomenon," "mutual support," "mutual demand," "rehearsal," and "individual problem-solving."

VIGNETTES

The following two vignettes illustrate just a few of the issues and diversity considerations presented and, additionally, illustrate and briefly explain the aforementioned dynamics of mutual aid.

Vignette 1

This vignette is a youth group (ages fourteen to twenty-one) who identify as LGBTQ. The purpose of this support, education, and socialization group is to provide a forum for youth to discuss issues of identity, coming-out, relationships, and learn issues facing the LGBTQ population. It meets once a week on Tuesdays after school, from four to six in the afternoon at a local LGBT community center. A social worker from a local HIV-prevention nonprofit agency is paid to facilitate the group. All parents or guardians of the group members have provided written permission for them to attend the group. The following is a hypothetical exchange that demonstrates different components of mutual aid. Let us assume that the group has been meeting for one month. Eight members regularly attend.

SOCIAL WORKER (SW): Thank you all for attending today. It is good to see everyone.

ERNIE: I don't think I can come again—my mother thinks this group is a waste of time. . . . Well, I mean she thinks that my being bisexual is something that will pass. She said she has a friend at work whose child was bisexual and it was just a stage he was going through. But for me it is different. I truly do like girls and boys. I don't even like to label myself.

SW: Ernie, thank you for sharing this. What would all other members like to say?

LI: I hate it when our parents interfere with our lives. It is our lives and they have no right to be part of this. It is hard enough to deal with being lesbian without having the support of your parents.

DARRELL: Yes, but you know my dad has come around a bit. He drives me here every week and while he is not thrilled about me being gay, he states he still loves me.

ERNIE: I hope my mother still loves me.

SW: I am hearing that your parents are having different reactions to you being in the group, with regard to your sexual orientation. I am also hearing you talk about the love your parents have for you and how strong that love is.

ERNIE: Well, I just feel that I could use some support . . . maybe it will get better, based on what you said, Darrell.

The mutual aid dynamic of *sharing data* has occurred as members are sharing information with each other about their parents. In addition, *the dialectical process* is occurring because within this exchange, group members hear the different experiences other members have had with their parents and as a consequence, Ernie is reformulating his view of his mother based on what Darrell stated.

SW: Do other group members have thoughts or feelings about their parents with regard to their sexual orientation or gender identity?

ADELA: I am staying with my grandmother because my parents had such a hard time with me identifying as a trans woman. They didn't want me and I really don't want to be with them. That is their loss—I hope they come around—I do talk to them now and then. I feel it is really hard to be African American and be trans. I mean my parents aren't that old but I feel that the prejudice in the African-American community is even stronger than in the white community. For me, it is about being comfortable in my body and having come out as a trans woman feels very good to me.

CINDY: I am glad you are feeling good about that.

ADELA: Thank you.

DARRELL: It is not easy to be black and be gay.

BRIAN: It is not that easy being white and gay either!

LI: Or Chinese!

SW: First, I would like to thank Adela for sharing. I am also hearing that it is not easy identifying as LGBTQ among different racial groups. Some of that is based on prejudice from society based on being LGBTQ and also on race, plus a lot of other different factors. However you identify, it is a challenging journey. I am glad we are all here for each other. Who would like to say more?

The mutual aid dynamic of *the all-in-the-same-boat phenomenon* is apparent as the members, though diverse in their own right, share a common experience of identifying as LGBTQ and talking about race. In addition, the *discussing a taboo area* has begun to occur as race, which is traditionally a difficult topic to discuss (even within the LGBTQ community), has been broached by the group. Finally, the social worker provided language (prejudice) that can help members *develop a universal perspective* where they can begin to talk about how prejudice such as homophobia and transphobia have impacted their lives.

ADELA: Well, I think people need to be educated in my community about race and trans issues. These are different than race and "being gay" issues.

LI: I agree with that.

BRIAN: So how do we educate people? Will people really change?

LI: We should give them a chance. I would like to have a community forum in the gay community about race and LGBTQ issues.

ADELA: Yes, this is a good idea.

SW: I support your ideas as well. Should we talk about how we might want to plan it?

This exchange is an example of the *strengths-in-numbers* mutual aid dynamic. This refers to a time when group members realize that they have the power to participate outside of the formal group in the community in a project devoted to social change. In this case, "social change" refers to educating the LGBTQ community about issues of race and racism.

Vignette 2

This vignette is a group of senior citizens who identify as lesbian. Most of the women recently came out (in the past ten years) and are talking about identity and relationships. This support group is facilitated by a social worker from a community-based agency. It meets on Saturday afternoons for ninety minutes at a local church. The following is a hypothetical exchange that demonstrates the remaining dynamics of mutual aid. Let's assume that the group has been meeting for three months. Six members regularly attend.

SOCIAL WORKER (SW): It is good to see everyone again. So what is new with everyone?

LANIE: I am glad to be here too. I need to talk with the group. I recently went to a new doctor and she asked me if I was married and once again, I was fed up! Everyone always assumes that I am "straight." So you know what I did? I walked out—believe it or not, this has happened to me enough and I got tired of it . . . so I walked out!

TRINA: You walked out? Wow . . . I know it can be frustrating when people assume we are straight. Hell, I assumed I was straight most of my life.

LIBBY: I know what you mean, Lanie—I hear and know how it can be frustrating.

SW: I am glad to see members supporting Lanie.

LANIE: Well, what I am supposed to do? I just get so fed up. For so long I was not happy with identifying as lesbian and then now that I am feeling comfortable with myself, I get so angry I just want to leave.

TRINA: Well what else can you do, Lanie? Maybe you can educate your doctors instead of walking out. Let them know you are a lesbian. Don't let your anger get the best of you 'cause you'll never see a doctor then!

LIBBY: I have done that before and I think you could do that—why don't you try that?

LANIE: I guess I could do that; it beats walking out.

Members are providing the mutual aid dynamic of *mutual support* by showing care and exhibiting empathy for Lanie. In addition, members are engaging in *mutual demand* with Lanie by challenging Lanie to try a different approach to talking to her doctor.

SW: So Lanie, how might you do "that"—talking to a doctor?

LIBBY: In the past, I avoided this and now I am so angry, it is hard.

MICHELLE: I know that you're angry; I have been like that before. What works for me is to be assertive and realize that most doctors aren't doing it on purpose; they just need to be educated. I talk to mine bluntly but try not to get too mad because when I have done this before, the doctors typically apologize.

LIBBY: So what should I do?

TRINA: Well, what do you think you can do?

LIBBY: I guess I can call the doctor and tell her how I feel.

SW: What would you say?

LIBBY: I could say, "Dr Ferguson, I wanted to tell you that I was a little upset when you asked whether I was married. I have had a hard time in my life not feeling good about being lesbian because society said it was wrong and I bought into it. Now that I am 'out,' I feel I need to tell you that I am in a relationship with a woman but not married in your sense."

Wow . . . that is a lot to say . . . but that feels better.

TRINA: You have to feel comfortable however you say it. But we need to let people know. When I go to a new doctor and am asked if I am married, I say, I am partnered. And that works for me.

LIBBY: Okay . . . good . . . well, thank you, I think I will talk to Dr. Ferguson again.

The last two mutual aid dynamics are evident here. The mutual aid dynamic of *rehearsal* is evident when Libby practiced what she might say to her physician. In addition, the entire discussion with Libby refers to the mutual aid dynamic of *individual problem solving* where members can help a particular member with an issue she or he would like assistance with.

CONCLUSION

This chapter highlights relevant issues in conducting group work with the LGBTQ population. It surveyed the literature on what types of groups and what types of specific issues may be important in conducting groups. Remember that conducting group work, regardless of population, requires a specific set of skills and a theoretical basis. Regardless of what theory or theories (e.g., solution-focused, cognitive-behavioral) is used, mutual aid provides a nice orientation in which to situate social work practice with groups. This mutual aid was illustrated in the two practice vignettes.

Although there is promising research on group work with this population, more research is necessary on group work with individuals who are Latino, African-American, Asian, Arab, and other racial groups, as well as individuals who are transgender, bisexual, and questioning, and face physical and other challenges. It is important that the notion of conducting group work practice with this population continues to expand to social action groups beyond the clinical setting. Equally important is that social workers advocate for the creation and continued support from their agencies for such groups. Not all community agencies are supportive, and therefore, it takes a social worker to understand the importance of advocating for this population.

The LGBTQ population has faced a number of challenges and successes in recent years on a societal level. These social dynamics filter down and are played out in groups, whether it has to do with identity; coming-out; social-ization; prejudice; romantic, family, and peer relationships; legal equality and social status; safety; violence; health; or mental health. By combining a genuine interest in learning about and helping this population with the exciting possibilities of conducting group work, a skilled social worker (you!) has the real possibility to help individuals within the group successfully reach their goals, both individually and collectively.

REFERENCES

Adelman, M. (1991). Stigma, gay lifestyles, and adjustment to aging: A study of later-life gay men and lesbians. *Journal of Homosexuality, 20*(3-4), 7-35.

American Psychiatric Association (2000). *Diagnostic and statistical manual of mental disorders,* Fourth edition, Text revision. Washington, DC: Author.

Ball, S. (1994). Group model for gay and lesbian client with chronic mental illness. *Social Work, 39*(1), 109-115.

Berger, R. (2000). Gay step-families: A triple-stigmatized group. *Families in Society, 81*(5), 504-516.

Blackburn, M. V. (2005). Agency in borderland discourses: Examining language use in a community center with black queer youth. *Teachers College Record, 107*(1), 89-113.

Boykin, K. (2005). *Beyond the down low: Sex, lies and denial in black America.* New York: Carroll and Graf.

Butler, S. S. (2004). Gay, lesbian, bisexual, and transgender (GLBT) elders: The challenges and resilience of this marginalized group. *Journal of Human Behavior in the Social Environment, 9*(4), 24-44.

Chan, C. S. (1989). Issues of identity development among Asian-American lesbians and gay men. *Journal of Counseling and Development, 68*(1), 16-20.

Conlin, D., & Smith, J. (1982). Group psychotherapy for gay men. *Journal of Homosexuality, 7*(2/3), 105-112.

Cramer, E. P., & Eldridge, T. L. (1997). Creating an education and support group for lesbians. *Journal of Gay & Lesbian Social Services, 7*(1), 49-72.

Crisp, D., Priest, R., & Torgerson, A. (1998). African American gay men: Developmental issues, choices and self-concept. *Family Therapy, 25*(3), 161-168.

DeLois, K., & Cohen, M. B. (2000). A queer idea: Using group work principles to strengthen learning in a sexual minorities seminar. *Social Work with Groups, 23*(3), 53-67.

Deren, S., Stark, M., Rhodes, F., Siegal, H., Cottler, L., Wood, M., et al. (2001). Drug-using men who have sex with men: Sexual behaviors and sexual identities. *Culture, Health & Sexuality, 3*(3), 329-338.

De Vidas, M. (1999). Childhood sexual abuse and domestic violence: A support group for Latino gay men and lesbians. *Journal of Gay & Lesbian Social Services, 10*(2), 51-68.

Dietz, T. J., & Dettlaff, A. (1997). The impact of membership in a support group for gay, lesbian, and bisexual students. *Journal of College Student Psychotherapy, 12*(1), 57-72.

Dilley, J. W., McFarland, W., Sullivan, P., & Discepola, M. (1998). Psychosocial correlates of unprotected anal sex in a cohort of gay men attending an HIV-negative support group. *AIDS Education and Prevention, 10*(4), 317-326.

Dunne, E. J. (1987). Helping gay fathers come out to their children. *Journal of Homosexuality, 14*(1/2), 213-222.

Drumm, K. (2004). An examination of group work with old lesbians with a lack of intimacy by using a record of service. *Journal of Gerontological Social Work, 44*(1-2), 25-52.

Firestein, B. A. (1999). New perspectives on group treatment with women of diverse sexual identities. *Journal for Specialists in Group Work, 24*(3), 306-315.

Flowers, J. V., Booraem, C., Miller, T. E., Iverson, A. E., Copeland, J., & Furtado, K. (1991). Comparison of the results of a standardized AIDS prevention program in three geographic locations. *AIDS Education and Prevention, 3*(3), 189-196.

Foster, S. B., Stevens, P. E., & Hall, J. M. (1994). Offering support services for lesbians living with HIV. *Women & Therapy, 15*(2), 69-80.

Getzel, G. (1991). Survival modes for people with AIDS in groups. *Social Work, 36*(1), 7-11.

Getzel, G. (1998). Group work practice with gay men and lesbians. In G. P. Mallon (Ed.), *Foundations of social work practice with lesbian and gay persons* (pp. 131-144). Binghamton, NY: The Haworth Press.

Gitterman, A., & Shulman, L. (Eds.) (1994). *Mutual aid groups, vulnerable populations, and the life cycle* (2nd ed.). New York: Columbia University Press.

Groves, P. A., & Scholdel, C. (1997-1998). Feminist groupwork with lesbian survivors of incest. *Groupwork, 10*(3), 215-230.

Halkitis, P. N., Shrem, M. T., & Martin, F. W. (2005). Sexual behavior patterns of methamphetamine-using gay and bisexual men. *Substance Use & Misuse, 40*(5), 703-719.

Hartley, C. F., & Whittle, S. (2003). Different sexed and gendered bodies demand different ways of thinking about policy and practice. *Practice, 15*(3), 61-73.

Hays, R. B., Rebochook, G. M., & Kegeles, S. M. (2003). The Mpowerment project: Community-building with young gay and bisexual men to prevent HIV. *American Journal of Community Psychology, 31*(3-4), 301-312.

Hetrick, E. S., & Martin, A. D. (1987). Developmental issues and their resolution for gay and lesbian adolescents. *Journal of Homosexuality, 14*(1/2), 25-43.

Isay, R. A. (1996). *Becoming gay: The journey to self-acceptance.* New York: Pantheon Books.

Johnson, T. W., & Keren, M. S. (1996). Creating and maintaining boundaries in male couples. In J. Laird & R. J. Green (Eds.), *Lesbians and gays in couples and families: A handbook for therapists* (pp. 231-243). New York: Jossey-Bass.

Kelly, J. A. (2000). HIV prevention interventions with gay or bisexual men and youth. *AIDS, 14*(2), 34-39.

Klein, R. (1999). Group work with transgendered male to female sex workers. *Journal of Gay & Lesbian Social Services, 10*(3/4), 95-109.

Kurland, R., & Salmon, R. (Eds.) (1998). *Teaching a methods course in social work with groups, 1.* Alexandria, VA: Counsel on Social Work Education.

Land, H., Hudson, S. M., & Stiefel, B. (2003). Stress and depression among HIV-positive and HIV-negative gay and bisexual caregivers. *AIDS and Behavior, 7*(1), 41-53.

Lewis, J. (1999). Status passages: The experience of HIV-positive gay men. *Journal of Homosexuality, 37*(3), 87-115.

Linn, G. L., Lewis, F. M., Cain, V. A., & Kimgrough, G. A. (1993). HIV-illness, social support, sense of coherence, and psychological well-being in a sample. *AIDS Education and Prevention, 4*(3), 254-262.

Lipton, B. (1996). Opening doors: Responding to the mental health needs of gay and bisexual college students. *Journal of Gay & Lesbian Social Services, 4*(2), 7-24.

Margolies, L., & Leeder, E. (1995). Violence at the door: Treatment of lesbian batterers. *Violence Against Women, 1*(2), 139-157.

Martin, D. J., Riopelle, D., Steckart, J., & Geshke, N. (2001). Support group participation, HIV viral load and sexual-risk behavior. *American Journal of Health Behavior, 25*(6), 513-527.

Masequesmay, G. (2003). Negotiating multiple identities in a queer Vietnamese support group. *Journal of Homosexuality, 45*(2-4), 193-215.

Medeiros, D. M., Seehaus, M., Elliott, J., & Melaney, A. (2004). Providing mental health services for LGBT teens in a community adolescent health clinic. *Journal of Gay and Lesbian Psychotherapy, 8*(3/4), 83-95.

Moore, L. S., Dietz, T. J., & Jenkins, D. A. (1996). Beyond the classroom: Taking action against heterosexism. *Journal of Gay & Lesbian Social Services, 5*(4), 87-98.

Moore, W. R. (2002). Lesbian and gay elders: Connecting care providers though a telephone support group. *Journal of Gay & Lesbian Social Services, 14*(3), 23-41.

Morrow, D. F. (1993). Social work with gay and lesbian adolescents. *Social Work, 38*(6), 655-660.

Morrow, D. F. (1996). Coming-out issues for adult lesbians: A group intervention. *Social Work, 41*(6), 647-656.

Morston, T., & McInnis, R. (1983). Sexual identity issues in group work: Gender, social sex role, and sexual orientation considerations. *Social Work with Groups, 6*(3/4), 67-77.

National Association of Social Workers (2003). *Social work speaks: NASW policy statements 2003-2006.* Washington, DC: NASW Press.

Orel, N. A. (2004). Gay, lesbian, and bisexual elders: Expressed needs and concerns across focus groups. *Journal of Gerontological Social Work, 43*(2-3), 57-77.

Peters, A. J. (1997). Themes in group work with lesbian and gay adolescents. *Social Work with Groups, 20*(2), 51-69.

Picucci, M. (1987). Planning an experimental weekend workshop for lesbians and gay males in recovery. *Journal of Chemical Dependency Treatment, 5*(1), 119-139.

Rankow, E. J., & Tessaro, I. (1998). Mammography and risk factors for breast cancer in lesbian and bisexual women. *American Journal of Health Behavior, 22*(6), 403-410.

Ratner, E. F. (1993). Treatment issues for chemically dependent lesbians and gay men. In L. D. Garnets & D. C. Kimmel (Eds.), *Psychological perspectives on lesbian and gay male experiences* (pp. 567-578). New York: Columbia University.

Richardson, D. (2000). The social construction of immunity: HIV risk prevention and prevention among lesbians and bisexual women. *Culture, Health & Sexuality, 2*(1), 33-49.

Roffman, R. A., Downey, L., Beadnell, B., Gordon, J. R., Craver, J. N., & Stephens, R. B. (1997). Cognitive-behavioral group counseling to prevent HIV transmission in gay and bisexual men: Factors contributing to successful risk reduction. *Research on Social Work Practice, 7*(2), 165-186.

Roffman, R. A., Stephens, R. S., Curtin, L., Gordon, J. R., Craver, J. N., Stern, M., et al. (1998). Relapse prevention as an interventive model for HIV risk reduction in a gay and bisexual men. *AIDS Education and Prevention, 10*(1), 1-18.

Rotheram-Boerus, M., Hunter, J., & Rosario, M. (1994). Suicidal behavior and gay-related stress among gay and bisexual male adolescents. *Journal of Adolescent Research, 9*(4), 498-508.

Sandstrom, K. L. (1996). Searching for information, understanding, and self-value: The utilization of peer support groups by gay men with HIV/AIDS. *Social Work in Health Care, 23*(4), 51-74.

Savin-Williams, R. C. (1994). Verbal and physical abuse as stressors in the lives of lesbian, gay male, and bisexual youths: Associations with school problems, running away, substance abuse, prostitution, and suicide. *Journal of Consulting and Clinical Psychology, 62*(2), 261-269.

Savin-Williams, R. C., & Ream, G. L. (2003). Suicide attempts among sexual-minority male youth. *Journal of Clinical Child and Adolescent Psychology, 32*(4), 509-522.

Schwartz, W. (1985). The group work tradition and social work practice. *Social Work with Groups, 8*(4), 7-27.

Shulman, L. (2006). *The skills of helping individuals, families, groups, and communities* (5th ed.). Itasca, IL: F.E. Peacock Publishers.

Snively, C. A. (2004). Building community-based alliances between GLBTQQA youth and adults in rural settings. *Journal of Gay & Lesbian Social Services, 16*(3-4), 99-112.

Stokes, J. P., Vanable, P., & McKirnan, D. J. (1997). Comparing gay and bisexual men on sexual behavior, condom use, and psychosocial variables related to HIV/AIDS. *Archives of Sexual Behavior, 26*(4), 383-397.

Toseland, R. W., & Rivas, R. F. (2005). *An introduction to group work practice.* Boston: Allyn and Bacon.

Wolfe, T. J. (1987). Group counseling for bisexual men. *Journal for Specialists in Group Work, 12*(4), 162-165.

Chapter 11

Social Work Practice with Lesbian, Gay, Bisexual, and Transgender People Within Families

Gerald P. Mallon

Are you out to your family?
How did your family deal with your being bisexual?
Do your children know that you are gay?
What was it like for your ex when you transitioned?

All these questions are those that almost inevitably arise in the process of getting to know a lesbian, gay, bisexual, or transgender person. Families supply physical and emotional sustenance, connect us with our past, and provide a context within which we learn about the world, including the attitudes and mores of our society (Berzon, 2001). An LGBT person's family is very important. Although some radical right ideologues erroneously promote the belief that homosexuality is a threat to the family, as if it were intrinsically antithetic to the idea of family life, nothing could be further from the truth. Lesbian, gay, bisexual and transgender (LGBT) persons need to be as much a part of their families as much as other individuals. Given the stigmatizing status that LGBT identity continues to hold for many in Western society, the family is one place where an LGBT person needs to feel accepted most. Most LGBT people hope that their families will continue to love and care for them after they disclose their gender or sexual identity. For many, this is the case, but sadly, for others, acceptance by one's family is not forthcoming.

Utilizing an ecological perspective of social work practice to work with LGBT people and families offers a broad conceptual lens for viewing family functioning and needs. Germain (1985) who led the development of this perspective in social work, noted that "practice is directed toward improving the transactions between people and their environments in order to enhance adaptive capacities and improve environments for all who function within them" (p. 31). As such, practitioners need to seek to influence the direction of change in both the person and the environment. With respect to LGBT persons within a family context, changing the environment means educating families and assisting them in dealing with heterocentric attitudes.

Consider the following example:

Damond is a sixteen-year-old Trinidadian youngster who has been sent to the United States to live with an aunt after his mother has been psychiatrically hospitalized. His aunt, a single mother, has lupus, works full-time, and has three other children to support in her home. Damond is depressed because of his mother's illness. He is feeling isolated by his separation from his mother and the difficult acclimation to a new country and culture. In addition, Damond is dealing, in silence, with his own emerging gay identity.

While cleaning Damond's room one afternoon, his aunt finds a letter that he wrote to a boy in school. Enraged, confused, and armed only with religious and culturally pejorative notions about homosexuality, even worrying that Damond's homosexuality might be contagious and put her own children at risk, she tells him that he is sick and needs help.

From this brief sketch, one can begin to see how and why this family is in crisis. There are numerous stresses in this environment. The economy requires that the aunt works to support her family despite her chronic illness; the young man is grieving over his mother's illness, his own relocation to a new environment, and dealing in silence with his own emerging gay identity. Adding to this case are cultural factors, in that, some cultures have a particularly negative view of individuals (even family members) who are LGBT and the fact that the young man was "found out" and did not chose to disclose his orientation. It is easy to see how this young person may become the target of his family's anger. As this example suggests, many personal, family, and environmental factors converge and interact with each other to influence the family. In other words, as Germain (1985, p. 43) so eloquently said over two decades ago, "human behavior is not solely a function of the person or the environment, but of the complex interaction between them."

All too often, despite the increasing emphasis on family-centered social work practice (Hartman & Laird, 1983), there is a tendency for social work practitioners to see LGBT persons primarily, if not solely, as individuals who are "gay," "lesbian," "bisexual," or "transgender," rather than as members of a family of origin and as possible creators of their own family systems, families of choice (Weston, 1997), or biological families. By not acknowledging that "human beings can be understood and helped only in the context of the intimate and powerful human systems of which they are a part," and of which the family is one of the most important (Hartman & Laird, 1983, p. 4), practitioners miss out on many important opportunities for fostering more positive relationships between LGBT persons and their families.

This chapter, based on the author's analysis of the existing literature, qualitative data analysis from interviews conducted with LGBT adolescents and their families, and more than thirty-one years of clinical practice with individuals and their families, examines the experience of LGBT persons and their families through an ecological lens. Such a perspective creates a framework where individuals and environments are understood as a unit, in the context of their relationship to one another (Germain, 1985). As such, this chapter examines the primary reciprocal exchanges and transactions that LGBT persons and their families face as they confront the unique person: environmental tasks involved in a society that assumes all of its members are heterosexual and oriented to the gender in which they were born. The focus of this chapter is limited to an analysis of LGBT persons within the context of their family system. As such the author explores the following areas: demographic issues; psychosocial risks and psychosocial needs of LGBT persons; the clinical assessment issues of working with an individual where sexual or gender orientation is the presenting issue; and recommendations for intervening with this population. Recommendations for social work practice with LGBT persons and their families are presented in the conclusion of the chapter. Issues pertaining to LGBT families created through adoption, foster care, alternative insemination, and surrogacy, are addressed later in this text.

DEMOGRAPHIC PROFILE

Although the stereotypes of the effeminate, white, meticulously groomed and dressed, middle- to upper-class, urban man living in a fabulously decorated house or apartment, or the butch, short-haired, husky, motorcycle-riding woman wearing no jewelry or makeup who carries her wallet in her back pocket, or the hip young urban woman who comfortably dates both men and women, or the man who dresses in woman's clothing secretly at home, but never in public, are the images that the popular media most perpetuates about LGBT persons, the reality is that LGBT persons are part of every race, culture, ethnic group, religious and socioeconomic affiliation, and family in the United States, and most likely all other countries as well.

As LGBT persons are socialized to hide their sexual or gender orientation, most are a part of an invisible population. In addition, in many areas of the United States (mostly outside of urban areas, although urban areas can also be unsafe), it is still unsafe for most LGBT persons to live openly and acknowledge their sexual or gender orientation. Therefore, there is no census data that support or deny the existence of this population. Individuals who are socialized to hide or who have real or perceived reasons to fear for their safety do not come forward to be counted. In fact, although there is an increasing awareness about LGBT persons, mainly from media representations of the population, it is safe to assume that most LGBT persons in the United States remain closeted and do not live as "out" or "openly" LGBT persons.

PSYCHOSOCIAL RISKS/PSYCHOSOCIAL NEEDS OF LGBT PERSONS

LGBT persons experience environmental and psychological stresses that are more elevated than most of their heterosexual counterparts, not necessarily because of their gay, lesbian, bisexual, or transgender orientation, but due in large part to the negative societal response to their LGBT orientation. Such conditions are unique to their membership in what remains in American society as a stigmatized and marginalized population.

As such, many LGBT persons experience difficulties in the following areas:

- Accessing systems of care (health, mental health, social services) (Appleby, 1998; Hunter & Mallon, 1998; Israel & Tarver, 1997; Lev, 2004; Page, 2004) that are affirming of and sensitive to the needs of LGBT clients.
- Mental health illness that is unique to their situation—especially anxiety-related disorders and mood disorders (Jones & Hill, 2003; Weitzman, 2006). Lesbian and gay youth, according to some studies (Garofalo, Wolf, Wissow, Woods, & Goodman, 1999; Remafedi, 1999; Rofes, 1983), are up to three times more likely to attempt suicide than their heterosexual counterparts. Trans youth may face many other challenges in their transition (Lesser, 1999).
- Substance abuse is generally thought to be elevated in the LGBT communities, since much of the initial coming-out process may center on the "bar" scene (Finnegan & McNally, 1996; Klein, 1993).

- The effects of trauma—psychological, political, and vicarious—are often reported by LGBT persons as issues of concern since living within the context of a "false sense of self" and hiding or monitoring one's behaviors, mannerisms, speech, and life can be very debilitating and lead to maladaptive responses (Bradford, 2004; Rust, 1996). Politically, LGBT persons are frequently the subjects of "moral" debates by politicians (Kluger, 2006); the issue of lesbian and gay marriage (Eskridge & Spedale, 2006) is one recently politicized issue that causes trauma for many lesbians and gay men who are tired of politicians who attempt to make their lives illegal or immoral. The issue of coming-out alone—since this is a process and not a one-time event— is exhausting to live through, which can even lead to trauma (LaSala, 2000). LGBT persons who are parents and have children may experience vicarious traumatization in watching their children struggle with homophobic comments or reactions from peers or their community (Mallon, 2004).
- Environmental risks/needs. Although it is a common myth that all LGBT persons are economically advantaged, many lesbians and gay men experience economic poverty (Lesbian & Gay, 2004), inadequate housing or threat of losing one's housing, and unemployment (Israel, 2005; Ochs, 1996, see www.aclu.org). The literature is replete with evidence that LGBT persons experience high levels of oppression and exploitation (Pharr, 1988) and incidents of community violence and discrimination on multiple levels (Herek, 1991). Racism is also an issue for LGBT persons to contend with, both from inside and outside the LGBT communities (Colon, 2001; Merighi & Grimes, 2000; Rodriguez, 1998; Walters, 1998).

CLINICAL ASSESSMENT FOR FAMILIES WHERE SEXUAL ORIENTATION IS AN ISSUE

Although not all LGBT persons need counseling, the fact that someone in the family has identified as gay, lesbian, bisexual, or trans can bring some families to the attention of a social services agency for a variety of reasons and services that might not at initial assessment seem to be pertaining to issues of sexual orientation (O'Dell, 2000; Oswald, 2002a,b). The following case example explores issues of sexual orientation from a family-centered perspective:

Shamir, a fifteen-year-old Pakistani male, is sitting in his bedroom in the apartment he shares with his mother, father, and three younger brothers, reading a very personal letter that a boy in school wrote to him. He has already read this letter several times, but like many adolescents venturing into the world of relationships, he is rereading it because it is a special letter to him. When his mother yells to him from the kitchen that he has a phone call, he puts the letter down on his bed and leaves his room to get the phone. During the time that he is on the phone his nine-year-old brother enters his room and begins to read the letter that Shamir has left on the bed. The younger sibling, realizing that its contents are questionable, shows the letter to their mother.

When Shamir returns from his phone call and finds his letter missing, he begins to panic. Shamir knows that it will be obvious to anyone who reads the letter that he is gay. Up to this point, Shamir has been successful at keeping his identity a secret. However, now that his secret is out in the open, he is angry that he did not have an opportunity to come out on his own terms; he has been found out, and there is a big difference! When he sees his mother's face, he knows that she has read the letter, but she says nothing to him. When he approaches her, she backs away and says, "We'll talk about this when your father gets home and when all of your brothers are asleep."

The next few hours are filled with dread and isolation for Shamir. What's going to happen? What is his father going to do? He is not prepared for this; he is terrified of the repercussions. What Shamir does not know is that his mother and father feel the same way: this is not the way things are supposed to be; they are not prepared for this. No one ever told them about the prospect of having a son who was gay. Should they send him for therapy? Should they send him away to protect the other boys? Should they even tell anybody about this?

For the social worker experienced in working with family systems, the situation in the above vignette presents the ideal opportunity for an intervention. A crisis has occurred, the family is in turmoil, and everyone is poised for something to happen. Family members are confused, frightened, shame-filled, unprepared, and angry. They can act in a reckless manner, lashing out at what the individual has disclosed, or they might fall into a conspiracy of silence and become completely paralyzed and numbed by the circumstances. Professionals who have spent years with families, or even those who have recently entered the field, know that what happens next is not always predictable. When the situation involves an issue of sexual orientation in the family, one can almost guarantee that there will be a great deal of ambivalence in this process. Coming out in the context of a family system can yield unpredictable outcomes.

THE COMING-OUT PROCESS WITHIN A FAMILY

Coming-out, a distinctively LGBT phenomenon (see Cass, 1979, 1983/ 1984, 1984; Coleman, 1981, 1987; Firestein, 1996; Fox, 1995; Lev, 2004; Troiden, 1979, 1988, 1989), is defined as a developmental process through which LGBT people recognize their sexual or gender orientation and inte- grate this knowledge into their personal and social lives (De Monteflores & Schultz, 1978). Although several theorists have written about coming-out from a uniquely adolescent experience (Hetrick & Martin, 1987; Mallon, 1998b,c; Malyon, 1981), developmentally, the coming-out process can even- tuate at any stage of an individual's life. Therefore, it is important to con- sider the consequences of a person coming out in the context of his or her family, as a child, as an adolescent, as an unmarried young adult, as a mar- ried adult, as a parent, or as a grandparent.

The events that mark coming-out and the pace of this process vary from person to person. Consequently, some people move through the process smoothly, accepting their sexuality or their gender fit, making social con- tacts, and finding a good fit within their environments. Others are unnerved by their sexuality, vacillating in their conviction, hiding in their uneasiness, and struggling to find the right fit.

Although the experience of an adolescent coming out is qualitatively dif- ferent from that of a parent or an adult who comes out, there are several con- ditions, broadly conceived, that all family members share. Earlier literature (Silverstein, 1977) focused primarily on the negative consequences of dis- closure, and indeed there can be many, but a range of responses to a family member's disclosure is perhaps a more appropriate characterization. The following description by Rothberg and Weinstein (1996) captures many of the salient aspects of this experience:

> When a family member comes out there are a multitude of responses. At one end of the spectrum is acceptance . . . but rarely, if ever, is this announcement celebrated. Take for example, the announcement a heterosexual person makes to his or her family of origin of an engage- ment to marry. This is usually met with a joyous response, a ritual party and many gifts. The lesbian and gay man does not receive this response. Instead, the coming-out announcement is often met with negative responses which can range from mild disapproval to com- plete nonacceptance and disassociation. These responses, though usually accepted, cause considerable stress and pain for the lesbian and gay person seeking approval. (p. 81)

Factors Affecting Disclosure

Religious Factors

Some families, particularly families with strong religious convictions, may openly condemn homosexuality, unaware that one of their own family members is lesbian, gay, bisexual, or trans (Helminiak, 1997; Herman, 1997).

Blumenfeld and Raymond (1993) note that families with strong religious convictions often support their views of their religion even against a family member. Personal biases, particularly cultural or religious biases that view an LGBT identity negatively, can make "coming out" to one's family a painful experience. This distress is manifest in this young person's narrative:

Everybody in the family knew that I was bisexual. The only person that couldn't deal with me being bi was my mother. Everyone else that I thought was going to have a hard time, didn't. My mother is a devout Baptist and she has a very hard time with my being bi. She has said that she hated me and to this very day she tells me that it is against God's will and it's against His proposition and when the day comes for Him to take over the world again I'm going to suffer. She always says that she doesn't want me to suffer because I am her son, but she doesn't realize that she is making me suffer because of the ways that she acts toward me.

Social workers must be aware of the strong anti-LGBT sentiment held by many religious groups and the impact that this has on family members for whom sexual or gender orientation is an issue. The Bible has historically been erroneously used as a weapon against lesbian and gay persons causing a great deal of distress in many families of faith. Several excellent resources (Cooper, 1994; Goodwill, 2000; Lease & Schulman, 2003; Metropolitan Community Church, 1990; Parents & Friends of Lesbians and Gays, 1997) exist that provide practitioners with an alternative lesbian and gay affirming perspective.

Cultural Factors

Race and cultural ethnicity can also play important roles in the disclosure process. Persons of color, many of whom have experienced significant stress related to oppression and racism based on skin color or ethnicity may experience even greater difficulty coming out within the family context as some may view a lesbian or gay sexual orientation as one more oppressed status to add to one's plate (Colon, 2001; Greene, 1994; Merighi & Grimes,

2000; Poon, 2004; Rodriguez, 1998; Savin-Williams & Rodriguez, 1993; Walters, 1998).

People of color who are LGBT are confronted with a tricultural experience. They experience membership in their ethnic or racial community and in the larger society. In addition, they are not born into the LGBT communities. Many become aware of their difference in adolescence and not only must they deal with the stigma within their own cultural/racial community but they must also find a supportive LGBT community to which they can relate. The lesbian/gay community is often a microcosm of the larger society, and many may confront racism there, as in the larger society. To sustain oneself in three distinct communities requires an enormous effort and can also produce stress for the adolescent (Chan, 1989; Hunter & Schaecher, 1987; Morales, 1989; Poon, 2004). The reality is that LGBT persons are part of every race, culture, ethnic grouping, class, and extended family.

Emotional Factors

If the LGBT identified individual chooses to come out voluntarily, then he or she has had time to prepare for the event. Some individuals may have role-played their coming-out process with a supportive friend or therapist; others may have written a letter or planned the event after experiencing positive disclosure events with several other trusted confidants. The truth, however, is that in most cases, even if the individual has had time to prepare for this event, the actual moment of disclosure catches most families off guard. Families have frequently not had this period of time to prepare and are often shocked by the disclosure. Jean Baker (1998), psychologist and mother of two gay sons, expresses these feelings as a parent perfectly:

> I still recall the night so vividly. Gary was helping me with dinner, which he occasionally did. He had just gotten a new haircut and immediately I hated it. I still don't know why, because it had never occurred to me that Gary might be gay, but for some reason I said to him, "With that haircut people will think you're gay." He hesitated for a moment and then, looking directly at me he said, "I think maybe I am."
>
> I stared at my son, totally speechless, stunned, momentarily unable to react. Then I started crying and found myself talking incoherently about the tragedy of being gay. . . . I rambled on senselessly about homosexuality as an adolescent phase, something people can grow out of, something that may be just a rebellion. . . . Knowing what I know about homosexuality and having examined my own feelings and atti-

tudes, I think my reactions that night were deplorable. My son deserved to hear immediately that I respected him for his honesty and his courage. What he heard instead was that his mother thought being homosexual was a tragedy.

As I think about my reactions that first night and during subsequent days and nights, I am still ashamed of what I learned about myself as a mother dealing with a son's homosexuality. Instead of thinking first about how I could help my son cope with what he might have to face in a society so condemning of homosexuals, I focused on how I felt. Though I didn't want to admit it, I was concerned about the prejudice and stigma I myself might have to face. (pp. 41-43)

Feelings surrounding the initial disclosure can range from shame, to guilt, to embarrassment or even complete disassociation. Acceptance is also a possible reaction, but one that is seldom experienced by most LGBT persons.

Managing Disclosure to Others

Deciding how to manage the disclosure of an LGBT orientation to the family is an important consideration at this point. The family that reacts extremely negatively to the disclosure, such as parents who throw a child out of the home or a spouse who is told to leave the home by his or her partner, may require outside intervention to assist them in dealing with the disclosure, which should be viewed as a crisis situation. Who to tell and who not to tell, and how to address the disclosure within the context of the family, are other issues that families must eventually discuss. Getting through the initial crisis of disclosure, however, should be the primary focus of the intervention.

Being "found out," as illustrated in Shamir's case presented earlier in this chapter, precipitates a somewhat different type of crisis, which may also require immediate intervention. In the sections that follow, we will explore the possibilities of a child or adolescent's coming out in his or her family system.

When a Child Comes Out Within the Family System

Although disclosure can occur at any point in the developmental process, for the purposes of this section, I will specifically address the issues as they pertain to a child or adolescent who comes out or is found out by his or her family.

Although one of the primary tasks of adolescence is to move away from one's family toward independence, families are still extremely important economic and emotional systems for the adolescent. Lack of accurate information about LGBT identity and fears about individuals who identify as LGBT lead many families to panic about how to manage the disclosure of a family member.

The following two case examples illustrate several points with respect to the coming-out process for adolescents.

Yuan Is Found Out

Yuan Fong is a Chinese-American eighteen-year-old senior in a public high school in a large West Coast city. He resides with his parents, who are Chinese born, in an apartment with an older brother, aged twenty, and two younger siblings, ages twelve and ten. Yuan is the captain of the football team, and well-liked by his peers and by teachers. He is a very handsome young man. Yuan has dated a few girls but is so into his football career that it leaves little time for anything else. Yuan has been aware of his feelings for guys for some time and has been trying to repress these feelings. Recently, however, he met a guy named Tommy whom he really likes, and Yuan's feelings have become more difficult to repress. Tommy and Yuan begin to see each other, first as friends, and then their friendship blossoms into a romance.

One evening, Mrs. Fong overhears a telephone conversation between Yuan and Tommy, It seems to her that Yuan is speaking to Tommy as she would expect him to speak to a girl that he is dating. When Yuan hangs up the phone his mother confronts him about what she heard. Yuan blows it off and laughs, blaming her interpretation on her imperfect English, but he knows that this is not the case. He is in a panic because he knows that his mother will not let this go.

Mrs. Fong becomes hypervigilant about Yuan and begins to search in his room for clues while he is at school. She finds letters that Tommy has written to Yuan, and then when she finds a small card from a lesbian and gay youth group, she takes it as confirmation that her son Yuan is gay. Mrs. Fong shares this information with her husband, who chastises her for snooping in their son's room. However, they are both upset and unprepared for how they should deal with this new information which changes their notion of their family.

When Yuan arrives home from football practice, both Mr. and Mrs. Fong ask to speak with him. They tell him what they have found and ask him if he is gay. Yuan, fearful and caught off guard, is unsure of how to respond, but it seems like there is no way out. Even though he is fairly sure that he is gay, Yuan tells them, "I think I am bisexual," rationalizing that being half gay is easier that being totally gay. Mr. and Mrs. Fong ask if he has ever been sexually abused by someone, or if he is just going through a phase, and insist that he is going to see their family doctor. Although they do not say it out loud, Mr. and Mrs. Fong are also concerned about how this will affect their two younger children. Yuan occasionally babysits when they go out; they wonder if Yuan might molest the younger children. This family is obviously in a crisis state.

Robin Comes Out

Robin is a seventeen-year-old Caucasian who lives with her mother, father, and two younger sisters on a small family-run farm in the Midwest. Robin is an average student in the eleventh grade in a public high school. Robin has a very close friend named Patsy who is a year older and attends the same school. After an initial period of confusion, Robin and Patsy realize that they have strong feelings for one another and that their feelings for each other are "more than just a phase." Although neither of them identify as lesbian at first, in time they first come to label their identity as gay first, and then later are comfortable calling themselves lesbian.

Robin has always been close to her family and has always been helpful around the farm. Not wanting to lie to her parents, Robin decides that she should tell her parents how she feels about Patsy. She plans the event, making sure that it is an evening when her sisters are already in bed and asks her parents to sit with her in her bedroom. She starts by telling her family that what she needs to tell them is not an easy thing to tell, but that she loves them and wants them to know her for who she really is. They seem puzzled, thinking that they already know their daughter quite well. She explains that since she was little, about six or seven, she has always liked other girls, not boys. She tells them that at first she thought the feelings would go away, but they did not. At this point, her mother and father are completely aghast about what she is trying to tell them. Robin makes it clear and says, "Mom, Dad, I still like girls and I have come to understand lately that I am a lesbian."

Robin's parents are without words. They are completely unprepared for having a lesbian daughter. They suggest therapy, they ask if she is sure, and suggest that it still might be a phase. They ask if it is her way of rebelling against them. Her answer to all their queries is no. Robin's parents are in shock, confused, embarrassed, and unsure of what to do. Robin's disclosure has created an imbroglio for the family that all are unprepared to deal with.

Like many families, these families had little accurate information about LGBT persons and as a consequence relied mostly on myths as their primary source of information. At first both families believed that their family member's differentness might be an adolescent phase. Both families suggested that the young person should attempt to change sexual orientation via therapy. In addition, although it was almost too frightening to mention, the families expressed fears about the possible molestation of younger siblings by their lesbian or gay child. These families, like most families who have had to deal with an unexpected disclosure, are clearly in a state of shock. Consequently, they are unprepared to see their teens growing up LGBT in a heterosexual world. Most parents never allow themselves to think that they might have a child who is LGBT. Parents are also aware of the shame and secrecy surrounding LGBT identity and as such are unsure of what their child's disclosure will mean for them and for the other family members (Lesser, 1999; Saltzburg, 2004).

In some cases, though not in Yuan's or Robin's case, the disclosure of an LGBT identity can lead to an array of abusive responses from family members. In other instances, an LGBT disclosure can lead to youths' expulsion from their homes, leading to out-of-home placement. In many families, the crisis of disclosure is resolved after the initial reaction of shock and the family moves forward. When a parent comes out in a family context, however, the issues are quite different.

When a Parent Comes Out Within the Family System

When a parent or a spouse comes out or is found out by family members, there are unique and distinctive repercussions. As observed in the previous case examples, lack of accurate information about LBGT identity and fears about individuals who identify as LGBT lead many families to panic about how to manage the disclosure of a family member. The issues of shame and stigma serve to further complicate these issues. The following two case examples illustrate several points with respect to the coming-out process for family members. A father discloses his bisexual identity to his son in the first case example, and a husband is unexpectedly "found out" by his wife as a trans person in the second scenario.

A Bi Dad's Disclosure

Pete, a Caucasian sixth grade child attending a private elementary school, resides in a large suburban environment in a small condo with his dad, Brendan, age thirty-six, and Jamie, his "uncle." Pete was ten when his dad decided to tell him that uncle Jamie, who had lived with the family for eight of Pete's ten years, was really his life partner.

Brendan decided to disclose his bisexual orientation to Pete because he felt that he was getting older and he wanted him to know the truth about his dad. He did not want anyone to make fun of Pete or for him to find out that he was bisexual before he had the opportunity to tell him. Brendan planned the disclosure and sat with Pete privately in their kitchen to tell him. Jamie, although not initially involved in the disclosure, joined them after Brendan had told Pete.

At first Pete was shocked and denied that his dad or Uncle Jamie, with whom he had an excellent relationship, were bisexual. Pete said he did not want to talk about it. Although he didn't say it at the time, he was embarrassed that his friends and teachers in school would find out about his dad and that he would be treated differently. After the initial disclosure, Pete began to distance himself from his dad and Uncle Jamie. When Brendan checked in to see how things were going with him, Pete simply replied that things were "fine."

However, things were not fine. Pete began to have problems in school (prior to the disclosure Pete was an A student) and on two occasions, Pete's dad received notices from school notifying him that Pete had gotten into trouble in the classroom.

Noting this marked change in behavior, the social worker at the school phoned Pete's dad and asked him to come into school for a conference.

Marcellino Is Found Out

Marcellino, a thirty-five-year-old Latino, has been married to Marta, a thirty-year-old Latina for eight years. They have two children, Pedro, age six, and Isabel, age four. They live in a small house in a suburb of a large southern city, which is comprised primarily of working-class Latinos like themselves. Although they have been married for eight years, Marcellino has always known since he was a teenager that he is "different." When he married, he thought that his feelings about himself would change, but they did not. He never discussed these feelings with Marta, but some part of him always thought that she knew that he always felt like a woman inside, not a man. Although Marcellino never talked openly about his trans identity, he did occasionally read a trans magazine called *Tapestry* and visited trans Web sites on his computer.

One evening, when Marcellino arrived home after work, Marta met him at the door and asked for an explanation about the *Tapestry* magazines she had in her hand and the visits to the Web sites on transgender persons that she found in files in the computer. Marcellino initially denied that the magazines were his and denied visiting the Web sites, but after a while he acknowledged that the magazines were his and that he had many times visited the Web sites for trans people. Marta told Marcellino that he had to leave their home immediately. She screamed that he had exposed her and her children to all kinds of things and that he had lied to all of them. Marcellino did not know where to turn. His family lived in Venezuela and he did not have a close family support system except for Marta and his children. Marcellino pleaded with Marta to go with him to see someone—a marriage or family therapist. Marta refused, telling him that he was disgusting, and told him to leave their home immediately.

Marcellino was confused, now estranged from his partner and his children, and feeling completely dejected. Marcellino went to the home of a co-worker to ask if he could stay overnight. In the morning, he went to visit his parish priest to ask for counseling. The priest referred him to a family center in the community. Marta was devastated, ashamed, and told no one about her separation from Marcellino except her sister.

Although the issues of disclosure for a parent coming out to his or her child are far different from those for a wife who finds out that her husband is exploring a transgender identity, both case examples reflect the level of denial, shock, and confusion that some family members experience in this process. In the first case, Brendan has clearly thought out his disclosure and it seems that he will work with his son to process this new information. In the second case, Marta and Marcellino have definitely not planned the disclosure and the consequences of his being found out seem to be, at this juncture, quite weighty for him and his family. Most families bring themselves out of a crisis without professional help; others will need support during the disclosure of the LGBT identity of a family member so that the family may remain intact and its members may grow through the experience (Fraser, Pecora, & Haapala, 1991; Kaplan, 1986; Tracy, Haapala, Kinney, & Pecora, 1991). The benefits of family support and family counseling have particular relevance in each of these four cases (Ariel & McPherson, 2000; Arnup, 1999).

TREATMENT CONSIDERATIONS WITH FAMILIES WHERE SEXUAL OR GENDER ORIENTATION IS THE ISSUE

Family-centered services often call for crisis intervention services, at least in the initial phases of the disclosure process. Families experiencing high stress, such as the disclosure of a lesbian or gay sexual orientation, may find that their regular coping mechanisms have broken down, leaving them open to change in either a positive or negative direction. The family member's increased vulnerability under these conditions can serve as a catalyst to seeking help to resolve their immediate issues (Tracy, 1991; Weissbourd & Kagan, 1989). If professionals trained in family preservation techniques can be available and gently encouraging, the pressure families feel can motivate them to change and to share their concerns. The immediate goal of this intervention is clearly to move the family out of crisis and to restore the family to at least the level of functioning that existed before the crisis (Kinney, Haapala, & Booth, 1991). Many family preservation professionals go well beyond that goal, increasing families' skill levels and resources so that they function better after the crisis than they did before.

Utilizing a family-centered approach (Brown & Weil, 1992; Hartman & Laird, 1983) for working with families, the following sections suggest some intervention guidelines for practitioners.

Intervention

Addressing issues of sexual or gender orientation disclosure requires professionals to first explore their own personal, cultural, and religious biases about persons who are LGBT-oriented. Although many professionals might believe that they are unbiased in their approach to LGBT persons, all professionals must first examine their own bias and be comfortable dealing with issues that are seen by most in Western society as "sensitive." Although most professionals receive little, if any, formal training in dealing with issues of sexual orientation in child welfare, several books published within the past decade provide a wonderful overview of the issues confronting LGBT persons in social work settings (Anastas & Appleby, 1998; Hunter & Hickerson, 2003; Mallon, 1998a; Morrow & Messinger, 2006; Van Wormer & Wells, 2000), which can be helpful for professional development.

Initial Preparations

Keeping people safe is one of the primary goals of this intervention. Workers should be aware that issues of sexual or gender orientation can frequently lead to violence within the family system. Being able to predict the potential for violence is an essential skill for workers to possess.

Preparing for the initial meeting by gathering information by talking to the referring worker (if the case has been referred) or by gathering information directly from the family members by calling them to schedule an interview can assist in forming a positive relationship that might make things easier when the worker arrives at the home. In some situations, as in Marcellino and Marta's case, it might be a good idea to schedule the initial meeting outside the family's home in a public, structured environment such as a restaurant or in a private meeting space in a community center. When situations are potentially volatile, meeting in a public place or a safe space can make it easier for family members to retain control.

The Initial Meeting

Whenever possible, the initial meeting should take place in the home of the family. In three of the four cases presented previously, this would be advisable. Meeting clients on their own turf, in their home, is an integral part of the philosophy of family preservation (Berry, 2005). Professionals should be conscious of being considerate and careful with all family members. In cases when a disclosure of sexual orientation is involved, family members might view the person who has come out or been found out as the only person who needs to be spoken with.

In some cases, family members should be met with one at a time. This is particularly true for the family members who are most upset, pessimistic, or uncooperative. In most cases, they should also be talked with first. This individual needs to feel important and understood. De-escalating this family member and gaining his or her confidence can be helpful in supporting the process and encouraging other family members to participate. Engaging in active listening techniques; using "I" statements (Kinney et al., 1991, Chapter 4); permitting the professional to share his or her own feelings about the situation; notifying family members of the consequences of their actions; calling for a time out; seeking the assistance of a supervisor, if necessary; reconvening at a neutral location; or actually leaving the home if the situation escalates to a point where police intervention is necessary are all options that professionals may need to consider and act upon during their initial visit.

Subsequent Contacts

The first session is usually the most fragile one. The family who has had a member disclose his or her sexual or gender orientation is, as noted, in a crisis mode. Family members in crisis feel vulnerable and anxious. Some may be angry, and others mistrustful. Many families feel secretive about disclosing family business to a stranger, especially when it pertains to a sensitive issue like one's sexual orientation. The goal in the first session is usually to calm everyone down. Establishing trust and forming a partnership between family members and the professional are the next steps.

Assessing Strengths and Problems and Formulating Goals

In subsequent sessions, the professional will need to assist the family in organizing information about their crisis. The social worker should work with family members to minimize blame and labeling and instead focus on generating options for change. This may be facilitated by working with the family to reach consensus about the fact that their family member is, in one way, not as they thought he or she was, but at the same time, still the same person that he or she has always been. Assisting family members with shaping less negative interpretations about a lesbian or gay identity is an important place to begin. Helping families to define problems in terms of their own skill deficits by setting goals, making small steps, prioritizing issues of concern for the family, and being realistic with family members can lead families back toward homeostasis. In the context of an emerging managed care environment, and as a means toward addressing issues of accountability, utilizing standardized outcome measures to test the veracity of clinical interventions with clients has increasingly become a significant aspect of practice (Bloom, Fischer, & Orme, 1995; Blythe, Tripodi, & Briar, 1994).

HELPING FAMILIES LEARN

One of the most dominant elements that is apparent in each of the case vignettes presented is the lack of accurate and relevant information about LGBT individuals. The myths and misconceptions that guide families are graphically present in their initial concerns about molestation, the need for therapy, and the possibility of changing one's sexual or gender orientation. Changing a family's notions about LGBT family members is not always a smooth or easy process. A great deal of the worry that families have about lesbian and gay persons is based on irrational fear and shame. The disclosure of an LGBT orientation within a family context spreads the societal stigmatization of homosexuality to all family members. Goffman called this phenomenon "courtesy stigma" (Goffman, 1963).

Although they caution about developing realistic expectations for all families, Kinney et al. (1991) posit that there are several ways to facilitate learning with clients: (1) direct instruction; (2) modeling; and (3) learning from one another. These strategies can be useful in helping families affected by issues of sexual orientation as highlighted in the following.

Direct Instruction

The social work professional who engages a family with issues of sexual orientation must be prepared to present and provide a great deal of direct instruction to family members. Providing families with accurate and relevant information about their child or family member's orientation is an essential part of this process. Bibliotherapy, or providing families with reading material, is an integral component of this strategy. Although finding this information is not the problem that it once was, as there is a plethora of information available, workers may have to access this information by visiting a local lesbian or gay bookstore or order it via the Internet, as the books are frequently not carried in mainstream bookstores. Increasing the family's knowledge about sexual or gender orientation (Baker, 1998; Boenke, 2003; Borhek, 1983, 1988; Dew, 1994; Fairchild & Hayward, 1989; Firestein, 1996; Fox, 1995; Griffin, Wirth, & Wirth, 1986; Israel, 2005; Lesser, 1999; Strommen, 1989; Switzer, 1996; Tuerk, 1995) and knowing about resources that support families, like Parents, Families and Friends of Lesbians and Gays (PFLAG) (Parents, Families and Friends of Lesbians and Gays, 1990, 1997; www.pflag.org) are important ways to strengthen and support the families of LGBT persons. Furnishing young people with literature, especially work written by LGBT young people for LGBT young people, is one of the most beneficial techniques that can be employed (see Alyson, 1991; Due, 1995; Heron, 1994; Kay, Estepa, & Desetta, 1996; Miranda, 1996; Monette, 1992; Reid, 1973; Savin-Williams, 1998; Valenzuela, 1996; Wadley, 1996a,b). Videos and guest speakers can and should also be utilized in this process. Such information is useful in assisting the LGBT oriented youngster in abolishing myths and stereotypes and correcting misconceptions about their identity. This information can also help educate non-LGBT teens about their lesbian and gay peers (Greene, 1996).

During the past decade, many high schools and colleges have housed lesbian, gay, and straight alliances (see www.glsen.org) and many cities have LGBT community centers (see www.lgbtcenters.org). These and other community-based organizations that might have lesbian- and gay-friendly programs in mainstream community centers are important referral sources for social work practitioners, and, as such, practitioners should know how to locate these organizations and be prepared to visit them.

Most lesbian, gay, and bisexual adolescents have little access to information about their emerging identity and few adult role models from whom to learn, but the Internet and the World Wide Web have liberated LGBT persons from their extreme isolation, supplying them limitless opportunities to communicate with other gays and lesbians in chatrooms and on bulletin boards. In recent years the Internet has grown exponentially. Its growth has permitted thousands of LGBT persons who may not be able to openly visit libraries or bookstores, or who may live in geographically isolated areas, to gain information and connect with others.

Although there is a very limited body of literature that focuses on the impact of disclosure on the nongay spouses of lesbian and gay persons (Buxton, 1994; Gochros, 1989, 1992), an excellent Web site, known as the

Straight Spouse Network, located at www.straightspouse.org, offers valuable support to the partners of lesbian or gay spouses. Klein and Schwartz (2001) also provide guidance on the topic from a bisexual perspective. Ali (1996), MacPike (1989), and Saffron (1997) have all addressed issues of parental disclosure to their children. An excellent Web site that addresses the concerns of the children of lesbian and gay parents (Children of Lesbians and Gays Everywhere [COLAGE]) is located at www.colage .org. Garner (2004) and Snow (2004) both address these issues in their books.

Although published sources can be purchased at LGBT bookstores in metropolitan areas, these sources and many others not mentioned here can also be ordered via the Internet through www.Amazon.com or www.Barnes andNoble.com.

Modeling

Modeling the behaviors ourselves in order to show clients how to do them is a very useful strategy for working with families who are dealing with issues of gender sexual orientation. The LGBT adolescent who comes out or the family who is affected by a disclosure by family members might benefit from attending a support group with other individuals or family members who share their experience. Individuals and family members, anxious about attending a support group for the first time, might very much benefit from a professional who agrees to accompany the client to the session. Accompanying the client to purchase books about LGBT topics at the bookstore or attending an LGBT-run function with clients can be other ways for workers to model acceptance for the client. Linking clients to religious leaders of their faith in their communities who have an affirming stance about lesbian and gay individuals can also be a useful modeling experience for family members.

Learning from Others

Families can also learn from one another by connecting with other families where sexual or gender orientation is an issue. If connections with other families cannot be made in person because of geographic distance, the Internet can be a useful substitute. Many sites include opportunities for LGBT individuals and families affected by issues of gender or sexual orientation to communicate with one another. It is the responsibility of the professional working with the family to identify and access resources for support within the community where the family lives. Workers need to be aware of these resources and visit them prior to making such referrals to clients.

Social workers must also be prepared to assist families in overcoming barriers that will inevitably occur while assisting them in the learning process. Acknowledging, validating, and rewarding small signs that family members are considering new options and beginning to try them is also an important task for workers.

Solving Problems

Social work practitioners trained in problem resolution strategies must incorporate issues of sexual or gender orientation into such designs. Professionals must focus on listening to and helping families to clarify what is causing them the most discomfort. Intervening with clients to assist them in intrapersonal problems can occur via direct interventions, cognitive strategies, values clarifications, and behavioral strategies, all methods suggested by Kinney et al. (1991).

Most families dealing with issues of sexual or gender orientation need help controlling and clarifying their own emotions. Assisting families to develop effective communication skills and problem solving strategies is a major focus of a family preservation model which can be effective with lesbian and gay children, youth, and families.

CONCLUSION

All family-centered services, notwithstanding issues of sexual or gender orientation, from family support to family preservation, maintain the position that children and adolescents are best reared by their own families. Viewed ecologically, both assessment and intervention with families must focus primarily on the goodness of fit (Germain & Gitterman, 1996) between the LGBT individual and those other systems with which he or she is in transaction, the most central of which in this case is the family. Many of the issues that surface when a family member discloses or is dealing with aspects of sexual or gender orientation can be best dealt with by a competent social worker trained in family systems. These issues must be viewed as deficits within the environment, dysfunctional transactions among environmental systems, or as a lack of individual or family coping skills or strategies (Loppnow, 1985). Providing education and intensive training effort for family-centered practitioners (Faria, 1994; Laird, 1996) that would help them feel competent about broadly addressing issues of sexual orientation could provide support for families in crisis and prevent unnecessary family disruption. Family-centered practitioners must also be prepared to serve as advocates for their clients, including the lesbian or gay child or adolescent; the parent who identifies as LGBT; or the couple in which one of the partners identifies as other than heterosexually oriented.

Family-centered social practitioners working with the primary goal of keeping families together can deliver these services within the context of the clients' natural environment—their community. Programs like the homebuilders model (Kinney et al., 1991) have opportunities to help families grappling with issues of sexual or gender orientation. Community-based family and children's services centers also provide many opportunities for addressing issues of sexual orientation within the family system. These approaches also have relevance for other situations where spouses or parents come out as lesbian or gay. Working with family systems in their communities makes social workers in family-centered programs ideally situated to see what is really going on in a family's natural environment. By being located in the home or in the community, the worker is able to make an accurate assessment and design an intervention that will support and preserve the family system. With a greater awareness of issues of sexual orientation, family-centered practitioners can educate parents, ease the distress experienced by couples where one partner is LGBT and the other is heterosexual, as well as model and shape new behaviors that can transform lives for young LGBT persons.

REFERENCES

Ali, T. (1996). *We are family: Testimonies of lesbian and gay parents.* London: Cassell.

Alyson, S. (1991). *Young, gay and proud.* Boston: Alyson Publications.

Anastas, J., & Appleby, G. (Eds.) (1998). *Not just a passing phase.* New York: Columbia University Press.

Appleby, G. A. (1998). Social work practice with gay men and lesbians within organizations. In G. P. Mallon (Ed.), *Foundations of social work practice with lesbian and gay persons* (pp. 249-270). Binghamton, NY: The Haworth Press.

Ariel, J., & McPherson, D. W. (2000). Therapy with gay and lesbian parents and their children. *Journal of Marital and Family Therapy, 26*(4), 421-432.

Arnup, K. (1999). Out in this world: The social and legal context of gay and lesbian families. *Journal of Gay & Lesbian Social Services, 10*(1), 1-26.

Baker, J. M. (1998). *Family secrets, gay sons: A mother's story.* Binghamton, NY: The Haworth Press.

Berzon, B. (2001). *Positively gay: New approaches to gay and lesbian life* (3rd ed.). Berkeley, CA: Celestial Arts.

Bloom, M., Fischer, J., & Orme, J. G. (1995). *Evaluating practice: Guidelines for the accountable professional* (2nd ed.). Needham Heights, MA: Allyn & Bacon.

Blumenfeld, W., & Raymond, D. (Eds.) (1993). *Looking at lesbian and gay life.* Boston, MA: Beacon Press.

Blythe, B., Tripodi, T., & Briar, S. (1994). *Direct practice research in human service agencies.* New York: Columbia University Press.

Boenke, M. (Ed.) (2003). *Transforming families: Real stories about transgendered loved ones* (2nd ed.). New Castle, DE: Oak Knoll Press.

Borhek, M. V. (1983). *Coming out to parents.* New York: Pilgrim Press.

Borhek, M. V. (1988). Helping gay and lesbian adolescents and their families: A mother's perspective. *Journal of Adolescent Health Care, 9*(2), 123-128.

Bradford, M. (2004). The bisexual experience: Living in a dichotomous culture. *Journal of Bisexuality, 4*(1/2), 7-23.

Brown, J., & Weil, M. (Eds.) (1992). *Family practice.* Washington, DC: Child Welfare League of America.

Buxton, A. P. (1994). *The other side of the closet.* New York: Wiley.

Cass, V. C. (1979). Homosexual identity formation: A theoretical model. *Journal of Homosexuality, 4,* 219-235.

Cass, V. C. (1983/1984). Homosexual identity: A concept in need of a definition. *Journal of Homosexuality, 9*(2/3), 105-126.

Cass, V. C. (1984). Homosexual identity formation: Testing a theoretical model. *Journal of Sex Research, 20,* 143-167.

Chan, C. (1989). Issues of identity development among Asian American lesbians and gay men. *Journal of Counseling and Development, 68*(1), 16-20.

Coleman, E. (1981). Developmental stages of the coming out process. *Journal of Homosexuality, 7*(2/3), 31-43.

Coleman, E. (1987). Assessment of sexual orientation. *Journal of Homosexuality, 13*(4), 9-23.

Colon, E. (2001). An ethnographic study of six Latino gay and bisexual men. *Journal of Gay & Lesbian Social Services, 12*(3/4), 77-99.

Cooper, D. (1994). *From darkness into light: What the Bible really says about homosexuality* (3rd ed.). Tucson, AZ: Cornerstone Fellowship.

Dew, R. F. (1994). *The family heart: A memoir of when our son came out.* Reading, MA: Addison-Wesley.

De Monteflores, C., & Schultz, S. J. (1978). Coming out: Similarities and differences for lesbians and gay men. *Journal of Social Issues, 34*(3), 59-72.

Due, L. (1995). *Joining the tribe: Growing up gay and in the 90's.* New York: Anchor Books.

Eskridge, W. N., & Spedale, D. R. (2006). *Gay marriage: For better or for worse? What we have learned from the evidence.* New York: Oxford University Press.

Fairchild, B., & Hayward, N. (1989). *Now that you know: What every parent should know about homosexuality.* New York: Harcourt Brace Jovanovich.

Faria, G. (1994). Training for family preservation practice with lesbian families. *Families in Society, 22,* 416-422.

Finnegan, D. G., & McNally, E. B. (1996). Chemical dependency and depression in lesbians and gay men: What helps? In M. Shernoff (Ed.), *Human services for gay people: Clinical and community practice* (pp. 115-130). Binghamton, NY: The Haworth Press.

Firestein, B. A. (Ed.) (1996). *Bisexuality: The psychology and politics of an invisible minority.* Thousand Oaks, CA: Sage Publications.

Fox, R. C. (1995). Bisexual identities. In A. R. D'Augelli & C. J. Patterson (Eds.), *Lesbian, gay, and bisexual identities over the lifespan* (pp. 112-142). New York: Oxford University Press.

Fraser, M., Pecora, P., & Haapala, D. (1991). *Families in crisis.* New York: Aldine de Gruyter.

Garner, A. (2004). *Families like mine: Children of gay parents tell it like it is.* New York: HarperCollins.

Garofalo, R., Wolf, C., Wissow, L. S., Woods, W. R., & Goodman, E. (1999). Sexual orientation and the risk of suicide attempts among a representative sample of youth. *Archives of Pediatric Adolescent Medicine, 153,* 487-493.

Germain, C. B. (1985). The place of community work within an ecological approach to social work practice. In S. H. Taylor & R. W. Roberts (Eds.), *Theory and practice of community social work* (pp. 30-55). New York: Columbia University Press.

Germain, C. B., & Gitterman, A. (1996). *The life model of social work practice* (2nd ed.). New York: Columbia University Press.

Gochros, J. (1989). *When husbands come out of the closet.* Binghamton, NY: The Haworth Press.

Gochros, J. (1992). Homophobia, homosexuality, and heterosexual marriage. In W. Blumenfeld (Ed.), *Homophobia: How we all pay the price* (pp. 131-153). Boston, MA: Beacon Press.

Goffman, E. (1963). *Stigma: Notes of the management of a spoiled identity.* Englewood Cliffs, NJ: Prentice Hall.

Goodwill, K. A. (2000). Religion and the spiritual needs of gay Mormon men. *Journal of Gay & Lesbian Social Services, 11*(4), 23-38.

Greene, B. (1994). Lesbian and gay sexual orientations: Implications for clinical training, practice and research. In B. Greene & G. M. Herek (Eds.), *Lesbian and gay psychology: Theory, research, and clinical applications* (pp. 1-24). Thousand Oaks, CA: Sage Publications.

Greene, Z. (1996). Straight, but not narrow-minded. In P. Kay, A. Estepa, & A. Desetta (Eds.), *Out with it: Gay and straight teens write about homosexuality* (pp. 12-14). New York: Youth Communications.

Griffin, C., Wirth, M. J., & Wirth, A. G. (1986). *Beyond acceptance.* Englewood Cliffs, NJ: Prentice Hall.

Hartman, A., & Laird, J. (1983). *Family-centered social work practice.* New York: Free Press.

Helminiak, D. A. (1997). *What the Bible really says about homosexuality.* San Francisco: Alamo Square Press.

Herek, G. M. (1991). Stigma, prejudice and violence against lesbians and gay men. In J. C. Gonsiorek & J. D. Weinrich (Eds.), *Homosexuality: Research implications for public policy* (pp. 60-80). Newbury Park, CA: Sage publications.

Herman, D. (1997). *The anti-gay agenda—Orthodox vision and the Christian right.* Chicago: University of Chicago Press.

Heron, A. (Ed.) (1994). *Two in twenty.* Boston: Alyson Publications.

Hetrick, E., & Martin, A. D. (1987). Developmental issues and their resolution for gay and lesbian adolescents. *Journal of Homosexuality, 13*(4), 25-43.

Hunter, J., & Mallon, G. P. (1998). Social work practice with lesbian and gay persons within communities. In G. P. Mallon (Ed.), *Foundations of social work practice with lesbian and gay persons* (pp. 229-248). Binghamton, NY: The Haworth Press.

Hunter, J., & Schaecher, R. (1987). Stresses on lesbian and gay adolescents in schools. *Social Work in Education, 9*(3), 180-188.

Hunter, S., & Hickerson, J. (2003). *Affirmative practices: Understanding and working with LGBT Persons.* Washington, DC: NASW.

Israel, G. E. (2005). Translove: Transgender persons and their families. *Journal of Gay and Lesbian Family Studies, 1*(1), 53-67.

Israel, G., & Tarver, D. E. (1997). *Transgender care.* Philadelphia: Temple University Press.

Jones, B. E., & Hill, M. (Eds.) (2003). *Mental health issues in lesbian, gay, bisexual, and transgender communities.* Washington, DC: APA.

Kaplan, L. (1986). *Working with multi-problem families.* Lexington, MA: Lexington Books.

Kay, P., Estepa, A., & Desetta, A. (Eds.) (1996). *Out with it: Gay and straight teens write about homosexuality.* New York: Youth Communications.

Kinney, J., Haapala, D., & Booth, C. (1991). *Keeping families together: The homebuilders model.* Hawthorne, NY: Aldine de Gruyter.

Klein, F. (1993). *The bisexual option.* Binghamton, NY: Harrington Park Press.

Klein, F., & Schwartz, T. (2001). *Bisexual and gay husbands: Their stories, their words.* Binghamton, NY: The Haworth Press.

Kluger, S. (2006, August 2). Give me your tired, your poor . . . or not. *USA Today,* p. 9A.

Laird, J. (1996). Family-centered practice with lesbian and gay families. *Families in Society, 22,* 559-572.

LaSala, M. C. (2000). Lesbians, gay men and their parents: Family therapy for the coming-out crisis. *Family Process, 39*(1), 67-82.

Lease, S. H., & Shulman, J. L. (2003). A preliminary investigation of the role of religion for family members of lesbian, gay male, or bisexual male and female individuals. *Counseling and Values, 47*(3), 195-209.

Lesbian and gay poverty [on-line]. From www.tased.edu.au/tasonline/tasqueer/nat_issu/poverty accessed August 10, 2006.

Lesser, J. G. (1999). When your son becomes your daughter: A mother's adjustment to a transgender child. *Families in Society, 80*(2), 182-189.

Lev, A. I. (2004). *Transgender emergence: Therapeutic guidelines for working with gender variant people and their families.* Binghamton, NY: The Haworth Press.

Loppnow, D. M. (1985). Adolescents on their own. In J. Laird & A. Hartman (Eds.), *A handbook of child welfare: Context, knowledge, and practice* (pp. 514-532). New York: Free Press.

MacPike, L. (Ed.) (1989). *There's something I've been meaning to tell you.* Tallahassee, FL: Naiad Press.

Mallon, G. P. (Ed.) (1998a). *Foundations of social work practice with lesbian and gay persons.* Binghamton, NY: The Haworth Press.

Mallon, G. P. (1998b). *We don't exactly get the welcome wagon: The experiences of lesbian and gay adolescents in child welfare systems.* New York: Columbia University Press.

Mallon, G. P. (1998c). Social work practice with lesbian and gay persons within families. In G. P. Mallon (Ed.), *Foundations of social work practice with lesbian and gay persons* (pp. 145-181). Binghamton, NY: The Haworth Press.

Mallon, G. P. (2004). *Gay men choosing parenthood.* New York: Columbia University Press.

Malyon, A. K. (1981). The homosexual adolescent: Developmental issues and social bias. *Child Welfare League of America, 60*(5), 321-330.

Merighi, J. R., & Grimes, M. (2000). Coming out to families in a multicultural context. *Families in Society, 81*(1), 32-41.

Metropolitan Community Church (1990). *Homosexuality not a sin, not a sickness: What the Bible does and does not say.* Los Angeles: Author.

Miranda, D. (1996). I hated myself. In P. Kay, A. Estepa, & A. Desetta (Eds.), *Out with it: Gay and straight teens write about homosexuality* (pp. 34-39). New York: Youth Communications.

Monette, P. (1992). *Becoming a man: Half a life story.* New York: Harcourt Brace Jovanovich.

Morales, E. S. (1989). Ethnic minority families and minority gays and lesbians. *Marriage and Family Review, 14,* 217-239.

Morrow, D. F., & Messinger, L. (2006). *Sexual orientation and gender expression in social work practice: Working with gay, lesbian, bisexual, and transgender people.* New York: Columbia University Press.

Ochs, R. (1996). Biphobia: It goes more than two ways. In B. A. Firestein (Ed.), *Bisexuality: The psychology and politics of an invisible minority* (pp. 217-239). Thousand Oaks, CA: Sage Publications.

O'Dell, S. (2000). Psychotherapy with gay and lesbian families: Opportunities for cultural inclusion and clinical challenge. *Clinical Social Work Journal, 28*(2), 171-182.

Oswald, R. F. (2002a). Inclusion and belonging in the family rituals of gay and lesbian people. *Journal of Family Psychology, 16*(4), 428-436.

Oswald, R. F. (2002b). Resilience within the family networks of lesbians and gay men: Intentionality and redefinition. *Journal of Marriage and Family, 64*(2), 374-383.

Page, E. H. (2004). Mental health services experiences of bisexual women and men: An empirical study. *Journal of Bisexuality, 3*(3/4), 138-160.

Parents, Families and Friends of Lesbians and Gays (1990). *Why is my child gay?* Washington, DC: Parents and Friends of Lesbians and Gays.

Parents, Families and Friends of Lesbians and Gays (1997). *Beyond the Bible: Parents, families and friends talk about religion and homosexuality.* Washington, DC: Author.

Pharr, S. (1988). *Homophobia: A weapon of sexism.* Inverness, CA: Chardon Press.

Poon, M. K. (2004). A missing voice: Asians in contemporary gay and lesbian social service literature. *Journal of Gay & Lesbian Social Services, 17*(3), 87-106.

Reid, J. (1973). *The best little boy in the world.* New York: Ballantine Books.

Remafedi, G. (1999). Sexual orientation and youth suicide. *Journal of the American Medical Association, 282,* 1291-1292.

Rodriguez, R. A. (1998). Clinical and practical considerations in private practice with lesbians and gay men of color. *Journal of Gay & Lesbian Social Services, 8*(4), 59-76.

Rofes, E. R. (1983). *I thought people like that killed themselves.* San Francisco: Grey Fox Press.

Rothberg, B., & Weinstein, D. L. (1996). A primer on lesbian and gay families. In M. Shernoff (Ed.), *Human services for gay people: Clinical and community practice* (pp. 55-68). Binghamton, NY: The Haworth Press.

Rust, P. C. (1996). Managing multiple identities: Diversity among bisexual women and men. In B. A. Firestein (Ed.), *Bisexuality: The psychology and politics of an invisible minority* (pp. 53-83). Thousand Oaks, CA: Sage Publications.

Saffron, L. (1997). *What about the children? Sons and daughters of lesbian and gay parents talk about their lives.* London: Cassell.

Saltzburg, S. (2004). Learning that an adolescent child is gay or lesbian: The parent experience. *Social Work, 49*(1), 109-118.

Savin-Williams, R. C. (1998). *And then I became gay.* New York: Routledge Press.

Savin-Williams, R. C., & Rodriguez, R. G. (1993). A developmental clinical perspective on lesbian, gay male and bisexual youth. In T. P. Gullotta, G. R. Adams, & R. Montemayor (Eds.), *Adolescent sexuality: Advances in adolescent development* (Vol. 5, pp. 77-101). Newbury Park, CA: Sage.

Silverstein, C. (1977). *A family matter: A parent's guide to homosexuality.* New York: McGraw Hill.

Snow, J. (2004). *How it feels to have a gay or lesbian parent.* Binghamton, NY: The Haworth Press.

Strommen, E. F. (1989). "You're a what?" Family member reactions to the disclosure of homosexuality. *Journal of Homosexuality, 18*(1/2), 37-58.

Switzer, D. K. (1996). *Coming out as parents.* Louisville, KY: Westminister John Knox Press.

Tracy, E. M. (1991). Defining the target population for family preservation services: Some conceptual issues. In K. Wells & D. Biegal (Eds.), *Family preservation services: Research and evaluation* (pp. 138-158). Newbury Park, CA: Sage Publications.

Tracy, E. M., Haapala, D. A., Kinney, J., & Pecora, P. (1991). Intensive family pres-
ervation services: A strategic response to families in crisis. In E. M. Tracy, D. A.
Haapala, J. Kinney, & P. Pecora (Eds.), *Intensive family preservation services:
An instructional sourcebook* (pp. 1-14). Cleveland, OH: Mandel School of
Applied Social Sciences.

Troiden, R. R. (1979). Becoming homosexual: A model of gay identity acquisition.
Psychiatry, 42, 362-373.

Troiden, R. R. (1988). *Lesbian and gay identity: A sociological analysis.* Dix Hills,
NY: General Hall, Inc.

Troiden, R. R. (1989). The formation of homosexual identities. In G. Herdt (Ed.),
Lesbian and gay youth (pp. 43-74). Binghamton, NY: The Haworth Press.

Tuerk, C. (1995, October). A son with gentle ways: A therapist-mother's journey.
*The Family: A Magazine for Lesbians, Gays, Bisexuals and Their Relations,
1*(1), 18-22.

Valenzuela, W. (1996). A school where I can be myself. In P. Kay, A. Estepa, &
A. Desetta (Eds.), *Out with it: Gay and straight teens write about homosexuality*
(pp. 45-46). New York: Youth Communications.

van Wormer, K., & Wells, J. (2000). *Social work with lesbians, gays, and bisexuals:
A strengths perspective.* New York: Allyn & Bacon.

Wadley, C. (1996a). Shunned, insulted, threatened. In P. Kay, A. Estepa, &
A. Desetta (Eds.), *Out with it: Gay and straight teens write about homosexuality*
(pp. 57-60). New York: Youth Communications.

Wadley, C. (1996b). Kicked out because she was a lesbian. In P. Kay, A. Estepa, &
A. Desetta (Eds.), *Out with it: Gay and straight teens write about homosexuality*
(pp. 58-60). New York: Youth Communications.

Walters, K. L. (1998). Negotiating conflicts in allegiances among lesbian and gays
of color: Reconciling divided selves and communities. In G. P. Mallon (Ed.),
Foundations of social work practice with lesbian and gay persons (pp. 47-76).
Binghamton, NY: The Haworth Press.

Weissbourd, B., & Kagan, S. L. (1989). Family support programs: Catalysts for
change. *American Journal of Orthopsychiatry, 59*(1), 20-30.

Weitzman, G. (2006). Therapy with clients who are bisexual and polyamorous.
Journal of Bisexuality, 6(1/2), 137-164.

Weston, K. (1997). *Families we choose: Lesbian and gay kinship.* New York:
Columbia University Press.

Chapter 12

Social Work Practice with LGBT Parents

Gerald P. Mallon

Lesbian, gay, bisexual, and transgender (LGBT) persons become parents for some of the same reasons that heterosexual people do (Bekov, 1994; Mallon, 2004; Martin, 1993; Pies, 1990). Some pursue parenting as a single person and some seek to create a family as a couple. Others became parents when they were in a heterosexual relationship (Buxton, 1994; Gochros, 1989). Although there are many common themes of LGBT parenting that readers will see reflected in the pages that follow, there are also some unique features.

Unlike their heterosexual counterparts, who couple, get pregnant, and give birth, most LGBT individuals and couples who wish to parent must consider many other variables in deciding whether to become parents. First, the couple must decide how they should go about creating a family: adoption (Mallon, 2004), foster parenting (Ricketts, 1991; Ricketts & Achtenberg, 1990), surrogacy (Bernfeld, 1995), shared custody from a heterosexual relationship (Buxton, 1994), or alternative insemination (Agigian, 2004).

RESEARCH ON LGBT PARENTING

Although a number of conservative politicians have noted that "studies show" that children are better off with a mother and a father—they are in fact referring to studies that compared children of two-parent heterosexual couples with those of single, presumably, heterosexual mothers. The findings of these studies do suggest that children are better off in two-parent families, but they do not suggest anything about sexual or gender orientation which was not measured or even considered. As Shuster (2005, p. 14) notes in quoting Charlotte Patterson (1992, 1994, 1995, 1996), the best-known researcher on issues of sexual orientation and parenting, these studies "don't have anything to do with sexual orientation, and are therefore irrelevant to the question about how 'children fare' in households headed by lesbian and gay parents."

But what do we know about how children and youth fare in households headed by LGBT persons? In this section, I will review the existing research to provide an overview of the research evidence on the impact of family life on children with LGBT parents. I will then use the research findings to examine (and *dispel*) the myths and facts about LGBT parents, and recommend future directions for research.

Research Limitations

The nature and scope of research studies on LGBT families continue to grow. The earliest documentation on lesbian mothers and gay fathers (Bozett, 1980; Osman, 1972) was mostly explored in the context of children born in heterosexual marriages which ended in divorce. Such early studies have been replaced by those focusing on children in planned LGBT-headed families, without the confounding variable of divorce and the coming-out process of the parents. There are, as with all research, some limitations to the research in the area of LGBT parenting. Since not all LGBT persons are "out," random representative sampling of LGBT parents is a challenge to methodology. This is particularly true as there is no reliable data on the number and whereabouts of LGBT parents in the general population in the United States, or elsewhere.

In the existing limited research, there are biases toward white, urban, well-educated, and mature lesbian mothers and gay fathers. I found no research on bisexual parents and limited literature on the experiences of trans parents (for information see http://www.transparentcy.org and http://www.firelily.com/gender/gianna/custody.html). The relatively small samples which do exist in the research are recruited through community networks. It is not easy to define groups that would be an appropriate comparison to LGBT parents—and comparing them to a heterosexual parenting population does not lend greater legitimacy either, as there are intrinsic differences. In her excellent review of the literature in this area, Scott (2002, p. 12) indicates:

There are also limitations in how far the findings of such research on biologically related parents and children can be simply "borrowed" to answer questions concerning the impact on children of being adopted or fostered by lesbians and gay men.

How are LGBT-headed families different from heterosexual families? One of the most consistent findings over the past ten years, according to Patterson (1996), is that same-gendered couples with and without children tend to establish a more even distribution of household tasks in comparison with heterosexual couples. Without socially prescribed guidance on gendered roles, LGBT parents tend to value equality in partnership and structure and equitable division of labor in housework, childrearing, and work outside the home. Even though this repeated finding seems to be well known in the mental health community, it is has not been discussed in the mainstream dialogue about the pros and cons of lesbian and gay marriage or parenting. The challenge for social services professionals, especially those interested in competent practice with LGBT parents, is to understand what this finding might mean for the children and their parents.

Stacey and Biblarz (2001) identify parental gender to be predictive of parenting skill. All mothers (heterosexual, trans women, lesbian, birth, and adoptive) are more likely than fathers to be more invested and skilled at caring for children. Therefore, when two women co-parent, gender and sexual orientation interact, with two mothers both committed to and working together toward creating an equitable and mutually caring environment that provides a loving and supportive foundation for their child's developing self-esteem.

The research on biological gay fathers and their children is extremely limited. There are no studies in the literature that have systematically examined the impact of their sexual identity on their children. Two studies (McPherson, 1993; Sbordone, 1993) show similar parenting styles and skills between gay and heterosexual fathers. Mallon's study (2004) of the parenting process in a group of twenty self-identified gay fathers found they were more likely to endorse a nurturing role for fathers, less likely to emphasize the importance of economic support, and less likely to show affection to their partner in the presence of the children (Barret & Robinson, 2000; Bigner & Jacobsen, 1992). Further results indicate that gay fathers are as effective as heterosexual fathers in caring for their children. They have been shown to be more consistent in limit-setting with their children than are heterosexual fathers. They have also been found to be more emotionally expressive and nurturing with their children, less likely to prioritize their "breadwinner" functions over their parenting roles, and less interested in conventional gender-role behaviors than heterosexual fathers (Mallon, 2004).

Fears About Lesbian and Gay Parents

Although there has been a wealth of literature about gay and lesbian parenting since the mid-1980s (Benkov, 1994; Bigner, 1996; Bozett, 1987; Martin, 1993; McGarry, 2004; Mitchell, 1996; Muzio, 1993, 1996; Pies, 1985) and very limited literature about trans parents (see http://www.transparentcy .org and http://www.firelily.com/gender/gianna/custody.html), the idea of an LGBT person as a primary nurturing figure rearing children is still remarkable to many. Many social work professionals still hold firm to a belief system grounded in the ubiquitous, negative myths and stereotypes about LGBT persons (Mallon, 1999a,b)—for example, that an LGBT person might abuse children, that children might be encouraged or "recruited" to be LGBT, or that LGBT persons are not suitable role models.

Those who oppose the idea of LGBT persons as parents base their thinking on a number of fears, for example:

- The child will be bullied or ostracized because of having LGBT parents.
- The child might become LGBT because of having an LGBT parental role model.
- Living with or having contact with an LGBT parent may harm the child's moral well-being (these beliefs may have their foundation in religious texts that condemn relationships that are other than heterosexual).
- The child will be abused (based on the myth that all LGBT persons are sexual predators).

None of these rationales is borne out or supported by evidence (Carey, 2005; Dunlap, 1996; Patterson, 1996; Stacey & Biblarz, 2001). Such attitudes can have a crucial impact on social work professionals working with LGBT parents.

The myth of LGBT persons (especially bisexual and gay men) as child abusers (Groth, 1978; Newton, 1978) remains ingrained in the psyche of many people, including professionals in the social work field, so much so that the idea that an LGBT person would be "allowed" to parent seems incredulous to some. These ideas are derived in part from the cultural myth that men in general, and gay men in particular, are sexual predators, unable to control themselves sexually, and prone to sexualize all situations.

The published social science literature (Cramer, 1986; Groth, 1978; Groth & Birnbaum, 1978; Herek, 1991; Newton, 1978) also confirms that the myth of child abuse by LGBT persons is a fallacy. Pedophilia is the attraction of an adult to children for sexual gratification and has nothing to do with the gender or sexual orientation of the perpetrator. One study examining sexual orientation and child sexual abuse (Jenny, Roesler, & Poyer, 1994), which looked at 269 cases of sexually abused children, found that only two offenders were identified as gay. These findings suggest that a child's risk of being sexually abused by the heterosexual partner of a relative is more than 100 times greater than the risk of being abused by somebody who might be identifiable as being LGBT.

Quality of Family Relations

Numerous studies show that the qualities which make good fathers or good mothers are universal and are not related to sexual orientation or gender. The need for fathers to be involved in the lives of their children has been very clearly established by many (Biller & Kimpton, 1997; Horn & Sylvester, 2002; Lamb, 1986, 1987, 1997; Popenoe, 1996). The ability to love and care for a child is not determined by one's sexual orientation (Sullivan, 1995). Furthermore, the desire to parent is not exclusive to heterosexuals, but is one shared by many LGBT persons (Benkov, 1994; Green, 1999; Mallon, 2004; Martin, 1993; Shernoff, 1996).

According to the meta-analysis of the relevant research spanning two decades conducted by Stacey and Biblarz (2001), none of the significant differences in parenting as reported in the research apply to children's self-esteem, psychological well-being, or social adjustment. Nor were there differences in parents' self-esteem, mental health, or commitment to their children. In other words, even though there are differences, they were not identified as deficits. In fact, the studies found no negative effects of lesbian and gay parenting. Bisexuals and trans parents were not included in the reviews of these studies.

A few studies reported some differences which could represent advantages of lesbian parenting. For example, several studies found that lesbian co-mothers share family responsibilities more equally than heterosexual married parents, and some research hints that children benefit from egalitarian co-parenting. A few studies found that lesbians worry less than heterosexual parents about the gender conformity of their children. Perhaps that helps to account for a few studies which found that sons of lesbians play less aggressively and that children of lesbians communicate their feelings more freely, aspire to a wider range of occupations, and score higher on self-esteem. Most professionals would see these differences as positive elements, but some critics of these studies have misrepresented these differences as evidence that the children are suffering from gender confusion. Finally, some studies reported that lesbian mothers feel more comfortable discussing sexuality with their children and accepting their children's sexuality—whatever it might be. More to the point are data reported in a twenty-five-year British study (Golombok & Tasker, 1996). Few of the young adults in this study identified themselves as gay or lesbian, but a larger minority of those with lesbian mothers did report that they were more open to exploring their sexuality and had at one time or another considered or actually had a same-sex relationship.

The Golombok and Tasker (1996) longitudinal study of children brought up in lesbian households assessed the quality of mother-child interaction (primary older children). They found that children with lesbian mothers had closer relationships with their mothers and were more likely to have a secure attachment style than those in a heterosexual family comparison group. As young adults, the respondents reported being able to communicate well with their mother about their own relationships, more so than did those in the comparison group.

Similarly, Chan, Raboy, and Patterson (2000) note that where the quality of family relationships is concerned research comparing various forms of lesbian and heterosexual families provides consistent evidence that children are more powerfully affected by *how* family members relate to each other than by family structure or parental sexual orientation.

Most children brought up in planned lesbian-led families and by previously heterosexual lesbian mothers have regular contact with adults beyond their immediate household, including grandparents, other relatives, and male and female family friends (Golombok, Spencer, & Rutter, 1983; Patterson, Hurt, & Mason, 1998).

Although most research to date on gay and lesbian parenting is based on those who are biological parents, researchers looking at LGBT parenting have reached the same, unequivocal conclusions. That is, the children of LGBT parents grow up as successfully as the children of heterosexual parents (Bronston, 2004; Elovitz, 1995; Golombok et al., 1983; Patterson, 1994, 1995, 1996; Tasker & Golombok, 1997).

Since 1980, more than twenty studies conducted and published in the United States, Australia, and the United Kingdom have addressed the way in which parental sexual orientation impacts on children. Another meta-analysis of eighteen such studies concluded:

> The results demonstrate no differences on any measures between the heterosexual and homosexual parents regarding parenting styles, emotional adjustment, and sexual orientation of the child(ren). (Allen & Burrell, 1996, p. 19)

Not one study has found that the children of LGBT parents face greater social stigma. There is no evidence to support the belief that the children of LGBT parents are more likely to be abused, or to suggest that the children of these parents are more likely to be gay, lesbian, bisexual, or transgender themselves. Children will, in fact, be who they are. It is important to bear in mind that the majority of LGBT persons have been raised by heterosexual parents.

Becoming a Parent: Making Decisions

Although LGBT persons become parents for some of the same reasons as heterosexuals, there are some unique circumstances as well (Mallon, 2004; Pies, 1990). Unlike their heterosexual counterparts, LGBT individuals and couples who wish to parent will have to give more careful consideration to how they will become a parent, and at the outset be open to different ways of becoming a family and parenting children, such as through adoption and fostering (Ricketts, 1991; Ricketts & Achtenberg, 1990), shared parenting (Martin, 1993), and surrogacy or donor insemination (Agigian, 2004; Mohler & Frazer, 2002). LGBT persons who choose to parent as single parents will face stresses more to do with single parenting than with their sexuality (Marindin, 1997; Melina, 1998, p. 292).

On the positive side, LGBT persons who choose to create families have the advantage of redefining and reinventing their own meaning for family and parenting, precisely because they exist outside of the traditionally defined "family." They have the unique opportunity to break out of preconceived gender roles and be a new kind of father or mother to a child (Benkov, 1994). Most LGBT persons who parent are not invested in raising LGBT children, as suggested by some, but in raising children who will be authentic, happy, self-confident, and have the ability to support them regardless of their expressions of gender or sexual orientation.

Myths versus Facts

Myth. The only acceptable home for a child is one with a mother and father who are married to each other.

Fact. Research shows that children thrive in many different types of family structure. In the United States there are increasingly more diverse types of families, as discussed in the introduction.

Myth. Children need a mother and a father in order to have proper male and female role models.

Fact. Children get their role models from many places besides their parents. These include grandparents, aunts and uncles, teachers, friends, and neighbors.

Myth. LGBT persons do not have stable relationships and would not know how to be good parents.

Fact. Many LGBT persons are in stable, committed relationships and many are successfully involved in the parenting of children. All of the evidence shows that LGBT parents can and do make good parents.

Myth. Children raised by LGBT parents are more likely to grow up LGBT themselves.

Fact. All of the available evidence demonstrates that the sexual orientation of parents has no impact on the gender or sexual orientation of their children, and that children of LGBT parents are no more likely than any other child to grow up to be LGBT. In fact, most LBGT persons have been raised by heterosexual parents. Of course, some children of LGBT parents will grow up to be LGBT, as will some children of heterosexual parents. These children will have the added advantage of being raised by parents who are supportive and accepting of their sexuality. There is some evidence that children of LGBT parents are more tolerant and open to difference.

Myth. Children reared by LGBT parents will be subjected to bullying and may be rejected by their peers.

Fact. Children make fun of other children for all kinds of reasons: for being too short or too tall, for being too thin or too fat, or for being of a different race or religion. Children can show remarkable resilience, especially if they have a stable, loving home environment, and parents who can support them. Owing to the bi/trans/homophobia that exists in society, some children will experience discrimination and negative comments for having LGBT parents. This needs to be acknowledged and addressed and children need to be given the strategies and supports necessary to deal with these experiences.

Myth. Gay/bi men are more likely to abuse children.

Fact. There is no connection between a gay or bisexual identity and pedophilia. All of the legitimate scientific evidence supports this assertion. In addition to the research mentioned previously (Jenny et al., 1994), of the cases studied involving sexual abuse of boys by men, 74 percent of the abusers were or had been in a heterosexual relationship with the boy's mother or another female relative.

Myth. Children raised by LGBT parents will be brought up in an "immoral" environment.

Fact. The research by Cameron, Cameron, and Landess (1996) is most frequently cited to support the claim that having an LGBT parent impacts adversely on children. They propose that LGBT identity is a "learned pathology" that parents pass on to their children by "modelling, seduction and contagion" (p. 388). There is ample evidence to discount this "research": the authors have been denounced by the American Sociological Association (ASA) for willfully misrepresenting research; Paul Cameron was expelled from the American Psychiatric Association and censored by the ASA for unethical scholarly practices, such as selective, misleading representations of research and making claims that could not be substantiated. Nonetheless, as Stacey and Biblarz (2001) note, bias against gay and lesbian parenting remains sufficiently strong for this work to continue to be cited in court cases and policy hearings.

Future Research

There is a need for a study on adoptive parents that compares children adopted by LGBT parents with children adopted by heterosexual parents. To my knowledge, no such study has yet been undertaken. There is also a need for more research on gay fathers, bisexual, and transgender parents, and for studies that include lesbian mothers who came to motherhood through alternative insemination, as well as studies that explore issues pertaining to gay fathers who have children through surrogacy or other means. It is also critical that research studies should have a more diverse representation of LGBT parents in terms of ethnicity, race, education, income, and nationality.

ISSUES FOR LGBT PERSONS
WHEN CONSIDERING PARENTING

The focus of this section is on the issues that LGBT persons face as they make the decision for becoming parents. As LGBT persons are becoming more visible in U.S. society, they are being considered more seriously as parents. Although LGBT persons become parents through a variety of means—alternative insemination, kinship, marriage—the increasing number of LGBT persons choosing to adopt or become foster parents has brought the issue of LGBT parenting to the forefront of the field of children, youth, and family services. There are a number of issues that social work practitioners need to consider in order to develop a knowledge base which will lead to competent practice with LGBT parents.

First, it is important to recognize that although there are many similarities, LGBT parenting families also differ from the heterosexually parented families. The conventional notion of a family presumes there will be two parents, one of each gender, that they will share a loving relationship and live under one roof, and that they will both be biologically related to the children they raise and recognized legally as a family. This mom-and-dad nuclear family is the baseline model in Western culture against which all other models of family are measured, and it is assumed by most to be the optimal family environment for child development; compared with such, all other types of families are viewed as deficient in some way.

This model, however, does not apply to most families with an LGBT parent(s). In families with an LGBT couple, usually there is at least one parent who has no biological relationship to the child. There is almost always a parent-child relationship not recognized or protected by the law.

We need to accept the premise that it is quality of care, and not family constellation, which determines what is optimal for a child's healthy development. The ability of LGBT parents to provide for the social and emotional health of their children just as adequately as heterosexual parents has been documented repeatedly in the research literature and has already been outlined in this chapter. We must also examine our own notions of family and learn to identify further what constitutes family, based on the loving bonds of responsibility that have been both intended and fulfilled, and not solely on biological, legal, or conventional definitions.

Decision to Explore Parenting

The following are narratives of gay men and lesbians who have consciously chosen to become parents:

> I have always loved children, and there has always been a part of me that wanted to be a dad. As a gay man, I thought it was impossible—who was going to let me be someone's parent? And it wasn't like I could just go out and get pregnant myself and have a baby. I guess I had internalized a lot of the homophobia that I had been fed—somewhere along the way, I believed that gay people could not be good parents, just because they were gay. It made me sad. I was always close to my sister's kids, but it wasn't enough to be the really devoted uncle; I wanted to be something more for a child.

> One day I thought, "Why not? Why can't I be a dad?' I could be a great dad for some child. I had a lot of the qualities that make for a great parent.

Some LGBT parents with whom I have worked noted that their longing to be parents stemmed from their own positive experiences with family, and the myth that LGBT persons could not parent was tinged with sadness, as this man noted here:

> I come from a very intact two-parent home, and family has always been the center of our lives, and my parents—being the very good parents that they were—instilled in us the value of family. Family was always very important. When it was clear to me that I was bisexual, there was a sadness that I could not have children and the coming-out process for me was not about people knowing I was bisexual; it was more about losing the idea of having children.

Another lesbian mother reconciled the desire to become a parent with living life as a lesbian who was out:

> I came out when I was twenty-four, but previous to that I always wanted children. I'm one of seven, all my siblings have lots of kids and I just always had in my head that I was going to have children. I just always wanted to have children. Then when I came out I thought, I guess I'm not having kids. I didn't really think twice about it. It didn't cross my mind to get married and have children. I thought, I'm not doing that, I'm not living a big lie or whatever, but that's what it felt like to me when women got married to have children and fulfill that parenting desire. So I just got totally into my career and then [I got] very active in the gay and lesbian community. I never heard of people having children as gays and lesbians; I never heard of that.

A trans woman echoed the sentiment of initial sadness about not being able to become a parent, and identified the life event that helped her see that she could indeed become a parent:

> Well, it was something that I had always wanted, actually. Probably the only problem I had with being transgender was that I couldn't be a parent. At least that was what I thought. But that changed when I was working in Boston and a friend was there—a friend from college and she was ill. She asked me if her son could stay with us until she got better. Her son was just sixteen months old. I was so excited, and he stayed with me for about nine months. When his mom got better he went back home with her, and at just about the same time that we moved to Los Angeles. His leaving left this huge, huge void. So I decided to fill that void by trying to adopt a child of my own. The LA Gay, Lesbian, Bisexual, and Trans Center was really helpful in

supporting me in this process—so was GLASS—Gay and Lesbian Adolescent Social Services which has a foster/adopt program.

For many LGBT persons, meeting another LGBT person who chose to be a parent was a transformative experience in their lives:

So when my friend, Ben, who was an openly bisexual man, adopted his first child and I spent time with him and his partner, I realized that I could do it and it opened up a whole new world to me.

As with other parenting couples, in some cases, there was one partner who wanted children more than the other:

Definitely Bill felt more strongly. He said that he couldn't live without being a parent and I felt, well, it's not that likely, but if it didn't happen, I would try to make something else important and that would be my life. Certainly my nieces and nephews would be more important, as they are to many gay people—kind of like substitute children. But my partner felt like he could not live without them, having children.

Becoming a Parent via Alternative Insemination

According to the LGBT Health Channel (downloaded, 09/20/06, http://www.lgbthealthchannel.com/AI/resources.shtml), alternative insemination (AI), also called artificial or donor insemination, is a method of conception whereby freshly gathered or frozen sperm is inserted manually into a woman's vagina or uterus to fertilize an egg. Insemination is usually performed on or near the day of ovulation, when a woman's egg is released from her ovary. AI is used among some lesbian, gay, bisexual, and transgender people (who are not taking hormones) as a means toward becoming parents. Some LGBT persons choose to utilize AI on their own without the assistance of professionals, others may be interested in participating in an AI Program such as the one held at the Fenway Community Health Center in Boston (see http://www.fenwayhealth.org/site/PageServer?pagename=FCHC_srv_services_alterninsem), which details a six step, well thought out program, including an AI orientation, medical tests, counseling sessions, and assistance in ordering sperm, for those considering AI as a means to becoming parents.

However, when LGBT persons choose to pursue this process, it begins when a woman obtains sperm from a male friend or from an anonymous donor at a sperm bank. There are several ways that LGBT persons may move toward utilizing AI as a means toward parenthood. A single bisexual woman may chose to conceive on her own without a partner; in other cases a lesbian couple may chose to conceive together as a couple, or in still other cases a woman may conceive and act as a surrogate mother for a gay man or trans person's child after being inseminated with his sperm. According to the LGBT Health Channel the conception rate through AI is similar to that through sexual intercourse. Approximately 11 percent of women who are trying to conceive are successful during a given menstrual cycle. Failure to conceive with AI is most often a result of fertility problems and not insemination error. There is a 20 percent rate of miscarriage among women who use AI and women who conceive during sexual intercourse. Age and medical history affect a woman's ability to conceive regardless of the method. It is a common misconception that more boys than girls are born of AI, but no data suggest that this is true.

AI can be a cost-effective alternative to adoption, which can cost anywhere from $10,000 to $30,000. AI using banked sperm may cost $500 to $1,000, depending on the number of inseminations that are needed to conceive.

Choosing between an anonymous or a known donor may however be complicated by logistical and social factors. Insemination with a known donor is cost-effective, can be done responsibly at home, and can provide a child with an identifiable father. General medical standards require a woman to use fresh sperm during home insemination, which can be difficult if the donor is not near. For most people, it results in a rewarding, personal environment for mother, father, and child. However, some difficulties can compel women to choose an anonymous donor, such as custody and visitation rights, legal issues, greater risk for sexually transmitted disease when using untested, familiar sperm, and parenting and family complexities.

Insemination with an anonymous donor is safer and more reliable, since the sperm is tested for sexually transmitted diseases (STDs), and because the procedure is managed by an experienced care team. Thawed, donated sperm lives for only one day, so conception is harder than with fresh sperm, which can live for several days in the uterus. Several factors make anonymous donation easier for some women; for example, sperm is medically tested, and, as there is no identifiable father, there are fewer legal issues regarding visiting and custody.

There are four types of insemination defined by where the sperm is placed: intracervical (ICI), just inside the cervix, the opening of the uterus; intrauterine (IUI), inside the uterus; pericervical (near the cervix); and vaginal-pool (inside the vagina).

A medical provider (nurse, physician, physician's assistant) performs ICI and IUI insemination using a sterile cannula (straw-like instrument) attached to a needleless syringe. These procedures require especially careful and sterile insertion. Sperm used in ICI is washed before it is inserted. All of the sperm inserted during IUI bypasses the cervix and enters the uterus, which means that most sperm reaches the fallopian tubes, where fertilization occurs. IUI is considered the most successful method, especially when combined with fertility drug therapy. Fertility drug therapy is determined by a woman's age and medical history and is not imperative for AI. It may be particularly useful in women whose cervical mucus, which lines the cervix during menstruation, is absent or detrimental to the sperm.

A support person, medical professional, the woman herself, or most commonly, a partner, inserts sperm into the vagina or uterus during vaginal-pool and pericervical insemination. Some of these methods are performed at home with a needleless or oral medication syringe and diaphragm or with a cervical cap. Some cervical caps feature a tube through which the sperm is injected; it is then placed over the cervix. The cap contains the sperm and encourages its flow into the uterus. Fresh sperm or bank sperm that has been properly thawed is used. As a medical professional must fit a cervical cap to a woman's cervix while she is ovulating, a syringe is the easiest method.

When a partner is involved in the insemination, the conception process can be a planned part of love-making, and not simply a "medical" procedure, as this woman recalled:

> When we decided to become parents, we had been together as a couple for over ten years. We talked about a number of ways to have children, foster care, adoption, but decided after a great deal of discussion to try to have a child through alternative insemination, using an anonymous donor. We did pick a donor who noted in his narrative that when the child became eighteen, he would be willing to be contacted if the child wished to do that. We wanted to keep that option open. Not everyone does, but for us, that was important that our child had the option of contacting his or her birth father at some point in time.
>
> I am a nurse so we purchased the frozen sperm from a reputable sperm bank in California. It came packed in dry-ice via Fed Ex—we thawed it out, and decided when the timing was right (within twenty-four hours after I started ovulating—we were fanatical about charting and timing my ovulation when we were trying to get pregnant) to have my partner perform a intracervical and intrauterine insemination using a sterile cannula attached to a needleless syringe, both of which I brought home from the hospital. I taught my partner how to do the insemination and we wanted to make this experience as much like a love-making experience as we could, given that a cannula and syringe were not a normal part of our love-making!
>
> We had to do this three times, the first two times it didn't take, but on our third try, we got pregnant. Nine months later, Josh was born—and our family was created!

Timing and Ovulation Prediction

Timing the insemination and accurately predicting ovulation are probably the most important aspects of AI. A woman is most likely to conceive during the twenty-four hours that follow ovulation, when the egg is viable. Over-the-counter ovulation kits test the urine for an increased level of luteinizing hormone (LH), which is released about twenty-four to thirty-six hours before ovulation. These kits typically cost approximately $25 to $35 and may contain five testing strips. Another method is to observe and note body signs of fertility, including elevated body temperature in the morning, consistently elevated temperature throughout the day, presence of cervical mucus, and lowered or "dipped" cervix. As noted in the previous narrative many women wishing to conceive record these signs on a calendar to predict ovulation.

Sperm

Some women obtain sperm from a friend, while others prefer sperm from an anonymous donor. Sperm banks provide women with frozen sperm from anonymous donors. Sperm stored at sperm banks is properly frozen and preserved in liquid nitrogen. It is tested for viability and STDs, including human immunodeficiency virus (HIV), and is accompanied by a profile of the donor's background.

Washing sperm before IUI kills some of the sperm and interferes with others. "Dizzy sperm," as they are called, may not be able to swim through the uterus and into the fallopian tubes. Still, IUI is successful because all of the sperm is inserted directly into the uterus. Sperm that has been frozen in a home freezer is not viable for insemination. There is a greater risk for sexually transmitted disease with fresh sperm, as it has not been tested.

Legal Issues

The laws regarding visitation rites and parent support among people who choose AI are undeveloped. There is a lack of statutes and precedent for unmarried partners. For these reasons, anyone donating or using sperm should consult a lawyer who is knowledgeable about legal issues surrounding AI. Women working with known donors should hire an attorney and make a legal agreement that protects everyone concerned, especially issues of visitation. Lesbian partners are advised to make co-parenting agreements that stipulate the care of the child in the event of separation. Though some states allow co-parent adoption, or same-sex parent adoption, and legally recognize both partners as parents, many do not. Parents should ask their attorneys about their legal rights with respect to these issues.

Practice Issues

Artificial insemination is one way that some LGBT persons are choosing to create families and become parents. There are however, several practice issues which should be considered in planning for the creation of families via AI. The first is educating family members about the process. Some families will be confused about the process and may be embarrassed to ask questions, such as "Who is the father of the baby?" Individuals and couples will need to be proactive in comfortably explaining the process to family members who may need to know. Family members will need to be taught the language of AI—for example, how should a family refer to the child's father? Later, as the children born via AI develop, they will also need parents to provide them with a language which they can use with friends to discuss, if they chose to, their birth situation. In many cases, the practice issues for families created via AI are not very different from those families created through adoption, kinship, or foster care.

Continuing to Parent After Coming Out As an LGBT Person

The issue of being a formerly married LGBT person is a phenomenon which is more prevalent than most might imagine. There are no statistics gathered on this population, but the numbers are most likely high as this is a topic that is highly charged emotionally and in many circles taboo to discuss. Some LGBT persons enter a heterosexual marriage to hide their orientation, or because they are not clear about their gender or sexual orientation at the time of their marriage. Once they come out, some previously heterosexual persons separate, ultimately divorce, and lead lives as LGBT persons. Others continue to remain within a heterosexual marriage and renegotiate their relationships. However, many LGBT persons claim that they initially married to create a family that included rearing children.

These men and/or women often feel like a minority within a minority as they walk the line between the heterosexually privileged world of "parent" and the less than privileged world as an LGBT person. There is often a sense of not fitting into either world, which adds to the sense of isolation and aloneness. With great effort, significant pain, and steadfast courage these men and women may come forth with their authentic identity to challenge the heterocentric definition of sexuality and parenting that Western culture dictates.

Gay dads, lesbian moms, bisexual moms or dads, and trans moms or dads who were previously married go through various stages in their coming-out process that are similar and yet different from their LGBT counterparts who have not been married or had children. The effects of their coming-out are felt not only by the LGBT person, but also by spouses, children, parents, friends, relatives, and new partners. Most formerly married LGBT persons with whom I have worked have not been aware of the difficulty of this coming-out in regard to the entire family system. The pain they feel in the process can, and has been for many, among the worst they have experienced in their lives. The difficulty in many instances is that the LGBT person may still love his or her spouse, and the sense of dedication to his or her children cannot be understated. The thought of separation and not seeing the children on a daily basis tears at their hearts, particularly for those who may have married with an expressed interest in having children. The process these LGBT persons go through, and the loss, and at the same time a sense of rebirth at each step, cannot be underestimated.

The sense of rebirth, called biphasic development by the late Alan Malyon (1982), the experience of being able to live one's life authentically, is best described by Mark, in the following narrative:

> I knew I was "different" since I was six or seven, but I did not come out until I was thirty-one years old. I got married when I was twenty-four years old, I desperately wanted to have a family which included children and I never thought that as a gay man that I could have that. I was married for seven years to a woman whom I loved and we had two great children, Luke, age six, and Andrew, age four. After a few years of being married, I just couldn't deny that I was a gay man. I knew that if I came out that it would also mean that my link to my children would possibly change and I didn't want to do anything that might damage that relationship. So I hid, I snuck around with men, I lied to my wife and felt horrible about being a "bad" husband.
>
> One day, it all broke wide open and I couldn't keep it all together anymore. My wife and I had an honest discussion. I told her I was gay and knew for a long time that I was a gay man; we agreed that we should separate—at least as a couple—and we continued to live together. It was so painful, so hard for me, for my wife, and ultimately for the kids, the worst time of my life. I liked the privileges I had in being seen as a married man by society and I feared giving that up if I came out as a gay man. After several months, we sat with the kids, talked to them about our separation, assured them that it was nothing that they had done, and told them that I would be getting my own place, three blocks away from our house. This was hard too, but better than trying to live together as a couple. My main focus was on continuing to be a real, involved parent in their lives, but not a married dad. We have had many ups and downs in this journey, but five years later, we are all still a family, albeit a very different kind of family. My

wife and I share custody of the boys; they have two homes and go back and forth every other week. My wife has a new man in her life who is a great guy, and I have a new partner, too. We have tried to be adults in this, making the kids our focus, not our former marriage. Sometimes we are great at being co-parents and sometimes it's a challenge, but overall, I think our kids are happy, well adjusted, and know that they are loved, and for us that is the most important thing.

To come out as an individual LGBT person or one who was married is no easy process. No one can do such work in isolation. Support during this time in the form of a trusted friend, a family member, or a professional (in either individual or group settings) is critical. As with anyone coming out, the fear of disapproval and exclusion is no different for these LGBT persons than anyone else. It is important to reframe this situation for the LGBT persons as what type of example they offer to their children when they do come out to them. The example being that despite fear, they take action to let others know who they are and live life as genuinely as possible. Certainly their children will have differences among their peers, and in relationships as they mature, so the example has been set to proudly and without apology be your authentic self despite the pressures to conform. This is an especially important lesson for children, particularly for adolescents who face such peer pressure as they mature.

Fronczak and Campanaro-Cummings (2006) note that it is their experience that the spouses of LGBT persons tend to try to cope alone and are unsure where to go for the sympathy and support they need. Groups focused on the unique needs of this population can provide an atmosphere of confidentiality, validation of feelings, constructive problem solving strategies, and guidance and resolution of issues in a positive direction (see Buxton, 1994; Gochros, 1989; Klein & Schwartz, 2002). The group emphasis should be on respect for individual circumstances, understanding, and compassion, all vital components in helping to rid the system of isolation and helplessness.

Many of the spouses of LGBT persons, note Fronczak and Campanaro-Cummings (2006), have recognized that there are stages of grieving and healing that occur for them. They have identified the stages as follows:

> *Stage one: Predisclosure or period of discontent.* This stage usually starts with identification by the non-LGBT spouse that something is wrong. There can be a tendency toward reduced intimacy, fear, and denial. There is confusion over the origin of the discontent.
> *Stage two: Disclosure or redisclosure.* The issue of being an LGBT person is identified for the first time or reidentified as a serious

area of concern. Feelings of shock, anger, guilt, blame, denial, and isolation occur.

Stage three: Trial accommodation and questioning. The couple tries to make sense of the issue and maintain their coupleness. The non-LGBT spouse exhibits empathy mixed with anger toward his or her spouse. Questions surface such as: Why is he or she LGBT? When did it start? Was it something I did? Can I fix this? There is often hope for a magic cure. Issues of love, trust, honesty, and spiritual beliefs begin to emerge.

Stage four: Awareness. There is awareness of one's own feelings apart from that of the LGBT spouse. The non-LGBT spouse has alternate feelings of disillusionment and hope. Symptoms of depression and heightened anxiety occur. This is often the stage where the non-LGBT spouse seeks help. The issues of fidelity, monogamy, and safer sex are confronted. If children are involved, decisions regarding disclosure are discussed (see MacPike, 1989).

Stage five: Renegotiating the relationship. Decisions are made about which direction the relationship should take. Options are discussed such as separation, divorce, mediation, couples' counseling, or staying together but redefining the relationship. The support system is enlarged as the couple reaches out and discloses the issue of gay/lesbian identity, bisexuality, or transgender identity to other people.

Stage six: Acceptance. A better understanding about the complicated issue starts to occur. The non-LGBT spouse reevaluates his or her own identity and becomes more autonomous. Often this is accompanied by fear of moving on and the realization that the relationship will be changed forever. This can be a stage of great growth.

Stage seven: Exploration and detachment. For those who stay married: The couple negotiates new rules and goals for their relationship. They are learning to cope with a newly defined relationship. Open communication is essential. Each individual gains more independence. The couple begins to build trust and commits to moving forward. For those who leave the marriage: The couple moves onto their separate lives. If children are involved, visitation, custody issues, boundaries, and rules are negotiated (children of LGBT parents should see Garner, 2004; Howey et al., 2000; Snow, 2004). The non-LGBT spouse defines new goals for themselves. Often careers are expanded. Education is pursued, culminating in an expanded vision of herself or himself. Although somewhat fearful, the non-LGBT spouse eventually considers dating and other relationships.

Stage eight: Resolution. Both parties get on with their lives, establishing healthy boundaries and a mutual respect.

These stages are often not in the exact order or sequence. They can last for differing amounts of time depending on the individual, the couple, and other life experiences. Grieving occurs in all stages—greater in the beginning and more tolerable in the end. There is no escaping the great struggle that occurs when a couple confronts LGBT identity together. However the closet that both were in can be a far more debilitating place. The following is one narrative from a woman whose husband transitioned to a female identity:

> I married Alex when I was thirty and he was thirty-two. We have a daughter, Jill, who is now age twelve. Two years ago, Alex told me that he was very unhappy and that he needed to tell me something that would be very upsetting to me, but that he had to tell me. He told me that all of his life he has felt trapped in his male body. He said that ever since he was a kid he really felt that inside he was a girl, not a boy. He said that at this point in his life he wanted to explore his female identity. I asked if he was gay and he said no, he was a woman, not a man. Well, I was clearly shocked and very dismayed. I could deal with him being attracted to another person, but to say that he was a woman not a man, was very difficult for me to take—I mean, we had a child together! Alex decided that it would be best if we separated while he was doing his exploration. I was so completely thrown off—I didn't know what to think. I called my therapist, who saw me immediately and then referred me to a Web site called the straight spouses support network—it was really so helpful to help me get through the initial crisis and to get some support for myself. The fact that it was online was helpful too. I wasn't sure I could go to a group or talk with others about this (see http://www.straightspouse.org/).
>
> Alex moved out of our home and into an apartment about ten blocks from our house. He stopped by every day to see Jill. After about two weeks when things calmed down a bit, we both spoke to our daughter and told her about Alex's decision. He made it very clear to her that even though we might no longer live together that he still wanted to be a parent to her. Alex and Jill were close and he had always been a great parent. Her only question was if her dad became a woman, would that mean she now had two moms? We both smiled, looked at each other, and said, "Yeah, I guess so."

Adoption and Fostering

Lesbian, gay, bisexual, and transgender persons are in a unique position with respect to adoption and fostering (Melina, 1998). Most heterosexuals come to the idea of fostering or adoption after trying or considering different ways of creating their own family, for example, infertility treatment or donor insemination. Although some women who identify as lesbian, bisexual, or trans may have infertility issues and may have tried sleeping with a man, tried to find a donor, or actually attempted donor insemination, for many LGBT persons, becoming a parent through fostering or adoption is a first choice.

Like all potential adopters and foster parents, LGBT persons have had to learn about the process. The women and men whom I met were resourceful and gathered information from books (Benkov, 1994; Martin, 1993), from other people who had adopted or fostered, including heterosexuals as well as other LGBT persons, and from agency social workers.

The issue of openness about one's sexual orientation was a clear theme for all of the LGBT persons who were considering fostering or adoption. The secondary theme was whether or not they could adopt:

> We wanted so much to become parents and often thought about and talked about adoption. We always kept hearing how many children were in need of homes. I thought that it would be great for a kid who had two parents that loved them. But I wasn't even sure that it was legally possible for gay men to adopt. (Mallon, 2004, p. 15)

Many LGBT prospective parents are also concerned that agencies may offer them the children who have traditionally been the most difficult to place. What strikes psychologist April Martin, author of *The Lesbian and Gay Parenting Handbook,* as ironic is that the same agencies which believe LGBT persons are not suitable parents will place with them children who require the most highly skilled parenting. She, and others, have pointed out that nontraditional families have unique strengths that make them excellent, and in some cases the best homes for certain children. The following quotation exemplifies this sentiment:

> When I went to the agency to find out more about adoption, they told me that I would have better luck by trying to become a foster parent first. That sounded fine to me, but then they told me that the only children they had for me were children that were born HIV positive. That sounded fine too, I had lots of experience with HIV, I had seen literally hundreds of friends die, but in retrospect, I did not realize at the time that it was a very different disease in children. My son, Julio, was placed with me; he was eighteen-months-old, underweight, sick quite a bit, and required lots of medical treatment. Being a parent to a HIV-positive child has a lot of ups and downs. It requires a style of parenting that most parents never have to deal with. But it was worth every doctor's visit. I am happy to say that today Julio is a healthy fifteen-year-old, managing and living with HIV. (Mallon, 2004, p. 121)

In addition to understanding the mechanics of the adoption process, it was important also to understand how forming a family by adoption differs from creating a family biologically:

> There was so much that we needed to learn about the adoption process, that we always had to keep clearly in our minds that what we were moving toward was going to be a very life changing event. Biologically, having a baby allowed you to prepare for nine months, adopting a child could take nine months, a year or even more. But more than that, we were talking about a child's life here, not just this intellectual process of being a family. Sometimes that was scary, but also very exciting.

Lesbian gay, bisexual, and transgender persons must also decide whether to be open or not about their gender or sexual orientation. Although foster care agencies approved single men and single women to become foster parents during the 1980s and early 1990s, most LGBT persons whom I met were determined early on, or had been warned by other LGBT persons who had become parents, that they should not be open about their gender or sexual orientation. Some still opt for the "don't ask, don't tell" policy. Many LGBT persons do choose to be open about their gender or sexual orientation, while others identify their partners as "friends" who will help raise the child. Despite the discomfort they felt about "going back in the closet," most took this approach as a matter of expediency, for fear of being rejected as parents. Most resented that they had to do so, but also believed it was the price they had to pay for the gift of becoming a parent.

Most LGBT persons who are considering fostering or adoption have probably openly identified as LGBT persons for some time (in fact, assessing a potential parent's level of "outness" is critical to the homestudy process), but as coming-out is a continual process and not a one-time event, these individuals will, as prospective adopters or foster parents, experience coming-out in ways that are uniquely different within their own families and communities. Becoming parents will inevitability increase their visibility within their communities in different spheres, such as school.

Dealing with Family of Origin Issues

Social workers will want to explore how the applicants' family of origin has responded to their desire to foster or adopt. For the LGBT persons I spoke to, there was some uncertainty, in general, about whether or not their families would support their decision to become parents. However, although there was a range of experiences reported, the overwhelming majority said their families had been very supportive.

Some families were initially shocked by their children's decision:

> At first my parents were taken aback. They just kept saying, "We don't get it; I thought gay people didn't want to have children." They kept telling me how hard it was going to be and asked if I was sure. After they realized that we had done our homework and had given this parenting thing a great deal of thought, they were very supportive, and have been great grandparents to Tanya. I have been very fortunate I have a very loving family.

Some recalled how their parents seemed to feel the need to warn them about the realties of parenting:

> When I told my father, after we had everything in process, that we were going to adopt, he first said, "Are you sure this is what you want to do?" When I told him yes, he said, "Well then, great, but be prepared to give up a lot of things that you used to do for yourself. Your focus now will have to be on those children."

One man recalled this heart-warming, welcoming ceremony from his family for his new son:

> My family was ecstatic when Josh came. I went down that next weekend and, unbeknownst to me, my entire family had assembled. They all showed up—all at one time, every single one of them. It was unprecedented—this only happened when we had weddings or funerals. I had no idea they were all gathering. When I got there, they all ran out of the house and my sister grabbed Josh and he didn't know this woman—he was being passed from one person to another. It was a very nice thing, we had a lovely dinner and it was great.

In contrast, one of the women met with complete rejection of her decision to parent by her own parents:

> My family has always been so nonsupportive of my life as a bi person, so it was no surprise when they were completely rejecting of my decision to parent. I told them I planned to adopt and they just rolled their eyes and said, "Do you really think that is fair to those children?" I have dealt with the pain I feel about their rejection of me, but in some small part of my heart, I wished they could have gotten over it and been there for my children as grandparents. I think I have reconciled this pain by realizing that my family is missing so much by not being a part of Joe and Jeremy's lives . . . they are such beautiful kids.

Whether it was assumed that parents would be supportive or not, a number of the men and women reported that they did not seek the input of their families:

> We didn't tell family, not until it was time; we discussed it a little bit with siblings beforehand, but not parents. I felt like I was over thirty, thirty years old, and I felt like this was my personal decision and they only needed to know when it happened. It was not something I really cared for any input on from people. It was between my partner and me, and other people didn't matter, except to be informed. I didn't feel like I needed approval from anyone. It was our decision. When we did tell our families, my family was fine, but my partner's family, especially his father, was very disapproving—so much so that they didn't meet our child until he was six months old. That was hard.

Most reported that their parents approved of their decision to become parents. Many were excited by the prospect of having a grandchild (one of the first laments from parents when their son or daughter comes out to them is, "But I wanted grandchildren!"). Their new role of parent often brought LGBT persons closer to their own parents. They found new appreciation and sensitivity for their parents' struggles to raise them, and they could rely on the support and guidance of their parents in raising their children. The narratives suggest that no matter how different their parenting style was from their own parents', or how different were the circumstances under which they became parents, LGBT persons' empathy for their parents increased when they stepped into the role of a parent.

Social workers need to be aware of the strong anti-LGBT sentiment held by many religious groups and the impact that this can have on family members for whom sexual orientation is an issue. Families, particularly families with strong religious convictions, may openly condemn homosexuality, unaware that one of their own family members is lesbian or gay (Helminiak, 1997; Herman, 1997). Religious views of homosexuality vary widely. According to many religious creeds and denominations, sexual relations between people who are not of the opposite sex are forbidden and regarded as sinful, and many religious teaching texts have been erroneously used as a weapon against lesbians and gay men, causing a great deal of distress in many families of faith. Several excellent resources, however, provide an alternative perspective (Cooper, 1994; Metropolitan Community Church, 1990; Parents, Families and Friends of Lesbians and Gays, 1997).

Second, the couple must decide whether to be open about their gender or sexual orientation. Although it is legal for LGBT persons to adopt, some fear that they would not be able to adopt if they disclosed their orientation. Some LGBT persons do choose to be open about their orientation, while others identify their partner as "friends" who will help raise the child. This is because in most states only one parent can be recognized as the legal parent, this establishes, as Hartman (1996, p. 81) points out, "an asymmetrical relationship between the two parents and the child." This asymmetry occurs on multiple levels: from school visits, to medical permission forms, to eligibility for Social Security survivors' benefits in the case of the death of a co-parent, to lack of support from family members, and to requirements for support and visiting arrangements in the case of a separation.

LGBT individuals who choose to adopt as single parents will also face stresses that may be more unique to single parenting than to their LGBT identification (Feigelman & Silverman, 1983; Marindin, 1997; Melina, 1998). However, it is not all struggle and hardship—on the positive side, LGBT persons who choose to create families have the advantage of redefining and reinventing their own meaning for family and parenting, precisely because they exist outside of the traditionally defined "family." They have the unique opportunity to break out of preconceived gender roles and be a new kind of parent to a child (Benkov, 1994).

Trends in Adoption: Dilemmas Agencies Face in Accepting Gay and Lesbian Prospective Parents

Numerous child welfare agencies across the country have broken through their own organizational bias against LGBT persons and are already placing children with LGBT parents (Evan Donaldson, 2003). The Evan B. Donaldson Adoption Institute issued a report in October 2003 that found that 60 percent of the country's adoption agencies accept applications from same-sex couples. The study further showed that 40 percent of U.S. agencies have already placed children in homes with gay or lesbian parents. In a report analyzing Census 2000 data, Arc's Family Net Project and the Urban Institute also found that same-sex parents are 1.7 percent more likely to have adopted than all other households.

However, by and large, few child welfare agencies seem to be openly discussing this process. Agency heads might be concerned that it will attract negative attention to their agency, or somehow be divisive among staff. There is a large adoption and foster parenting network within LGBT communities across the country as well as a virtual community found on many Internet Web sites, all of which assist LGBT persons interested in adoption or foster parenting in identifying the names and address of "safe" child welfare agencies where they can be certified (see www.aclu.org/issues/ gay/parent and www.aclu.org/issues/gay/child and www.lambdalegal.org).

Historically perceived as a preferential service granted only to those couples who were Caucasian and infertile, and who could afford to take a healthy, same-race infant into their home, adoption is now viewed in a much broader context. Contemporary adoption has made it possible for a broader range of children to be adopted—children of color, children with a range of disabilities, children with medical and developmental issues, and preschoolers and adolescents.

Similarly, policies have made it possible for a broader range of adults to adopt, including foster parents, families of color, single individuals (both male and female), older individuals, individuals with disabilities and families across a broad economic range. At one time or another, many of these groups were excluded from the adoption process. Inclusion of some of these groups caused great controversy when initiated. In the process of moving toward inclusiveness, however, many professionals voiced concern about "lowering" the standard of adoption and thereby "damaging" the field.

The trend toward inclusiveness, and a broader understanding of who makes a suitable parent, has had a major impact on the more than 519,000 children in out-of-home care, some of whom have waited for extended periods for permanent homes. Such changes have allowed children and youth previously considered "unadoptable," or not suitable for family foster care, to be provided with permanent homes with caring adults, some of whom are LGBT persons. Although accurate statistics on the number of LGBT people do not exist, it has been estimated that up to 10 percent of the population (twenty-five million individuals) identify as having a sexual orientation other than heterosexual. Excluding twenty-five million individuals from becoming adoptive parents, solely on the basis of sexual orientation, seems preposterous considering how many children and youth are in need of permanent families.

Although some child welfare agencies are struggling to develop policies about LGBT parenting, many agencies appear to believe "the less said the better" (Sullivan, 1995, p. 3) and therefore do not publicize the fact that they place children with LGBT people. Perhaps they are afraid of being stigmatized as "the gay adoption or foster care agency." Organizational structures, which operate in the absence of written policies, frequently compel staff members to develop their own policies. The lack of written policies, in and of itself, is a strategy that many child welfare agency executives and boards have permitted to exist with respect to the issue of LGBT adoption and foster parenting. When individuals design their own policies to guide agency practice, the agencies run the risk of personal, cultural, and religious bias. Child welfare agencies, some of which continue to avoid written policies, do not provide the opportunity for the community to resolve the issue. Policies responding to the needs of children and families need to be written and clearly communicated to all interested groups.

OTHER ISSUES FOR LGBT PARENTS

Becoming a family is far more complex than simply getting a child and this was what each of the LBGT persons who were parents discovered from day one.

The Homecoming: The Initial Reactions

After many months, and in some cases years, of anticipation and preparation, the day arrived when the wished-for child finally comes home. The homecoming process is an occasion mixed with great emotion for both the parent and the child. Even with the best-laid plans, it did not happen the way they fantasized it would.

What Have We Done?

It's not uncommon for new parents to feel inadequate (Brazelton, 1992). Second-guessing and questioning one's ability are universal sentiments for all new parents. This mom recalled her ambivalence vividly:

> I was so happy, but also so scared, I think I was sick for three days after he came. I kept thinking, What have we done? We have no business being a parent to anyone; we have no idea what we are doing. I kept looking at this little scrawny baby and thinking we will never be able to do this. . . . But then I got over it and got on with being a parent.

Preparing the home for a child seldom seemed to go smoothly for most LGBT parents. Most recalled having a definite plan before the child arrived. They had a plan for where the child would sleep, how they would cook for the child, and how they would do things, but almost immediately they had to modify their plans when the reality of having a child in the home set in. One couple recalled:

> The day he came to our home was such a joy for us. The first few weeks of parenting were a blur, the house turned upside down, our workout room quickly became his playroom. We were so caught up in the whirl of diapers, formula, and baby Tylenol and everything else that we barely had time to think about how Perry had settled into his own home. I was initially worried about whether or not he would mess up the living room, but within two or three days we didn't even try anymore or care.

Initial reactions to parenting may not always have prepared the new parent for their new role; child care for a new baby is one major issue:

> Well, my initial intention was I had this woman I set up to watch him. My plans were that I had my own business and I would bring Wade to work a lot of times and at least three times a week I would have a babysitter. I found this woman from our neighborhood and she babysat for me three days a week, six hours a day. It was a couple months. And I expected that kind of support at work and I expected family support more. My mother was alive at the time; she died a year after Wade was born. She had been a really good grandmother; she babysat her grandchildren and was a very active grandparent. I didn't realize that she was so gravely ill at the time when Wade was a baby. So I expected all of this family support and I ended up with zero family physical support.

All parents have dreams and fantasies about becoming a family. Sometimes the fantasy matches the reality and sometimes it does not. Most LGBT persons acknowledged that things changed when they added a child to their lives. Many, as do all first time parents, have well-developed fantasies about what having a child will be like. The stress of becoming a family depends on many factors. Some of these forces are predictable, and some are beyond our immediate control. The temperament of the parent is a key component in this process. Martin (1993) suggests that parents ask themselves the following questions in evaluating their temperament for parenting: How well do we adapt to change in general? How quickly do we recover from disruption? How high is our tolerance for chaos, noise, sleep deprivation, intrusion, and lack of solitude? Most parents go into a kind of shock when a child arrives. They may have dreamed about parenthood, but they could never imagine how relentlessly and completely it changes time, space, sleep, and every other aspect of one's former, child-free life. Most LGBT parents, like other parents, had no idea if they could handle it, or what their limits might be, or what their capacity to rise to the task might be. One mom recalled it this way:

> What surprised me most about parenting was how incredibly unselfish I had become. All my thoughts were about him, making sure that he was safe and nurtured. Before becoming a parent, my check, my discretionary funds, everything, was all about me, and now I am worried about, do I have enough money to do that kind of stuff. And from the first day, until Josh was about nine or ten, I never slept an entire night without waking up about three to four times a night to make sure that there were blankets on his bed and that he was safe, and that he was breathing, the whole ideal that he was okay. My whole waking moments were about my child. So that is a very unusual feeling to have and the whole thing about that when he first

> came in was that there was no bond between us. I think we both felt this maternal bond that I think mothers have when they first give birth to kids. There is something in that first twenty-four hours that connects them to their child, an emotional attachment. I had read about that, and I had heard people talk about that, but you don't know what it is until you experience it. It's when it just clicks and that's what happened—we were inseparable, I mean literally inseparable. He lived and breathed me, and I lived and breathed him.

In addition to parental temperament, the individual child's temperament is also a key factor in the family-making process. All infants require an enormous amount of attention and are by virtue of their development demanding, but there are differences between those who are cheerful and those who are fussy. It does not take a difficult child to complicate the emotional adjustment to parenthood (Brazelton, 1992). Even when LGBT parents love their child completely, they experience many other emotions as well—feelings of loss, depression, loneliness, and frustration among them. Having a new baby is such a transformative experience for all parents. Many parents note that activities they used to do for intellectual stimulation or exercise or accomplishment also had to change.

Single Moms and Dads

Some LGBT persons become single parents by choice. Quite simply, there was a time in their lives when they were ready to become parents, but they had not found a life partner, and so they moved ahead anyway and decided to parent alone. While there are some obvious hardships associated with single parenting, there are some advantages of single LGBT parenthood. One dad, who adopted two children as a single man, recalled:

> I feel guilty for saying this, but I think it's easier to be a single parent, in many ways. I see, and I could be wrong because I'm not in a gay coupled relationship, but by outside observance of gay couples, you have more of a built-in set of roles for parenting. With just me as a parent, there are no roles to play, no male/female roles to play. For many gay male couples who are parents, and from what I have witnessed, there is a lot of fighting over how to do everything. Then you have the two of them constantly fighting. I've seen it in all the couples, where they are both trying to be the mom and the dad. As the only parent, I make the rules, I make the decisions, and I don't have to negotiate with the other partner.

Of course, dating for single parents can be a challenge. One lesbian mom said:

> In the beginning, I had a lot of girlfriends and brought them home comfortably and didn't think too much of it. As my kids have gotten older there are such a multitude of issues and concerns and I have changed how I deal with dating. So many issues come into play . . . especially during the teenage years. You kind of remember the discovering of your own sexuality so you know what it's like . . . and I guess I have had to put my own needs second to what I think my child needs from her parent.

One trans parent, although obviously delighted with her role as parent, had this lament, which resonates more with the experiences of single parenthood cited in the research (Feigelman & Silverman, 1983; Marindin, 1997; Melina, 1998, p. 292):

> I feel very alone sometimes being a single parent—it's lonely sometimes—it's not a sexual thing; I just kind of want someone to hold me and say, "You're doing all right—you're a good person and a good parent."

Couple Relationships Change

Many couples find that their relationship changes when a child becomes a member of the family constellation. A relationship between two adults is a complex process. There are always conflicting needs and desires between partners, all of which require communication, negotiation, and a willingness to tolerate the flaws that are inherent in everyone. When a child comes into the picture, interpersonal dynamics can become more complex (as most of us know well from our own families of origin). Parenting a child means that the relationship between partners will change, as this gay dad recalled:

> We were so happy to be parents, but I don't think we had any idea about how much our lives as a couple would change once Josh came into our lives. We were busier than ever. We had less time for each other; our focus became Josh, not each other; sometimes that was really hard.

After a child is adopted by an LGBT couple, many questions come to the surface, including who will take responsibility for what areas of parenting, how to navigate legal issues, and how to handle emotional issues including bonding and attachment. If a couple already has subterranean communication problems, it will come to the surface with full force when children enter the family, and will contribute to already substantial parenting challenges (Lancaster, 1996).

Dividing Roles and Duties

Having a child is a labor-intensive enterprise, as any parent will corroborate (Brazelton, 1992). Living outside the patriarchal norms set for men and women, same-gender couples have a unique opportunity to redefine their roles and responsibilities in the family according to their strengths and skills, rather than their gender. Since gay men do not have to divide the labor of parenthood according to prescribed, gendered roles, there is a lot more room for conversation and, as always, negotiation. One of the positive outcomes of deciding who does what is that LGBT parents were free to come to a decision about what works best for them and their child.

Despite their planning and discussions, one parent may end up doing the bulk of the nurturing, either because that is how they planned it, or because one partner is clearly more suited for that role than the other. However, modification of their original intention to parent equally may cause the parent who is less involved to feel left out. The child may also become much more intensely bonded during the first few years to the parent who is the primary caretaker. As Martin (1993, p. 221) so aptly points out, "the unabashed love affair between child and primary parent may further contribute to the other parent's feeling shut out." The recollections of this dad clearly illustrate Martin's point:

> After the initial shock of parenting wore off, we had this plan. I would work three days a week, stay home with Andrew on one day and write the other day. Craig would work four days and stay home with Andrew the day I wrote. But even though that was the plan, it almost never worked. Craig frequently worked on the day he wasn't supposed to. Because of that our bond grew stronger. I was resentful that Craig didn't hold up his part of the parenting agreement, but in reality, I was more the primary parent. My relationship with Andrew became closer and my relationship with Craig became more distant—he felt left out, and in some ways, he was.

Nonlegal Parents

Since many LGBT persons who choose to become parents together cannot be legally recognized as parents in most states, one parent in the couple is likely to receive less validation and support from the outside world than the other "real parent." In a heterosexual couple, a father may not be seen as the primary caregiver, yet he will clearly be recognized as a real parent. With only one recognized in a legal capacity as the parent, the second father or mother often has to go out of his or her way to assert true parenthood, which is often stressful to both partners. Both persons in the couple may be profoundly disturbed by the fact that one parent is left out. And the one left out may feel increasingly insecure about his or her role in the family if his or her partner is not sensitive to the particular situation.

Communication, Arguments, and Negotiations

Although the necessity of negotiation and good communication between co-parents escalates once a child enters the picture, there is less and less time for couples to talk things over. Finding time to communicate was a challenge for most of the LGBT parents I worked with, as this dad recalled:

> We were always sleep deprived and just plain tired from all of the energy that is consumed by active parenting. We could rarely find time to spend together—never mind having a real heart-to-heart talk. I had a harder time with loss of independence than my partner did. Becoming a parent was a big adjustment for me. We both continued to work; we both tried to parent equally, but one partner always seems to be doing more. We fought about a bunch of things that we never even had to think about before we had children—like whose turn it was to go get the Pampers in the middle of the night when we realized we were out of them. The first year was the hardest; it got better after that.

Another mom had a different take on finding time to communicate. Conscious of the effect their arguments were having on their child, she and her partner became more diligent about communicating well with each other:

> There are many times when we can't discuss something right then and there. If we really get loud or start to raise our voices, the kids get this really wide-eyed upset look, so we have to wait until they go to bed or they are out of earshot before we resume our discussion. It's hard to wait when you're upset; stuffing feelings can really build up to a bigger argument. But we have recently gotten to a point where we look at one another and say, "Let's talk about this later."

When Parents Separate

Lesbian, gay, bisexual, and transgender people who become parents, like their non-LGBT counterparts, may also split up (Melina, 1998). Problems that existed in the relationship before children sometimes rise to the surface with the demands of child rearing, as this narrative suggests:

> We were both so in love with the idea of being parents that we forgot to take care of and communicate with each other. Like most parents the energy goes into being a parent and not being a partner; and we were not always

good about acknowledging it. My partner felt left out of the relationship that I shared with our son, and when he got home from work I was so tired from parenting that I didn't have the strength to give him the attention that I had before our son came into our lives.

Feeling emotionally deprived and excluded are painful feelings. Another person who comes along offering affection, attention, and comfort may make a partner vulnerable to an affair, or may lead to anger and resentment, which can be toxic to the relationship. Some couples may seek support and assistance from the social work or mental health community:

We had a lot of conflicts in our relationship when we became parents. Money issues, scheduling issues, parenting styles, were all issues. Our sex life had deteriorated and our communication had broken down. We needed tools to help us reconnect. We went to a therapist, someone who understood gay people and parenting issues. It really saved our relationship and made us better parents too. It wasn't as easy as I am making it seem; it was a lot of work, but it was worth it.

When a coupled relationship ends, the family relationships were reconfigured to create a responsible parenting plan:

When we finally decided to separate after a lot of painful discussion, once again, we had to figure out everything about being divorced gay parents by ourselves. It's not like with straight couples where they can go to an attorney and have someone mediate the separation agreement. Since gay people do not have sanctioned legally recognized unions, they once again, have to figure out how to do things without sanctioned legal guidance. No one we knew had ever had to figure out how to develop a separation agreement with a gay couple who had children. We now had to learn to be co-parents who lived separately. It's really hard to work out an amicable agreement with someone who you used to love, especially when you are really angry with them—but you have to forget your own pain and focus on being a good parent.

Brodzinsky and Schechter (1990) found that adopted and nonadopted children were similarly affected by the separation and divorce of their parents. Although the breakup of a relationship is always disruptive to the couple and to the children involved, the LGBT parents who experienced separation from their original partners kept the well-being of their children as their primary focus.

ISSUES FOR CHILDREN OF GAY PARENTS

Children move through infancy, toddlerhood, preschool, school-age, and then adolescence, and the shifts and changes that parents must weather as a child ages present numerous challenges for all parents (Brazelton, 1992; Gordon, 2000; Larson & Richards, 1994; Wolf, 2002). The most common issues LGBT parents dealt with were summarized into four main themes: (1) What do we tell them? (2) Where did I come from? (3) I wish I had a mom/dad. (4) Growing up with LGBT parents.

What Do We Tell Them? (Where Do I Come From?)

The majority of the LGBT parents I spoke with were very comfortable talking with their children about their adoption, insemination, foster, or kinship process. One dad's trajectory about talking to his children about this process captures all of the elements of the other parents' narratives:

> We have always told them about their birth families and about how they were adopted. They love hearing the story of how we picked them up at the airport and how we brought them home. As they got older they have had questions about their birth families and we have told them as much as we know about them. We have also made it clear that we will help them to find their birth families when they are eighteen if that is something that they want to do. I think we just kept our discussions very natural—every now and then I try to check in with them to just see how they are feeling about things and their birth families is an area that we frequently talk about.

LGBT parents I spoke with were clear that they needed to keep the communication open with their children about adoption, insemination, their family configuration, and LGBT-headed families. They also noted that most children were not that interested in communicating about these topics on a daily basis. Knowing when to address these issues and when not to talk about them was key. One mom described it this way:

> We try to weave things into the conversation normally; like when we are talking about our lives before we had children, we might say, "before we adopted you." Our oldest child thought for the longest time that being gay meant that you were in a committed relationship with another person of the same gender. It wasn't completely accurate, but we didn't go out of our way to correct him. Kids don't generally associate being gay with sex, but I think most children don't think of their parents as sexual beings. Sometimes we

were, I think, overly sensitive about gay issues, and the kids would set us straight and let us know right away that whatever it was had nothing to do with their unique family situation.

These experiences seem to be corroborated by the work of H. David Kirk (1964) when he notes that adopted persons handle adoption best when they are raised in families that allow them the freedom and opportunity to explore adoption-related issues (and, in this case, issues related to being in an LGBT-headed family) whenever they arise.

I Wish I Had a Mom/Dad

Most children live in worlds that are dominated by moms, not dads. Moms are highlighted in cartoons, on TV commercials, in videos, and are usually the ones in the family who bring younger children to school in the morning and pick them up in the afternoon. Most LGBT parents we spoke to did not seem to feel the need to intentionally connect their children with mother or father figures; they did acknowledge that there were times when their children verbalized a desire at one time or another for a mom or a dad. This desire for a mom or a dad took on several forms, and parents were aware of what the verbalization for a mom or a dad meant for their own child. One dad's narrative recalls how his child expressed an interest in a mom:

One day Wade just started talk about his birth mom—it was near his birthday and I think that often adopted kids think about their birth families during those anniversary times—but he just said, kind of sadly, "I love you, Dad, but wish I had a mom." I felt bad for him. I knew that there wasn't anything that I could do to make it better, but I just felt sad for him.

Other parents noted that their children's lack of a dad was pointed out more by other children:

My kids were obviously comfortable with their own family, but other kids who were my children's friends frequently mentioned about the lack of a dad in our family. In some cases, the kids who were my children's friends were from single-mom families or divorced families where they lived with their mom, with very little involvement with their dad, so the fact that our children had two moms was quite a different experience for them.

Children utilize parents in ways that make them feel safe and comfortable. One dad recalled how his son needed to be physically close to him and that he equated that need for closeness with a mom figure:

> Drew was a very tactile child; he needed at times to be close physically to me and in times when he was very stressed, he used to snuggle up close and say, "I love to be all mushy with you—you are like a big fat mother pig." He meant this as the highest compliment and he clearly selected the mushier dad since my partner is the more physically fit of the two of us.

The following narrative of this mom suggests that her child had clearly thought about having a dad. It also points to the concrete ways that children think about their own lives:

> When I asked my son if he ever misses having a dad, he kind of looked at me incredulously and said, "How can you miss something that you never had?"

Growing Up Gay

During infancy and toddlerhood the issues of having an LGBT parent are subtle and, for most children, irrelevant, as children are unaware of gender roles in the home. The children of LGBT parents whom I met seemed to bond to their parents, and parents were accepting of their child, praising them, correcting them when necessary, and creating a conscious environment of affection and warmth. Kirk (1964), in his classic work on adoption, offers a perspective that may explain why the bond between the adopted child and adoptive parent can be so strong, which I believe can also be applied to LGBT parents and their children. According to Kirk's hypothesis, they all have suffered a deep sense of loss: the LGBT parent experienced loss because of the exigencies associated with coming-out as an LGBT person in a heterocentric, bi/transphobic, and sexist world that presumes that they will never be a suitable primary parent, and the adopted children experience the loss of their birth families. When the parents understand the shared nature of their loss, they can be more empathic toward their child and better able to raise him or her in a sensitive and understanding way.

As children develop into middle childhood (ages six through twelve), they began to further develop their sense of self (Brodzinsky and Schechter, 1990), including the development of gender, racial, and cultural difference, and, in the case of the children of LGBT parents, differences in their family composition. Many of the issues brought to light by these LGBT parents seem to be more related to issues of adoption than to issues pertaining to their LGBT parent, but in some cases there are more subtle complexities that are inextricably linked to insemination, adoption, foster care, and having a family that is considered to be different from the norm.

The Pain of Being Different

In middle childhood and then adolescence, children become acutely aware of being different or being perceived as being different. Some children may relish their differentness, but most do not. Sometimes LGBT parents report that their child was teased in school for being adopted and for being the child of gay parents. Like the training that parents of color provide for their children to combat prejudice (Crumbley, 1999), most of the LGBT parents we worked with spoke about providing their child with emotional armor to protect against the pain of a taunt. However, even with this emotional preparation by their parents, the children had to learn to protect themselves at school:

> My eleven-year-old son, who struggles with being perceived as different and having a different kind of family, came home from school one day and said, "You don't get it do you? Do you know what they say to me in school? They say, 'Like father, like son.' You know, they make these cracks trying to say that I'm gay, which I'm not, because you are. It pisses me off!"

As the children became teenagers, many of the parents noted there were new issues that they had to address in their families. Huge changes occur in the years between thirteen and nineteen. Physically, children grow faster during their teens than at any time since the prenatal period (Marcia, 1980; Offer, 1969). Biological and emotional changes in adolescents strain most family systems (Wolf, 2002). Most of the LGBT parents were clear that the changes their children experienced had less to do with their LGBT identity and more to do with the emerging identity of the teenager (Wolf, 2002). There were some cases, however, when parents did feel that their LGBT identity was an issue for their children. The comments of one dad are representative of many of the issues discussed in interviews about the changes brought about by adolescent development:

> The onset of junior high school caused our son to deal with our family situation in different ways. While in grammar school all of his friends knew our family and had sleepovers, spent time with us—our being gay was no big deal. We knew their families, we socialized with their parents, and our gayness was a nonissue. However, when our son went to a new school, he had to meet new friends, and make decisions about how much or how little he told them about his family. It was like the first day of camp, but on a bigger scale. He now had the control over telling others about his gay dads, not us. It was sometimes difficult for him. But he learned to tell friends when he felt comfortable, and he did not necessarily do that on day one. He also had to tell them he was adopted, and I think, in some ways, not having a mother was a bigger issue than having too many fathers.

As parents of adolescent children, the LGBT parents whom we talked with described how they had to learn a new set of rules about parenting. They had to get used to knocking on closed bedroom doors, they had to learn not to take adolescent moodiness personally, and they had to learn to let go. The hallmark of adolescence is moving toward independence, and for very involved parents such as the LGBT parents with whom I worked, allowing their children to move away from them was a necessary, but sometimes painful, process. Most of the parents acknowledged that this had less to do with them as LGBT persons and more to do with the development of their teenaged children. Nonetheless, caring for a teenage child was a new phenomenon for the LGBT parents, and many were weighed down as well with memories of their own tumultuous adolescence. Some equated their own coming-out process as adolescents to the coming-out that their children had to experience as the children of an LGBT parent:

> I felt guilty sometimes that adolescence which is difficult enough without having this extra layer of having to come out to your friends about having a gay, lesbian, bisexual, or trans parent. My child also had to come out about being adopted and not having a mom. In some ways these issues are really the bigger ones.

CONCLUSION

This chapter has focused on the evidence in relation to LGBT persons *choosing* parenthood and the effects on the children they parent. I would not argue that all LGBT people should be adoptive parents. In the same way, I would never argue that all non-LGBT people would make suitable adoptive parents. There are thousands of untold narratives by LGBT parents, who are caring parents for children who needed temporary or permanent families. The question is not whether LGBT persons will be parents, but how publicly they will be, and whether these families will be offered the same fair process and open opportunity as non-LGBT people who parent. Sidestepping of the issue of parenting by LGBT persons, or pretending that the issue does not exist, does not protect children. LGBT parenting challenges the traditional notions of family and in turn challenges practitioners to examine their own views of what constitutes a family.

The body of literature on this topic is nascent and relatively homogeneous. Numerous authors reviewing the research relevant to LGBT parenting have concluded that there is no evidence that LGBT parents are less capable of being effective parents than heterosexuals (Brooks & Goldberg, 2001; Hicks, 2000; Stacey & Biblarz, 2001). Although more research specific to the reality of LGBT parents, especially for bisexual and trans persons, should certainly be undertaken, a foundation of evidence indicates that the sexual or gender orientation of parents makes very little difference to outcomes for children.

While the research and practice findings summarized here are highly relevant to the concerns raised by those opposed to the consideration of LGBT persons as parents, further research into the specific experiences of children reared by LGBT persons is clearly needed.

As social work practitioners, particularly those working with LGBT parents, it is essential for us to read the research and to analyze, interpret, and discuss the research findings and practice implications for effective practice with this population. It is incumbent upon us as a professional community to be clear about the facts, able to rebut the misinformation presented by those who may not see LGBT persons as "appropriate" resources for children in need of homes, and nurture the narratives of truth that we have witnessed through case examples. Research findings and their interpretation have enormous impact in many influential arenas, including court cases for custody and visiting rights, judges, child advocates, professionals in the health and mental health communities, and those charged with developing and enacting legislation that guides our laws. In the midst of a politically charged environment in which negative stereotypes and ideological assertions can easily gain status as "truth," it is essential for social work practitioners to become familiar with what is known and not known from the research studies and practice implications so that LGBT parents work with and are supported by informed and competent practitioners.

REFERENCES

Agigian, A. (2004). *Baby steps: How lesbian alternative insemination is changing the world*. Wesleyan, CT: Wesleyan University Press.

Allen, M., & Burrell, N. (1996). Comparing the impact of homosexual and heterosexual parents on children: Meta-analysis of existing research. *Journal of Homosexuality, 32*, 19-35.

Barret, R., & Robinson, B. E. (2000). *Gay fathers*. New York: Jossey-Bass.

Benkov, L. (1994). *Reinventing the family: The emerging story of lesbian and gay parents*. New York: Crown Publishers.

Bernfeld, R. (1995). A brief guide regarding donor and co-parenting agreements. In M. E. Elovitz & C. Schneider (Eds.), *Legal issues facing the nontraditional family—1995* (pp. 135-169). New York: Practicing Law Institute.

Bigner, J. (1996). Working with gay fathers. In J. Laird & R.-J. Green (Eds.), *Lesbians and gays in couples and families: A handbook for therapists* (pp. 370-403). San Francisco: Jossey-Bass.

Bigner, J. J., & Jacobsen, R. B. (1992). Adult responses to child behavior and attitudes towards fathering: Gay and non-gay fathers. *Journal of Homosexuality, 21,* 173-186.

Biller, H. B., & Kimpton, J. L. (1997). The father and the school-aged child. In Lamb, M. E. (Ed.) *The role of the father in child development* (pp. 143-161). New York: John Wiley & Sons.

Bozett, F. W. (1980). Gay fathers: How and why they disclose their homosexuality to their children. *Family Relations, 29,* 173-179.

Bozett, F. W. (Ed.) (1987). *Gay and lesbian parents.* New York: Praeger Press.

Brazelton, T. B. (1992). *Touchpoints: Your child's emotional and behavioral development.* Reading, MA: Perseus Books.

Brodzinsky, D. M., & Schechter, M. D. (Eds.) (1990). *The psychology of adoption.* New York: Oxford.

Bronston, B. (2004, November 14). Children of same-sex parents fare well in research: Early studies find positive outcomes, but more work remains. *New Orleans Times Picayune,* p. 14.

Brooks, D., & Goldberg, S. (2001). Gay and lesbian adoptive and foster care placements: Can they meet the needs of waiting children? *Families in Society, 46*(2), 147-157.

Buxton, A. P. (1994). *The other side of the closet: The coming out crisis for straight spouses and families.* New York: Wiley.

Cameron, P., Cameron, K., & Landess, T. (1996). Errors by the American Psychiatric Association, the American Psychological Association and the National Education Association in representing homosexuality in aminus briefs about Amendment 2 to the U.S. Supreme Court. *Psychological Reports, 79,* 383-404.

Carey, B. (2005, January 29). Experts Dispute Bush on Gay-Adoption Issue. *New York Times,* p. A23.

Chan, R. W., Raboy, B., & Patterson, C. J. (2000). Psychosocial adjustment among children conceived via donor insemination by lesbian and heterosexual mothers. *Child Development 69,* 443-457.

Cooper, D. (1994). *From darkness into light: What the Bible really says about homosexuality* (3rd ed.). Tucson, AZ: Cornerstone Fellowship.

Cramer, D. (1986). Gay parents and their children: A review of research and practical implications. *Journal of Counseling and Development, 64,* 501-507.

Crumbley, J. (1999). *Transracial adoption and foster care: Practice issues for professionals.* Washington, DC: CWLA Press.

Dunlap, D. W. (1996, January 7). Homosexual parents raising children: Support for pro and con. *New York Times,* p. L15.

Elovitz, M. E. (1995). Adoption by lesbian and gay people: The use and misuse of social science research. In M. E. Elovitz & C. Schneider (Eds.), *Legal issues facing the nontraditional family—1995* (pp. 171-191). New York: Practicing Law Institute.

Evan B. Donaldson Adoption Institute (2003). *Adoption by lesbians and gays: A national survey of adoption agency policies, practices, and attitudes.* New York: Author.

Fronczak, T., & Campanaro-Cummings, V.J. (2006). *Gay parenting.* Providence, RI: Straight Spouses Support Network.

Garner, A. (2004). *Families like mine: Children of gay parents tell it like it is.* New York: HarperCollins.

Gochros, J. (1989). *When husbands come out of the closet.* Binghamton, NY: The Haworth Press.

Golombok, S., Spencer, A., & Rutter, M. (1983). Children in lesbian and single-parent households: Psychosexual and psychiatric appraisal. *Journal of Child Psychology and Psychiatry, 24*(4), 551-572.

Golombok, S., & Tasker, F. (1996). Do parents influence the sexual orientation of their children? Findings from a longitudinal study of lesbian families. *Developmental Psychology, 32*(1), 3-11.

Gordon, T. (2000). *Parent effectiveness training: The proven program for raising responsible children.* New York: Three Rivers Press.

Green, J. (1999). *The velveteen father: An unexpected journey to parenthood.* New York: Villard.

Groth, A. N. (1978). Patterns of sexual assault against children and adolescents. In A. W. Burgess, A. N. Groth, L. L. Holmstrom, & S. M. Sgroi (Eds.), *Sexual assault of children and adolescents* (pp. 221-264). Lexington, MA: Lexington Books.

Groth, A. N., & Birnbaum, H. J. (1978). Adult sexual orientation and attraction to underage persons. *Archives of Sexual Behavior, 7*(3), 175-181.

Hartman, A. (1996). Social policy as a context for lesbian and gay families: The political is personal. In J. Laird & R.-J. Green (Eds.), *Lesbians and gays in couples and families: A handbook for therapists* (pp. 69-85). San Francisco: Jossey-Bass Publishers.

Helminiak, D. A. (1997). *What the Bible really says about homosexuality.* San Francisco: Alamo Square Press.

Herek, G. M. (1991). Stigma, prejudice and violence against lesbians and gay men. In J. C. Gonsiorek & J. D. Weinrich (Eds.), *Homosexuality: Research implications for public policy* (pp. 60-80). Newbury Park: Sage Publications.

Herman, D. (1997). *The anti-gay agenda—Orthodox vision and the Christian right.* Chicago: University of Chicago Press.

Hicks, S. (2000). Good lesbian, bad lesbian: Regulating heterosexuality in fostering and adoption assessments. *Child & Family Social Work, 5*(2), 157-168.

Horn, W. F., & Sylvester, T. (2002). *Father facts* (4th ed.). Lancaster, PA: National Fatherhood Initiative.

Howey, N., Samuels, E., Cammermeyer, M., & Savage, D. (2000). *Out of the ordinary: Essays on growing up with gay, lesbian, and transgender parents.* New York: Stonewall Inn Editions.

Jenny, C., Roesler, T. A., & Poyer, K. L. (1994). Are children at risk for sexual abuse by homosexuals? *Pediatrics, 94*(1), 41-44.

Kirk, H. D. (1964). *Shared fate.* Glencoe, IL: Free Press.

Klein, F., & Schwartz, T. (Eds.) (2002). *Bisexual and gay husbands: Their stories, their words.* Binghamton, NY: The Haworth Press.

Lamb, M. E. (Ed.) (1986). *The father's role: Applied perspectives.* New York: John Wiley & Sons.

Lamb, M. E. (Ed.) (1987). *The father's role: Cross cultural perspectives.* Hillsdale, NJ: Erlbaum.

Lamb, M. E. (1997). The development of father-infant relationships. In M. E. Lamb (Ed.), *The role of the father in child development* (pp. 104-120). New York: John Wiley & Sons.

Lancaster, K. (1996). *Keys to parenting an adopted child.* Hauppauge, NY: Barrons.

Larson, R., & Richards, M. (1994). *Divergent lives: The emotional lives of mothers, fathers, and adolescents.* New York: Basic Books.

MacPike, L. (1989). *There's something I've been meaning to tell you.* New York: Naiad Press.

Mallon, G. P. (1999a). *Let's get this straight: A gay and lesbian affirming approach to child welfare.* New York: Columbia University Press.

Mallon, G. P. (1999b). Lesbians and gay men as foster and adoptive parents. In *Let's get this straight: A gay and lesbian affirming approach to child welfare* (pp. 112-131). New York: Columbia University Press.

Mallon, G. P. (2000). Gay men and lesbians as adoptive parents. *Journal of Gay and Lesbian Social Services, 11*(4), 1-21.

Mallon, G. P. (2004). *Gay men choosing parenthood.* New York: Columbia University Press.

Malyon, A. K. (1982). Psychotherapeutic implications of internalized homophobia in gay men. *Journal of Homosexuality, 7*(2/3), 59-69.

Marcia, J. E. (1980). Identity in adolescence. In J. Adelson (Ed.), *Handbook of adolescent psychiatry* (pp. 159-187). New York: John Wiley & Sons.

Marindin, H. (1997). *The handbook for single adoptive parents.* Chevy Chase, MD: Committee for Single Parents.

Martin, A. (1993). *The lesbian and gay parenting handbook: Creating and raising our families.* New York: Harper Perennial.

McGarry, K. (2004). *Fatherhood for gay men: An emotional and practical guide to becoming a gay dad.* Binghamton, NY: The Haworth Press.

McPherson, D. (1993). *Gay parenting couples: Parenting arrangements, arrangement satisfaction, and relationship satisfaction.* Unpublished doctoral dissertation, Pacific Graduate School of Psychology, CA.

Melina, L. R. (1998). *Raising adopted children.* New York: Quill.

Metropolitan Community Church (1990). *Homosexuality not a sin, not a sickness: What the Bible does and does not say.* Los Angeles: Author.

Mitchell, V. (1996). Two moms: Contribution of the planned lesbian family and the deconstruction of gendered parenting. In J. Laird & R.-J. Green (Eds.), *Lesbians and gays in couples and families: A handbook for therapists* (pp. 343-357). San Francisco: Jossey-Bass Publishers.

Mohler, M., & Frazer, L. (2002). *A donor insemination guide: Written by and for lesbian women.* Binghamton, NY: The Haworth Press.

Muzio, C. (1993). Lesbian co-parenting: On being/being the invisible (m)other. *Smith College Studies in Social Work, 63*(3), 215-229.

Muzio, C. (1996). Lesbians choosing children: Creating families, creating narratives. In J. Laird & R.-J. Green (Eds.), *Lesbians and gays in couples and families: A handbook for therapists* (pp. 358-369). San Francisco: Jossey-Bass Publishers.

Newton, D. E. (1978). Homosexual behavior and child molestation: A review of the evidence. *Adolescence, 13,* 205-215.

Offer, D. (1969). *The psychological world of the teenager: A study of normal adolescence.* New York: Basic Books.

Osman, S. (1972). My stepfather is a she. *Family Process, 11,* 209-218.

Parents, Families and Friends of Lesbians and Gays (1997). *Beyond the Bible: Parents, families and friends talk about religion and homosexuality.* Washington, DC: Author.

Patterson, C. J. (1992). Children of gay and lesbian parents. *Child Development, 63,* 1025-1042.

Patterson, C. J. (1994). Lesbian and gay couples considering parenthood: An agenda for research, service and advocacy. In L. A. Kurdek (Ed.), *Social services for gay and lesbian couples* (pp. 33-56). Binghamton, NY: Harrington Park Press.

Patterson, C. J. (1995). Lesbian mothers, gay fathers, and their children. In A. R. D'Augelli & C. J. Patterson (Eds.), *Gay, lesbian, and bisexual identities over the lifespan* (pp. 262-292). Oxford: Oxford University Press.

Patterson, C. J. (1996). Lesbian mothers and their children: Findings from the Bay area families study. In J. Laird & R.-J. Green (Eds.), *Lesbians and gays in couples and families: A handbook for therapists* (pp. 420-438). San Francisco: Jossey-Bass Publishers.

Patterson, C. J., Hurt, S., & Mason, C. D. (1998). Families of the lesbian baby-boom: Children's contact with grandparents and other adults. *American Journal of Orthopsychiatry, 68,* 390-399.

Pies, C. (1985). *Considering parenthood: A workbook for lesbians.* San Francisco: Spinsters/Aunt Lute.

Pies, C. (1990). Lesbians and the choice to parent. In F. W. Bozett & M. B. Sussman (Eds.), *Homosexuality and family relations* (pp. 138-150). Binghamton, NY: The Haworth Press.

Popenoe, D. (1996). *Life without father.* New York: Free Press.

Ricketts, W. (1991). *Lesbians and gay men as foster parents.* Portland, MN: University of Southern Maine.

Ricketts, W., & Achtenberg, R. A. (1990). Adoption and foster parenting for lesbians and gay men: Creating new traditions in family. *Marriage and Family Review, 14*(3/4), 83-118.

Sbordone, A. J. (1993). *Gay men choosing fatherhood.* Unpublished doctoral dissertation. Department of Psychology, City University of New York, NY.

Scott, S. (2002). *Research Briefing: The impact on children of having lesbian or gay parents.* London: Barnardo's.

Shernoff, M. (1996). Gay men choosing to be fathers. In M. Shernoff (Ed.), *Human services for gay people: Clinical and community practice* (pp. 41-54). Binghamton, NY: The Haworth Press.

Shuster, S. (2005). Can we speak freely? What research has told us about LGBT parenting. *In the Family, 10*(4), 14-17.

Snow, J. E. (2004). *How it feels to have a gay or lesbian parent: A book by kids for kids of all ages*. Binghamton, NY: The Haworth Press.

Stacey, J., & Biblarz, T. (2001). (How) Does the sexual orientation of parents matter? *American Sociological Review, 66,* 159-183.

Sullivan, A. (Ed.) (1995). *Issues in gay and lesbian adoption: Proceedings of the Fourth Annual Pierce-Warwick Adoption Symposium*. Washington, DC: Child Welfare League of America.

Tasker, F. L., & Golombok, S. (1997). *Growing up in a lesbian family: Effects on child development*. New York: Guilford Press.

Wolf, A. E. (2002). *Get out of my life: The parent's guide to the new teenager*. New York: Farrar, Straus, Giroux.

Chapter 13

Community Practice
with LGBT People

Eli C. Nealy

LGBT CONTEXT

Much like immigrants in a new country, lesbian, gay, bisexual, and transgender (LGBT) persons grow up surrounded by a history and culture that is not their own (Hogan & Hudson, 1998). The rituals, relationships, and language all seem disconnected from their experience of themselves. From an early age, they often know that their lives and choices (children, careers, partners, and religion) will play out differently than the paths of those around them. Unlike ethnic immigrants, even their own families are different, a dynamic that creates an even more profound sense of being a stranger in a foreign land. Today, however, there are over 150 community centers throughout the country, with new centers forming on a regular basis. Collectively, their combined membership, client base, visitors, newsletter readership, and event attendees represents one of the largest constituencies in the LGBT movement. Centers are the primary point of contact for people coming-out, seeking LGBT health services, community information, and referrals. In many cities and towns, community centers are the only local LGBT community resource. Whether organizing for social change, providing direct services, or educating the public, community centers work more closely with their LGBT constituency and engage more community leaders and decision makers than any other LGBT network in the country (see http://www.lgbtcenters.org/). This chapter reviews the current knowledge and practice available within the social work context for working with LGBT communities.

While most immigrants can choose to live in, or near, their own ethnic communities, queer people for many generations have had no visible community. Even today, despite meccas like San Francisco and New York City, young lesbians, gay boys, and gender-different youth typically find themselves isolated from others who are like them. This lack of visible, healthy community creates a lack of role models and limits opportunities. As Edward, a thirty-three-year-old gay male substance user put it:

> Growing up gay, the image of gay that was always depicted was the subservient, sex maniac person who hung out at the bars. Like that was the only thing that existed as something visible for the gay community. You always heard about the gay bars, and then there was the sex room, and all that kind of stuff. It was almost like, if that was the picture that was out there in front of you, how can you not become that—because you don't know anything else.

Many times, the power of stigma and shame creates an enforced silence that typically leads to experiences of loss of self, isolation from family and friends, and concomitantly, a sense of alienation from the larger community and culture. In a study exploring whether ongoing discrimination fuels anxiety, depression, and other stress-related mental health problems among LGBT people, Cochran and Mays (2000) found a strong relationship between perceived discrimination and substance abuse and mental health status. Other risk factors related to increased rates of substance use and abuse within the LGBT communities include: the impact of stigma and discrimination against LGBT persons upon self-concept and self-esteem; the lack of access to affirmative health promotion and disease prevention resources in the larger society; the impact of multiple stigmas and problems including concurrent poverty, racism, HIV/AIDS-related issues, and/or other concerns; reliance upon the LGBT bar scene for socialization and identity affirmation; family, religious, and social intolerance of LGBT lifestyles; and the threat and/or experience of anti-LGBT violence.

Traditional social service treatment models locate the problem within the individual or, in some instances, the family. Consequently, they tend to treat individuals not communities. In contrast, community building models of practice may offer the greatest hope for work with oppressed groups. Briggs (2003) defines community building as an effort to organize and strengthen social connections and build common values that promote collective goals. Similarly, Fabricant and Fisher (2002) define community building as an activity that is defined by the intersection of four dynamics: rights, relationship, reciprocity, and responsibilities.

The current larger U.S. social context is powerfully marked by the driving forces of globalization intertwined with notions of privatization and an increasing focus on the individual as opposed to the community or common/public good (Anton, 2000; Macarov, 2003). With the concomitant decline of civic participation, described by Putnam's (2000) work, *Bowling Alone,* the consequent need for community practice with marginalized communities, and LGBT persons in particular, becomes even more pressing. Within this context of LGBT oppression and societal individualism, individual interventions alone are inadequate. For example, couples counseling alone is not enough; LGBT couples and families need basic human rights and social protections. Similarly, it is not sufficient to utilize individual psychotherapy alone to support a young trans woman through transition; that same trans woman needs and deserves to be safe on the streets, able to obtain employment without discrimination, and find access to the basic health care needed to support her transition (Currah et al., 2006).

These dynamics are even truer for LGBT persons facing multiple stigmas and oppression. While this is to some extent a generalization, psychotherapists and agencies that deliver services to white, heterosexual, middle- to upper-class individuals have less of a need to be concerned with the development of social capital—largely because these communities are the ones that dominate social capital (social networks with resources and power) in our country. However, more marginalized communities tend by definition to be isolated from dominant power structures and systems of access. From a social capital perspective, it is insufficient to simply treat an individual's substance abuse or depression, no matter how holistic the service delivery may be.

Social service needs like mental health and addiction, housing, and access to health insurance/healthcare are significantly affected by an individual's or a community's experiences of oppression, isolation, and alienation (Smith & Mancoske, 1997). Consequently, these experiences must be addressed through the building of relationships (between clients, between client/worker, between client/worker and larger systems) based on mutual exchange, respect, and reciprocity. This community building work leads to a greater acknowledgment of social rights for all persons/communities and an increased understanding of our responsibilities to one another for maintaining those relationships and rights.

Against the backdrop of societal harassment, discrimination, and violence (see Hanson, 1996), community building models are well-suited to provide LGBT-identified clients an opportunity to recover from the intersecting dynamics of addiction, oppression, and alienation (Gutierrez, Oh, & Gillmore, 2000; Huebner, Rebchook, & Kegeles, 2004). Jones et al. (as cited in Meyer, 2003) explicate the significance of community connections by describing the ways minority group affiliations enable oppressed individuals to experience social environments free of stigma. Consequently, members of stigmatized groups who have a strong sense of "community cohesiveness" are better able to reappraise societal stigma and reclaim a positive sense of identity (Goffman, 1963).

The community-building environment promotes a sense of affiliation with something larger than oneself. It decreases feelings of isolation and alienation by promoting pride and empowerment. These changes are essential for individuals who have been trivialized and marginalized by mainstream society, isolated from one another, and often rejected by heterosexual and/or nontransgender family and friends. While personal resources can sometimes be utilized for these purposes, Meyer (2003) posits group-level resources as essential, noting that when the latter are absent, even very resourceful individuals may experience deficient coping skills.

This need for community connections is essential to understanding the links between substance use and sexual risk taking. For example, among HIV-negative gay men, dissatisfaction with social support predicts unprotected anal intercourse (UAI) (Dilley, McFarland, Sullivan, & Discepola, 1998). In addition, social support has been associated with factors of mental health, as those with less support and more isolation have more mental health problems (Ayala & Coleman, 2000; Turner, Hays, & Coates, 1993).

Community-building models have been found effective in HIV prevention with gay men (Hays, Rebchok, & Kegeles, 2003), in work with lesbian and bisexual women (Nystrom & Jones, 2003; Steinhouse, 2001), and in HIV prevention and general health promotion with transgender individuals (Kammerer, Mason, & Connors, 1999). Finnegan and McNally (2002) reinforce the importance of these approaches, noting that LGBT individuals in recovery need a sense of belonging, social networks, connection to LGBT culture, and avenues for political action.

WHAT IS LGBT COMMUNITY PRACTICE?

Several points have to be taken into consideration when discussing LGBT community practice. First, traditional notions of community are frequently limited to geographic neighborhoods. However, the LGBT community typically spans the world. Social workers need to embrace Halperin's (1998) challenge to rethink and redefine community, "not as a geographical and bounded place," but instead as a "dynamic, contentious, and changing process that plays out as a series of everyday practices" by a network of people who have or have had some link to one another (p. 13).

Second, related to that concept is the recognition that the "LGBT community" is not a singular notion. LGBT individuals come from every conceivable community: they are black, white, Latino, and Asian; young, old, and differently abled; rich, middle class, working class, and poor; high school educated and college graduates; urban, suburban, and rural; Jewish, Christian, Muslim, and nonreligious. In reality, there are many LGBT communities.

Third, community is not equivalent to uniformity. Fabricant and Fisher (2002) note that community building must emphasize both partnership and the importance of difference, stating "people must revel in diversity and inclusion" (p. 288). They go on to emphasize that any understanding of community building "must incorporate conflict and tensions, not simply cohesion and consensus building" (p. 289).

From these starting concepts, community-building interventions are rooted in the efficacy of empowerment, a concept increasingly important to the philosophy and practice of health promotion. Empowerment is a participatory process through which individuals, organizations, and communities gain greater control, efficacy, and social justice (Peterson & Zimmerman, 2004). Key empowerment concepts include beliefs about control (perceived locus of control and self-efficacy beliefs); values, such as self-esteem; social and personal skills; and an ability to conceptualize the ways societal stigma and powerlessness contribute to individual problems (Crossley, 2001; Gutierrez, 1990).

A collaborative approach to service delivery is essential to an empowerment-focused, community-building approach. Simon (1994) defines authentic collaboration as an ongoing reciprocity of effort, ideas, resources, and respect. In a collaborative model clients are not patients but community partners. They are not "the other," or separate from community workers, but instead collaborators in a united movement for freedom from addiction and oppression. As Fabricant and Fisher (2002) conclude, collaboration implies "not only partnership but the transformation of clients into leaders in the day-to-day life of the agency" (p. 262).

Recent HIV prevention efforts have often been built around a peer-based, collaborative model of service delivery. One example is the "Mpowerment Project," which relied on peers as change agents in the delivery of sex-positive, gay-identified, HIV prevention messages within the context of an empowerment-based, community-building initiative (Hays et al., 2003). This model draws on Rogers's (1995) theory of diffusion of innovations, which holds that group members are most likely to adopt behavioral changes when conveyed positively by respected peers. These models bring workers, peer leaders, and participants together in an environment that reduces shame and isolation and fosters affirmative identity development and community empowerment. Studies show that peer-based services have been effective HIV prevention and substance abuse harm reduction tools for reaching gay men, transgender individuals, youth, women, sex workers, and injection drug users (Bockting, Rosser, & Coleman, 1999).

Enabling positive connections and reconnections to queer strengths and queer culture is another essential element of community building practice. Peter Bell (2002), a substance abuse expert who has worked extensively with cross-cultural issues in addiction prevention and treatment, wrote about the concept of cultural pain. He defined it as a feeling of insecurity, embarrassment, anger, confusion, or inadequacy due to the conflicting expectations and pressure of being a minority. Bell argued that people from oppressed communities must learn to deal with the ongoing challenge of this pain. Community-building models of practice help LGBT persons move through their cultural pain to discover cultural identity and pride, a process essential to healthy sober LGBT communities.

Facilitating cultural pride necessitates a focus on individual and community strengths. As McKnight (cited in Fabricant & Fisher, 2002) and others note, community is not built with a focus on deficiencies and needs. Instead, healthy, sober communities are built by valuing and sharing cultural strengths and traditions, while building on the capacities and gifts of those who live there (Delgado, 1998; Hess, McGowan, & Botsko, 2003; National Community Building Network, 2003). The Kretzman and McKnight model of community building (as cited in Nystrom & Jones, 2003) assumes that community members have the resources needed to bring people together, to make consensus-based decisions about the community's needs, and to provide necessary services and programs.

Essential to this work is the development of comprehensive community-level interventions, as a wraparound to individual and group-level interventions. Swenson (as cited in Lee, 1994) notes a connection between the absence of constructive community relationships and individual fragmentation, purposelessness, addiction, and violence. She goes on to say that for oppressed groups in particular, the community is a critical mediating structure between empowerment, liberation, and oppression. Community-building models such as these are not simply about treating individuals or addressing an interpersonal conflict or problem. Instead, their work is about building a community of empowered consumers, citizens, and activists. Their focus is on returning people to community in an effort to decrease isolation and increase self esteem. Community-building models enable clients to participate meaningfully in society; they empower LGBT people to become agents of social change in the places where they live.

Authentic community-building models call for empowerment at both the interpersonal and structural levels. However, the empowerment literature and established treatment systems often remain focused on the individual and frequently neglect larger systems of oppression and power (Crossley, 2001). By contrast, Gutierrez et al. (2000) suggest that gaining a sense of personal power is only the first step toward the ultimate goal of changing oppressive structures. It is essential that empowerment theory and social work services move beyond an individual perspective to encompass both interpersonal factors, such as social support and connections to community, and more macro issues of power, privilege, and societal change (Mays, Cochran, & Zamudio, 2004).

LGBT COMMUNITY CENTER MOVEMENT

Prior to 1969, there were no community centers and only a few lesbian and gay organizations scattered throughout the country. The growth of the LGBT service industry burgeoned during the 1980s with the spread of the HIV/ AIDS epidemic and the accompanying growth in activism within the gay community. Today, there are over 150 LGBT community centers throughout the United States in major and smaller metropolitan, suburban, and rural areas. The National Association of LGBT Community Centers was founded in 1994 to support the growth and development of this industry. These centers, scattered across the United States in small towns and communities as well as large urban areas, are designed to facilitate community building, cultural celebration, caring for LGBT persons in need, and the social change necessary for LGBT persons to live healthy and full lives.

There is something unique and powerful about the delivery of social services within the context of a local LGBT organization dedicated to community building, celebration of culture, and social change. In contrast to receiving services in a more traditional medical facility or a freestanding treatment clinic, clients do not need to identify as "sick" when they walk through the doors of a community center. Instead, entering the center is about embracing the fullness and the goodness of who they are. It is about finding themselves in a physical space surrounded by positive images, sounds, and experiences of LGBT history and culture. It involves becoming a part of an organization that is an advocate for equality and justice for LGBT persons in their local community.

With LGBT identity historically being defined as criminal, sinful, pathological, aberrant, and the result of dysfunctional parenting, LGBT individuals live within a societal context permeated with heterosexist assumptions that often renders queer identities and relationships invisible and/or marginal. Against the backdrop of these realities, participating in activities at an LGBT community center offers an affirming, empowering, and normative experience that yields a transformative and healing effect for many individuals. Against the norms of powerlessness inherent in oppression, becoming an active member of this kind of center offers a route to visibility, personal and communal empowerment, and becoming a participant in creating societal change.

The marginalization and oppression of individuals and communities can create tremendous struggles with internalized shame and self-hatred, as well as a pervasive sense, even the reality, of isolation and alienation. From the onset, the National Association of LCBT Community Centers' mission has been about community building, the work of moving LGBT persons from isolation and invisibility to inclusion and active participation in social change. Fabricant and Fisher (2002) outline the goals of this work: from client/consumer engagement to increasing participation in the life of the agency, to the development of a membership relationship with the organization, and then with the wider community and society. This movement is guided and facilitated by relational principles rooted in reciprocity, respect, inclusiveness, and accountability.

Case Study: The New York City LGBT Community Center

The New York City Lesbian, Gay, Bisexual and Transgender Community Center (the Center) became a reality in 1983 when a handful of community groups and a fledgling board of directors raised over $150,000 in just two weeks to put a down payment on an unused public school building at 208 West 13th Street in Manhattan. From the beginning, the Center's mission was clearly articulated:

> The Lesbian, Gay, Bisexual & Transgender Community Center provides a home for the birth, nurture and celebration of our organizations, institutions and culture; cares for our individuals and groups in need; educates the public and our community; and empowers our individuals and groups to achieve their fullest potential. (www.gaycenter.org)

Today, the Center functions as a hub of the queer community in New York City and is home to over 300 different social, recreational, cultural, spiritual, and advocacy groups, including eighty twelve-step meetings. Some 6,000 people come through the doors of the Center each week looking for information and referrals, community support, professional networking, educational resources, cultural programming, avenues for activism, and mental health and social services (see www.gaycenter.org).

The mission and work of the Center has much in common with early settlement house history. Originally emerging in the late 1800s and early 1900s, settlement houses were founded to help new European immigrants in urban areas acculturate to U.S. language, civic life, and culture (Fabricant & Fisher, 2002, Husock, 1993). These institutions offered a wide range of social services—English, educational groups, job development, nurseries and kindergarten, mental health—and a diverse array of services that were not problem-focused, including recreation, libraries, and cultural activities such as art exhibits, theater, music, and folk festivals. These community-building efforts were designed to create stronger neighborhoods. However, settlement houses quickly discovered that emerging social problems required more than just concerted community effort. Consequently, they quickly became engaged in social reform activities, such as setting aside parks and playgrounds, improved sanitation and public health, and city, state, and federal efforts regarding minimum age, child labor laws, and women's suffrage. As Fabricant and Fisher (2002) note, settlement houses were known for the collaborative delivery of services in a context of community building and social change.

As a contemporary settlement house, the Center creates a safe space for LGBT persons to build self-esteem and decrease isolation, educate LGBT "immigrants" about their own history and culture, deliver a wide array of services designed to meet LGBT-specific needs in an LGBT-affirmative and identified environment, and provides space for community organizing. This fits with Husock's (1993) description of settlement houses as an alternative to current social welfare policy, in that they exist not simply to treat specific problems or "problem people," but rather aspire to be a community recreational, educational, and cultural institution.

Center members talk frequently about the value of the "safe space" provided by the Center. For example, when Guatemalan immigrant Eduardo was asked about his participation in groups and meetings at the Center, he replied:

> I come to this group because I am part of the gay community now, and I know you are worried (concerned) for us; it doesn't matter what religion, what country we are from. I feel support here: I can talk if I need to, find advice. It's like my country's representative here. How do you say, like the "Embahada"? Every country has some house—in other countries you have a place from the United States . . . an embassy, that's what I mean. It's like I am at the embassy. This is my embassy in New York City. . . . I feel comfortable to come over here. I am not afraid of the police here. I feel like you guys take care of me, so I feel that comfort . . . I feel like in this place you care about our community and that is very important.

The Center offers a wide range of cultural programs, such as rotating visual arts exhibits, bingo, dances, lecture series, Lesbian Cinema Arts, Queer Book of the Month, Queer Songbook: Emerging LGBT Artists, and Out & Faithful: a series on LGBT folks and religion/spirituality. Many educational activities take place including yoga, dance classes, foreign language clubs, an extensive lending library, and a state-of-the-art cyber center. Professional groups like LGBT social workers, nurses, and firefighters meet at the Center, as well as infant-toddler play groups and LGBT parenting groups. Like other settlement houses, these activities offer a "comprehensive approach that strengthens individual and neighborhood assets, while building collective capacity to address social problems" (Hirota, Brown, & Martin, 1996, p. 233).

Nestled within these community activities, the Center offers both adolescent (YES [Youth Enrichment Services]) and adult (Center CARE [Counseling, Advocacy, Recovery and Education]) social service programs. Rooted in the Center's overall mission, these programs exist to bring LGBT people out of isolation, to build self-esteem and empowerment, and connect them to proactive, healthy, and affirmative counseling services, activities, and avenues for activism. This involves engaging theoretical models, such as community building, empowerment, prevention, and relational cultural approaches that readily translate the mission into service effectiveness. From this mission, it follows that Center CARE and YES are not simply about providing "clinical" or "treatment" services to clients, but instead, about partnering with clients to enable them to move through internalized shame and isolation, and into a community of LGBT activists empowered for social change.

In the Center's adult counseling program, staff provide individual, group, and community-level interventions. The goal of these interventions is never simply about individual change—a gay man getting sober, a lesbian feeling less depressed, and a transgender person finding housing. The Center's goal is always about empowering individuals in a way that links people together to create community health and empowerment. As Kawachi, Kennedy, and Lochner (1997) note in an article titled "Long Live Community: Social Capital As Public Health," higher levels of social connection and cohesiveness are correlated to lower mortality rates. Further, when working with marginalized communities it is essential to address the ways public health and social change are intertwined. If social cohesion is essential to health and wellness, then community mobilization toward social change efforts focused on undoing the effects of oppression, marginalization, and isolation must be incorporated into models of service delivery. This means moving beyond the individualized approaches located in free market models and traditional social service organization literature and embracing the importance of community participation and change (Gittell, Ortega-Bustamante, & Steffy, 2000).

Another parallel of the original emphasis of settlement houses is the Center's role as an "engine for social change." This work is reflected in programs like the Center's extensive voter registration and mobilization campaign, Promote the Vote; Causes in Common, a project that works to build coalitions between the LGBT rights and reproductive freedom movements; the historical formation of groups like ACT-UP (an early HIV/AIDS activist group) and the Gay and Lesbian Activists Against Defamation (GLAAD); and regular candidates' forums and well-attended postelection gatherings and strategy sessions. This social change work flows directly from the creation of social capital through community-building activities. Linked together, these twin forces enable community residents to understand the ways in which personal needs and community problems are often rooted beyond the immediate "neighborhood" to the systems and structures of society as a whole (Fabricant & Fisher, 2002, p. 259).

This final stage of community building results in both a "broader communal sense of identity and more political and economic clout," noting that if the process of building social capital stops at the level of the organization, the larger community will be shortchanged (Fabricant & Fisher, 2002, p. 258). Saegart, Thompson, and Warren (2001) describe social capital as the "set of resources that inhere in relationships of trust and cooperation between people" (p. 1). As such, it is both an individual and a collective asset.

When lesbian and gay parents began to meet at the Center in 1989, forming Center Kids, they discovered that they were not alone and began to build peer support networks they could rely on for resource sharing and emotional support (individual assets). Over time, Center Kids grew larger, becoming more visible and vocal within the New York City community and resulting in public good, such as LGBT parental involvement with local school PTAs and the advocacy for Dignity for All Students legislation. This reflects what Gittell and Vidal (1998) describe as "bonding social capital." More recently, Center Kids has spawned a new community organizing initiative, Causes in Common, which focuses more on "bridging social capital" in its work to build collaborations between LGBT and reproductive rights organizations across the country. The evolution of LGBT family connections in New York City illustrates the ways social networks create new opportunities, resources, and even new communities (Fabricant & Fisher, 2002). This community building or social capital development among participants has over time resulted in political capital with the NYC Board of Education, the

Administration for Children's Services, and City Council, as well as social solidarity with other groups concerned with reproductive access.

A second illustration of increasing community diversity and inclusion leading to increased social and political capital outcome of community practice involves the Center's Gender Identity Project (GIP). When birthed in 1989, there was little visible or organized transsexual community. Initially headed by a psychologist, the GIP was largely staffed by peer educators and counselors. With the advent of the New York State AIDS Institute funding, the GIP developed a strong peer education training model that provided a wide range of individual and group services for the transgender community. Over the years many of these peer counselors pursued professional education. Today, there are more than a dozen trans-identified MSWs who began as peers in the GIP and now work in agencies throughout New York City. GIP capacity building efforts also include the development of a transgender training program. These sessions are designed to build capacity at other agencies and organizations, such as local colleges, medical schools, HIV/AIDS community-based organizations, outpatient mental health clinics, city agencies and bureaus, and substance abuse treatment programs. Through the development of trans-identified social work practitioners and their educated allies, the GIP and other trans organizations successfully completed many years of advocacy with the New York City Department of Homeless Services, resulting in policy changes that now allow transgender clients to be housed in the facility matching their self-identified gender.

It is relevant to note the importance of matching community practice to the varying stages of community development that may be evident. For example, the Stonewall Rebellion in 1969 is largely recognized as the emergence of a visible and organized lesbian and gay community. As noted earlier, the number of gay and lesbian groups in urban areas grew substantially during the 1980s and early 1990s. However, visible community growth has been slower in many smaller or rural areas. The emergence of organized transgender community groups occurred even later and, in some areas around the country, is still at a very early stage.

WHAT IS NEEDED TO MOVE FORWARD

- *Vision:* Look beyond the individual and his or her personal needs and recognize that individual services are insufficient unless nestled within the context of community building and social change.
- *Capacity building:* There is a tremendous need for competent LGBT-identified social workers and non-LGBT-identified social work allies,

as well as for capacity building work on group and organizational levels.

- *Community building:* Engage others, both "old-timers" and emerging segments of the LGBT communities, to tell their personal stories of transformation and their visions for change. From these conversations, build a shared vision of an increasingly diverse LGBT movement aligned with other movements for human rights and justice. Remember that community building is about building relationships—with staff, volunteers, and community members; this means modeling interaction, affirmation, and authenticity (Fabricant & Fisher, 2002).

- *Leadership*: Develop models of shared leadership where others with less authority gain power while no leader loses power. Create systems and programs of leadership development that multiply power, thus building increased social and political capital. This is particularly critical given the impending retirement of baby boomer leaders during the next twenty years. Utilize joint projects and events to create new social capital, for both bonding to LGBT folks and bridging with other communities.

- *Activism:* Create new avenues for community members to become engaged in activism and social change, to build bridges with other communities, and to become active participants in the larger civic life of their neighborhoods, cities, states, and country. Commit to bringing people together around shared interests and needs. Provide space for LGBT persons to organize themselves.

- *Community challenges:* The diversity of LGBT communities demands a need for communication (skills) across differences. This includes the need for complete inclusion of transgender persons and for an explicit antiracist, antioppression lens that goes beyond the history of traditional identity politics. Social work leaders are needed who will push community building beyond the chief critique of settlement houses: their penchant for functioning more as agents of social control than for empowering members for participation in social change.

IMPLICATIONS FOR SOCIAL WORK PRACTICE

In attempting to work within communities where LGBT persons can find a "fit" that both affirms their lives and promotes health, social workers must be willing to move beyond the stereotypes and mythology that surround the lives of LGBT persons (Mallon, 1998). Those who work with LGBT persons must be comfortable addressing issues of gender and sexual orientation and be open to developing community strategies using a variety of approaches, many of which have proven to be useful with other oppressed communities (Guttierrez, Alvarez, Nemon, & Lewis, 1996; Hasenfeld & Chester, 1987; Kemp, 1995; Rivera & Erlich, 1995; Rofes, 1996; Weil, 1986, 1996), designed to address the unique needs of each community.

Ecologically oriented social workers who are interested in working with LGBT communities should be prepared to do the following:

1. Engage in conscious, purposeful, and differential use of themselves as professionals, advocates, and change agents in promoting improvement and change in LGBT communities, and equally be prepared to confront those social policies that affect their clients' welfare.
2. Possess a commitment to entering this process with the collaboration of partnership with members of the community.
3. Recognize the risks that confront highly vulnerable populations while participating in efforts to change communities and social policies that affect LGBT persons.
4. Possess a willingness to educate the members of the community, increasing their sense of ownership in community projects and demystify the planning process, and thereby facilitating a move toward active subjects rather than objects of assessment.
5. Possess a willingness to approach the community from the position of "respectful" outsider—one who is willing to abandon the role of expert and to allow the participants to become collaborators in the discovery process.
6. Possess a professional commitment to pursuing economic and social justice for diverse and at-risk client populations through community practice.
7. Be able to assess the need for advocacy and social action in collaboration with clients in the community.
8. Expand one's knowledge base regarding the ways in which the interests, traditions, and expectations of diverse clients with whom they are working coincide and collide with the interests, traditions, and expectations of relevant community leaders.

Most LGBT persons are living their lives within the context of a hostile environment because the societal norm is that heterosexuality is the dominant orientation. Negotiating life in a hostile environment undoubtedly produces stress and strain. Although a great deal has been written about the impact of stress on the lives of LGBT persons, one must ask this question: If this community has been so stressed, then why have so many LGBT persons done so well? Perhaps the research conducted with populations who have experienced high levels of stress suggest some answers. Those individuals who have experienced undue stress, particularly those who band together and form family units, emerge from such stress-filled situations as strong and resilient, as contrasted with those who have been previously described in the literature as "at risk." This metaphor of resilience is appropriate for describing most LGBT persons who have come together in communities to support one another.

The fact that so many LGBT persons survive, thrive, and become successful functioning adults is a testament to their resilience. Resilience studies (Aldwin, Levenson, & Spiro, 1994; Brooks, 1994), which have provided data in regard to the benefits of adaptability and perseverance in the face of adversity, suggest that the development of strong family-like communities, similar to those families of creation for LGBT persons, provide opportunities for the development of a strong sense of identity and pride in the community. Perhaps social workers would do better to foster resilience within LGBT communities rather than to look for the deficiencies that bind groups together.

Fabricant and Fisher (2002) propose that community building may be the most important social service work in the near future. While a fair amount of literature has been written exploring the development of the HIV/AIDS service industry, little has been written about the emergence and growth of LGBT community centers. I believe that LGBT community building offers a model for twenty-first-century practice. Studying the emergence, philosophy, and service approaches of LGBT community centers may well offer useful tools for developing the community building and social change approaches that can be so effective in oppressed and marginalized communities.

REFERENCES

Aldwin, C. M., Levenson, M. R., & Spiro, A. (1994). Vulnerability and resilience to combat exposure: Can stress have lifelong effects. *Psychology and Aging, 9,* 34-44.

Anton, A. (2000). *Not for sale: In defense of public goods.* Boulder, CO: Westview Press.

Ayala, J., & Coleman, H. (2000). Predictors of depression among lesbian women. *Journal of Lesbian Studies, 4*(3), 71-87. Retrieved November 27, 2004, from CSA Illumina database.

Bell, P. (2002). *Chemical dependency and the African American.* Center City, MN: Hazelden.

Bockting, W., Rosser, S., & Coleman, E. (1999). Transgender HIV prevention: Community involvement and empowerment. *The International Journal of Transgenderism, 3*(1/2). Retrieved October 23, 2004, from http://www.symposion .com/ijt/hiv_risk/bockting.htm.

Briggs, X. (2003, April 16). *A post to NCBN's community list from Xavier de Souza Briggs* [Msg. 1]. Message posted to http://www.ncbn.org/Media/EDocs/ definition.pdf.

Brooks, R. B. (1994). Children at risk: Fostering resilience and hope. *American Journal of Orthopsychiatry, 64,* 545-553.

Cochran, S., & Mays, V. (2000). Relation between psychiatric syndromes and behaviorally defined sexual orientation in a sample of the U. S. population. *American Journal of Epidemiology, 151*(5), 516-523.

Crossley, M. (2001). The "Armistead" project: An exploration of gay men, sexual practices, community health promotion, and issues of empowerment. *Journal of Community & Applied Social Psychology, 11,* 111-123.

Currah, P., Juang, R.M., & Minter, S. (2006). *Transgender rights.* Minneapolis, MN: University of Minneosta Press.

Delgado, M. (1998). Cultural competence and the field of ATOD: Latinos as a case example. In M. Delgado (Ed.), *Alcohol use/abuse among Latinos: Issues and examples of culturally competent services* (pp. 5-19). Binghamton, NY: The Haworth Press.

Dilley, J., McFarland, W., Sullivan, P., & Discepola, M. (1998). Psychosocial correlates of unprotected anal sex in a cohort of gay men attending an HIV-negative support group. *AIDS Education & Prevention, 10*(4), 317-326.

Fabricant, M., & Fisher, R. (2002). *Settlement houses under siege: The struggle to sustain community organizations in New York City.* New York: Columbia University.

Finnegan, D., & McNally, E. (2002). *Counseling lesbian, gay, bisexual, and transgender substance abusers: Dual identities.* Binghamton, NY: The Haworth Press.

Gittell, M., Ortega-Bustamante, I., & Steffy, T. (2000). Social capital and social change: Women's community activism. *Urban Affairs Review, 36*(2), 123-147.

Gittell, R., & Vidal, A. (1998). *Community organizing: Building social capital as a development strategy.* Thousand Oaks, CA: Sage Publications.

Goffman, E. (1963). *Stigma: Notes on the management of a spoiled identity.* Englewood Cliffs, NJ: Prentice Hall.

Gutierrez, L. (1990). Working with women of color: An empowerment perspective. *Social Work, 35*(2), 149-153.

Guttierrez, L., Alvarez, A. R., Nemon, H., & Lewis, E. A. (1996). Multicultural community organizing: A strategy for change. *Social Work, 41*(5), 501-508.

Gutierrez, L., Oh, H., & Gillmore, M. (2000). Toward an understanding of (Em)Power(Ment) for HIV/AIDS prevention with adolescent women. *Sex Roles, 42*(7/8), 581-611.

Halperin, R. (1998). *Practicing community: Class, culture and power in an urban neighborhood.* Austin: University of Texas.

Hanson, B. (1996). The violence we face as lesbians and gay men: The landscape both outside and inside our communities. In M. Shernoff (Ed.), *Human services for gay people: Clinical and community practice* (pp. 95-114). Binghamton, NY: The Haworth Press.

Hasenfeld, Y., & Chester, M. (1987). Client empowerment in the human services: Personal and professional agenda. *Journal of Applied Behavioral Science, 25,* 499-521.

Hays, R., Rebchook, G., & Kegeles, S. (2003). The Mpowerment project: Community-building with young gay and bisexual men to prevent HIV. *American Journal of Community Psychology, 31*(3/4), 301-312.

Hess, P., McGowan, B., & Botsko, M. (2003). *Nurturing the one, supporting the many.* New York: Columbia University.

Hirota, J. M., Brown, P., & Martin, N. (1996). *Building community: The tradition and promise of settlement houses.* Chicago: Chapin Hall Center for Children. Retrieved February 10, 2005, from http://www.chapinhall.org.

Hogan. S., & Hudson, L. (1998). *Completely queer: The gay and lesbian encyclopedia.* New York: Henry Holt & Co.

Huebner, D., Rebchook, G., & Kegeles, S. (2004). Experiences of harassment, discrimination and physical violence among young gay and bisexual men. *American Journal of Public Health, 94*(7), 1200-1204.

Husock, H. (1993). Bringing back the settlement house. *Public Welfare, 51*(4), 16-25.

Kawachi, I., Kennedy, B., & Lochner, K. (1997). Love live community: Social capital as public health. *The American Prospect, 35,* 56-59.

Kammerer, N., Mason, T., & Connors, M. (1999). Transgender health and social service needs in the context of HIV risk. *International Journal of Transgenderism, 3,* 1-2.

Kemp, S. (1995). Practice in communities. In C. Meyer & M. A. Mattaini (Eds.), *Foundations of social work practice* (pp. 176-204). Washington, DC: NASW Press.

Lee, J. (1994). *The empowerment approach to social work practice.* New York: Columbia University.

Macarov, D. (2003). *What the market does to people: Privatization, globalization and poverty.* Atlanta, GA: Clarity Press.

Mallon, G. P. (Ed.) (1998). *Foundations of social work practice with lesbian and gay persons.* Binghamton, NY: The Haworth Press.

Mays, V., Cochran, S., & Zamudio, A. (2004). HIV prevention research: Are we meeting the needs of African American men who have sex with men? *Journal of Black Psychology, 30*(1), 78.

Meyer, I. (2003). Prejudice, social stress, and mental health in lesbian, gay, and bisexual populations: Conceptual issues and research evidence. *Psychological Bulletin, 129*(5), 674-697.

Nealy, E. (2006, April). *Client interviews.* New York: LGBT Center.

Nystrom, N., & Jones, T. (2003). Community building with aging and old lesbians. *American Journal of Community Psychology, 31*(3/4), 293-300.

Peterson, N. A., & Zimmerman, M. (2004). Beyond the individual: Toward a nomological network of organizational empowerment. *American Journal of Community Psychology, 34*(1/2), 129-145.

Putnam, R. (2000). *Bowling alone.* New York: Simon & Schuster.

Ratner, E. F. (1993). Treatment issues of chemically dependent lesbians and gay men. In L. D. Garnets, K. G. Rivera, & J. L. Erlich (1995). Organizing with people of color: A perspective. In J. E. Tropman, J. L. Erlich & J. Kolhman (Eds.), *Tactics and techniques of community intervention* (pp. 196-213). Itasca, NY: Peacock.

Rofes, E. (1996). *Reviving the tribe: Regenerating gay men's sexuality and culture in the ongoing epidemic.* Binghamton, NY: The Haworth Press.

Saegart, S., Thompson, J. P., & Warren. M. (2001). The role of social capital in combating poverty. In S. Saegart, J. P. Thompson, & M. Warren (Eds.), *Social capital and poor communities* (pp. 211-254). New York: Russell Sage Foundation.

Simon, B. (1994). *The empowerment tradition in American social work: A history.* New York: Columbia University.

Smith, R., & Mancoske, R. (1997). *Rural gays and lesbians: Building on strengths of communities.* Binghamton, NY: The Haworth Press.

Steinhouse, K. (2001). Bisexual women: Considerations of race, social justice and community building. *Journal of Progressive Human Services, 12*(2), 5-25.

Turner, H., Hays, R., & Coates, T. (1993). Determinants of social support among gay men: The context of AIDS. *Journal of Health and Social Behavior, 34*(1), 37-53.

Weil, M. (1986). Women, community, and organizing. In N. VanDenBergh & I. B. Cooper (Eds.), *Feminist visions for social work* (pp. 187-210). Silver Spring, MD: NASW.

Weil, M. O. (1996). Community building: Building community practice. *Social Work, 4*(5), 481-499.

Chapter 14

LGBT Communities and Health Care

Brian J. Flynn

This chapter addresses health care issues for lesbian, gay, bisexual, and transgender (LGBT) communities. Testimonials and descriptions of barriers in accessing health care will be provided, followed by a brief history of the struggle for quality health care for LGBT communities. A discussion of significant health concerns that impact LGBT adults and adolescents will be provided, and although health care concerns of LGBT patients across the life span will be covered, particular attention will be given to aging LGBT individuals due to the lack of attention paid to this population's specific health care needs. This will be followed by discussions covering issues regarding caregiving, residential care, grief and loss issues, and disaster work with LGBT populations. Finally, information and resources are included, which social workers and other health care providers can use to become more culturally competent when providing services to LGBT communities.

The purpose of this chapter is to highlight discriminatory practices, identify the specific needs of those with other than heterosexual sexual and gender orientations, and to provide recommendations in order to fill the gaps that exist in the delivery of effective and equitable health care resources for LGBT communities. It is important to note that the health care experiences of LGBT communities, although at times similar, are also quite diverse from person to person. There are both discriminatory differences and similarities among LGBT consumers and in no way is it the intention of this chapter to cluster these experiences into a common collection. Although there has been a good deal of research done on the needs of gay men and lesbians in health care (Shankle, 2006; Shernoff & Scott, 1998; White & Martinez, 1997), very little has been studied or documented that addresses the needs of gender-variant individuals, and there are even fewer resources that speak to the health care needs of bisexual consumers. When reading this chapter please consider and challenge the following assumptions and "suppositions about human sexuality and relationships," as outlined by Paul and Nichols in their article, "'Biphobia' and the Construction of a Bisexual Identity," in Sher-noff and Scott's second edition of *The Sourcebook on Lesbian/Gay Health Care:*

> (1) the idea that sexual orientation is a fixed, invariant aspect of per-sonality, (2) that sexual orientation is a variable that readily differenti-ates the population into two discrete groups, (3) that gender is necessarily the dominant variable in determining a person's sexual orientation, (4) that homosexuality is a consequence of failed hetero-sexuality, an option in relationships only to be "chosen" due to an in-ability to sustain heterosexual relations, and (5) that monogamy is the only means of sustaining a long-term relationship. (Paul & Nichols, 1988, p. 263)

TESTIMONIALS

The following testimonials highlight the experiences of LGBT people attempting to access health care:

> When I say that I'm bisexual, they look at me like, sure you are. And I want to hit them, because it's like, I know who the hell I am. I'm the only one in the world who knows who I am, and so what I say is true.

> I said I was bisexual and he looked at me like, what? He really didn't know what to say next. Finally he said, "So you sleep with men and women?" I said, "Not at the same time." I thought it was funny, but he didn't. There certainly wasn't a smile on his face. (The Lesbian, Gay, Bisexual, Transgender Community Center of Greater Cleveland Web site, 2004)

> I hear a lot of fear on the part of gay men and women thinking about entering the health care system, [in] the nursing home . . . or at any kind of senior care level. I mean, we're coming out of an experience of being badly treated in society, and there's no sense that the treatment is going to get any better when you get older and more vulnerable within the system. (CLSC Rene-Cassin Web site, 2004)

The following is from Tina Donovan, who offers her perspective of her experiences as a transgender person:

> One incident in particular that took place in a hospital emergency room was extremely traumatic for me. I was in the emergency room seeking treatment, which under the best of conditions is already a stressful experience. One of the nursing staff members saw on my chart the name "Timothy Donovan." The name and face did not go together. He asked me some questions, and did not like my answers. He proceeded, in a very nasty and belittling manner, to try and lift my skirt to show the other nurses and patients that I was not what I appeared to be. He should have treated me first as a patient and as a person; my gender identity should not have been an issue for ridicule. Certainly, the nurse should have shown far more sensitivity than he did. Instead, his behavior was malicious and abusive. I was tied down and sedated. I spent two weeks under sedation before I was released. It took me a long time to get over this episode. (Donovan, 2001, p. 21)

An older gay man offers this account of his experiences with the medical system during his partner's illness:

> A recent widower at age seventy, John fears he may be forced to sell his home that he and his partner of thirty years shared because of various estate taxes and the significant drop in household income. John met Paul in 1970, and they moved in together two years later. They were always present at family members' weddings, birthdays, funerals, relocated for one another's jobs, and considered themselves spouses even though they were not able to legally marry. When Paul was diagnosed with Lou Gerhig's disease, he and John completed health care proxy documents and filed them with their attorney. John went with Paul to almost every doctor's appointment over his ten years of illness. John recalled that most experiences with Paul's health care providers and hospitals were sensitive and respectful, but getting access to his medical records required faxes and signatures, which proved more difficult especially when Paul was heavily sedated. When John's partner Paul died in their home, as he had wished, John was not allowed to sign the death certificate because they were not married. Now, John fears he may have to sell their home because he lacks the legal and financial protection that would come automatically if he had been married. Even though their house was purchased in both names with rights of survivorship, John must pay taxes on Paul's share of the house, which would not be the case if they had been married. John won't get his partner's Social Security benefits and pension, either. The survivor of a married couple would have collected both.

Finally, the following highlights the pervasiveness of heterosexism and transphobia in the medical system:

> A rather butch lesbian in San Francisco recently had cancer in one breast, and decided in consultation with her doctor to have a full mastectomy. She thought it was a good idea to have the other breast removed as well, since she wanted to minimize the chances of a recurrence. The choice was made easier for her because she had no strong emotional attachment to her breasts; they did not form an important part of her gendered or sexual self-understanding. Whereas her insurance company agreed to pay for the first mastectomy, they worried that the second breast was "elective surgery" and that, if they paid for that, it would be setting a precedent for covering elective transsexual surgery. The insurance company thus wanted to limit both consumer autonomy in medical decision making (understanding the woman as someone who wanted for medical reasons to have the second breast removed), and to dismiss autonomy as the basis for a transsexual operation (understanding the woman as a possible transitioner). (Butler, 2004, pp. 85-86)

These distressing accounts of how Tina, John, and the others were treated while attempting to access medical care is unfortunately similar to what many members of the LGBT community have faced at the hands of the health care system.

BARRIERS TO ACCESS

Despite the achievements of the LGBT equality in health care movement, heterosexism, homophobia, transphobia, and biphobia continue to permeate the medical system. Discrimination and bias are ubiquitous in the majority of the experiences of LGBT patients within the health care system. Many LGBT patients experience barriers to accessing and receiving quality medical care and treatment. According to the Institute of Medicine, the three types of barriers to accessing quality health care are: (1) structural barriers (e.g., availability of services, organizational structure of health care facilities), (2) financial barriers (e.g., insurance coverage), and (3) personal and cultural barriers (e.g., attitudes of patients and providers) (Institute of Medicine, 1993, 1999). All three types of barriers impact LGBT consumers as indicated in the following examples.

One recent study states approximately one-quarter of transgender respondents reported having been denied medical care because of their transgender status (Kenagy, 2005). In one study, 84 percent of lesbian respondents reported reluctance in seeking health care, finding it nonempathic, and 96 percent of the respondents "anticipated situations in which it could be harmful to them if their health care provider knew they were lesbian" (Seattle and King County Public Health Web site, 2004).

Managed care limits its participants as to which health care provider they can receive care from, which may exclude providers who are openly savvy to the specific needs of the LGBT community. Many insurance companies do not provide domestic partner coverage or benefits and fail to provide reimbursement for procedures and treatment which are specifically pertinent to the LGBT community. For example, transgender individuals are excluded particularly from benefiting from insurance coverage when it comes to treatments that address gender identity disorder as many insurers consider the treatment purposes cosmetic. In addition, although gender identity disorders are considered capable of causing "significant impairment" (Dean et al., 2000), those diagnosed with gender identity disorder are "specifically excluded from the Americans with Disabilities Act and thus do not receive its benefits or protections" (Dean et al., 2000). There are ongoing debates and controversies surrounding the psychiatric diagnosis of gender identity disorder (GID). On the one hand, the existence of GID in the *Diagnostic and Statistical Manual of Mental Disorders,* Fourth Edition (DSM-IV) allows for many transgender individuals to gain the psychiatric support needed to undergo surgeries and other treatments, as such a diagnosis is typically required to be "approved" for surgery, many hormone treatments, and some related interventions. On the other hand, GID's existence promotes seeing transgender identity as a pathological state of being. There is no doubt the debate will continue and social workers should be serving as advocates for the wishes and well-being of their transgender clients.

Assessment and intake tools often exclude language that resonates with LGBT patients who are left to feel that their specific health concerns are not heard nor taken seriously by providers. Many health care institutions fail to recognize the legitimacy of LGBT relationships and many members are denied the right to be kept informed about their loved one's health condition and treatment. Confidentiality is extremely important for many LGBT patients and because of their prior experience in a hostile health care environment they may be less likely to seek care due to a fear of backlash or stigmatization.

BRIEF HISTORY

The struggle for equality in health care by members of LGBT communities has been ongoing. Throughout history, the medical system and mental health world overwhelmingly treated homosexuality and gender variation as diseases and any help sought by nonheterosexual patients, regardless of their complaints, has often resulted in treatment that assumed pathology. A study published in 1957 by psychologist Dr. Evelyn Hooker maintained there was no variation in the mental health needs of heterosexual and nonheterosexual men. Although disputed by some members of the psychiatric community, Dr. Hooker's research findings prevailed and became the foundation for many researchers and activists in the LGBT equality in health movement. In 1973, the APA (the American Psychiatric Association) removed homosexuality from the DSM. Deyton and Lear cite Howard Brown who commented on this change of position by the APA by stating, "Since it is doctors who ultimately determine whether people are mentally ill or well, the board's vote made millions of Americans who had been officially ill that morning officially well that afternoon. Never in history had so many people been cured in so little time" (Brown, as cited by Deyton & Lear, 1988, p. 16). The result of this ruling and years of advocacy was the creation of a number of agencies and institutions designed to meet the specific needs of LGBT communities. In the early 1980s, the AIDS crisis rallied the LGBT communities in the fight against HIV and AIDS. The response of the LGBT communities to the AIDS crisis "has been marked by unequalled vigor, creativity, scientific soundness and effectiveness" (Deyton & Lear, 1988, p. 19).

HEALTH CARE CONCERNS AMONG LGBT PEOPLE

The following health issues hold particular significance for members of LGBT communities. When providing treatment and intervention to LGBT individuals, families, and communities, social workers and other providers need to be aware of the specific needs and health care concerns of these populations. Although this section is not meant to be exhaustive of all the health care issues that may impact an LGBT person, its purpose is to help highlight some of the screening, prevention, and treatment needs of LGBT patients.

The Effects of Hate Crimes and Other Types of Violence

In 2001, 2,475 Americans reported being victimized by antigay violence, up 10 percent from 2,249 in 1999. In 2004, according to the FBI, 15 percent of hate crimes were committed against people because of their perceived nonheterosexual orientation. Lesbians at universities report being victims of sexual assault twice as often as heterosexual women (White, 1995). Many crimes go unreported as victims fear that disclosing their orientation will only place them at risk for more violence (Dean et al., 2000; Community United Against Violence Web site, 2006). Transgendered individuals are at even greater risk. The April 13, 2001, edition of the *San Francisco Chronicle* reported, from statistics gathered by Community United Against Violence, a San Francisco antiviolence advocacy group, that one in six attacks nationwide were against transgender people (Community United Against Violence Web site, 2006). According to the Gay and Lesbian Medical Association (GLMA):

> Virtually every transgendered person is likely to experience some form of victimization as a direct result of his or her transgender identity or presentation. . . . Victimization includes subtle forms of harassment and discrimination as well as blatant verbal, physical and sexual assault. The last may include physical and sexual assault and even homicide. The majority of assaults against transgender persons are never reported to the police. This situation exists because transgender individuals have little societal support or access to legal recourse. (Dean et al., 2000, p. 133)

For LGBT adolescents, the impact of discrimination, harassment, and violence can be even worse. The emotional and physical turmoil many adolescents face as part of the maturation process can be further complicated in LGBT adolescents who struggle with the conflicts of how they are feeling and the expectations placed on them by society. Adolescents are particularly concerned about how they are being accepted by their peers and losing that acceptance because of actual or perceived differences in sexual orientation can be especially detrimental to the emotional well-being of an adolescent. Conformity is crucial for many teenagers and those who are different often face taunting, harassment, and violence. Many LGBT adolescents fall victim to violent acts every year, the majority of incidents are a direct result of their differences in orientation. The perpetrators of these acts are not just limited to peers, but parents and other adults often victimize adolescents who appear different or who make their orientation known. This violence both in and out of the home often leads teenagers to run away or look for other avenues to escape or cope with the aggression they face.

When working with LGBT adults and adolescents, social workers and other providers need to be aware of the high probability their clients have been the victims of verbal and/or physical abuse. They also need to be aware of the level of fear and anxiety present in someone living with this constant threat. Creating a safe environment is crucial when attempting to build rapport with LGBT patients. This can be accomplished by ensuring patient confidentiality. The social worker must provide, clarify, and make readily available to all patients the agency and legal policies that protect their privacy and explain the consequences inflicted on those who breach confidentiality. Validate the experiences of LGBT consumers by asking specific questions that inquire as to whether they have been victims of discrimination, harassment, verbal abuse, or physical abuse based on their status as a sexual or gender minority. Offer to victims of these offenses specific supportive interventions that can provide culturally competent and compassionate mental health services.

Breast Cancer

According to the GLMA, lesbians are at greatest risk for breast cancer than any other subset of women in the world due to risk factors such as nulliparity and increased tobacco and alcohol use. This is further complicated by the fact that many lesbians do not receive any routine preventive or pre-cancer screening care, which would include breast examination and mammograms, because of past experiences with an unwelcoming and dismissive health care system. This puts them at higher risk for late stage diagnosis (GLMA Web site, 2006). For transgendered patients who have had one or more gender reconstruction surgeries or who are transitioning, it is important for providers to recognize that screening examination may be necessary as not all sexual organs may have been removed during surgery, and breast exams in this case may be needed for male-to-female (MTF) and/or female-to-male (FTM) patients (Seattle and King County Public Health Web site, 2004). Social workers and other providers need to insist their that patients who are at risk of breast cancer receive the routine screenings necessary to detect cancer at its earliest stage. They should remain cognizant of the apprehension many women who are members of sexual and gender minorities feel regarding the health care system and should be advocates in helping their clients to regain the confidence many have lost in providers.

Tobacco Use

LGBT individuals are more inclined to use tobacco products to help combat the stress of societal discrimination and hostility that they face (U.S. Department of Health and Human Services Web site, 2006). The stress resulting from discrimination, low self-esteem and, for some, having to live a secretive life all put LGBT individuals at greater risk for using tobacco products. Many tobacco companies specifically target gays and lesbians in advertising campaigns. Using tobacco increases risk for many types of cancers and heart and lung disease.

Heart Disease

Heart disease is one of the leading causes of death in the United States and the number one killer of both men and women. Symptoms of heart disease and heart attacks in women are different than what men experience and often providers and patients alike are unfamiliar with specific warning signs to watch for and therefore, many women's symptoms go undiagnosed. Risk factors for women, including stress and tobacco use, are higher for lesbian and bisexual women (U.S. Department of Health and Human Services Web site, 2006). LGBT individuals need to be educated on the impact that obesity, tobacco use, and stress have on the heart. When patients identify and report the early warning signs and symptoms of a heart attack and/or heart disease, social workers can help to guarantee that their possibly apprehensive clients will seek treatment by referring them to providers that are LGBT friendly. Specific support groups intended and created for addressing the concerns of LGBT individuals who are living with congestive heart failure (CHF), coronary artery disease, arrhythmias, and other forms of heart disease are needed.

HIV/AIDS

The introduction of highly active antiretroviral treatment (HAART) has dramatically decreased mortality rates for HIV-infected individuals. However, the side effects of these medications can be debilitating for many patients, causing physical and emotional stress and impacting relationships, employment, and caregiving responsibilities. The long-term effects of these treatments are unclear. Recent studies of the effects of HIV medications have shown an increase in diabetes, hypoglycemia, skin conditions, and lipodystrophy. The perception that HIV is no longer a threat due to advances in HIV treatment has increased risky sexual behavior, particularly among young gay and bisexual men of color. According to the Centers for Disease Control (CDC):

> The success of highly active antiretroviral therapy (HAART) may have had the unintended consequence of increasing some men who

have sex with men (MSM)'s risk behaviors. Some research suggests that the negative aspects of HIV infection have been minimized since the introduction of HAART, which has led to a false understanding of what living with HIV means and thus can lead to increased risk behaviors. (CDC Web site, 2005b, citing Ostrow, Fox, Chmiel, et al., 2000; Suarez & Miller, 2001)

Providers need to be sensitive to the difficulties of HIV drug regimens, recent advances in treatment and the changing behaviors of their LGBT patients. Social workers who provide services to consumers who are infected or affected by HIV should educate themselves regarding medications and side effects.

Education is critical when providing prevention techniques for LGBT patients but is only effective when it includes language that "speaks to" and pertains to the particular audience for whom it is meant. Many gay men and lesbian women do not prefer the term "homosexual" and feel that it is more of a clinical term and is not how many people choose to identify themselves. If a social worker is unsure of the terminology a client prefers, they should simply ask him or her. Asking a client or patient how they would like to be addressed is easier and more comfortable than offending someone later on because of an assumption made by the provider. When working with adolescents it can be particularly challenging to find language and interventions that relate well to young people. Many existing prevention strategies have proven to be ineffective because they fail to "speak to" adolescents in their language and on their terms. Aggleton and Warrick state:

> Few approaches engage either with young people's sexual desires, motivations and behaviors in ways that are likely to be meaningful to the individuals concerned. Indeed in perhaps the majority of contemporary accounts, sexuality is not discussed at all, it being assumed that all young people are unequivocally heterosexual; and sexual behavior is reduced to the effects of biology, poor socialization and faulty learning, boredom and frustration, among other factors. More often than not it is the negative consequences of sexual behavior that are focused on, such as unwanted teenage pregnancy and the acquisition of sexually transmitted diseases. This emphasis is unfortunate in two respects: not only does it provide a limited understanding of young people and their HIV and AIDS-related needs, it also encourages us to see young people's sexuality in negative terms as something that needs to be restrained and controlled, not as creative force capable of offering pleasure, fulfillment and growth. (Aggleton & Warrick, 1997, p. 81)

Social workers and other providers should be familiar with practices and interventions that are best suited to meet the needs of LGBT adults and adolescents who are struggling with behaviors that may put them at risk for contracting HIV and other STDs. Harm reduction, although often used when working with consumers struggling with addiction, is a type of intervention that has gained increased attention in the area of HIV prevention. Harm reduction, also called risk reduction, meets patients "where they are at," and is best used for people who have expressed or demonstrated that, for them, abstinence at the present time is not an option. Harm reduction attempts to reduce negative consequences of risky behaviors by using a nonjudgmental and flexible approach to prevention. The Body Web site (2006) reports:

> Consistent with the tenets of normalization, supporters argue that the focus of early prevention efforts ignored the degree to which various sexual acts were a "normal" part of people's lives. Officials tried to stop transmission by eliminating all risk behavior, in the same way that deterrence seeks to eliminate all drug use. Harm reduction suggests that prevention focus on informing people of the risks of the various practices and on promoting sexual activities that are least likely to transmit HIV. The goal of stopping all risky sexual activity would be abandoned as unrealistic. Further, harm reduction would not stigmatize those who practice higher-risk sex, recognizing that sexual behavior is the result of various complex situational, cultural, social, and personal factors.

Hepatitis

Hepatitis is an inflammation of the liver. Several different viruses cause viral hepatitis. Hepatitis A is caused primarily by eating or drinking food and water that has been contaminated by the feces of an infected person. Hepatitis B is spread through blood and occurs when blood from an infected person enters the body of an uninfected person through sexual contact, the sharing of needles during IV drug use, or from mother to baby during the birthing process. There are vaccines available for both hepatitis A and B. Hepatitis C is a liver disease caused by the hepatitis C virus (HCV), which is found in the blood of persons who have this disease. HCV is spread by contact with the blood of an infected person, primarily through the sharing of needles and from infected mothers to babies during the birthing process. Hepatitis C is particularly problematic because there is no vaccine and 80 percent of those infected experience no symptoms (CDC, 2005b).

Individuals who are co-infected with HIV and hepatitis C face many challenges. Coinfection leads to liver damage more quickly than being infected
with HCV alone and may also affect the treatment of HIV infection (CDC,
2005a). There is treatment for chronic hepatitis C which has been shown to
be successful for some patients. Treatment for both diseases entails taking
powerful medications which can be accompanied by debilitating side effects. Adherence to treatment regimens is challenging for many patients
and requires the support of health care providers.

Alcohol and Drug Use

Due to the overall lack of services and avenues for socializing and networking among LGBT people, particularly in rural areas, many have had to
turn to bars and nightclubs where alcohol is served in order to connect with
and meet others. For this reason, combined with the stressors of living in a
heterosexist society, many LGBT individuals have turned to alcohol and illegal substances as ways of coping and socializing. In the National Lesbian
Health Care Survey of 1987, 14 percent of respondents expressed concern
regarding their own alcohol use and, in contrast with heterosexual women,
alcohol use among lesbians increased with age (Van Wormer, Wells, & Boes,
2000). Alcohol and drug use lowers inhibitions and often makes it easier for
people to approach someone else in pursuit of friendship, sexual contact, or
relationship potential. Mood altering substances also cloud judgment and
can often put people more at risk for unsafe sexual experiences (Eliason,
1996).

The CDC (2005b) reports on its Web site that the use of alcohol and illegal drugs continues to be prevalent among some men who have sex with
men and is linked to HIV and STD risk (CDC Web site, 2005b, citing Stall,
Paul, Greenwood, et al., 2001). Substance use can increase the risk of HIV
transmission by increasing the tendency to engage in risky sexual behaviors
while under the influence of the drugs and through the sharing of needles or
other injection equipment. In recent years, the use of methamphetamine has
gained significant attention (CDC, 2005b). Street methamphetamine is referred to by many names, such as "speed," "meth," and "chalk." Methamphetamine hydrochloride, which looks like clear chunky crystals resem-
bling ice and can be inhaled by smoking, is referred to as "ice," "crystal,"
"glass," and "tina" (National Institute on Drug Abuse Web site, 2006). Reports of the increased use of methamphetamines across the country have
raised public health concerns because methamphetamine use has been
associated both with sexual risk behaviors for HIV and other STDs and
sharing injection equipment when the drug is injected (CDC Web site,

2005b, citing Diffusion of Effective Behavioral Interventions Web site). Methamphetamine and other "party" drugs (such as Ecstasy and ketamine) may be used to decrease social inhibitions and enhance sexual experiences (CDC Web site, 2005b, citing Mansergh, Colfax, Marks, et al., 2001). These drugs, along with alcohol and nitrate inhalants ("poppers"), have been associated with risky sexual practices, particularly among MSM (CDC Web site, 2005b, citing Purcell, Parsons, Halkitis, Mizuno, & Woods, 2001).

As noted earlier, the need to escape from hostile environments and the pre-existing desire for exploration and growth lead many LGBT individuals into situations that put them particularly at risk for substance abuse and sexually transmitted diseases. Bars and clubs are often the only outlet for LGBT individuals to meet and connect with others who are like-minded. The use of mood altering substances helps to numb the pain of rejection, loneliness and the fear of further aggression. LGBTquestioning teens may also turn to alcohol and drugs to help lessen inhibitions when considering engaging in socializing or sexual exploration. Sexually active teens, particularly males, are just as at risk for contracting STDs as their adult counterparts (Gochros & Bidwell, 1996, pp. 8-9). An article in the journal *AIDS Education and Prevention,* as cited by Aggleton and Warrick in Lorraine Sherr's *AIDS and Adolescents,* claims that

> adolescents have developmental capabilities that may serve to limit their understanding of the consequences of their actions and put them at greater risk for inadvertent exposure to HIV disease (Newman et al., 1993, as cited by Aggleton & Warrick, 1997, p. 80) and the tendency to underestimate susceptibility may be especially true among adolescents, who characteristically view themselves as invincible. (Mickler, 1993, as cited by Aggleton & Warrick, 1997, p. 80).

Research has also found that smoking rates are higher among LGBT adolescents compared to the general population. Smoking during adolescence increases the risk of smoking as an adult; 90 percent of adult smokers started smoking as teenagers (U.S. Department of Health and Human Services Web site, 2006). As there is a lack of education and information provided to LGBT or questioning adolescents by the medical community as a whole, many of them feel isolated, confused, and lonely. These feelings and the absence of viable alternative avenues to connect with and meet other teens, particularly in rural areas, make LGBT adolescents particularly vulnerable. LGBT adolescents are often dealing with their own fears regarding coming out to families, peers, teachers, etc., and may have very distorted images regarding what reactions to expect from others. Health care providers need to be vigilant when working with adolescents to create environments that are safe, receptive, and attentive to the needs of those who may be LGBT or questioning. This can be accomplished through building rapport, explaining how confidentiality protects patients, and working to replace adolescents' preconceived notions and myths regarding other LGBT teens, adults, and communities.

Social workers should also facilitate the formation of safe, alternative outlets for LGBT individuals to meet and socialize with other like-minded individuals. The creation of support groups, social clubs, and networking organizations, particularly in demographic areas in which there is a gap in these kinds of resources, is essential in meeting the emotional and social needs of many LGBT individuals.

Social workers should provide education to LGBT patients regarding the physical, emotional, and psychosocial effects of alcohol and illegal drug use. As mentioned, harm reduction techniques can be particularly beneficial in meeting the needs of LGBT individuals, who may also be living with HIV or at risk for HIV infection, but are most effective when combined with education and/or counseling (Reid, 2002). According to the Harm Reduction Coalition, harm reduction "recognizes that the realities of poverty, class, racism, social isolation, past trauma, sex-based discrimination and other social inequalities affect both people's vulnerability to and capacity for effectively dealing with drug-related harm" (Harm Reduction Coalition Web site, 2005). Harm reduction programs, such as needle or syringe exchanges, which allow injection drug users to trade used needles for clean, should also "include a broad array of services such as referrals to chemical detoxification and methadone maintenance, AIDS education and prevention materials, and methods for reducing the risk of infection (e.g., distributing condoms and instructing injection drug users on how to use bleach to disinfect their needles). Programs that emphasize a strong behavioral component, in conjunction with programmatic activities, could result in more averted HIV infections" (Reid, 2002). The National Association of Social Workers (NASW) also shares these views:

> All social workers have a responsibility to educate clients about risk reduction behaviors, including safer injection practices and harm reduction. . . . Needle exchange programs should be part of a comprehensive HIV prevention program for drug users, including efforts to reduce sexual risk behaviors, to increase the quantity and quality of drug abuse treatment, and to reduce drug use in the community. (NASW, as cited by Reid, 2002, p. 22)

Depression/Anxiety

Many LGBT people suffer from symptoms of depression and anxiety due to a lifetime of discrimination and ridicule. LGBT individuals are often "socialized to hide" their identity and feelings from the rest of the world (Appleby, 2001, p. 56). Many have been forced into concealing all or part of their orientation from loved ones, co-workers, supervisors, landlords, etc., and have had to risk possible alienation from family members or friends in the event they decide to reveal their orientation. These stressors can cause increased feelings of loneliness, isolation, suspicion, guilt, and anger. Symptoms associated with the coming-out process can often be misdiagnosed (Faria, 1997). The stress associated with self-disclosure and the coming-out process can be accompanied by feelings of guilt, shame, hopelessness, and isolation as one realizes they are a member of a group that is marginalized and discriminated against (Swindell & Pryce, 2003). Transgender individuals very often struggle with preconceived notions from therapists and other providers when seeking help from the mental health system. Arlene Istar Lev (2004) writes:

> The difficulty lies not in professional assessment processes or diagnostic competency, but rather in the perspective that assumes psychopathology in all-gender variant people without understanding the context for their difficulties . . . transgendered and transsexual people who desire body modification must seek out services to live authentically and, paradoxically, the very criteria which make them eligible for these services also determine that they have mental health issues. For example, the need to prove that one is transsexual has historically depended on one's distress in his or her body and hatred of his or her genitals to the point of expressing suicidality and self-harm behaviors. These same behaviors lead clinicians to label such clients as borderline, obsessive, depressed, and impulsive. (p. 190)

When working with LGBT clients, social workers and other providers need to be especially familiar with accurately recognizing and identifying symptoms of depression and/or anxiety. Support and education need to be provided to anyone grappling with feelings of sexual and/or gender variance and particular attention needs to be paid when LGBT individuals make the difficult decision to come out to themselves, loved ones, co-workers, and/or employers.

CHILD CARE

LGBT couples who parent are not entitled to the same protection as heterosexual couples in the event of separation. There is no guarantee an LGBT parent will be entitled under the law to child support, custody, or visitation.

For LGBT patients who are ill, child care can be an ever-present anxiety. The question of who will take care of children in the event that a parent dies or becomes incapable of caring for them is also a concern for domestic partners who are raising children. LGBT parents have called for legal reform, and some states—New York, for example—have adopted laws which allow for a parent to legally appoint someone to care for their children in the event of the parent's death. This is referred to as a standby guardian and it allows an ill parent to appoint a loved one to take over responsibility and care of children. This can be especially comforting to same-sex couples and partners (Ettlebrick, 1996). Social workers can assist in these matters by advocating for the rights of their clients and by providing education to parents regarding the options available to them.

AGING

The number of aging LGBT people has grown and will continue to grow as the U.S. population as a whole grows older and LGBT individuals become increasingly comfortable in self-disclosing their orientation. Although the numbers vary from source to source, there are anywhere from two to four million LGBT people over the age of sixty-five in the United States. Many of these individuals have endured a lifetime of dealing with an antagonistic and unsympathetic society and are skeptical of a health care system that has been unwelcoming of them in the past. A study of gay, lesbian, and bisexual (GLB) individuals over the age of sixty reported almost two-thirds (63 percent) of participants were the victims of verbal abuse based on their sexual orientation and more than a quarter (29 percent) received threats of physical violence. Twenty-nine percent of the GLB participants reported being victimized by someone who threatened to disclose their sexual orientation to friends, family, and co-workers (Grossman, D'Augelli, & O'Connell, 2001).

When working with older clientele, social workers need to be aware of the specific needs of aging LGBT individuals. Many in LGBT communities have experienced the loss of friends and loved ones due to the AIDS crisis. Enduring the loss of such a big part of a generation of gay men has left those who are now approaching their old age wondering why and how they survived. Survivor guilt is prevalent in many older gay men and the feelings of remorse, shame, and "Why me?" or "Why not me?" can be overwhelming. These feelings can certainly become a risk to one's emotional and physical well-being. The lack of and decline in attention given recently to the AIDS epidemic has many in LGBT communities at a loss and many have been left with feelings of abandonment from a cause that many identified with so closely. For more than a decade many LGBT communities rallied around the fight for accessible, affordable, and effective responses to the epidemic. Now, with so little attention being given to the epidemic, many who were once ardent activists are left feeling increasingly secluded and frustrated.

Isolation is a risk for anyone approaching old age. For those in the LGBT community it is even more of a possibility; as mobilization in later years becomes a concern, so does the inability to connect and network with the group of friends, something many LGBT people come to rely on. Many LGBT individuals have been abandoned by their families of origin, are not part of traditional families and so have had to depend on the community as a whole for their socialization and sense of belonging. If one becomes homebound or has increased anxiety around leaving home, networking with friends and natural support systems can become a challenge. There are some organizations that are designed to meet the needs of older LGBT clients, such as the newly renamed Services and Advocacy for Gay, Lesbian, Bisexual, and Transgender Elders, formerly called Senior Action in a Gay Environment (SAGE), in New York City, which offers outreach programs and volunteers who assist with meeting the needs of homebound older LGBT individuals (Genke, 2004).

Accessing and utilizing home care is also an issue that can be a challenge to LGBT clients who could benefit from services. As stated earlier, many members of LGBT communities are distrustful of the healthcare system that has in the past failed them. Going to a clinic or health care provider's office can be challenging for many whose lifestyles have not been embraced by many providers. Allowing someone into the safe haven of your home can be even more frightening, particularly given statistics such as these: "a 1988 survey of nursing students showed that 8 to 12 percent (depending on whether the rated gay, lesbian, or bisexual) despised lesbian, gay, and bisexual people, 5 to 12 percent found lesbian, gay, and bisexual people disgusting and 40 to 43 percent believed that lesbian, gay and bisexual people should keep their sexuality private" (Seattle and King County Public Health Web site, 2004). Many older LGBT individuals live alone and because of the lack of LGBT friendly home care services available, a disproportionate number of neglect cases involve older LGBT people (Cook-Daniels, 2004, as cited by

Genke, 2004). Genke (2004) also lists other objections one might have to accepting home care as inability to afford services because of ineligibility for insurance benefits and "denial of need" (p. 92). This is coupled by the "not unfounded fear of discrimination" (p. 92). Social workers involved in home care need to be creating services that are geared toward LGBT consumers and providing LGBT culturally competent trainings to physicians, nurses, aides and technicians.

What happens when a partner becomes ill or is injured? Many hospitals only allow patients to have visitors or people speaking on behalf of the patient who are "next of kin." This term usually only includes biological ties and can refer to those who are tied together by legal marriage, thus excluding same-sex domestic partners. However, there is some protection through advance directives and health care proxies, which allow a patient to appoint someone they trust as their agent to make health care decisions in the event they lose the capacity to make decisions or speak on their own behalf. Hospitals, physicians, and other health care providers must follow the agent's decisions as if they were the patient's. Advance directives and health care proxies ensure that health care providers abide by the patient's wishes, particularly if those wishes include a partner or close friend following through on and voicing the wishes and decisions of the impaired patient.

A living will is a health care declaration that a patient can complete prior to their decline in health which specifically states their wishes regarding their medical treatment in the event they become unable to communicate. A power of attorney can also be executed to make medical decisions on ones behalf. Most states have provisions for living wills, health care proxies, and powers of attorney, although many of them differ in specific guidelines and terminology. Social workers need to be familiar with the requirements necessary to gain this kind of protection and peace of mind for the LGBT clients whom they serve.

The financial matters of a deceased loved one are not always as easily settled and agreed upon. Many surviving same-sex partners are unable to take advantage of their deceased loved one's pension and Social Security benefits as married spouses would be entitled to. Not all life insurance policies include domestic partner benefits. Same-sex partners must seek out specific coverage that will protect and provide for their loved ones in the event something should happen to them.

Despite the difficulties, many older members of the LGBT community are better equipped to deal with the natural stressors that accompany the aging process. Because of their past experience of having to deal with discrimination and an overall lack of resources, many have learned to become self-sufficient and have created effective and healthy coping strategies early on in life. Older LGBT individuals, who have learned to foster their own independence, are particularly more equipped to handle life changes than their heterosexual counterparts. Researchers have dubbed this phenomenon as "mastery of stigma":

> Gay people—and no doubt members of other oppressed groups—have a unique advantage. In their adolescence and young adulthood, gay men had to learn how to manage the stigma of being gay. They had to salvage their self-esteem, for example, in the face of societal disapproval. Most gay people do this successfully. It is suggested here that when, in later life, they must face the stigma of being old, they are in a better position to adapt than their heterosexual counterparts. They have already had a successful mastery of stigma experience. (Berger & Kelly, 2001, p. 63)

CAREGIVING

With few exceptions, very little has been researched regarding the specific needs and experience of LGBT caregivers (Fredriksen, 1999; Hash & Cramer, 2003). It would be expected that LGBT caregivers would have similar challenges to those of heterosexual caregivers—the physical and emotional strain, an absence of support and affordable and accessible resources for caregivers and conflicts with familial and vocational responsibilities. However, some LGBT caregivers face a lack of support during caregiving and post-caregiving from family or co-workers who are not accepting of the relationship between the caregiver and the patient (Hash & Cramer, 2003). Many LGBT caregivers and their partners experience rude or slighting remarks from health care providers and many organizations are not in the practice of recognizing the legitimacy of these partnerships by enforcing "next of kin" policies that only recognize legal unions or biological family members (Hash & Cramer, 2003, p. 56).

RESIDENTIAL LIVING

The sexuality of older residents in nursing and assisted living facilities is virtually ignored by American society, and sexuality among the elderly is often joked about as the majority of the aged are seen as asexual and incapable of feeling sexual or having desires to be intimate with others. The wants and desires of elderly members of the LGBT community in residential care are even further overlooked.

Having to enter a residential care facility is a frightening experience for many people. For LGBT seniors this can be even more troublesome as their care and well-being is now in the hands of a system that has not been welcoming of them in the past. In one study of undergraduate nursing students, more than half felt "homosexual relationships were not true expressions of human sexuality" (Randall, as cited in Christensen, 2005) and a similar study of nurses' attitudes toward leukemia and AIDS patients of varying sexual orientations showed respondents expressing more negative attitudes toward nonheterosexual patients regardless of their illness (Kelly et al., 1988, as cited in Christensen, 2005). Many older LGBT individuals have experienced a great deal of bias, hostility, and legalized discrimination in their lifetimes and deserve a living environment that is safe and accepting of who they are as individuals and members of a community. Unfortunately, many adult care facilities lack the understanding and the vigilance necessary to create this type of environment. Social workers employed in nursing facilities, adult day care centers, and other venues designed to meet the needs of older persons need to advocate for the needs of LGBT individuals by creating safe and welcoming environments for clients who are both already accessing services and those who are looking for assistance and support.

Assessment tools and intake forms for care facilities are often gender specific and fail to inquire about sexual orientation, domestic partnerships, or affiliation or involvement within a specific community. Many older residents do not feel comfortable disclosing their sexual orientation due to a fear of retaliation or other negative consequences from staff. Upon entering a residential care facility, residents should be encouraged to share feelings of loss of a partner, same-sex relationship, or community involvement. Most nursing facilities lack access to media and publications that deal with issues that are of interest to the LGBT population. Social workers can educate other staff on the feelings of isolation this can create in LGBT residents and advocate for the inclusion of publications, movies and other types of media that pertain to LGBT audiences. LGBT families do not often have the same framework as traditional families and LGBT seniors may have a larger network of support systems that include friends and non-blood-related family members than their heterosexual counterparts. It is important not to limit visitations to a legal spouse or "next of kin." LGBT seniors in residential care should be encouraged to participate actively in activities that allow them to openly share memories, mementos, and anecdotes of past and current same-sex partners or friends without risk of ridicule from other residents or staff. They should feel safe in actively seeking companionship and intimacy with other LGBT residents.

While there are some residential care facilities and senior centers that cater specifically to the needs of older LGBT people, more steps need to be taken to ensure all older LGBT residents, regardless of where they are cared for, can be provided a safe, accepting, and nurturing environment. Social workers can lobby state and local governing bodies to respond to the needs of communities by providing funding that will allow for the creation of LGBT residential facilities, day care, and community centers.

GRIEF AND LOSS

Grieving LGBT individuals often experience the same range of emotions as heterosexuals. However, some of their experiences can be quite different and usually have to do with how their relationship is or had been perceived by mainstream society. Many LGBT individuals who are grieving experience a lack of support or concern from extended families, friends and/or co-workers (Holleran, 2006; Shernoff, 1998). Devaluing a relationship or the impact the death of a partner has on the surviving member can be particularly painful when already dealing with feelings of loss and loneliness. The grief of a surviving partner or friend can be complicated by the anger and resentment that can be felt toward families, co-workers, and other societal pressures that may have forced some relationships to be clandestine.

The grieving process is often interrupted or hindered because the surviving partner may have been denied from taking part in the dying process by extended family or institutional barriers. Without having access to their friend or partner during the most critical time, many LGBT individuals are deprived of taking part in the anticipatory grief process (reactions to current or future losses) which can further complicate bereavement (Faria, 1997). There may be no "formal recognition of loss and little or no sympathy for the grieving partner" (Faria, 1997), and the surviving partner or partners may also be excluded from planning or participating in funeral rituals.

Funerals and other end-of-life arrangements can often be marred by conflicting views of the deceased's wishes. Family members who do not respect the legitimacy of LGBT relationships can interfere with the carrying out of final wishes and agreements between partners. If those involved in the relationship have been forced to keep their affiliation a secret, these secrets may become revealed when a crisis or tragedy occurs. Funeral, cremation, and other end-of-life rituals can be arranged and explicitly outlined in a last will and testament. With clearly outlined instructions and wishes, there is little room for interpretation and disagreement between family members. A will is a legally binding document and it will protect the surviving member(s) of the relationship in carrying out what was mutually agreed upon prior to the death of their loved one. Without these prior wishes clearly documented, many state laws allow for the "next of kin to take ownership of the body" (Ettlebrick, 1996, p. 105). Social workers can help to facilitate the kinds of discussions between LGBT friends and partners that include end-of-life wishes and concerns.

DISASTER WORK

When a disaster happens in a community, everyone is affected. Members of marginalized groups or disenfranchised populations within the community are even more vulnerable during and following a disaster as many of them are not entitled to the same kind of relief and assistance afforded to other groups in the community. When working in disaster social work it is imperative to consider the impact of disasters on LGBT victims.

Many LGBT people receive emotional support and socialization through community agencies or establishments. These are considered natural support systems and the effects of the sudden loss of this support can be detrimental to a community already struggling with the trauma of the disaster. Natural support systems are defined by the Sacramento, California, Lanterman Developmental Disabilities Services Act, Section 4512 of the Welfare and Institution Code, Part (e), as "personal associations and relationships typically developed in the community that enhance the quality and security of life for people, including, but not limited to, family relationships; friendships reflecting the diversity of the neighborhood and the community; association with fellow students or employees in regular classrooms and work places; and associations developed through participation in clubs, organizations, and other civic activities" (Allen, 2005). These supports can often be rendered ineffective or inaccessible following a disaster due to the destruction of infrastructure, lack of power or loss of funding, thus leaving the members that rely on them with increased risk for isolation, feelings of loneliness and/or depression.

Many federal aid and relief organizations fail to recognize domestic partnerships when providing financial, medical, or mental health assistance to survivors or victims' loved ones. LGBT people may also be more skeptical of receiving assistance based on prior negative experiences with governmental or regulatory agencies. There may be feelings of distrust and suspicion on the part of LGBT communities when seeking out these services and relief workers need to be aware of how LGBT individuals may have been treated when they have asked for help in the past. The goal for any relief and disaster social work effort is to return individuals and communities to their prior state of functioning and self-reliance. Disaster and relief workers are most effective when they are flexible and cognizant of the cultural norms and attitudes of the individuals and communities they set out to assist. When delivering relief and support, social workers need to consider the specific needs of impacted LGBT communities. Members of the LGBT community will require specific interventions that allow them to feel safe, valued, and included in the relief efforts. For example, disaster information, guidelines, and applications for relief assistance should contain language every member of the community can relate to and understand, shelters should accommodate LGBT residents, and emotional support and grief work should validate the losses of LGBT victims.

WHAT DO SOCIAL WORKERS NEED TO KNOW? HOW TO HELP OURSELVES AND OTHER HEALTH CARE PROVIDERS TO BE MORE CULTURALLY COMPETENT WITH LGBT COMMUNITIES

In addition to what has already been listed, in the following text are some strategies we as social workers and other providers can implement in our agencies and facilities to ensure the delivery of the highest level of quality health care to LGBT clients.

Working with Vulnerable Populations

Provide ongoing, in-service training to all staff that prepares them to provide LGBT culturally competent health, mental health, and primary care. Educate staff on the specific health care concerns and needs of gender and sexual minorities. In addition to the techniques listed below, teach medical staff and other employees to avoid making assumptions regarding the sexual orientation or gender of clients, even if they have identified themselves as belonging to one group or another. For many LGBT individuals, it may take some time before they are comfortable revealing their sexual or gender minority status. If an adolescent client identifies themselves as LGBT, be supportive and avoid making the assumption they are passing through "a phase" (Seattle and King County Public Health Web site, 2004). Do not make assumptions about a person's orientation or gender based on whether the person has children. Many LGBT individuals are caring for either their biological or adopted children. Ensure that all staff are educated on the language and terminology that is acceptable and inoffensive to LGBT clients and/or patients; this includes using the proper pronouns for patients. If you are unsure of how to address patients, ask them. Provide staff with readily available brochures and pamphlets of community resources and agencies that meet the specific needs of LGBT communities and educate staff on the appropriate and safe manner in which to distribute these materials. All employees need to be made aware of the employment and legal consequences of breaching any portion of patient confidentiality, which includes sexual orientation, gender identity, or HIV status.

Assessment/Intake Tools

Social workers and other providers need to help create and utilize intake/assessment/demographic tools that do not negate or omit LGBT people or their relationships. When inquiring about gender include transgender, MTF, FTM, or "other (please explain)." Relationship status should include questions regarding domestic partners, not just whether people are single or married. Questions regarding the gender of current or potential sexual partners should also be included. Ensure confidentiality to all patients and make them aware that confidentiality is taken seriously where they receive care. Include statements on intake sheets that allow for the clients' decision to forgo the completion of forms in place of one-on-one, private conversations with the health care provider. Revisit sexual histories and inquiries regarding sexual partners at each appointment, home visit, or encounter to see if sexual practices have changed.

Interview Techniques

Providers should avoid asking close-ended questions or questions that omit certain relationships, such as these: "Are you married?" "How often do you have intercourse?" or "Do you have children?" Instead, focus on fact finding in a more open and all inclusive way. Ask questions similar to these: "Who do you live with?" "Who would you consider your significant other(s)?" "Do you have sex with men, women, both, MTF, FTM, or other?" "Who does your family consist of?" Keep in mind answers regarding a patient's gender may change over time.

Making Waiting Rooms and Sitting Areas LGBT Friendly

Include in waiting rooms publications that are intended for LGBT audiences. Provide posters and brochures that are of interest to LGBT patients. Make information readily available regarding community services and agencies intended to meet the needs of LGBT clients and, as noted, publicly provide your agency's policies regarding confidentiality so that all clients can rest assured their privacy will be taken seriously. Advocate for your agency to adopt nondiscrimination policies which include sexual orientation and gender identity for both employees and the populations served. Once these guidelines are implemented, post them conspicuously in waiting rooms and other rooms where clients and employees alike can see and read them clearly (GLBT Health Access Project, 2004).

As social workers, we may be familiar with considering race, ethnicity, age, ability, and class as factors in how health care is accessed and utilized, and less adept at taking into account how sexuality and/or gender impact delivery of services. Sexual and gender minorities face many challenges when it comes to receiving quality, unbiased health care. The majority of their experiences in the medical system have been less than helpful. Experiencing an injury or illness and having to seek medical care for yourself or a loved one can be stressful enough without having to deal with the added fear of being denied services, ridiculed, or having your sexual or gender minority status disclosed to others and your confidentiality breached. By becoming aware of the health care needs and concerns of LGBT individuals and how many LGBT patients have experienced the American health care system, we as social workers are better situated to provide education, to advocate for the reduction of barriers to access, and to fight discrimination and inequality in the delivery of health care to LGBT communities.

WEB RESOURCES

Gay and Lesbian Medical Association
http://www.glma.org/

This Web site of the well-known public policy advocacy group includes their recent *Healthy People 2010 Companion Document:*

> The Companion Document focuses on approximately 120 objectives and 12 focus areas from the recently published Healthy People 2010 document—the federal blueprint for public health for the next ten

years. The document examines these areas and lists specific recommendations regarding improved access, preventative medicine, and cultural competency. The document also examines and makes recommendations in the following areas: quality health services, mental health, public health infrastructure, HIV, immunization and infectious diseases, tobacco, injury and violence prevention, and substance abuse.

Gay, Lesbian, Bisexual and Transgender Health Access Project
http://www.glbthealth.org/

Provided by the Massachusetts Department of Public Health, it offers *Community Standards of Practice,* training and free materials, including posters and stickers that address homophobia and transphobia in health care.

Gayhealth.com
http://www.gayhealth.com

This site includes sections for providers and information regarding current news, food and fitness, drugs, sex, image, and "ask the doctor," "ask the pharmacist," and "ask the therapist." A state-by-state list of LGBT-friendly providers and clinics is also provided.

National Center for Transgender Equality (NCTE)
http://www.nctequality.org/

Offering information on civil liberty law and policies impacting transgender individuals, this site includes sections on how to get involved on local, state, and federal levels. The mission of the NCTE is listed on its Web site as follows:

> NCTE is a national social justice organization devoted to ending discrimination and violence against transgender people through education and advocacy on national issues of importance to transgender people. By empowering transgender people and our allies to educate and influence policymakers and others, NCTE facilitates a strong and clear voice for transgender equality in our nation's capital and around the country.

GMHC: Gay Men's Health Crisis
http://www.gmhc.org/

"Established in 1981, Gay Men's Health Crisis Inc. is the oldest not-for-profit AIDS service organization in the United States. GMHC is dedicated to providing direct services, education, and advocacy to men, women, and children living with HIV/AIDS." Located in New York City, GMHC provides extensive information regarding HIV testing, treatment, HIV policies and legal issues, advocacy, peer counselors, a phone hotline and Web inquiries, opportunities for volunteerism, and case management services.

SAGE: Services and Advocacy for Gay, Lesbian, Bisexual, and Transgender Elders
http://www.sageusa.org/

The oldest and largest organization devoted to meeting the needs of aging LGBT individuals, SAGE provides individuals and caregivers with information, training and education, crisis intervention, counseling, support and recreational groups, assistance with shopping, "help finding homecare you can trust," and "help finding a safe and friendly long-term care facility." For information, e-mail caregiving@sageusa.org.

Queers on Wheels
http://www.queersonwheels.com/

This is the Web site of a Pasadena, California, based organization that provides services to LGBT individuals with disabilities. Web site resources include message boards, links, volunteer opportunities, and a link to a resource guide for LGBT people with disabilities.

Gayscape
http://www.gayscape.com/aa.html

This site provides a directory of Web sites and resources for, by, or about gay and lesbian African Americans.

Lambda Legal
http://www.lambdalegal.org/cgi-bin/iowa/index.html

"Lambda Legal is a national organization committed to achieving full recognition of the civil rights of lesbians, gay men, bisexuals, transgender people, and those with HIV through impact litigation, education, and public policy work." The Web site provides resources for LGBT youth as well as information on creating safe and nondiscriminatory environments in schools, universities, and the workplace.

Bitheway.org
http://bitheway.org/

This Web site provides bisexual resources, including the brief history of the bi movement, politics, chat, message boards, and pride-related graphics.

LGBT Health Channel
http://www.lgbthealthchannel.com/

Healthcommunities.com (HC), Inc., "provides reliable, physician-developed patient education to consumers and medical Web site design services for doctors. By delivering condition and treatment information that patients and their physicians have grown to trust, HC improves quality of care and enhances the patient-physician relationship." This Web site provides relevant and current information regarding a number of health topics, including alternative insemination, anal cancer, hormone therapy, and party drug use.

BFLAG: Blind Friends of Lesbians and Gays
http://www.bflag.org/

This organization serves the blind LGBT communities. BFLAG's objectives are as follows:

1. "To provide a forum for the views and concerns of visually impaired persons interested in issues facing those who are gay, lesbian, bisexual, or transgender."
2. "To provide information about publications of interest to members, that is produced in accessible format and by encouraging the production of such material in accessible format."
3. "To facilitate the free exchange of ideas, opinions and information relative to matters of concern to blind people who are lesbian, gay, bisexual or transgender."
4. "To seek to assure adequate services to those who are gay, lesbian, bisexual, or transgender by agencies and institutions serving the blind."

The Body
http://www.thebody.com/

The HIV/AIDS resources on this site include "ask the experts" forums, treatment information for patients who are recently diagnosed, coinfected with hepatitis C, discontinuing treatment, or finding or switching providers, and information on side effects, Medicare, and the Ryan White Care Act.

Bisexual Resource Center
http://www.biresource.org/

This site is a clearinghouse of articles, resources, publications, volunteer opportunities, conference information, and pertinent links.

OutProud
http://www.outproud.org/

OutProud is the National Coalition for Gay, Lesbian, Bisexual, and Transgender Youth. The site includes testimonials, chat groups, resources, online magazine, brochure, school resource library, as well as online support for LGBT or questioning youth and their providers, teachers, schools, and communities.

PFLAG—Parents, Families and Friends of Lesbians and Gays
http://www.pflag.org/

Topics on this site include making schools safe environments, providing education regarding LGBT civil rights and legal protections, hate crime legislation, workplace and employment nondiscrimination, and issues facing families including marriage, adoption, custody and visitation, immigration, and tax equity.

Safe Schools Coalition
http://www.safeschoolscoalition.org/about_us.html#OurMission

This side includes resources for LGBT youth, parents, educators, and school systems, as well as specific resources for LGBT youth of color and LGBT youth with disabilities. Its mission "is to help schools—at home and all over the world—become safe places where every family can belong, where every educator can teach, and where every child can learn, regardless of gender identity or sexual orientation."

REFERENCES

Aggleton, P., & Warwick, I. (1997). Young people, sexuality, and HIV and AIDS education. In L. Sherr (Ed.), *AIDS and adolescents* (pp. 79-90). Amsterdam, The Netherlands: OPA.

Allen, J. B. (2005). *Community mental health promotion (CMHP) project: Enhancing recovery through linkage with indigenous natural supports.* The Mental Health Association in New York State, Inc. Web site. Retrieved April 22, 2007, from www.mhanys.org/cmhp/ cmhp_ressdsnaturalsupports.htm.

Appleby, G. (2001). Ethnographic study of gay and bisexual working-class men in the United States. In G. Appleby (Ed.), *Working-class gay and bisexual men* (pp. 51-62). Binghamton, NY: The Haworth Press.

Berger, R., & Kelly, J. (2001). What are older gay men like? An impossible question? In D. C. Kimmel & D. L. Martin (Eds.), *Midlife and aging in gay America* (pp. 55-64). Binghamton, NY: The Haworth Press.

Butler, J. (2004). *Undoing gender.* New York: Routledge.

The Body Web site (2006). *The complete HIV/AIDS resource.* Retrieved October 10, 2006, from http://www.thebody.com.

Centers for Disease Control, National Center for HIV, STD and TB Prevention, Divisions of HIV/AIDS Prevention Web site (2005a). *Coinfection with HIV and hepatitis C virus.* Retrieved January 31, 2006, from http://www.cdc.gov/hiv/pubs/brochure/coinfection.htm.

Centers for Disease Control, National Center for HIV, STD and TB Prevention, Divisions of HIV/AIDS Prevention Web site (2005b). *HIV/AIDS among men who have sex with men.* Retrieved January 31, 2006, from http://www.cdc.gov/hiv/PUBS/Facts/msm.htm.

Christensen, M. (2005). Homophobia in nursing: A concept analysis. *Nursing Forum, 40,* 60-72.

CLSC Rene-Cassin Web site (2004). *Improving the quaility of services via client satisfaction.* Retrieved October 1, 2005, from http://www.santemontreal.gc.ca/css/cavendish/en/default.aspx?sortcode=2.13.

Community United Against Violence Web site (2006). *Hate crime statistics.* Retrieved January 23, 2006, from http://www.cuav.org/.

Dean, L., Meyer, I. H., Robinson, K., Sell, R., Sember, R., et al. (2000). Lesbian, gay, bisexual, and transgender health: Findings and concerns. *Journal of the Gay and Lesbian Medical Association, 4,* 101-149.

Deyton, B., & Lear, W. (1988). A brief history of the gay/ lesbian health movement in the U.S.A. In M. Shernoff & W. Scott (Eds.), *The sourcebook on lesbian/gay health care* (2nd ed.) (pp. 15-19). Washington, DC: National Lesbian/Gay Health Foundation.

Donovan, T. (2001). Being transgender and older: A first person account. In D. C. Kimmel & D. L. Martin (Eds.), *Midlife and aging in gay America* (pp. 19-22). Binghamton, NY: The Haworth Press.

Eliason, M. (1996). *Institutional barriers to health care for lesbian, gay & bisexual persons.* New York: NLS Press.

Ettelbrick, P. (1996). Legal issues in health care for lesbians and gay men. In K. J. Peterson (Ed.), *Health care for lesbians and gay men* (pp. 93-109). Binghamton, NY: The Haworth Press.

Faria, G. (1997). The challenge of health care social work with gay men and lesbians. *Social Work in Health Care, 25*(1/2), 65-72.

Fredriksen, K. I. (1999). Family caregiving responsibilities among lesbians and gay men. *Social Work, 44*(2), 142-155.

Gay and Lesbian Medical Association Web site (2006). *Cancer in our lives.* Retrieved October 13, 2006, from http://www.glma.org.

Gay, Lesbian, Bisexual and Transgender Health Access Project (2004). *Community standards of practice for the provision of quality health care services to lesbian, gay, bisexual, and transgender clients.* Retrieved November 28, 2005, from http://www.glbthealth.org/.

Genke, J. (2004). Resistance and resilience: The untold story of gay men aging with chronic illnesses. In B. Lipton (Ed.), *Gay men living with chronic illnesses and disabilities* (pp. 81-95). Binghamton, NY: The Haworth Press.

Gochros, H., & Bidwell, R. (1996). Lesbian and gay youth in a straight world: Implications for health care workers. In K. J. Peterson (Ed.), *Health care for lesbians and gay men* (pp. 1-18). Binghamton, NY: The Haworth Press.

Grossman, A., D'Augelli, A., & O'Connell, T. (2001). Being lesbian, gay, bisexual, and 60 or older in North America. In D. C. Kimmel & D. L. Martin (Eds.), *Midlife and aging in gay America* (pp. 23-40). Binghamton, NY: The Haworth Press.

Harm Reduction Coalition Web site (2005). *Principles of harm reduction.* Retrieved on November 12, 2006, from http://www.harmreduction.org.

Hash, K., & Cramer, E. (2003). Empowering gay and lesbian caregivers and uncovering their unique experiences through the use of qualitative methods. *Journal of Gay & Lesbian Social Services, 15,* 47-63.

Holleran, A. (2006). *Grief.* New York: Hyperion Books.

Institute of Medicine (1993). *To err is human: Building a safer health care system.* Washington, DC: Author.

Institute of Medicine (1999). *Redesigning care delivery.* Washington, DC: Author.

Kanapaux, W. (2003). Homosexual seniors face stigma. *Geriatric Times, 4,* 22-26.

Kaplan, L., Tomaszewski, E., & Gorin, S. (2004). Current trends and the future of HIV/ AIDS services: A social work perspective. *Health and Social Work, 29,* 153-161.

Kenagy, G. P. (2005). Transgender health: findings from two needs assessment studies in Philadelphia. *Health and Social Work, 30*(1), 19.

Lesbian, Gay, Bisexual, Transgender Community Center of Greater Cleveland Web site (2004). *Health needs of the bisexual and transgender communities.* Retrieved December 6, 2005, from http://www.lgcsc.org/healthassessment.html.

Lev, A. I. (2004). *Transgender emergence: Therapeutic guidelines for working with gender-variant people and their families.* Binghamton, NY: The Haworth Press.

Mansergh, G., Colfax, G. N., Marks, G., et al. (2001). The circuit party men's health survey: Findings and implications for gay and bisexual men. *American Journal of Public Health, 91,* 953-958.

National Institute on Drug Abuse Web site (2006). *Medical consequences of meth use.* Retrieved November 2, 2006, from http://www.drugabuse.gov/consequences/neurological/.

Ostrow, D. G., Fox, K., Chmiel, J. S., et al. (2000, July). *Attitudes towards highly active antiretroviral therapy predict sexual risktaking among HIV-infected and uninfected gay men in the multicenter AIDS cohort study (MACS).* XIII International Conference on AIDS; Durban, South Africa. Abstract ThOrC719. Retrieved April 25, 2005, from http://www.iac2000.org.

Paul, J., & Nichols, M. (1988). "Biphobia" and the construction of a bisexual identity. In M. Shernoff & W. Scott (Eds.), *The sourcebook on lesbian/gay health care.* (2nd ed.) (pp. 259-264). Washington, DC: National Lesbian/Gay Health Foundation.

Purcell, D. W., Parsons, J. T., Halkitis, P. N., Mizuno, Y., & Woods, W. J. (2001). Substance use and sexual transmission risk behavior of HIV-positive men who have sex with men. *Journal of Substance Abuse, 13,* 185-200.

Reid, R. (2002). Harm reduction and injection drug use: Pragmatic lessons from a public health model. *Health and Social Work, 27,* 223-227.

Seattle and King County Public Health Web site (2004). *Culturally competent care for GLBT people: Recommendations for health care providers.* Retrieved November 9, 2005, from http://www.metrokc.gov/health/.

Shankle, M. D. (2006). *The handbook of gay, lesbian, bisexual, and transgender public health.* Binghamton, NY: The Haworth Press.

Shernoff, M. (1998). *Gay widowers: Life after the death of a partner.* Binghamton, NY: The Haworth Press.

Shernoff, M., & Scott, W. (Eds.) (1998). *The sourcebook on lesbian/gay health care* (2nd ed.). Washington, DC: National Lesbian/Gay Health Foundation.

Stall, R., Paul, J. P., Greenwood, G., et al. (2001). Alcohol use, drug use and alcohol-related problems among men who have sex with men: The urban men's health study. *Addiction, 96,* 1589-1601.

Suarez, T., & Miller, J. (2001). Negotiating risks in context: A perspective on unprotected anal intercourse and barebacking among men who have sex with men—Where do we go from here? *Archives of Sexual Behavior, 30,* 287-300.

Swindell, M., & Pryce, J. (2003). Self-disclosure stress: Trauma as an example of an intervening variable in research with lesbian women. *Journal of Gay & Lesbian Social Services, 15,* 95-108.

U.S. Department of Health and Human Services Web site (2006). *Smoking and tobacco statistics.* Retrieved January 7, 2006, from http://www.hhs.gov/.

Van Wormer, K., Wells, J., & Boes, M. (2000). *Social work with lesbians, gays, and bisexuals.* Boston: Allyn & Bacon.

White, J. (1995). Lesbian health care: What a primary care physician needs to know. *The Western Journal of Medicine, 162,* 463-467.

White, J., & Martinez, M. C. (1997). *The lesbian health book.* Seattle: Seal Press.

Chapter 15

Social Work Practice with LGBT People Within Organizations

George A. Appleby
Edgar Colon

The premise of this chapter is that U.S. society will continue to discriminate against LGBT persons in the name of "family values" or "special rights" or "preservation of morale" or any other meaningless slogan. Such discrimination will be seen for what it really is: bigotry. However, social change is slow and discriminatory attitudes and behaviors will continue to be oppressive environmental and organizational influences on LGBT social workers employed by human service agencies. This vestige of homophobia and heterosexism, therefore, must become the target of social work intervention (Appleby, 1995).

Drawing upon the extensive research on organizational structures and their psychosocial impact has directed specific attention to the employees of social service agencies (Sussal, 1994). A convincing case was made for the workplace having the potential to promote feelings of personal validation and a source of mental health. The workplace itself, however, can also become a source of emotional distress. Menzies-Lyth (1988) studied the ways in which the workplace can become destructive. She noted that anxieties not handled openly through discussion may result in an increased likelihood that rigid and injurious defenses against conflict interactions may be developed. These include "prohibitions against talking about uncomfortable anxiety producing topics, unnecessarily harsh disciplinary practices, rigid lines of hierarchical relationships, and the impact of scapegoat behaviors on the individual employee in these circumstances can result in feelings of worthlessness and self-devaluation" (p. 91). She suggested that lesbians and gays are subjected to a breadth of discriminatory feedback in their daily lives that no other segment of the population must undergo. "It is not uncommon for public policies and practices to disregard lesbian and gay special needs, while at the same time not even acknowledging their existence. [This is an exercise of the most destructive defense, denial.] A conspiracy of silence exists which is anxiety producing and painful" (Sussal, 1994, pp. 90-91).

While the dynamics of homophobia and heterosexism have been considered in detail elsewhere, the present discussion warrants at least an examination of some of the key correlates. Power and powerlessness are the most weighty of these correlates. Pellegrini (1992) in her study of gender inequality indicated that oppression, a key concept that ties sexism and homophobia together, is all about power: the power to enforce a particular worldview; the power to deny equal access to housing, employment opportunities, and health care; the power to alternately define and to efface difference; and the power to set the terms of power. Pharr (1988), in her examination of homophobia as a weapon of sexism, noted that some of the following are elements of all oppression: the imposition of normative behavior supported by institutional and economic power; social definition as "other"; invisibility of the "outsiders"; distortion and stereotyping; blaming the victim; and internalized oppression. Power exists on various levels: individual, interactive, as well as societal. Power is the capacity to produce desired effects on others, perceived mastery over self and others, and the capacity to influence the forces that affect one's life.

Most gay and lesbian scholars who view power and oppression from a social-psychological or sociopolitical framework reference each of the previous elements in their analysis of homophobia and heterosexism (Appleby & Anastas, 1998; Blumenfeld, 1992; D'Emilio, 1983; Herek & Berrill, 1992). LGBT persons share similar life experiences with all other oppressed people, and power or the lack thereof is central to their social functioning (Appleby, Colon, & Hamilton, 2002).

The converse of power, powerlessness is the inability to exert such influence. It is painful because the feeling of controlling one's destiny to some reasonable extent is the essential psychological component of all aspects of life. A sense of power is critical to one's mental health. Power is manifest in the individual's sense of mastery or competence. Social work has been ambivalent about its own power or the use of power in general. Throughout the profession's literature there appears to be a reluctance to discuss professional power, as if the discussion alone might imply collusion in the misuse of power, oppression. Social work scholars concerned with individual or societal oppression have all come to the conclusion that power is core to an understanding of person: environment as experienced by all minorities or to the development of appropriate social work interventions with these groups (Germain & Gitterman, 1996). This contemporary understanding of power is also reflected in the growing influence of "empowerment" as primary outcome and process in practice theory.

Social work has had a long and proud tradition of advocating on behalf of vulnerable and oppressed people—that is, accessing power for others— and lesbian and gay clients have not been exceptions. Self-advocacy, unfortunately, has too often been interpreted by some social workers in the past as crass self-interest, and thus less worthy of attention. In recent years, with the advent of unions and legislative lobbying around professional licensing and standards, third-party payment, and managed care policies, this trend is being reversed. It is the position taken in this essay that all social workers, especially minorities, and specifically lesbian or gay social workers, must begin to reframe self-advocacy as a matter of gaining personal and societal power in the areas of civil rights, organizational (agency) recognition and equity, and mental health in the workplace. It will be argued that the profession's self-advocacy is mandated by the code of ethics, that it is supported by organizational and political realities, and that it is consistent with contemporary practice perspectives and skills. The case will be made that LGBT workers should begin to focus on their own workplace to create an inclusive productive environment for everyone. Finally, it will be argued that LGBT social workers should form coalitions with other minorities and like-minded people to press for a specific strategy of "diversity management" that is both inclusive and clearly stated in terms of outcomes that are tied to professional productivity.

CODE OF ETHICS

The National Association of Social Workers (NASW) joined the American Psychological Association and the American Psychiatric Association in the 1970s to challenge the indefensible position that homosexuality is a mental illness resulting from pathological development. The mental health professions came to this position after an extensive review of the existing research and the clinical experiences of its members. Each profession now views homosexuality not as an illness but as another path to psychosocial adaptation. In 1999, the social work profession included nondiscrimination language based on sexual orientation in its newly developed *Code of Ethics*. The code is based on the fundamental values of the social work profession that include the worth, dignity, and uniqueness of all persons as well as the advancement of their rights and opportunities. It is also based on the nature

of social work, which fosters conditions that promote these values as ingredients of optimal social functioning. The code offers general principles to
guide conduct in situations that have ethical implications. Specifically,
social workers shall not "practice, condone, facilitate or collaborate with
any form of discrimination on the basis of race, color, sex, sexual orientation . . ." (National Association of Social Workers *Code of Ethics,* Section
II., F., 3., 1999).

The individual social worker and agency are expected to deliver appropriate and nondiscriminatory services to all clients. While this language is
specific to the worker's ethical responsibility to clients, it can be logically
generalized to his or her ethical responsibility to colleagues because of the
code's emphasis on respect, courtesy, fairness, and good faith. General
language is again introduced in reference to employers and employing organizations: ". . . to improve the employing agency's policies and procedures . . ." (IV., L., 1.) and "act to prevent and eliminate discrimination in
the employing organization's work assignments and in its employment policies and practices" (IV., L., 3., 1999). Finally, restated in the code in relation to ethical responsibility to society is the same language: "The social
worker should act to prevent and eliminate discrimination against any person or group on the basis of . . . sexual orientation . . ." (VI., P., L., 1999).
The revised code, adopted by the 1996 Delegate Assembly and enacted in
1999, is a clearer articulation of the profession's values of service, social
justice, dignity and worth of the person, importance of human relationships, integrity, and competence. The language related to sexual orientation
is as emphatic as the original document. The code goes well beyond advocacy on behalf of clients, to mandate self-advocacy as a means of ending
discrimination against lesbian and gay social workers in social agencies
and professional organizations (Code of Ethics Revision Committee,
1996). While most agencies are effective in the application of the code to
clients, some have yet to move beyond cultural homophobia in relation to
policies governing the workplace. The code, then, has the potential to be one
of the most powerful tools in support of ending bigotry and agency-based
discrimination.

Initially, NASW adopted an educational strategy to advance the code.
Eventually, the association formed state and national committees on inquiry
(COI) to adjudicate violations of the code. The code and the related adjudi-
cation procedures are powerful instruments of social justice for lesbians and
gay men, holding both the practitioner and the social agency accountable.
Violation of the code may bring public censure that could result in public
humiliation and possible loss of funds and accreditation status for an agency

and loss of employment for the individual. Most COI cases related to sexual orientation focused on client discrimination and seldom on agency-based worker discrimination. For those social workers whose work environment negates their personhood and denies their unique needs, self-advocacy apparently has not become the norm.

ORGANIZATIONAL AND POLITICAL REALITIES

In recent years, NASW has taken on an advocacy role in relation to expanding the civil rights of this still-marginalized group. Social policy now reflects an appreciation that gay and lesbian discrimination is a violation of both the right of privacy and equal protection under the law as guaranteed by the U.S. Constitution and the Bill of Rights. These are the basic rights of citizenship. The Constitution does not allow for exceptions. This change from an educational focus on the mental health consequences to an emphasis on civil rights has not been an easy task. Nonjudgmental attitudes are necessary to support social change and to end individual and organizational prejudice. Homophobia and heterosexism are social forces that permeate all aspects of social life; social service agencies, and social work professionals are not immune. Attitudes about homosexuality in the helping professions as a whole have been changing markedly since the 1970s. Unfortunately, both workers and clients may still be affected by the residue of outmoded psychological theory that until recently viewed homosexuality as pathology. Scholars warn that the worker's feelings, attitudes, and level of comfort with gay or lesbian orientation must be examined; they require self-exploration over time. Studies continue to suggest that negative attitudes toward homosexuality and homosexual clients persist among some social workers and social work students (Bahr, Brish, & Croteau, 2000; Bochenek, 2002; DeCrescenzo, 1984; Eliason, 1995; Greene, 1994; Harris, Nightengale, & Owen, 1995). Prejudice toward lesbian, gay, and bisexual social workers results in discriminatory personnel practices and unnecessary stress.

In 1999, the Delegate Assembly of the NASW approved a policy statement on gay issues, affirming the association's understanding of the social, economic, political, and mental health consequences of discrimination and prejudice, and thus outlined a modest action plan focusing on the education of the profession. The following year, the NASW Board of Directors established its first Task Force on Gay Issues to help carry out the earlier mandate. In 1979, the task force was restructured as an authorized committee of the association, and in 1982 it was renamed the National Committee on Lesbian and Gay Issues (NCOLGI), with resources to advance the education of membership. The committee supported the development of a mono-graph, *Lesbian and Gay Issues: A Resource Manual for Social Workers* (Hidalgo, Peterson, & Woodman, 1985), encouraged NASW Press to solicit articles related to lesbian and gay issues, and identified relevant workshops for the annual conference. Throughout this period, the energy of the commit-tee, and thus the association, was directed toward mounting a response to the AIDS pandemic and, to a lesser extent, educating membership about gay and lesbian issues. In 1993, the committee became a bylaws-mandated eq-uity unit, along with the National Committee on Women's Issues (NCOWI) and the National Committee on Minority Affairs (NCOMA), each account-able to the board. It took ten years, 1977-1987, after the first social policy statement was adopted, for the Delegate Assembly to significantly revise the original document and to rename it *Lesbian and Gay Issues.* Monumen-tal change took place in 1996 when the Delegate Assembly approved a by-laws amendment that added sexual orientation to its list of protected classes in the association's affirmative action plan. Along with this change, which places the profession in the forefront of its sister disciplines, a major revi-sion of its 1987 policy statement was adopted. This latest statement, *Lesbian, Gay, and Bisexual Issues* (National Association of Social Workers, 1996), is probably the most progressive position taken by any of the legal, educa-tional, health, human service, and mental health professional associations:

> It is the position of NASW that same-gender sexual orientation should be afforded the same respect and rights as opposite-gender orientation. NASW asserts that discrimination and prejudice directed against any group are damaging to the social, emotional, and economic well-being of the affected group and of society as a whole. NASW is committed to advancing policies and practices that will improve the status and well-being of all lesbian, gay and bisexual people.

> NASW believes that nonjudgmental attitudes toward sexual orientation allow social workers to offer optimal support and services to lesbian, gay, and bisexual people. The profession supports and empowers les-bian, gay, and bisexual people through all phases of the coming out process and beyond. The profession believes discriminatory statutes, policies, and actions that diminish the quality of life for lesbian, gay, and bisexual people and that force many to live their lives in secrecy should be prevented and eliminated. NASW supports the right of the individual to self-disclosed sexual orientation. NASW encourages the development of supportive practice environments for lesbian, gay, and bisexual clients and colleagues. The rights and well-being of the

children of lesbian, gay, and bisexual people should be an integral part of all these considerations.

NASW affirms its commitment to work toward full social and legal acceptance and recognition of lesbian, gay, and bisexual people. To this end, NASW supports legislation, regulation, policies, judicial review, political action, and changes in social work policy statements and the NASW Code of Ethics and any other means necessary to establish and protect the equal rights of all people without regard to sexual orientation. NASW is committed to working toward the elimination of prejudice and discrimination both inside and outside the profession. (NASW, 1996, pp. 2-3)

This same Delegate Assembly gave approval to policy statements and resolutions related to full representation at all levels of leadership and employment; the broadening of nondiscrimination statements to include sexual orientation in all social agencies, universities, professional associations, and funding organizations; exacting the association to campaign against any laws allowing discriminatory practices in immigration, employment, housing, professional credentialing, licensing, public accommodation, child custody, and the right to marry; and opposing exclusion from the military and other forms of government services. "All social work practitioners, administrators, and educators are encouraged to take action to ensure that the dignity and rights of lesbian, gay and bisexual employees, clients and students are upheld and that these rights are codified in agency policies" (NASW, 1996, pp. 5-6). Policy became more than an abstraction when in 1996 the NASW Board of Directors charged the National Committee on Lesbian, Gay, and Bisexual Issues to go beyond education to achieve its purpose: "to further the cause of social justice by promoting and defending the rights of persons suffering injustices and oppression because they are lesbian, gay, or bisexual" (NASW, 1996). The committee has been charged to address policy development and practice standards; to engage in civil rights activities and advocacy; to continue pressing for professional education; and to assist the association in its own organizational development in relation to gay, lesbian, and bisexual rights and privileges. The corporate political and organizational will has been clearly stated. This, then, is another powerful resource for practitioners committed to changing the climate of social agencies.

More recently, NASW (2003) supports curriculum policies in schools of social work that eliminate discrimination against people of diverse gender and encourages the implementation of continuing education programs on practice and policy issues relevant to gender diversity. In addition, to foster public awareness, NASW supports collaboration with organizations and groups supportive of the transgender community to develop programs to increase public awareness of the mistreatment and discrimination experienced by transgender people and of the contributions they make to society. NASW also urges development within schools and other child and youth services agencies of programs that educate students, faculty, and staff about gender diversity and the needs of transgender children and youth (NASW, 2003).

CONTEMPORARY PRACTICE

Social work is an agency-based profession with well-recognized organizational skills in service delivery and formal and informal resources management. These skills evolved over the last hundred years as the profession matured within its organizational context. Today, this knowledge, and these skills and processes have become the core of all social work practice, commonly referred to as generalist or foundation practice. The emphasis of this section is the environmental focus of practice, the goal of empowerment, and the organizational skills of self-advocacy.

The generalist social worker possesses an integrated view of people and environments and uses appropriate interventions to empower consumers at all social system levels. Nurturing environments have been given much more theoretical attention with the introduction of Germain and Gitterman (1980) and Germain's (1991) advancement of the ecological perspective. Much of the empirical work in this area has sought to understand various client environments and to reassess the effectiveness of social work interventions. Scholars focusing on either clinical or generalist approaches to practice have drawn heavily on the ecological metaphor.

Another Theme of Contemporary Practice Is Empowerment

Empowerment may be defined as the enabling of a client population to handle problems on their own, with the feeling of a growing capacity, to take their lives into their own hands. Gutierrez (1990, p. 151) defines empowerment as "a process of increasing personal, interpersonal, or political power so that individuals can take action to improve their situation . . . [the] development of increased power or control." It is a process necessary to cope in a hostile world and may mean (1) increasing self-efficacy; (2) developing a sense of mastery, initiative, and action; and (3) fostering group consciousness and a "sense of shared fate." This facilitates a person's ability for reducing self-blame and seeing many problems as being collective rather than just theirs alone. Problems are often a function of societal power arrangements. Self-blame is often responsible for feelings of depression and immobilization. When people feel competent and self-assured, they are more capable of assuming personal responsibility for change (Morales, 1995). The shades of mental health theory and practice run through these discussions of empowerment.

In relation to LGBT social work, Sussal (1994) reminded us that the workplace provides a unique situation in which an environment supportive of mental health can be structured by influencing and setting policies that obviate discrimination, developing programs to raise consciousness about gay and lesbian issues, and delivering direct services to LGBT persons and their family members or co-workers.

Generalists regard clients in relation to the social milieu, view problems in the context of the situation, and seek solutions within both personal and environmental structures. Many of the empowering processes, as well as the functions of generalist social work entail some degree of organizational sophistication. Many scholars studied the array of professional and client roles in relation to organizational processes associated with clients' and workers' tasks, for example, accessing, processing, utilizing, and communicating information. McPheeters (1971), Teare and McPheeters (1970, 1982), Pincus and Minahan (1976), and Johnson (1995) analyzed helping roles, while Siporin (1975) analyzed role models, and Compton and Galaway (1994), and Conaway and Gentry (1988) studied role sets and intervention roles. DuBois and Miley (1996) extend this scholarship by identifying the organizational nature of practice implicit in the core roles and functions of generalist practice. The role of consultant (for problem giving) includes activities directed toward empowering clients to resolve problems, fostering organizational development, coordinating program and policy development, and mentoring. A second role, resource manager, includes activities commonly thought of as brokering, convening, and mediating. The third role, educator, covers a range of teaching and training activities aimed at clients, colleagues, and the public.

One specific skill continually referenced by each of the scholars mentioned is advocacy. In situations where adequate services do not exist or are not accessible, the social worker assumes an advocacy function. As an advocate, he or she is concerned with making the social welfare system responsive to the unmet needs of the client. According to Briar (1968), the social worker as advocate is the client's supporter, advisor, champion, and if need be, representative in his or her dealings with the court, the police, the social agency, and other organizations that affect the client's well-being. Advocacy, then, is an organizational skill. Owing to the currency of this skill, social workers understand the pervasiveness and extensiveness of organizations in our national life, and that organizations determine what and how resources are to be distributed to both consumers of our services and to those of us who provide the service. They determine the direction (or what appears to be nondirection) of the society. Also, they are barriers to social change and social justice, just as they are the very basis of change and the guarantor of the benefits of social justice.

Social workers have come belatedly to appreciate the unique organizational dynamics of agency-based practice, with its own well-developed theoretical base (organizational theory) and its range of macro-intervention skills, which are similar and unlike those of clinical or interpersonal practice. Inappropriately, practitioners tend to draw upon interpersonal and developmental theory and, too often, upon a family systems metaphor when analyzing organizational behavior. This is akin to explaining soil erosion as the result of the land's weakened immunologic reaction to ozone depletion in the stratosphere. Interventions also tend to be more interpersonal than task group or administrative. A composite view of organizations that blends content from sociology, psychology, economics, management, anthropology, political science, and industrial relations should inform assessment at this level. The point is worth emphasizing that this is an important body of theory to inform practice designed to empower LGBT clients, as well as employees in their pursuit of a nondiscriminatory workplace environment.

What, then, from this body of practice knowledge, theory, and research, helps us to understand the unique reality of LGBT persons within human service organizations and directs energy toward the improvement of that reality? Theory suggests that organizations tend to grow. Growth is equated with success. Even in a no-growth economy, public and private organizations try to grow at one another's expense. In addition to their growth in size, another important consideration gives contemporary organizations an unprecedented role in contemporary society: the modern organization is a *legal* entity, just like the individual (Coleman, 1974). The legality is granted by the state, itself a legal creation. While the individual is given a set of rights and responsibilities by the state, these same rights and responsibilities are extended to organizations. These rights, coupled with size, give organizations an enormous amount of power within the state. The state or government is more comfortable dealing with other organizations than with individual persons, and thus tends to provide more preferential treatment in terms of taxation or rights to privacy.

Hall (1977), in his classic summary of organizational theory, pointed out that government organizations receive power through mandates from the legislature and will seek to maintain that power even if no purpose is being served. In other words, organizations grow, maintain themselves, and continue their operations regardless of the motivations of their members. Organizations process information, and to accomplish this end, they structure themselves by establishing roles, lines of communication, and ranks. Procedures are established in advance to deal with most possible events. These structures virtually force certain things to be communicated and suppress other things. Individuals who process and interpret the information that is passed on to people in decision-making positions have influence or power. Professionally, social workers have come to respect the inexorable power of organizations and have used this power to expand the health, mental health and human service rights and benefits of clients. Thus, following an understanding of organizational theory and the professional experience with the manipulation of power, the strategy should then be to change the agency's environment with the goal of increasing the power of lesbian and gay workers as they coalesce with other devalued constituencies.

STRATEGIES FOR AN INCLUSIVE WORKPLACE

Those charged with the management of any organization do not typically address a problem until two things happen. First, they become reasonably sure that a problem exists, and second, they become convinced that trying to solve the problem will be good for agency growth and survival. Winfeld and Spielman (1995) suggested that public and private organizations are attempting to adapt to the changing demographics of both their clients/consumers and their employees. The vogue strategy is diversity management, which is now viewed more as a core administrative issue and less strictly as a human resources issue. The distinction is a crucial one. Although administrators have not doubted that proper management and support programs are important, those programs have not been tied into performance outcomes. Some vague relationship between caring for staff and their resulting performance has always been acknowledged, but it was never considered an empirical cause and effect. This is changing in industry and in some sectors of the public arena. If the point of a diversity management effort is to create a harassment-free, satisfactory, cooperative, productive, and profitable/effective workplace for all, then it must include sexual orientation as a diversity factor.

The business and industrial relations literature offers evidence that companies with progressive, people-oriented strategies experience better results in terms of customer satisfaction, profitability, and global competitiveness (Lyndenberg, Marlin, & Strub, 1986). While the terms may be different, the underlying concepts are relevant to the environment both within and out-side a social agency. A progressive company or social service organization benefits from the ability to take full advantage of the skills and knowledge of all of its employees. A big part of this benefit is felt in allowing each person to perform to his or her greatest potential, unfettered by fear of prejudice; but it is demonstrated in another way as well. Members of a given group often understand the customs, practices, and requirements of that group better than people who are not members. Therefore, tapping into the cultural expertise and knowledge of certain employee constituencies can pay rich dividends in new and relevant services.

Another significant factor is the very real issue of productivity. Work is a task, but it is also a social activity. People need and expect to be able to express themselves to the fullest, and when they cannot, they are unhappy. That unhappiness may eventually sabotage the efforts of the work group and by extension weaken the performance of the whole organization.

There are other reasons to include LGBT employees into an overall diversity strategy: law, service effectiveness, and common sense. The legal landscape in relation to LGBT rights changes continually. Even at the time this chapter is written, LGBT rights are not protected by the U.S. Constitution, in addition, there is no federal job protection for LGBT persons. The Employment Non-Discrimination Act (ENDA), which would provide such protection, has yet to be passed by Congress. According to Lambda Legal and Educational Defense, fifteen states—California, Nevada, Oregon, Hawaii, New Mexico, New Hampshire, New York, New Jersey, Illinois, Connecticut, Vermont, Massachusetts, Minnesota, Rhode Island, and Wisconsin—and the District of Columbia offer full civil rights legal protection to gay and lesbian people; seven other states—Washington, Montana, Arizona, Colorado, Indiana, Pennsylvania, and Delaware—offer protection to public employees (http://data.lambdalegal.org/pdf/enda_llanalysis_20071016.pdf). Between fifteen and eighteen other states cover some degree of protection with very tenuous executive orders. Approximately 165 cities and counties have ordinances that do not carry the weight of law (http://thetaskforce.org/reports_and_research/nondiscrimination_laws). While these laws and ordinances vary in power, each represents a building block upon which precedents are being set. Many of these precedents have implications for employers. Agencies that operate in a state, city, or county with a sexual orientation nondiscrimination law or order are in violation of the law if it does not include sexual or gender orientation as a protected characteristic in its written nondiscrimination policy. Violators can be sued or brought before the state's human rights commission.

Organizations can expect more of their LGBT employees to insist upon discrimination protection and equitable benefits in the workplace. Those organizations would do well to listen. The reason is simple. In those places where the law does not protect and provide for inclusion of sexual minorities, LGBT people work under enormous strain. They cannot perform at their best under these oppressive circumstances. In many cases, discrimination is unlawful; it is always unproductive and unprofitable (Winfield, 2005; Winfeld & Spielman, 1995).

Effectiveness is another reason for organizations to take a proactive stance. The experience of industry suggests that adopting discriminatory policies is detrimental to economic health. Human rights are never far divorced from economics. According to a 1996 *Newsweek* poll, nearly 84 percent of Americans support equal employment rights for LGBT persons. The Human Rights Campaign found that, in 1994, 70 percent of the voting population did not realize that antigay job discrimination is still widespread and predominantly legal (Goldberg, 1996). Organizations that support LGBT employees and their requirements will be rewarded, and those that resist inclusion will see the results in their annual reports, decreased service caseloads, and funding sources.

Common sense is perhaps the most compelling reason for including gay and lesbian workers in the agency's diversity mix. They are already there. About 10 percent of the population is believed to be gay or lesbian, yet a much higher but unconfirmed percentage is estimated for the health and social services workforce. About twenty-one million (conservative estimate) LGBT persons live and work in the United States alone. Some studies estimate that they are the single largest minority in the workforce (Williamson, 1993). They need and want the quite ordinary freedom of visibility without reprisals.

Winfeld and Spielman (1995) in their analysis of human diversity in private industry sum up by observing that all organizations have it within their power to a take an affirming position on nondiscrimination and to proactively ensure that all members understand the dynamics of the nondiscrimination policy. The reason is simple: Unless organizations take a proactive stance, they can be sure that they will lose customers/clients and talented employees to competitors who have a nondiscriminatory policy. Inclusion is a very small price to pay for effectiveness and productivity. It must be acknowledged that some agencies, either through religious conviction or homophobia or both, are hesitant or want to avoid this subject altogether. Some fear that they will lose clients or community support if they take an ethical/legal stance. They are afraid that having an inclusive policy will be interpreted as giving tacit approval, and those clients who hold the opposite view will seek services elsewhere. This argument would have little merit if the discussion were to focus on racism or sexism, but because homophobia is so institutionalized, this contradiction is seldom raised. Leaving the ethics of this situation aside, the answer is simple: Acknowledgment of and education about something does not equal endorsement of it. Providing for the concerns of a particular constituency in the agency does not mean that you endorse the members of that constituency, their behavior, or their beliefs. It is quite pragmatic, in that it simply signals that the agency is committed to all its employees with no exceptions.

The agency can do many things to secure and maintain the best efforts of its employees. In return for equitable benefits, programs, and policies, the employer has the right to expect dedication, loyalty, self-motivation, and cooperation from all employees at all times. From an LGBT perspective, the trade is a simple one, the same as is expected by and granted to heterosexual employees: a safe working environment, equitable benefits, and appropriate public support (Winfeld & Spielman, 1996).

A safe work environment is demonstrated and encouraged by three things: (1) a nondiscrimination policy that expressly includes sexual and gender orientation; (2) diversity education that includes a comprehensive module on gender and sexual orientation; and (3) equitable human resource policies, and the support of an LGBT/straight employee's alliance. Equitable benefits means providing to the partners of lesbian and gay employees the same benefits, including health coverage, which are accorded the families of other employees,in essence, equal pay for equal work.

Equitable benefit plans may include hard benefits, such as medical and dental care, and soft benefits, such as adoption benefits, bereavement and family leave policies, employee assistance programs, parenting leave, use of health and fitness programs, relocation policy, and sick leave.

While these benefits are commonly available in the private sector, access to school records, visiting rights in hospitals and prisons, and home purchase loans are usually offered by the public sector. Other areas in which agencies can take a proactive stance toward equity are agency-paid pension plans and benefits under the Consolidated Omnibus Budget Reconciliation Act (COBRA) and the Family and Medical Leave Act (FMLA) of 1993.

The law and justice are not the same thing, but the terms are frequently used interchangeably. While there are few direct legal precedents for domestic partner benefits, there are ample precedents of justice. Both as a matter of justice and law, an employer is obligated to provide equal pay for equal work to its employees. By providing benefits to the families of married employees and denying the same to families of unmarried employees, the employer is violating that obligation and discriminating according to the marital status and sexual orientation of its employees. By refusing to provide the same benefits to unmarried employees as it provides to married employees, the employer may be violating any number of previously mentioned city, county, and state laws.

COMING OUT AT THE WORKPLACE

LGBT persons are different from visibly recognizable minorities because they must decide whether to come out whenever meeting someone new or every time a personal topic comes up at work. If they stay in the closet, they may cope by not telling the whole story or by simply avoiding personal conversations. This takes a lot of energy.

The stress of not being open either to oneself or to co-workers is taxing. LGBT persons and their heterosexual allies who deal every day with the silence and intolerance of their agencies or organizations deserve a lot of affirming messages. They need to hear that they are not shameful and that even the smallest details of their lives that reflect their sexual orientation are worthy of having someone hear them. The growing literature on LGBT persons in the workplace (Anastas, 1998, 2001a, 2001b; Appleby, 1995, 2001; Mallon, 1999) suggests that the most effective weapon against homophobia is for LGBT social work employees to come out (DeCrescenzo, 1997; Ellis & Riggle, 1996; Griffith & Hebl, 2002). This action will counter stereotypes and end the isolation and the institutional process of blaming the victim as they present themselves publicly as competent, functioning, visible representatives of their community (Pharr, 1988).

While coming-out appears to be most effective, there are several other steps that can be taken in response to questionable personnel practice: file an objection, and if that does not work, bring a legal suit against overt discrimination. It is important to remember that coming-out is a painful and liberating process involving complex decisions under the best circumstances, but when it pertains to the workplace, it is affected by the socioeconomic climate, perceived job risk, prior loss of job due to coming-out, income, child-related work, gender structure of the workplace, as well as religion and self-hate (Schneider, 1986).

Social workers must respect that although coming-out will promote self-esteem and renewed energy with the removal of significant psychological and social barriers, it also entails risks and courage and timing.

SELF-ADVOCACY REVISITED

It is too easy to overestimate the climate of acceptance. Collective action is more effective than individually playing Don Quixote fighting windmills. The process of building the support of other minorities and like-minded allies will prove more fruitful. LGBT persons and heterosexuals have been working together successfully since the beginning of time. What is different today is that many people now openly live out their sexual orientation. This challenges straight and LGBT people alike to deal with their fears and prejudices on the job so that all can be creative and productive together.

The following steps are recommended in the process of assisting agencies to become nurturing environments that champion the civil rights and the well-being of LGBT employees: (1) start with an educational program related to sexual and gender orientation for all employees and (2) follow this up with supportive programs that offer mentoring by someone with organizational status, or arrange an opportunity to work with a coming-out coach who has had a successful experience, and finally, organize programs that encourage joining support groups and networks of LGBT persons, and their allies. Understandably, such a network might become the constituency group, the medium for self-advocacy, most invested in pressing for a safe work environment, equitable benefits, and appropriate public support and that could certainly be a factor in reconfiguring the power balance in most organizations.

REFERENCES

Anastas, J. W. (1998). Working against discrimination: Gay, lesbian and bisexual people on the job. *Journal of Gay & Lesbian Social Services, 8*(3), 83-98.

Anastas, J. W. (2001). Economic rights, economic myths, and economic realities. *Journal of Gay & Lesbian Social Services, 13*(1-2), 99-116.

Appleby, G. A. (1995). AIDS and homophobia/heterosexism. In G. A. Lloyd & M. A. Kuszclewicz (Eds.), *HIV disease: Lesbians, gays and the social services* (pp. 1-24). Binghamton, NY: The Haworth Press.

Appleby, G. A. (2001a). Ethnographic study of gay and bisexual working-class men in the United States. *Journal of Gay & Lesbian Social Services, 12*(3/4), 51-62.

Appleby, G. A. (2001b). Framework for practice with working-class gay and bisexual men. *Journal of Gay & Lesbian Social Services, 12*(3/4), 5-46.

Appleby, G. A., & Anastas, J. (1998). *Not just a passing phase: Social work with lesbian, gay and bisexual people.* New York: Columbia University Press.

Appleby, G., Colon, E., & Hamilton, J. (2002). *Diversity, oppression and social functioning.* Waltham, MA: Allyn and Bacon.

Bahr, M. W., Brish, B., & Croteau, J. M. (2000). Addressing sexual orientation and professional ethics in the training of school psychologists in school and university settings. *School Psychology Review, 29,* 222.

Blumenfeld, W. J. (Ed.) (1992). *Homophobia: How we all pay the price.* Boston: Beacon Press.

Bochenek, M. (2002). School practitioners supporting LGBTQ students. *Journal of Child and Youth Care, 15*(3), pp. 69-80.

Briar, S. (1968). The casework predicament. *Social Work, 13*(1), 5-11.

Code of Ethics Revision Committee (1996, August 7). *Memorandum: Code of ethics revised draft.* Washington, DC: National Association of Social Workers.

Coleman, J. S. (1974). *Power and the structure of society.* New York: W.W. Norton and Company.

Compton, B., & Galaway, B. (1994). *Social work processes* (5th ed.). Pacific Grove, CA: Brooks/Cole Publishing Company.

Conaway, R., & Gentry, M. (1988). *Social work practice.* Englewood Cliffs, NJ: Prentice Hall.

DeCrescenzo, T. A. (1984). Homophobia: A study of the attitudes of mental health professionals toward homosexuality. *Journal of Social Work and Human Sexuality, 2,* 115-136.

DeCrescenzo, T. (1997). *Gay and lesbian professionals in the closet: Who's in, who's out and why?* Binghamton, NY: The Haworth Press.

D'Emilio, J. (1983). *Sexual politics, sexual communities: The making of a homosexual minority in the United States, 1940-1970.* Chicago: University of Chicago Press.

DuBois, B., & Miley, K. K. (1996). *Social work: An empowering profession* (2nd ed.). Boston: Allyn and Bacon.

Eliason, M. J. (1995). Attitudes about lesbians and gay men: A review and implications for social service training. *Journal of Gay & Lesbian Social Services, 2*(2), 73-90.

Ellis, A. L., & Riggle, E. D. B. (Eds.) (1996). Sexual identity on the job: Issues and services [Special Issue]. *Journal of Gay & Lesbian Social Services, 4*(4).

Germain, C. B. (1991). *Human behavior and the nodal environment: An ecological view.* New York: Columbia University Press.

Germain. C. B., & Gitterman, A. (1980). *The life model of social work practice.* New York: Columbia University Press.

Germain, C. B., & Gitterman, A. (1996). *The life model of social work practice* (2nd ed.). New York: Columbia University Press.

Goldberg, S. B. (1996, Summer). No special rights: Supreme Court's amendment 2 decision has long-range implications. *HRC Quarterly,* pp. 4-5.

Greene, R. R. (1994). Social work practice within a diversity framework. In R. R. Greene (Ed.), *Human behavior theory: A diversity framework* (pp. 1-18). New York: Aldine de Gruyter.

Griffith, K. H., & Hebl, M. R. (2002). The disclosure dilemma for gay men and lesbians: "Coming out" at work. *Journal of Applied Psychology, 87*(6), 1191-1199.

Gutierrez, L. (1990). Working with women of color: An empowerment perspective. *Social Work, 35*(2), 149-152.

Hall, R. H. (1977). *Organizations: Structure and process* (2nd ed.). Englewood Cliffs, NJ: Prentice Hall, Inc.

Harris, M. B., Nightengale, J., & Owen, N. (1995). Health care professionals' experience, knowledge, and attitudes concerning homosexuality. *Journal of Gay & Lesbian Social Services, 2*(2), 91-108.

Herek, G., & Berrill, K. (1992). *Hate crimes: Confronting violence against lesbians and gay men.* Newbury Park, CA: Sage Publications.

Hidalgo, H., Peterson, T. L., & Woodman, N. J. (Eds.) (1985). *Lesbian and gay issues: A resource manual for social workers.* Washington, DC: NASW Press.

Johnson, L. C. (1995). *Social work practice: A generalist approach* (4th ed.). Boston: Allyn and Bacon.

Lyndenberg, S., Marlin, A. T., & Strub, S. O. (1986). *Rating America's corporate conscience: A proactive guide to the companies behind the products you buy.* New York: Addison-Wesley.

Mallon, G. P. (1999). A call for organizational trans-formation. *Journal of Gay & Lesbian Social Services, 10*(3/4), 131-142.

McPheeters, H. L. (1971). *A core of competence for baccalaureate social welfare.* Atlanta, GA: The Undergraduate Social Welfare Manpower Project.

Menzies-Lyth, I. (1988). *Containing anxiety in social institutions: Selected essays.* London: Free Association Press.

Morales, J. (1995). Gay Latinos and AIDS: A framework for HIV/AIDS prevention education. *Journal of Gay & Lesbian Social Services, 2*(3/4), 89-105.

National Association of Social Workers (1996, June). *Lesbian, gay and bisexual issues (Revised Social Policy Statement).* Washington, DC: National Association of Social Workers National Committee on Lesbian, Gay, and Bisexual Issues (NCOLGABI).

National Association of Social Workers (2003). *Social work speaks NASW policy statements 2003-2006.* Washington, DC: NASW Press.

Newsweek (1996, June 7). Poll on gay and lesbian rights. *Newsweek,* pp. 50-52.

Pellegrini, A. (1992). Shifting the terms of heterosexism: Gender, power, homophobia. In W. J. Blumenteld (Ed.), *Homophobia: How we all pay the price* (pp. 39-56). Boston: Beacon Press.

Pharr, S. (1988). *Homophobia: A weapon of sexism.* Little Rock, AR: Chardon Press.

Pincus, A., & Minahan, A. (1976). *Social work practice model and method.* Itasca, IL: Peacock Publishers.

Schneider, B. E. (1986). Coming out at the workplace: Bridging the private/public gap. *Journal of Work with Groups, 5*(3), 71-79.

Siporin, M. (1975). *Introduction to social work practice.* New York: Macmillan Publishing Co.

Sussal, C. M. (1994). Empowering gays and lesbians in the workplace. *Journal of Gay & Lesbian Social Services, 7*(1), 89-103.

Teare, R. J., & McPheeters, H. L. (1970). *Manpower utilization in social welfare: A report based on a symposium on manpower utilization in social welfare services.* Atlanta, GA: Southern Regional Educational Board.

Teare, R. J., & McPheeters, H. L. (1982). A framework for practice in social welfare: Objectives and roles. In D. S. Sanders, O. Dunen, & J. Fischer (Eds.), *Fundamentals of social work practice* (pp. 56-72). Belmont, CA: Wadsworth Publishing Company.

Williamson, A. D. (1993, July/August). Is this the right time to come out? *Harvard Business Review,* 26-34.

Winfield, L. (2005). *Straight talk about gays in the workplace.* Binghamton, NY: The Haworth Press.

Winfeld, L., & Smelman, S. (1995). *Straight talk about gays in the workplace: Creating an inclusive, productive environment for everyone in your organization.* New York: AMACOM.

Winfeld, L., & Spielman, S. (1996, Summer). The workplace is a happening place. *HRC Quarterly,* pp. 12-13.

Appendix

Key Definitions and Terms

Although no one owns definitions, the definitions are constantly evolving over time, and many of the definitions below are based on previous work developed by Mallon and Betts (2005).

TERMINOLOGY

Language is often a source of confusion and misinformation, and as such, it is important that service providers have accurate definitions. Heterosexually oriented practitioners are often unfamiliar or uncomfortable with the vernacular of the gay and lesbian "culture." It should be recognized that as with any subculture—particularly that of oppressed groups—language is constantly changing. Usage may vary with different generations, geographic areas of the country, socioeconomic status, or cultural backgrounds. Which terms are acceptable and which are offensive varies widely and is also culturally dependent.

homosexual: The use of the word *homosexual* in describing individuals and same-sex relationships may be inaccurate. When referring to people, as opposed to behavior, *homosexual* is considered derogatory and places the emphasis on sex. The preferred terms used by most are *gay* and *lesbian,* which stress cultural and social matters more than sex. In addition, prior to 1972, the term *homosexual* was a diagnostic term used to pathologize gay men and lesbians.

So that adoption and foster care social workers are clear about terminology and language, the following describes terms that relate to lesbians and gay men, and to sex, gender, and sexuality.

sex, gender, and sexuality: The English noun *gender* is derived from the Old French word *genre,* meaning "kind of thing." It goes back to the

Social Work Practice with LGBT People

Latin word *genus* (meaning "kind" or "species"). *Gender* is often, but decreasingly, used as a synonym for *sex,* which refers to the physical ana-tomical differences that are commonly used to differentiate male from female.

Many people, among them social scientists, use *sex* to refer to the biolog-ical division into male and female, and *gender* to refer to gender roles as-signed to people on the basis of their apparent sex and other associated factors. Society tends to assign some social roles to males and others to females (as society perceives their sex).

A person's gender is usually assigned at birth. The "male" or "female" recorded on the birth certificate can affect much of what happens to that child, socially, for the rest of his or her life. Gender is social, cultural, psy-chological, and historical. It is used to describe people and their roles in so-ciety, the way they dress, and how they are meant to behave.

It is assumed by some that sex, gender, and sexuality naturally follow on from each other, but different societies and cultures have had very different notions of sex, gender, and sexuality and how people express them. It is per-haps more helpful to consider "What is sexuality, and how do people in dif-ferent places and at different times understand their bodies and desires?" *Sexuality* is usually defined as the expression of sexual desire.

sexual orientation: This is the commonly accepted term for the direction of a person's sexual attraction, emotional, or physical attraction, and its ex-pression. Examples of sexual orientation are heterosexuality, homosexual-ity, and bisexuality. In a sense, sexual orientation is a social construct, and a relatively new one, most likely determined by a combination of continually interacting sociocultural influences and biological tendencies. Most cultures have a sexual object preference for the opposite sex.

For many years, the common assumption, shared by many scientists and religious communities, was that the natural and normal human sexual ori-entation is exclusively for the opposite sex (i.e., heterosexual). In 1976, the historian Michel Foucault argued that homosexuality as a concept did not exist as such in the eighteenth century, that people instead spoke of sodomy (which involved specific sexual acts, regardless of the sex or sexuality of the people involved). Sexual studies carried out during and after the 1950s led psychologists and doctors to recognize homosexuality as a second ex-clusive orientation. Since then, similar acceptance has grown for nonexclu-sive orientations, such as bisexuality.

heterosexuality: This term relates to sexual attraction, both physical and emotional, which is primarily directed toward people of the opposite gender.

homosexuality: This term relates to sexual attraction, both physical and emotional, which is primarily directed toward people of the same gender. The word *homosexual* translates literally as "of the same sex," being a hybrid of the Greek prefix *homo-* meaning "same" (as distinguished from the Latin root *homo* meaning *human*) and the Latin root *sex* meaning "sex."

Although some early writers used the adjective *homosexual* to refer to any single-gender context (such as the Roman Catholic clergy or an all-girls' school), today the term implies a sexual aspect. The term *homosocial* is now used to describe single-sex contexts that are not specifically sexual. Older terms for homosexuality, such as *homophilia* and *inversion* (in which a gay individual would be called a "homophile" or an "invert") have fallen into disuse. The term *homosexual* can be used as a noun or adjective to describe same-sex-oriented individuals as well as their sexual attractions and behaviors.

It is recommended that the terms *homosexual* and *homosexuality* be avoided—in particular, describing individuals as homosexual may be offensive, partially because of the negative clinical association of the word, stemming from its use in describing same-sex attraction as a pathological state, before homosexuality was removed from lists of mental disorders. For example, the American Psychiatric Association's 1968 list of mental disorders still regarded homosexuality as confused or disturbed sexuality. In the United States in 1975, the *Journal of the American Medical Association* was still publishing articles on possible treatments for ego-dystonic homosexuality,* including hormonal therapy and aversion therapy.

It was not until the late 1980s that journals began to focus on research and articles that were lesbian and gay affirming in their approach to treatment.

bisexuality: This term refers to sexual attraction toward people of both genders. Someone who identifies as bisexual is attracted to and may form sexual and affectionate relationships with both men and women, though not necessarily at the same time. The term may refer to a sociopolitical identity or to sexual behavior, or both. Most known societies have included people who have exhibited some degree of bisexuality.

Although bisexuality is an identified sexual orientation, it is sometimes transitional for those coming to terms with their lesbian or gay identity. Some

---

*Ego-dystonic homosexuality is a psychosexual disorder in which an individual has persistent distress associated with same-gender sexual orientation and is unable to initiate or maintain heterosexual relationships, usually experiencing a strong need to change the behavior or, at least, to alleviate the distress associated with the gay or lesbian sexual orientation.

people identify as bisexual before identifying as gay or lesbian, because bisexuality can represent a mediating position between homosexual and heterosexual in the traditional cultural system.

gay: In addition to meaning "merry," "joyous," or "glad," *gay* also means homosexual. *Gay* also refers to homosexually oriented ideas (e.g., literature or values). The word *gay* has had a sexual meaning since at least the nineteenth century (and possibly earlier; Chauncey, 1994). In Victorian England, female and male prostitutes were called "gay" because they dressed gaily. Eventually, "gay boys" (male prostitutes) became used as a term for any male homosexual. It has also been claimed that *gay* was an acronym for "Good As You," another popular etymology with its supposed origin emanating from a street called Gay Street in New York's West Village, a focal point of lesbian and gay culture. The term also seems, from documentary evidence, to have existed in New York as a code word in the 1940s, where the question, "Are you gay?" would denote more than it might have seemed to outsiders (Chauncey, 1994).

The term *gay* can be used to refer only to male homosexuals. Used inclusively, it refers to homosexual men and women, and arguably to bisexuals. When used in the phrase *the gay community,* it may also include transgender people and transsexuals, although this is also a subject of some debate, and these issues will not be fully addressed in this book.

Gay originally was used purely as an adjective ("He is a gay man" or "He is gay"). Gay is now also used as a collective noun (e.g., "Gays are opposed to that policy"), but rarely as a singular noun ("He is a gay"). When used as an adjective not describing a person who is part of the gay community (as many children and youth are now popularizing in school settings, e.g., "That shirt is so gay."), the term *gay* is purely pejorative and deeply offensive. The derogatory implication is that the object (or person) in question is inferior, weak, effeminate, or just stupid.

lesbian: A lesbian is a woman whose homosexual orientation is self-defined, affirmed, or acknowledged as such. *Lesbian* also refers to female homosexually oriented (and can refer to women-oriented) ideas, communities, or varieties of cultural expression. The word *lesbian* originally referred to an inhabitant of the Greek island of Lesbos. It came to have its current meaning because of the ancient Greek poet Sappho, who lived on Lesbos; some of her poems concerned love between women.

Whether Sappho was a lesbian, in the modern meaning of the term, or simply a poet who described lesbians, is open to question. Nevertheless, this association with Sappho led to the term *sapphism* being used as another term for lesbianism.

transgender: *Transgender* is a term created by people with trans histories to refer to trans people. It is now generally considered an umbrella term encompassing many different identities. It is commonly used to describe an individual who is seen as "gender-different." Outside the transgender communities, people identified as transgender are usually perceived through a dichotomous lens and are commonly described as transgressing gender norms, gender variant, or gender deviant. This traditional misreading is predicated a conception of transgender within a pathologically oriented perspective framed in a language layered in heterosexist, sexist, bigenderist, and transphobic context and meaning.

Transgender is often used as a euphemistic synonym for transsexual people. One set of reasoning for this is that it removes the conceptual image of "sex" in *transsexual* that implies transsexuality is sexually motivated, which it is not.

The term *transgender* is also used to describe behavior or feelings that cannot be categorized into other defined categories, for example, people living in a gender role that is different from the one they were assigned at birth, but who do not wish to undergo any or all of the available medical options, or people who do not wish to identify themselves as transsexuals, either men or women, and consider that they fall between genders or transcend gender.

By using the words "transgender" and/or "trans" in this text the authors look for a common language, communities, and purposes and are not seeking to erase any of the diverse identities of those individuals who identify themselves and/or are seen as: androgyne, bi-gendered, butch queen, CD, cross-dresser, drag king, drag queen, female-to-male, femme queen, FTM, gender bender, gender blender, gender challenged, gender fucked, gender gifted, gender nonconforming, gender-queer, male-to-female, MTF, new man, woman, non-op, nonoperative transexual, passing man, passing woman, phallic woman, post-op, post-operative transexual, pre-op, pre-operative transsexual, sex-change, she-male, stone butch, TG, third sex, trannie/tranny, trannie-fag, trans, trans butch, transexual/transsexual, transgender, transgenderist, transie, trans man, trans person, transexed, transexed man, transexed woman, transexual, transexual man, transexual woman, transvestic fetishist, transvestite, trans woman, tryke, TS, two-spirit, and the like.

transvestite/cross-dresser: This is a person who, for any reason, wears the clothing of a gender other than that to which the person was assigned at birth. Cross-dressers may have no desire or intention of adopting the behaviors or practices common to that other gender and do not necessarily wish to undergo medical procedures to facilitate physical changes. Contrary to common belief, most male-bodied cross-dressers prefer female partners.

bull dyke, fag, and queer: These terms are sometimes used to refer negatively to lesbians and gay men. They are equivalent to hate terms and epithets used against racial and ethnic minorities. A political usage exists for words such as *queer, dyke,* or *faggot* by some gays and lesbians who, in a reclamation process, redefine and use with pride words formerly used as pejorative. As these words still carry a negative connotation in society, however, their positive usage is restricted to political lesbians and gay men active in the reclamation struggle and as words used by in-group members to define themselves.

drag: The term *drag queen* originates in Polari, the language of gay men in England in the early part of the last century. *Drag* meant *clothes,* and was also theatre slang for a woman's costume worn by a male actor. A *queen* is an effeminate gay man. Drag is a part of Western gay culture—drag involves wearing highly exaggerated and outrageous costumes or imitating movie and music stars of the opposite sex. It is a form of performing art practiced by drag queens and kings. Female-bodied people who perform in usually exaggerated men's clothes and personae are called *drag kings,* though this term has a wider meaning than drag queen.

Drag kings should not be seen just as female equivalents of drag queens, because the term covers a much wider field of gender performance and political activism. Gender identity among drag kings is far more varied, too. Drag kings are largely a phenomenon of lesbian culture; they have only recently begun to gain the fame or focus that drag queens have known for years.

heterosexism (or heterocentrism or heterosexualism): This is the assumption that everyone or a particular person is heterosexual. It does not necessarily imply hostility toward other sexual orientations (as does homophobia), but is merely a failure to recognize their existence. Heterocentrism is culturally, religiously, and socially sanctioned by most major institutions in American culture, including the family.

homophobia: This term is most frequently used to describe any sort of opposition to homosexual behavior or the political causes associated with homosexuality, though this opposition may more accurately be called "anti-gay bias."

The term also describes a phobia triggered by an encounter (in oneself or others) with same-sex physical attraction, love, and sexuality. The term was finally described by George Weinberg (1972), the clinical psychologist who coined the term, to mean a morbid and irrational fear of homosexuals.

homo-ignorant: *Homo-ignorant* is a term developed to describe individuals with a very limited knowledge about gays, lesbians, bisexuals, and transgender individuals.

coming-out: Coming-out, a distinctively lesbian and gay phenomenon (see Cass, 1979, 1984; Coleman, 1981; Troiden, 1979, 1993), is defined as "the developmental process through which gay and lesbian people recognize their sexual orientation and integrate this knowledge into their personal and social lives" (DeMonteflores & Schultz, 1978, p. 59). Coming-out is the process of first recognizing and then acknowledging nonheterosexual orientation in oneself, and then disclosing it to others. Coming-out often occurs in stages and is a nonlinear process. Coming-out can also be used to mean "disclosure," as in "I just came out to my parents."

disclosure: The point at which a lesbian or gay man discloses his or her sexual orientation to another person. It is not appropriate to use terms such as *discovered, admitted, revealed, found out,* or *declared,* which are pejorative terms, suggesting judgment.

being out: This term is used to describe persons who are open about their sexual orientation to friends, family, colleagues, and society. Not everyone who is "out" is out to all of these groups; some people may be out to their family, but not to their colleagues.

being closeted or in the closet: These terms refer to someone who is not open about his or her sexual orientation. This person, for his or her own personal reasons, chooses to hide his or her sexuality from others.

The language in this publication is intended to be understandable and acceptable. "Same-sex," "gay," "lesbian," "heterosexual," "transgender," and "bisexual" are used to describe sexuality and partnerships.

SYMBOLS AND SITES

Some definitions and images are from the Web page "The Origin of Gay and Lesbian Symbols," at SwadePages (www.swade.net) and are used with permission.

lambda: The eleventh letter of the Greek alphabet. "Lambda was first chosen as a gay symbol when it was adopted in 1970 by the New York Gay Activists Alliance. It became the symbol of their growing movement of gay liberation. In 1974, lambda was subsequently adopted by the International Gay Rights Congress held in Edinburgh, Scotland. As their symbol for lesbian and gay rights, lambda has become internationally popular" (SwadePages, www .swade.net).

pink triangle: In Nazi Germany, homosexuals were forced to wear the pink triangle and were treated as the lowest status individuals by the Nazis. Gay men and lesbians have reclaimed the pink triangle and wear it as a badge of honor and also as a symbol of militancy against institutionalized oppression.

black triangle: "The black triangle was used to identify 'socially unacceptable' women, according to the Nazis. Lesbians were included in this classification. Now, lesbians have reclaimed the black triangle as their symbol in defiance of repression and discrimination, much as gay men have reclaimed the pink triangle" (SwadePages, www.swade.net).

intertwined male genetic symbol: Identifies gay men.

intertwined female genetic symbol: Identifies lesbians.

labrys: "The labrys, or double-bladed ax, comes from the goddess Demeter (Artemis). It was originally used in battle by Scythian Amazon warriors. The Amazons ruled with a dual-queen system and were known to be ferocious and merciless in battle, but just and fair once victorious. . . . Today, the labrys has become a symbol of lesbian and feminist strength and self-sufficiency" (SwadePages, www.swade.net).

transgender symbol: "The IFGE (International Foundation for Gender Education) logo, or transgender symbol, is the widely recognized symbol for cross-dressers, transvestites, transsexuals, and transgenderists" (SwadePages, www.swade.net).

freedom rings: "Designed by David Spada with the rainbow flag in mind, the freedom rings are six colored aluminum rings. They have come to symbolize independence and tolerance of others. Freedom rings are frequently worn as necklaces, bracelets, rings, and key chains. Recently, freedom triangles have emerged as a popular alternative to the rings, though the meaning remains the same" (SwadePages, www.swade.net).

rainbow flag: "Created in 1978 for San Francisco's Gay Freedom Celebration by Gilbert Baker, depicts not the shape of the rainbow but its colors in horizontal stripes. The rainbow flag has been adopted as the gay and lesbian flag. It represents the diversity yet unity of gays and lesbians universally" (SwadePages, www.swade.net).

Stonewall: Is the site where, in 1969, gays and lesbians fought police for five days. This event marks the independence day of gay and lesbian culture. Although it is generally accepted that the Stonewall Rebellion marks the start of the gay and lesbian movement, two other liberation organizations preceded this event: the Mattachine Society was founded in 1950, and the Daughters of Bilitis in 1955.

REFERENCES

Cass, V. C. (1979). Homosexual identity formation: A theoretical model. *Journal of Homosexuality, 4,* 219-235.

Cass, V. C. (1984). Homosexual identity formation: Testing a theoretical model. *Journal of Homsexuality, 4,* 143-167.

Chauncy, G. (1994). *Gay New York: Gender, urban culture and the making of the gay male world.* New York: Basic Books.

Coleman. E. (1981). Developmental stages of the coming out process. *Journal of Homosexuality, 7(2/3),* 31-43.

DeMonteflores, C., & Schultz, S. J. (1978). Coming out: Similarities and differences for lesbians and gay men. *Journal of Social Issues, 34(3),* 59-72.

Mallon, G., & Betts, B. (2005). *Recruiting, assessing and retaining lesbian and gay foster and adoptive families: A good practise guide for social workers*. London: British Association of Adoption and Foster Care.

Troiden, R. R. (1979). Becoming homosexual: A modle of gay identity acquistion. *Psychiatry, 42,* 362-373.

Troiden, R. R. (1993). The formation of homosexual identities. In L. D. Garntes & D. G. Kimmel (Eds.), *Pychological perspectives on lesbian and gay male experiences* (pp. 191-217). New York: Columbia University Press.

Weinberg, G. (1972). *Society and the healthy homosexual*. New York: St. Martin's Press.

Index

As a general rule, the term *gay* used in this index refers to men who have sex with men. Page numbers followed by the letter "f" indicate a figure.

Social Work Practice with LGBT People